MUSÉUM

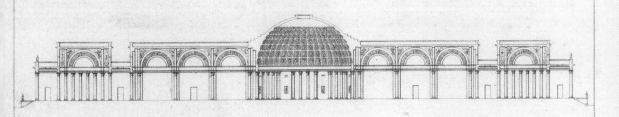

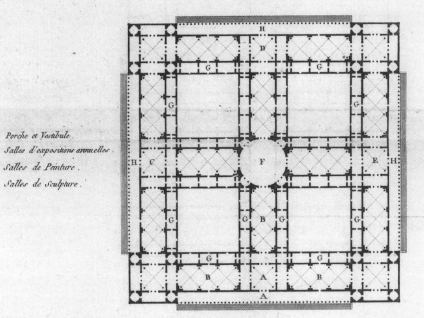

A . *Porche et Vestibule.*
B . *Salles d'expositions annuelles.*
C . *Salles de Peinture.*
D . *Salles de Sculpture.*

E . *Salles d'Architecture.*
F . *Salle de Réunion.*
G . *Cabinets des Artistes.*
H . *Entrées particulières.*

Gravé par C. Normand.

Précis of the Lectures on Architecture

Published by the Getty Research Institute

Jean-Nicolas-Louis Durand

Précis of the Lectures on Architecture

Précis of the Lectures on Architecture
with **Graphic Portion of the Lectures on Architecture**
Jean-Nicolas-Louis Durand
Introduction by Antoine Picon
Translation by David Britt

Texts & Documents

The Getty Research Institute Publications Program

Texts & Documents
Julia Bloomfield, Kurt W. Forster, Harry F. Mallgrave, Thomas F. Reese, Michael S. Roth, and Salvatore Settis, *Editors*

Précis of the Lectures on Architecture
with *Graphic Portion of the Lectures on Architecture*
Barry Bergdoll, *Editorial Consultant*
Steven Lindberg, *Manuscript Editor*

Jean-Nicolas-Louis Durand, *Précis des leçons d'architecture données à l'École Royale Polytechnique* (Paris: the author, 1802–5) and *Partie graphique des cours d'architecture faits à l'École Royale Polytechnique depuis sa réorganisation; précédée d'un sommaire des leçons relatives à ce nouveau travail* (Paris: the author, 1821), were translated by David Britt

Antoine Picon's introduction was translated by David Britt

The plates of the *Graphic Portion of the Lectures on Architecture* have been reproduced with the permission of Yale University Library

Published by The Getty Research Institute, Los Angeles, CA 90049-1688
© 2000 by The Getty Research Institute
All rights reserved. Published 2000
Printed in the United States of America

04 03 02 01 00   5 4 3 2 1

Cover: *Précis*, part II, plates 3, 4, 10, and 16
Frontispiece: *Précis*, part III, plate 11

Library of Congress Cataloging-in-Publication Data
Durand, Jean-Nicolas-Louis, 1760–1834.
    [Précis des leçons d'architecture données à l'Ecole polytechnique. English]
    Précis of the lectures on architecture ; with, Graphic portion of the lectures on architecture / Jean-Nicolas-Louis Durand ; introduction by Antoine Picon ; translation by David Britt.
        p. cm.—(Texts & documents)
    First work originally published: Précis des leçons d'architecture données à l'Ecole polytechnique. Paris : J. Durand, 1802–1805. 2nd work originally published: Partie graphique des cours d'architecture faits à l'Ecole royale polytechnique depuis sa réorganisation. Paris : J. Durand, 1821.
    Includes bibliographical references and index.
    ISBN 0-89236-580-3
    1. Architecture. 2. Architecture—Designs and plans. I. Title: Précis of the lectures on architecture ; with, Graphic portion of the lectures on architecture. II. Durand, Jean-Nicolas-Louis, 1760–1834. Partie graphique des cours d'architecture faits à l'Ecole royale polytechnique depuis sa réorganisation. English. III. Title: Graphic portion of the lectures on architecture. IV. Title. V. Series.
NA2520 .D8213 2000
720—dc 21

99-057591

Contents

Graphic Portion of the Lectures on Architecture

The contents pages have been translated faithfully from the original publications. Thus the minor discrepancies that existed between the contents pages and the text are reproduced here.

Acknowledgments

This edition in English of the *Précis des leçons d'architecture données à l'École Polytechnique* by Jean-Nicolas-Louis Durand springs from a fruitful collaboration between the translator, David Britt, and myself. It owes a great deal to Jean-Louis Cohen, who prompted me to embark on the project, and to Harry Francis Mallgrave, whose support and advice have been invaluable at every stage. Finally, it was Steven Lindberg who made it possible for this edition to assume its final form.

The work of providing illustrations was considerably simplified thanks to the help of Werner Szambien, Director of Research at the Centre National de la Recherche Scientifique, who generously placed at my disposal the picture material that he had collected on Durand and on his work. Barry Bergdoll, Professor of Art History at Columbia University, kindly reviewed the text of my introduction and thus enabled me to make several improvements.

— Antoine Picon

From "Poetry of Art" to Method: The Theory of Jean-Nicolas-Louis Durand

Antoine Picon

A Durable Impact

When the *Précis des leçons d'architecture données à l'École Polytechnique* (Précis of the Lectures on Architecture Given at the École Polytechnique) first appeared in 1802–5, there was nothing to indicate its future success.[1] Forbidding in appearance, written for students at a school where—as Durand himself acknowledges in his introduction—they had very little time to devote to architecture, the *Précis* did not look like a work with a great critical reputation ahead of it. Its author had made his mark during the French Revolution by winning a number of governmental competitions for public monuments; but none of these projects was ever built, and he had subsequently devoted himself mainly to theory and to his teaching at the École Polytechnique. Although Durand's first publication, his *Recueil et parallèle des édifices de tous genres, anciens et modernes* (Collection and Parallel of Edifices of All Kinds, Ancient and Modern), completed in 1801,[2] had attracted some attention, the *Précis* was too different to benefit immediately from its success. The *Recueil et parallèle* takes the form of a sequence of large engraved plates that are of the greatest interest to anyone interested in architectural programs and their historical evolution. The *Précis des leçons d'architecture données à l'École Polytechnique* is just what its title indicates: a basic course in architecture for future engineers. Its more limited illustrative content inevitably suffers by comparison with the plates of the *Recueil et parallèle*.

Despite this initial handicap, the work soon became a classic of architectural education. Under the familiar appellation *le petit Durand,* the Little Durand (as distinct from *le grand Durand,* which was the *Recueil et parallèle*), the *Précis* was soon to outgrow its intended audience of Polytechnicians to become a staple work of reference at the École des Beaux-Arts itself. Thumbed by generations of students throughout the nineteenth century, it lost its influence only with the triumph of the modern movement and its rejection of the academic tradition. It was eventually rediscovered by the theorists of postmodernism, and by all those fascinated by its ambition of refocusing architectural thought on the issue of design: "The *Précis* is the first architectural treatise to take as its subject architecture itself, architecture without reference to building. For Durand, what counts in architecture is the inaugural act, that

1

is, design."[3] The words are those of Bernard Huet in his preface to Werner Szambien's monograph on the architect, written in the early 1980s.

In addition to Szambien's fundamental work, there have been numerous discussions of Durand over the past few decades: declarations by architects—both theorists and practitioners, among them Robert Krier and Livio Vacchini—and essays in historical interpretation—such as Alberto Pérez-Gómez's chapter on the author of the *Recueil et parallèle* and *Précis* in his *Architecture and the Crisis of Modern Science* or the more recent book by the Italian art historian Sergio Villari, *J. N. L. Durand, 1760–1834: Art and Science of Architecture*.[4] From the early nineteenth century to the end of the twentieth, there seems to have been no end to the discussion of Durand's theoretical work—some commentators lauding it to the skies, others pointing out its limitations and its dangers.

The success of a theoretical work is measured at least as much by its bad reviews as by its good ones. The praise of such authors as Bernard Huet is matched or exceeded in quantity by adverse comment, ranging from Durand's contemporary Athanase Détournelle, who condemned his "unduly energetic manner of stating a truth,"[5] to Pérez-Gómez, who portrays him as a desiccated functionalist, the embodiment of architecture's loss of symbolic meaning—a loss caused, in Pérez-Gómez's view, by the advent of modern science.

Not only did Durand's work survive the decline in the teaching of architecture at the École Polytechnique and the demise of the École des Beaux-Arts, today, after nearly two centuries, it still seems to retain its power to disturb. So durable an impact is intriguing. It is true, first, that Durand's books appeared at a key moment in the evolution of French architecture, namely, the emergence of the early-nineteenth-century neoclassical style associated with the names of Charles Percier and Pierre-François-Léonard Fontaine.[6] With its sober, not to say ascetic, line engravings in which echoes of antiquity mingle with the influences of Italian vernacular architecture, the *Précis* looks, in many ways, like a manual of French neoclassicism. Furthermore, transcending that specific moment in architectural history, Durand's writings offer one of the earliest formulations of the concepts *composition* and *type* that were to guide the teaching of the Beaux-Arts until it collapsed under the onslaught of modernity. And yet their historical importance alone is not enough to explain their continuing relevance.

One corner of the veil is lifted by Bernard Huet, who describes Durand as the heroic pioneer of a process whereby architecture was refocused on design—with, as its corollary, the search for a method specific to design.[7] The possibility of such a refocusing is still a live issue to this day. When Durand gave one of the plates in his 1813 edition of the *Précis* the ambitious title "Marche à suivre dans la composition d'un projet quelconque" (Procedure to Be Followed in the Composition of Any Project), he was adopting a position that still has its adherents.

The material conditions governing this hypothetical "procedure to be followed" have of course changed since the early nineteenth century. Even diehard historicists among the champions of the "generic project" would be unlikely to take as a model the "Édifice destiné à la réunion des savants, des hommes de lettres, et des artistes" (Building Designed as a Meeting Place for Scholars, Men of Letters, and Artists), a simplified version of a project by Percier,[8] that Durand holds out as an example to readers of the 1813 edition of the *Précis*.

What has not changed, however, is the nature of the challenge that Durand confronted: the possibility of maintaining architecture as an autonomous discipline on the threshold of a world increasingly dominated by scientific and technological rationality. He was a former pupil of Étienne-Louis Boullée, who had been aware of the incipient confrontation between architecture, on the one hand, and science and technology, on the other; and the resultant tensions were brought home to him by his own position as a professor at the École Polytechnique. Set up in 1794 to educate scientists and engineers, in the early decades of its existence the École Polytechnique was a focal point of the formulation and transmission of scientific and technological knowledge. Mathematics, mechanics, physics, and chemistry were very much to the fore—far ahead of the teaching of architecture, which the early curricula of the École Polytechnique presented as a straightforward application of Gaspard Monge's descriptive geometry. Such was the context in which Durand composed his *Précis;* and indeed this book looks very like a manifesto in favor of an architecture as rigorous as the sciences of observation and deduction and as efficient as engineering.

What is the path that leads from the "poetry of art" proclaimed by Boullée and Claude-Nicolas Ledoux to the combinatorial techniques of the *Précis*? What part do scientific and technological references play in this transition? These questions may serve as a guiding thread for a study of Durand's approach.

A Man of "Classic Merit"

The life of the author of the *Précis* offers few salient features; it was almost exclusively devoted to theoretical reflection and teaching. Born in Paris in 1760, in very modest circumstances—his father was a shoemaker—the young Durand went to school at the Collège de Montaigue before turning to architecture. In 1775 he entered the office of the architect Pierre Panseron. The next year he moved to that of Boullée, and in two successive years, 1779 and 1780, he obtained second place in the Grand Prix de l'Académie d'Architecture (figs. 1, 2).[9] He visited Italy around this time, though the exact date is not known.[10]

Until the closing days of the ancien régime, Durand's activities were limited to architectural draftsmanship and engraving. Only in 1788 did he obtain his first commission to design a building, a family house for a contractor named Lathuille, on rue Faubourg-Poissonnière, in Paris (fig. 3).[11] Around the same time he followed the example of his master, Boullée, by turning to theoretical speculation. The result was a series of 168 pencil

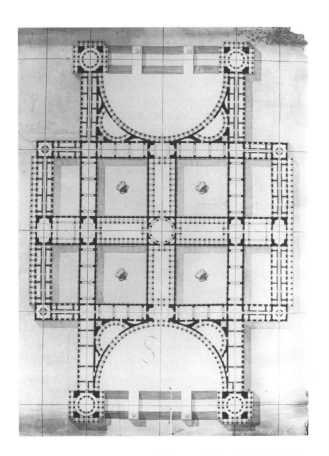

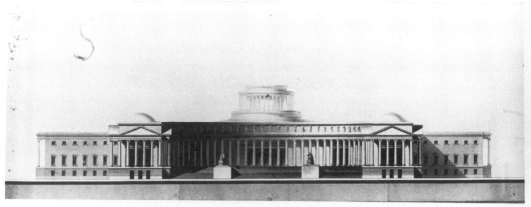

Fig. 1. Jean-Nicolas-Louis Durand, architect
Museum design for the Grand Prix de l'Académie d'Architecture of 1779, plan
Paris, École Nationale Supérieure des Beaux-Arts

Fig. 2. Jean-Nicolas-Louis Durand, architect
Museum design for the Grand Prix de l'Académie d'Architecture of 1779, elevation
Paris, École Nationale Supérieure des Beaux-Arts

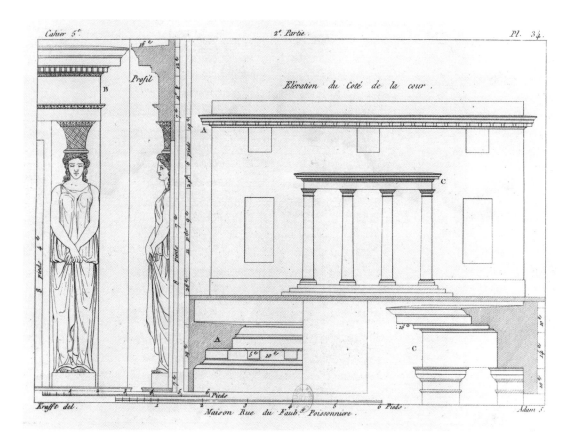

Fig. 3. Jean-Nicolas-Louis Durand, architect
Maison Lathuille
From Jean-Charles Krafft, *Recueil des plus jolies maisons de
Paris et de ses environs* (Paris: J. L. Scherff, 1809)
Photo: Paris, Bibliothèque Nationale de France

sketches (figs. 4, 5) to which his contemporary Antoine Rondelet gave the title *Rudimenta operis magni et disciplinae…* (Rudiments of the Great Work and Discipline; ca. 1790).[12] This was inspired by the pioneer work of Boullée and of Giovanni Battista Piranesi. The reference to Piranesi is evident in a number of drawings that either refer directly to motifs from his *Carceri* (Prisons) or use the formula of a view through an arch. The influence of Boullée and his *Essai sur l'art* (Essay on Art; written ca. 1780–90) goes far deeper: it leads Durand to reflect on the concepts *character* and *type*. From one sketch to the next, he reviews a succession of architectural contexts and assembles a kind of inventory of architectural means and ends: a repertoire of formulas and programs that he would attempt to systematize, not long afterward, in the *Recueil et parallèle*.

The French Revolution marked a turning point in a hitherto obscure career. Working in association with the architect Jean-Thomas Thibault, Durand designed the decor for the festival in honor of the "Martyrs of Liberty," Joseph Bara and Joseph Viala; he then entered the competitions organized in Year II (1793–94) by the Comité de Salut Public (Committee of Public Safety).[13] In the course of a few months, Durand and Thibault submitted no fewer than fifteen projects: a column inside the Panthéon, a triumphal arch, a Temple of Equality, proposals for a primary assembly, a common house, public baths, a primary school. One project stands out amid this prolific output: the Temple of Equality, with its "Revolutionary" order adorned by a woman's head on the capital, probably inspired by the Temple of Dendera in Egypt. The Year II competition jury awarded first prize to the Temple of Equality by Durand and Thibault, and it was marked "To Be Executed as a National Monument" (fig. 6). It was never built, however. Like the other winners of the Year II competitions, Durand and Thibault gained nothing but prestige.

Durand's newfound reputation nevertheless helped to secure him rapid promotion at the École Polytechnique, where he was engaged as a draftsman, on Fontaine's recommendation, in 1794. He became an assistant professor three years later and was eventually appointed professor of architecture, the post that he was to occupy until 1833. Such was the context in which he developed the material of his *Précis*. In gratitude to the institution that had taken him under its protection, Durand made over the copyright of the book to the École Polytechnique in 1805.

The compilation of the *Recueil et parallèle des édifices de tous genres, anciens et modernes*, 1799–1801, absorbed much of his energy during the final years of the French Revolution. Taking up the principle of comparative plates at a constant scale—used by the architect and engraver Juste-Aurèle Meissonnier in his *Parallèle général des édifices les plus considérables depuis les Égyptiens, les Grecs, jusqu'à nos derniers Modernes* (General Parallel of the Most Considerable Edifices from the Egyptians and Greeks to Our Most Recent Moderns; circa 1750), by Julien-David Le Roy in the 1770 edition of his *Ruines des plus beaux monuments de la Grèce* (Ruins of the Finest Monuments of Greece; originally 1758; fig. 7), and by Victor Louis in his *Plan sur la même échelle des théâtres modernes les plus connus* (Plans, to a Single Scale, of the Most Noted Modern Theaters; 1782)[14] — Durand applied it to the whole known history of architecture down to the close of the eighteenth century. In his juxtapositions of temples, forums, basilicas, theaters, colleges, and libraries, the concept of the building type, already adumbrated in the *Rudimenta,* took clear shape. Accompanied by a text written by the architect Jacques-Guillaume Legrand, the *Recueil et parallèle* was a great success (fig. 8). Shortly afterward, in 1802–5, the first edition of the *Précis des leçons d'archi-tecture données à l'École Polytechnique* appeared, bringing to a close the most brilliant phase of Durand's career, in which his projects and later his writings made him a major figure on the French architectural scene.

With the end of the revolutionary period, the author of the *Recueil et paral-lèle* and the *Précis* gradually withdrew into his work as a teacher. He trained several generations of Polytechnicians, along with a number of French and foreign architects, the most famous of whom was undoubtedly the German architect Leo von Klenze, who attended his lectures in 1804–5.[15] Durand's high reputation as a teacher should not obscure the fact that his place in the world of architecture was increasingly marginal. He built little: all that we have is a small number of houses, built in a neoclassical style entirely in keep-ing with his principles. Three of these, two of which were built for his own use, are in the commune of Thiais, south of Paris, where he lived (fig. 9). Also close to Paris, at Chessy, Durand built one for the administrator of the École Polytechnique, Claude Lermina.[16] This modest building record was the main obstacle to the award of any public honors. He was, for example, unsuccess-ful in securing election to the Institut de France.

Theoretical reflection continued to absorb Durand's attention. It led him, for instance, to recast volume 1 of his *Précis* for the editions of 1809 and 1813 and to publish his *Choix des projets d'édifices publics et particuliers com-posés par MM. les élèves de l'École Polytechnique* (Selection of the Projects for Edifices, Public and Private, Composed by the Students of the École Polytechnique) in 1816 — and, most importantly, in 1821 the *Partie graphique des cours d'architecture faits à l'École Royale Polytechnique* (Graphic Portion of the Lectures on Architecture Given at the École Royale Polytechnique), a kind of abstract of his teaching, which was attached to the end of the *Précis* in subsequent reprints.[17]

After a long illness, Durand finally made up his mind to apply for retire-ment in 1833. He died in December 1834. After a brief interim tenure by his close collaborator François-Tranquille Gaucher, who was followed by Martin-Pierre Gauthier, Durand's true successor at the École Polytechnique was a for-mer pupil, the engineer and architect Léonce Reynaud. One of Reynaud's first

(pp. 8–9, 10–11)
Figs. 4, 5. Jean-Nicolas-Louis Durand, draftsman
Rudimenta operis magni et disciplinae, folios 1, 2, ca. 1790
Rouen, Musée des Beaux-Arts

Croquis de Mr Durand.

Rudimenta Op...

8

Cathédrale de Sienne. · à Florence.

Croquis de Mr Brunel d'Architecte · Rudimenta · ouvi

10

Cheminée.

A Discipline.

**Fig. 6. Jean-Nicolas-Louis Durand and Jean-Thomas
Thibault, architects**
Clemens Wenzeslaus Coudray, copyist
Temple of Equality, Year II project, 1794
Weimar, Kunstsammlungen

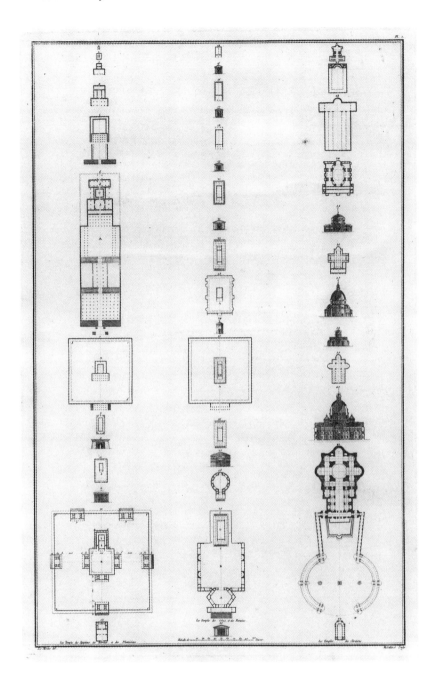

Fig. 7. Le Moine, draftsman
Michelinot, engraver
Parallel between ancient and modern temples
From Julien-David Le Roy, *Les ruines des plus beaux monuments de la Grèce,* 2d ed.
(Paris: Louis-François Delatour, 1770), plate 1
Photo: Getty Research Institute

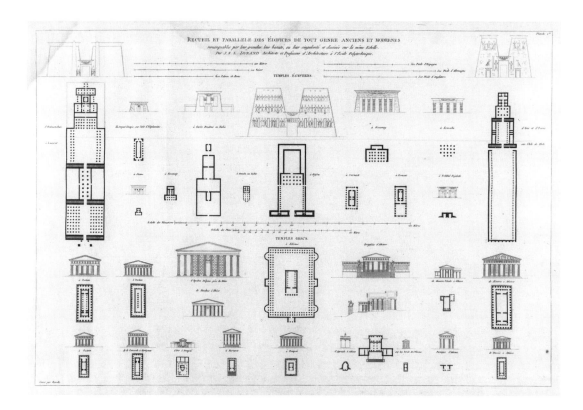

**Fig. 8. Jean-Nicolas-Louis Durand and
Jacques-Guillaume Legrand, draftsmen
Jean-Baptiste Reville, engraver**
Egyptian temples; Greek temples
From Durand, *Recueil et parallèle des édifices de tout
genre, anciens et modernes* (Paris: the author, 1800)
Photo: Getty Research Institute

Fig. 9. Jean-Nicolas-Louis Durand, architect
Country house at Thiais, garden front
Photo: Werner Szambien

tasks was to rethink the whole of a system of teaching whose principles had scarcely changed since the beginning of the nineteenth century.

In 1820 the director of the École des Ponts et Chaussées, Gaspard Riche de Prony, paid tribute to a colleague, the professor of architecture at that school, Charles-François Mandar, by calling him a man of "classic merit."[18] It is an expression that seems equally apt for the personality of Jean-Nicolas-Louis Durand. Though less advanced than the fascinating, unfinished propositions of his master, Boullée, Durand's theoretical synthesis has something "classic" about it, both in its restraint and in its efficiency.

"Revolutionary" Architecture: An Abortive Revolution

Historians of eighteenth-century French architecture tend to be rather hard on Durand, especially if they are specialists in Boullée, Ledoux, and the whole unique episode that Emil Kaufmann dubbed "revolutionary architecture."[19] "The theorist of an impoverished architecture, Durand had himself emerged from a background that was close to poverty," remarks Michel Gallet in his biographical and critical dictionary of Parisian architects.[20] In saying this, Gallet—who is Ledoux's biographer—is affecting ignorance of all the ties that link the architectural speculations of the 1780s and 1790s with Durand's theoretical approach.

Like the generation of revolutionary architects, his own teachers, Durand takes as his point of departure the exhaustion of the classical tradition based on the teachings of Vitruvius.[21] The exhaustion of that tradition was already implicit, by contraries, in the doomed attempt to restore the classical ideal mounted in the early 1770s by Jacques-François Blondel, professor at the Académie d'Architecture.[22] Boullée and Ledoux, both of whom had been Blondel's pupils, could see that the discipline of architecture needed to be reconstituted on some basis other than the manipulation of orders and proportions. In his theoretical writing, Le Roy often came close to their positions—not that this prevented him from acting as Blondel's deputy for a dozen years before taking over as professor at the Académie. Nor were Boullée, Ledoux, and Le Roy the only ones who felt this need for renewal. A slightly older man, Nicolas Le Camus de Mézières, the architect of the Halle aux Blés in Paris, arrived at the same analysis in his book *Le génie de l'architecture* (The Genius of Architecture), published in 1780.[23] Mathurin Crucy, by some years their junior, interpreted Blondel's death in 1774 as a liberation from the yoke of Vitruvian tradition.[24]

Kaufmann's epithet *revolutionary* has been much criticized;[25] perhaps the only justification for its continued use lies not in any supposed commitment on the architects' part to the French Revolution, or even to the political ideas that it expressed, but in their desire to liberate themselves from tradition. Boullée and Ledoux did indeed have a revolution in mind, but it was primarily an architectural one.

The reasons why that revolution was inevitable are many. Some of them lie in the qualities of Enlightenment culture in general: its empiricism, its critical attitude to any tradition that presented itself as a series of postulates seemingly devoid of rational foundation. By presenting architectural proportions as a kind of dogma, like religious articles of faith, the Vitruvian tradition renders itself liable to be falsified by experience. The falsification was supplied by eighteenth-century travelers, who revealed the diversity of exotic architectures, ancient and modern, Egyptian, Arab, and Chinese, and who also explored the variations in Greco-Roman architecture itself. Revealed to the French public by Charles-Nicolas Cochin II, Gabriel Dumont, and Jacques-Germain Soufflot, the squat columns of the Temples of Paestum shook the foundations of Vitruvianism as surely as did the study of Chinese pagodas. Moving on from Magna Graecia to Attica and the Peloponnese, Le Roy completed the demonstration with his *Ruines des plus beaux monuments de la Grèce* (fig. 10).[26]

Decisive changes also took place in the architectural profession itself, relative to the nature of commissions and to the relationship with clients. In France, Vitruvianism had allowed the architect to emerge as an artist working in the service of the king, the church, and the magnates of the realm. This figure, responsible for a variety of prestigious programs—châteaus, churches, town mansions—was gradually undermined by a twofold tendency to rationalize public commissions and to diversify private ones. Public rationalization took the form of the replacement of the notion of the monument with that of the facility, *l'équipement*. Schools, courthouses, bourses, and markets were facilities, with functional objectives that soon took over from the monumental imperatives of the assertion of royal power.[27] In the architect's private work, diversification took two forms. Some programs, such as great town houses (*hôtels*) for aristocratic or bourgeois clients, became more and more complex, undermining the traditional hierarchies of architecture. Their planning underwent a process of refinement, confronting architects with new problems in which tradition was no help to them.[28] At the other end of the scale, a proliferation of speculative programs soon included the first buildings designed specifically for rental.[29] Here, too, tradition had almost no contribution to make.

Whether in responding to more and more detailed functional specifications, or in adapting to the new habits and aspirations of the aristocracy and the bourgeoisie, or again in satisfying the constraints imposed by real estate speculation, the architect had to establish new relationships with his clientele founded not on traditional forms of patronage but on the recognition of his professional competence. Le Camus de Mézières argues for such relationships in his book *Le guide de ceux qui veulent bâtir* (The Guide for Those Who Wish to Build; 1780), which represents the architect as a specialist employed, like a lawyer or a physician, to give practical advice to his client.[30]

Such a specialist can no longer leave the contractors and workmen to do as they please—if only because he has to keep their costs under control. *Le guide de ceux qui veulent bâtir* is a work expressly designed to help the client forestall the peculations of craftsmen. The final decades of the ancien régime

Fig. 10. Julien-David Le Roy, architect and draftsman
Pierre Patte, engraver
Reconstruction of the Propylaea
From Le Roy, *Les ruines des plus beaux monuments de la Grèce,* 2d ed. (Paris: Louis-François Delatour, 1770), plate 24
Photo: Getty Research Institute

Fig. 11. Louis-Jean Desprez, draftsman and engraver
École des Ponts et Chaussées, ca. 1780, an imaginary view based on the traditional representation of Academies
Paris, Musée Carnavalet

saw the emergence of a desire to impose tighter control on the building production process; this in itself was a break with Vitruvian tradition, which always took an easygoing view of the relationship between conception and realization. The relationship between the rules of art and their application was no longer negotiable; it was time to look for new principles that could be rigorously adhered to.

The technical aspects of building, which Vitruvianism regarded as subordinate to issues of ordonnance, now became crucial. In particular, the pursuit of structural innovation—which had been marginalized in the French classical tradition—now came to the fore. It was no coincidence that it was the architects of the late Enlightenment who rediscovered the teaching of Philibert de l'Orme, with its emphasis on technical experimentation,[31] or that they made use of one of his most remarkable inventions, the roof truss system using short wooden members described in his *Nouvelles inventions pour bien bastir et à petits fraiz* (New Inventions for Building Well at Little Cost; 1561).[32]

All of this may be summed up in a single concept, the imperative of utility. Architecture must be useful: it must conform to needs, habits, and customs, and to their evolution. "Utility circumscribes everything. In a few centuries' time it will set bounds to experimental physics, as it is about to do to geometry"[33]—as Denis Diderot had written in his *Pensées sur l'interprétation de la nature* (Thoughts on the Interpretation of Nature; 1754). Though the pursuit of utility might well one day put a brake on scientific progress, for an art such as architecture it was a spur to self-renewal in depth.

In the second half of the eighteenth century, the issue of the utility of architecture was thrown into prominence by the nascent rivalry between architects and engineers.[34] In France those engineers who belonged to the various state corps—and especially those of the Ponts et Chaussées, who were responsible for the building and maintenance of bridges and highways—sought to appear as the most useful servants of the community. At the École des Ponts et Chaussées (fig. 11), in 1778, the dissertation topic set for budding engineers was "What is the utility of the Ponts et Chaussées, relative to commerce and agriculture?" In 1789 students were required to consider, more generally, "the utility of the École des Ponts et Chaussées to the state and society since its establishment in 1747."[35]

By postulating that all human ideas and judgments, even the most complex, ultimately derive from the sensations, the sensationalist philosophy of John Locke and Étienne Bonnot de Condillac imparts a moral quality to utility. The pursuit of utility is not to be equated with that of material happiness alone. Since physical enjoyments condition those of the mind and soul, the sphere of utility embraces that of private and public morality. This makes it easier to understand why, in 1783, the students of the Ponts et Chaussées were asked to consider the need for an engineer to have "an enlightened mind and a good heart." The topic chosen for 1787 explicitly identifies loving humanity with being useful to it.[36]

Utility, in the context of Enlightenment culture, is also bound up with the idea of human beginnings. Our most pressing needs, of body and mind alike, are those that date back to the very dawn of civilization. And so, by definition, the question of the utility of architecture refers us to that of its origins. This was clear early on to the Abbé Marc-Antoine Laugier, whose *Essai sur l'architecture* (Essay on Architecture; 1753) harks back to the very earliest days of humanity (fig. 12). "Let us," he says, "consider man in his earliest origins, without aid or guide other than the natural instinct to satisfy his needs."[37] Laugier goes on to describe the original shelter, the hut or cabin, from which art ought never to have departed. As proof of this, he adduces our perennial fascination with the temples of antiquity, the columns and entablatures of which look to him like an almost literal transposition of the tree trunks and branches of the primitive shelter. The detached column and its entablature: this and nothing else is the starting point from which the author of the *Essai sur l'architecture* sets out to regenerate architecture in his own time, and to give it both beauty and utility.

Laugier's ideas were undeniably attractive—if only because they offered the beginnings of a theoretical justification for the churches with detached columns that were then multiplying, from Pierre Contant d'Ivry's Saint-Vaast in Arras to Soufflot's new basilica of Sainte-Geneviève in Paris (now the Panthéon).[38] But by the 1770s and 1780s Laugier was no longer enough. The gulf between primitive hut and contemporary building was too wide to allow the whole discipline of architecture to be reformed on the basis of a single archetype. Because of their slender proportions, and the need to counter the lateral thrust of their vaults with devices reminiscent of the flying buttresses of the medieval cathedrals, the churches with detached columns that referred to that archetype worked on structural principles closer to Gothic than to Greek architecture.[39] The question of the origins of architecture—the roots of its utility—remained open.

The question was taken up by Boullée (fig. 13), Ledoux, and Le Camus de Mézières in an attempt to move on from the answers supplied by Laugier and other previous authors. They set themselves a multistage program. Leaving the orders to one side, they first tried to identify more fundamental components on which to rebuild the discipline of architecture. Most of the revolutionary architects concentrated on two lines of investigation: first, the sensations produced by elementary forms and volumes, and second, the functional elements of architecture. Elementary forms and volumes feature prominently in Boullée's *Essai sur l'art*, which sets out to elucidate the impression that they produce on the mind.[40] From these basic shapes of architectural invention, described by Ledoux as "letters of the alphabet used by the best authors,"[41] we may pass on to rhythms and proportions, posing once more the question of their impact on the viewer. An intuition of the same kind appears in the introduction to Le Camus de Mézières's *Le génie de l'architecture:* "No one," he complains, "has yet written on the analogy of the proportions of architecture with our sensations."[42] In its analysis of the various rooms of a dwelling, *Le génie de l'architecture* is nevertheless fundamentally

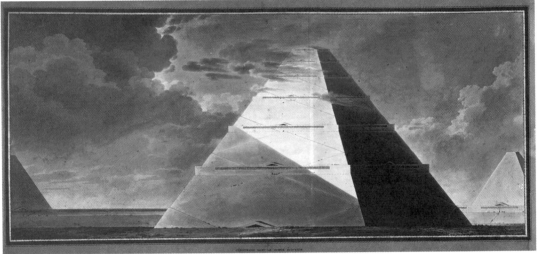

Fig. 12. Charles-Joseph-Dominique Eisen, draftsman
Jacques Aliamet, engraver
Frontispiece
From Marc-Antoine Laugier, *Essai sur l'architecture*, 2d ed.
(Paris: Nicolas-Bonaventure Duchesne, 1755)
Photo: Getty Research Institute

Fig. 13. Étienne-Louis Boullée
Design for a cenotaphe in the Egyptian manner
Paris, Bibliothèque Nationale de France

engaged in the second line of investigation: functions and the corresponding spatial sequences.

Not content with identifying these new constituents of the discipline of architecture, we must describe the ways in which they combine. Here sensationalist philosophy, with its "analytical method," offers a valuable source of inspiration. Analytical method, introduced by Locke in his *Essay Concerning Human Understanding* (1690), is intended to enable us to reconstruct the mental processes that lead from elementary sensations to complex judgments, from the first inarticulate cries to language. Condillac, in his *Essai sur l'origine des connaissances humaines* (Essay on the Origins of Human Knowledge; 1746), defines the analytical process as "composing and decomposing our ideas in order to make a variety of comparisons between them, and by this means discovering their relationships among themselves and the new ideas that they are able to produce."[43] As an art of composition and decomposition, the analytical method grew increasingly generalized in its application as the eighteenth century proceeded. In 1775 Condillac himself, in his *Cours d'études,* defined it as "the complete decomposition of an object, and the distribution of its parts into an order in which its generation becomes easy"[44]—without specifying the object involved. Seen thus, it seems to apply to almost all of the sciences and to the most diverse branches of art.[45] Antoine-Laurent de Lavoisier's revolution in chemistry is surely analytical, as is the desire of artists—musicians, painters, sculptors, gardeners—to found their own practice on a precise study of the sensations produced by nature. In his lecture course at the École Normale in Year III (1794–95) the Ideologue Joseph-Dominique Garat went so far as to describe analysis as the "method of the human mind."[46]

There is certainly something analytical in the revolutionary architects' quest for constituents of architecture more basic than the orders of Vitruvian tradition—as there is in their attempt to combine the new elements as rationally as possible. This is not to say that their analytical approach keeps all of its promises. Whatever the philosophers may say, an almost unbridgeable gulf continues to separate our sensations from the complex judgments of the human mind. It is a gulf of the same kind as that between simple volumes (or elementary functions) and the buildings that architects are actually asked to construct.

This is no easy obstacle to surmount. It tends to show that the analytical method cannot be directly transposed into architecture. And so the notions of "type" and "character" emerge as necessary buffers between architecture's primary constituents and its products. The type, a generic combination of forms, masses, and functions answering to a certain form of use, takes the place of the actual edifices—temples, basilicas, theaters—that were offered as examples by Vitruvian tradition. More abstract than the ancient concept of the example or model, the notion of the type begins to emerge in the work of Boullée and Ledoux, without ever achieving the clarity that Durand gives it. Thus, Boullée had a variety of residential types in mind when, between 1792 and 1796, he worked on a series of designs for "private architecture."[47] Significantly, this undertaking was to remain a collection of fragments—as indeed was his *Essai sur l'art,* which is primarily concerned with works of public architecture.

It was not enough, however, to pass from the elementary constituents of architecture to the various types capable of advancing the project. Even more than the engineers, the revolutionary architects were responsive to the moral dimension of utility. Without this there could be no "poetry of art," and therefore nothing to distinguish architecture from mere building. The type is a generic formula, a crystallized usage; it is the physical correlative of utility. It attains its true dignity only when accompanied by character. Whether cheerful or austere, grand or intimate, character is there to manifest the moral dimension of utility: the meaning that always transcends those material needs that utility satisfies. "To instill a work with character," writes Boullée in his *Essai sur l'art,* "is to make accurate use of all the means proper to make us feel no other sensations than those that arise from the subject."[48]

For the revolutionary architects, "to instill a work with character" is to work on two seemingly disparate levels at the same time: that of the immediate effect produced by the built masses and that of an ornament that is firmly symbolic in character. The first of these two levels addresses sensations that are in some way antecedent to language. Masses, or the contrast of shade and light, operate without reference to the world of spoken or written meanings. By contrast, the symbolism employed by Boullée and Ledoux presupposes the existence of a fully formed language. Their projects for public monuments frequently feature inscriptions. These monuments are the manifestos of a "speaking" architecture;[49] they seek to express themselves in ways that both predate and postdate the invention of language. Simultaneously, revolutionary architecture sets out to convey the nature of the long march from the laborious beginnings of humanity to civilization. In the course of that process, utility asserts itself in both of its dimensions, physical and moral; need and virtue progress together. Revolutionary architecture aspires to be the bearer of collective values. It regards itself as profoundly public-spirited: a civics lesson in stone.

At this point the break with Vitruvian tradition is complete. The meaning of architecture, for the heirs of Vitruvius, was that it manifested an order external—as divine creation is external—both to man and to society. From the speculations of Juan Bautista de Villalpando, on the proportions assigned by God to the Temple of Jerusalem, to those of René Ouvrard, on the conformity of those proportions to musical intervals,[50] numerous attempts had been made to reconcile the teachings of Vitruvius's *Ten Books on Architecture* with those of divine revelation. If—as Jacques-Bénigne Bossuet supposed in his *Introduction à la philosophie* (1722)—God created the world by giving it order and proportion,[51] then the canons of architectural beauty were necessarily related to that general order and proportion.

This idea of the rules of architecture, as something totally external to man and to society, was now opposed by a new interpretation, whereby architecture is a prime manifestation of the process that creates the social bond. This does not mean that all of the elements of the discipline relate to human origins—far from it. But architecture has its place at the origin of society, alongside the primary needs to which it responds.

In this radical redefinition of the ambitions of the discipline, design becomes the instrument of choice. "What is architecture?" asks Boullée:

> Am I to define it, with Vitruvius, as the art of building? No, Vitruvius's definition contains a flagrant error. He mistakes the effect for the cause. To execute, you must first conceive. Our earliest forefathers did not build their huts until they had first conceived the image of them. That production of the mind, that creation, constitutes architecture.[52]

To shift architecture's center of gravity in this way, toward design, is in itself to attempt a revolution against the tradition of Vitruvius, biased as this was toward the building rather than the concept. Such a revolution must necessarily restore architects to their position of supremacy. In their eyes, engineering—confined as it is to material utility—can never rival a discipline that is able to reconcile the inspired freshness of the dawn of humanity with the refinement of a mature civilization. In the name of this wide spectrum of means and effects, Boullée and Ledoux take it upon themselves to correct the designs for bridges produced by their engineer contemporaries and to rearchitect them with the aid of a symbolic decoration that recalls their mythic origin.[53]

By the turn of the century the defeat of revolutionary architecture was becoming apparent. The "poetry of art" so dear to Boullée and Ledoux abruptly vanished from sight in favor of the colder, more abstract architectural idiom later known as neoclassicism. The great programs of public works with which the revolutionary architects had dreamed of covering France made way for less-ambitious undertakings. After their long struggle to block the expansionist ambitions of the engineers, architects now had no choice but to accept their growing power, one of the symbols of which was the new École Polytechnique.

Numerous reasons for this defeat can be advanced. There is a certain impracticality in Boullée's and Ledoux's definitions of the constituent elements of architecture—to which should be added their inability to theorize their design-centered approach by applying the concepts of type and character. Such vagueness might well be explained by the chronic tension between their desire to retain architecture's special link with nature and their simultaneous affirmation of its eminently social function. On the one hand, architecture appeals to natural sensations and needs; on the other, it depends on historical laws of the formation and evolution of societies. On the one hand, it is the work of genius, to which nature dictates its laws; on the other, it has to cater to uses that do not seem particularly natural. The Enlightenment had seen no necessary contradiction in either of these two sets of propositions, since man is himself both a child of nature and a socialized individual. Around 1800, however, it began to be apparent that there was some degree of incompatibility between the natural and the societal. The early writings of Count Henri de Saint-Simon reveal a profound break with eighteenth-century philosophy.[54] There now emerged the first symptoms of the grieving process that marked the loss of some of the revolutionary ideals—one of which was the hope of reconciling a return to origins, inspired by Jean-Jacques Rousseau, with the idea of social progress.

Durand's theoretical work bears the mark of this new context, while remaining surprisingly loyal to the inheritance of revolutionary architecture. In many respects—whether in defining the status of the elements of architecture or in theorizing the use of the architectural types—it takes up and completes the unfinished work of Boullée and Ledoux. But there is a heavy price to be paid. The "poetry of art" disappears, and in its place is a "method" that has nothing like the same enticing appeal.

The Teaching of Architecture at the École Polytechnique

The context in which Durand taught architecture conditioned his awareness of the limitations of revolutionary architecture. At the École Polytechnique, working alongside some of the leading scientists and engineers of the day—including Claude-Louis Berthollet, Jean-Antoine Chaptal, Joseph-Louis Lagrange, and, of course, Gaspard Monge, the father of the new institution—he was in a position to observe the widening gap between scientific and technological definitions and the logical processes observed in architecture. Durand tried to bridge this gap, though he no longer cherished the illusion that architecture would ever regain its dominance over engineering—a discipline that had been dynamized by its close ties with science.

The École Polytechnique (initially known as the École Centrale des Travaux Publics) was both an offspring of the French Revolution and the heir to an ancien régime policy of setting up schools for governmental engineers.[55] The École des Ponts et Chaussées was founded in 1747 to provide a unified recruitment system for civil engineers employed to build the transportation infrastructure. The École du Génie, for military engineers specializing in fortifications, opened at Mézières in the following year. The École des Mines followed in 1783. The rise of the engineer was thus accompanied by the creation of a series of educational establishments. This was a radical development in a profession for which training had traditionally been by apprenticeship.

Until the French Revolution, the training of future engineers had nevertheless remained highly traditional, focused—like that of architects—on draftsmanship and design. Only the École du Génie had begun to break free of this obsolete framework by assigning a major role to the sciences.[56] Here the presence of the mathematician Gaspard Monge was crucial. Appointed to Mézières as a mere draftsman at the age of eighteen in 1764, Monge soon attracted attention by the force of sheer intellect and was appointed first a *répétiteur* (teaching assistant) and then a professor.[57] The direct application of science to engineering was the keynote of his work at Mézières, just as it was later to guide him in creating the École Polytechnique. For example, his system of descriptive geometry was first devised to deal with concrete propositions concerned with the cutting of stones and the profiles of fortifications (figs. 14, 15).[58]

The foundation of the École Polytechnique was thus the culmination of an institutional process begun under the ancien régime. Even so, it owed a great deal to revolutionary ideas about the organization of public education. Resolutely encyclopedic in its inspiration, the École Polytechnique bears a close resemblance to certain proposals drawn up by Marie-Jean-Antoine-Nicolas de Caritat de Condorcet, and above all by Charles-Maurice de Talleyrand, whom Monge advised on scientific and technological matters. As Jean-Nicolas Hachette related in his *Notice sur la création de l'École Polytechnique* (1828), Monge had "long since conceived the plan of an advanced school to which only the most distinguished pupils of the secondary schools would be admitted."[59] The numerous debates on public education that took place during the French Revolution afforded opportunities to refine his ideas and to put them into practice.

In at least two respects, France's war against the rest of Europe also played an essential role.[60] First, it led to a shortage of engineers, and this necessitated a reorganization in depth of the systems by which they were trained. Then the Comité de Salut Public began to mobilize scientific manpower in order to improve the production of gunpowder and weaponry.[61] Along with the likes of Berthollet, Chaptal, Jean-Henri Hassenfratz, and Alexandre Vandermonde, Monge distinguished himself in the role of scientific and technical consultant. It was therefore not surprising that his proposals for the creation of a new school, summarized in his paper "Développemens sur l'enseignement adopté pour l'École Centrale des Travaux Publics" (Remarks on the Instruction Adopted for the Central School of Public Works),[62] were given an attentive hearing by the Comité de Salut Public, most particularly by those two among its members who were alumni of the École du Génie at Mézières, Lazare Carnot and Claude-Antoine Prieur de la Côte-d'Or.

On 3 Vendémiaire, Year III (24 September 1794), the final project for the new school was presented to the Convention. It provided for all the future engineers and officers of the state corps to be brought together in a central establishment, the École Centrale des Travaux Publics. All of the schools created by the ancien régime were to be replaced by a single establishment. In the event, this merger proved impracticable and was abandoned. In 1795 the former engineering schools were reopened as practical training establishments for graduates of the institution created by Monge, which was henceforth to be known, for political reasons,[63] as the École Polytechnique. Their function would be to provide specialized teaching for each of the three state corps of engineers, subsequent to the generalist training dispensed by "Polytechnique."

Initially designed for an annual graduating class of four hundred, later three hundred, this training is detailed in the *Programmes de l'enseignement polytechnique de l'École Centrale des Travaux Publics* (Curricula for the Polytechnic Instruction at the Central School of Public Works) published in the fall of 1794.[64] It provides for a highly advanced course of scientific and

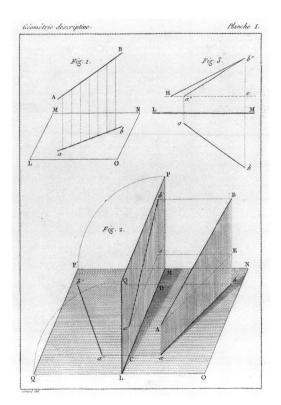

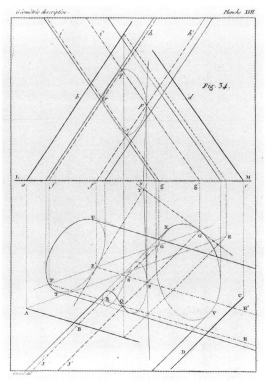

Fig. 14. Gerard, draftsman
Basic principle of descriptive geometry
From Gaspard Monge, *Géométrie descriptive,* 5th ed. (Paris: Bachelier, 1827), plate 1

Fig. 15. Gerard, draftsman
Intersection of two cylindrical surfaces
From Gaspard Monge, *Géométrie descriptive,* 5th ed. (Paris: Bachelier, 1827), plate 17

technological studies, to include mathematics, mechanics, physics, chemistry, and the principal branches of engineering itself: mines, bridges and highways, and fortification. The greatest departure from the syllabi of the ancien régime lies in the importance allotted to science. In accordance with Monge's desire to conduct the students from theoretical speculation to the concrete problems of engineering, two subjects are favored on account of their many applications: descriptive geometry and chemistry.

Developed, as we have seen, by Monge at Mézières, descriptive geometry was a rationalization of the techniques of projection long used by stonecutters and master carpenters. This rationalization made descriptive geometry into a relatively powerful tool for solving problems—a tool, what is more, that was in active contact with the latest findings of one of Monge's favorite subjects, the analytic geometry of surfaces. According to the *Programmes de l'enseignement polytechnique,* it is the function of descriptive geometry to describe all those objects that are "susceptible of rigorous definition."[65] In his own teaching, Monge described it as a language "necessary to the man of genius who conceives a project, to those who must direct its execution, and finally to those artists who must themselves execute its different parts."[66] The projected École Centrale des Travaux Publics would thus teach stereotomy, public works, architecture, and fortification as so many applications of descriptive geometry.

At the outset, the teaching of architecture was thus clearly subordinate to that of the sciences. Presented as a mere application of their general principles, it was treated as an ultimately minor specialty within the wide range of disciplines that engineers needed to master.

As if the context in which he worked were of slight importance, its first professor, Louis-Pierre Baltard, made few innovations with respect to the content of his course. He maintained the traditional tripartite division into decoration, distribution, and construction—a modernized version of the Vitruvian triad beauty, commodity, and solidity used by François Blondel at the Académie d'Architecture.

Under Durand, the teaching of architecture moved away from this obsolete theoretical framework. It also shook off the tutelage of descriptive geometry, the limitations of which had soon become evident. In spite of Monge's declarations to the contrary, descriptive geometry proved to be of little practical use. It dominated the course at the École Polytechnique at the very time when in construction work its major practical application, stereotomy, was declining in importance.[67] The complex forms—pendentives, interpenetrations—that arise from stereotomy are utterly foreign to the purist geometry of revolutionary and neoclassical architecture. Nor did the use of descriptive geometry in the design of machines ever prove totally convincing.[68] Its importance in the training of French engineers throughout the nineteenth century had more to do with the mental habits of order and precision that it tended to establish.[69] This, in fact, was the basis of the close links between the descriptive geometry course and the architecture course. It was Durand's major

Fig. 16. Auguste Geoffroy
Exercise in drawing with wash, École Polytechnique, 1828
Palaiseau, École Polytechnique

Fig. 17. Unknown artist
Portraits of Durand, from a student's lecture notes
Palaiseau, École Polytechnique

achievement to structure his own teaching in a way sufficiently close to that of the sciences to ensure that architecture would not look like an excuse to relax between classes in mathematics and mechanics.

In this he faced a steeper challenge in every successive year. Abandoning its initial encyclopedic ambitions, the Polytechnique made its training ever more mathematical.[70] Analysis and rational mechanics were to dominate the syllabus until the turn of the twentieth century. The importance of chemistry declined, and most engineering classes were transferred to the specialist schools. The subjects public works and fortification therefore disappeared. Only the teaching of architecture remained, thanks to Durand's success in making it a generalist course. In 1806 this part of the curriculum consisted of 58 one-hour classes, plus 25 three-and-a-half-hour study sessions, plus 8 ten-hour competitions. In 1811 the number of classes was reduced to 38 and the number of study sessions raised to 30, the number and duration of the competitions remaining unchanged.[71] Until Durand's retirement, the organization of architectural tuition remained broadly the same: classes, study sessions devoted to a variety of drawing tasks, and competitions (fig. 19).

The durability of the architecture course at the École Polytechnique is all the more remarkable since architecture courses were also offered at specialized schools, notably the École des Ponts et Chaussées and the École de l'Artillerie et du Génie in Metz. However, none of these was comparable in scope with Durand's. At the École des Ponts et Chaussées, Charles-François Mandar left aside matters of composition and concentrated on construction.[72] And those Ponts et Chaussées engineers who had attended both courses tended to remember Durand rather than Mandar. Thus, when Claude Navier, one of the founders of the science of strength of materials, edited the 1813 republication of Bernard Forest de Bélidor's *La science des ingénieurs* (originally published in 1729), he wrote in his notes to the chapter on the orders of architecture that:

> The maxims given here by Bélidor were enshrined and developed by Monsieur Durand in classes whose memory of which will always be cherished by the students of the École Polytechnique.... Monsieur Durand was the first who succeeded in putting the principles of architecture onto a solid foundation. He recognizes no other foundation than fitness [*convenance*], that is, a perfect rapport between the planning of a building and the use for which it is destined. Thus, to project a building is to solve a problem whose given factors consist in the conditions of solidity, economy, and utility, to which it is subject.[73]

"To project a building is to solve a problem": Navier's formula may seem overstated. But it is entirely in keeping with the spirit of Durand's course, and with his intention of giving architecture a method that could be advantageously placed alongside that of science.

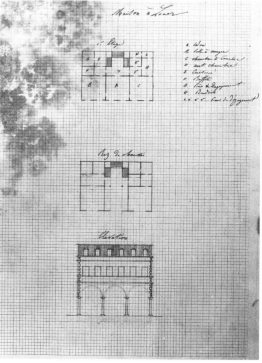

Fig. 18. Unknown artist
Exercise in drawing with wash, École Polytechnique, early nineteenth century
Palaiseau, École Polytechnique

Fig. 19. Félix de Juge
Design for an apartment building, for architectural competition, École Polytechnique, 1831
Palaiseau, École Polytechnique

The Foundations of Theory: From Imitation of Nature to Utility
In establishing this method, Durand turns his back more decisively than any predecessor on the temptation to base the discipline of architecture in the imitation of nature. The first pages of the introduction to the *Précis* leave this matter in no doubt. Durand undertakes to discredit the Vitruvian creed once and for all by demonstrating that the proportions of the orders of architecture cannot possibly be based on those of the human body. He follows the theorist Claude Perrault in pointing out that the proportions in question have varied considerably over the centuries and that the ancients themselves never observed a fixed system of ratios. Above all: "What comparison is there between a man's body, which varies in width at different heights, and a kind of cylinder with a constant diameter throughout?"[74]

The first objects fashioned by man in response to the challenges of nature are equally unsuitable to serve as a basis for the discipline of architecture. The primitive hut so dear to the Abbé Laugier comes in for particular criticism. Is it really all that primitive? This crude artifact, "the inchoate production of the first falterings of art,"[75] neither has anything natural about it nor casts any light whatever on the genesis of those infinitely more complex structures, the Greek temples. Through his critique of the Abbé Laugier, Durand is challenging the quest for origins that was still a preoccupation of the revolutionary architects.

The scope of this challenge is not to be underestimated. Not only was Durand abandoning a quest that had run like a thread through Enlightenment culture: in Boullée and Ledoux, in particular, such a quest led directly onto a symbolic level on which a mature architecture harked back to its beginnings, real or mythical, in order to dramatize the transition from the state of nature to that of civilization. The constant references in revolutionary architecture to the four traditional elements and to their use by man, or the fondness for such motifs as the juxtaposition of rock and column, raw material and shaped material, were all expressions of the symbolic dimension of the architectural project itself.[76] Durand will have none of this; in fact, he makes a point of dissociating the design-oriented approach from the manipulation of signs and symbols. In this respect, the *Précis* occupies a position diametrically opposed to that of the *Lettres sur l'architecture des Anciens et des Modernes* (1787) of Jean-Louis Viel de Saint-Maux, which professed to be a demonstration of the symbolic origins of architecture.[77] Above and beyond the role of imitation and the hut model, we realize the true distance that separates Durand from such a writer as Antoine-Chrysosthôme Quatremère de Quincy, who remains committed to the symbolic vocation of architecture.[78]

An architecture deprived of symbols might still seek to give pleasure through its decoration. Here, again, the author of the *Précis* firmly distances himself from Boullée and Ledoux by making clear his disdain for the very idea of decoration. Any concession to the exclusive pursuit of beauty is futile, says Durand, who goes on to announce in peremptory tones: "Whether we consult reason or examine the monuments, it is evident that pleasure can never have been the aim of architecture; nor can architectural decoration have been its object."[79]

Durand's break with the natural order thus leads to a major exercise in demolition. From the very first pages of his book, the author of the *Précis* sweeps away practically all previous attempts to find the historical foundation of architecture. He then goes on to make short work of a number of previously sacrosanct architectural ideals, such as the desire to make architecture significant and the pursuit of beauty. Of the ideas of the revolutionary architects, all that he retains is the imperative of utility. But Durand's utilitarianism has all the dryness of a scientific axiom. Utility here is physical rather than moral; it is characteristic of humanity, without bearing any particular relation to the question of its origins—on which Durand has this to say: "If we examine the sequence and development of intelligence and feeling, we shall find that, in all ages and in all places, all of men's thoughts and actions have sprung from two principles alone: love of comfort and dislike of all exertion."[80] These are words that Claude-Adrien Helvétius or Paul-Henri d'Holbach would not have disavowed.[81] Love of comfort and dislike of all exertion: such is the reason for architecture, its true foundation.

For Durand, utility as applied to architecture finds expression in two ways: in making buildings suitable for their intended use and in minimizing the physical or financial effort required for their completion. *Convenance* (fitness) and *économie* (economy) are the terms that he uses to designate these two aspects of utility. The history of these two terms did not begin with Durand's *Précis*, however. Innovative though he was in his approach to the basic concepts of architecture, Durand was also the heir to a long line of theorists who had progressively defined the range of possible meanings of fitness and economy.

The term *convenance* appeared in the treatises at a very early date, at first to designate the agreement supposed to exist between a building and its purpose. Already present, albeit in a minor key, in Jean Martin's French translation of Alberti (1547),[82] it began to play a more assertive role in the work of a later theorist, Claude Perrault, who, in the notes to his translation of Vitruvius (1673) defined it as "the usage and the useful and necessary end to which an edifice is made, as in solidity, salubrity, and commodity."[83] For Perrault, from whom Durand draws inspiration more than once, fitness had a dual aspect. It pointed, first of all, to the social purpose of architecture, the harmony between its productions and the various social conditions and uses. But it also corresponded to those "positive beauties" in architecture that Perrault contrasted with the "arbitrary beauties" of proportions and orders, both in his translation of Vitruvius and in his *Ordonnance des cinq espèces de colonnes selon la méthode des Anciens* (Ordonnance for the Five Kinds of Columns after the Method of the Ancients; 1683).[84] By the end of the seventeenth century, the concept of fitness made it possible to raise questions that were later to become essential ones, that of the social utility of architecture and that of its true foundations—as distinct from those foundations that were to prove incidental, such as proportions and orders.

A physician and a scientist above all, Perrault tried to revolutionize architectural theory on the strength of his own anatomical and physiological knowledge, which led him to take a skeptical view of Vitruvius's claim to have taken his principles from nature. Like his brother Charles, the author of *Parallèles des Anciens et des Modernes* (Parallels between the Ancients and the Moderns; 1688–97) and *Contes* (Fairy Tales; 1697), Claude was a protégé of Jean-Baptiste Colbert, Louis XIV's chief minister, and a servant of Colbert's grand design of bringing the sciences and the arts under governmental control.[85] Claude Perrault sought to replace Vitruvian principles with a recognition of architecture as a social and political institution. Taste and the norm, rather than nature, were to be the foundations of the architectural discipline.[86] Though rejected by the architects of his own time, Perrault's theory came to the fore once more in the 1780s — as may be seen from the lengthy discussion of it in Boullée's *Essai sur l'art*.[87]

In the meantime, fitness had become one of the key ideas in Enlightenment architectural theory. Conscious of the need of a closer link between architectural production and society, Jacques-François Blondel made it into the touchstone of his teaching, though without adopting Perrault's proposed distinction between positive and arbitrary beauty. Durand was the heir to Perrault, but also to Blondel, who — for all his longing to restore the French classical tradition — was well aware of the new challenges that now confronted architecture.

Fitness, as defined in the *Précis*, owes far more to Perrault than to Blondel. Like Perrault, Durand divides it into solidity, salubrity, and commodity. This division, as with Perrault, goes hand in hand with the determination to consider only the positive virtues of architecture. *Positive:* an adjective constantly used by late-eighteenth-century philosophers and scientists, from Jean Le Rond d'Alembert to Condorcet, to reflect an attitude that consists in focusing on tangible fact rather than on engaging in gratuitous speculation.[88] The word *positive* was soon to acquire a new dignity in the hands of Saint-Simon and Auguste Comte.[89] Contrary to widespread belief, Comtian positivism is not about banishing all theoretical concerns in favor of pure empiricism: it teaches that all theory must rest on verifiable facts and proscribes the use of concepts and terms that have no concrete counterpart.[90] In many ways, Durand stands between Perrault and Comte in seeking to deconstruct everything that might appear chimerical in the chosen objectives of architecture.

Durand's emphasis on economy reflects the same determination to stick to the indisputably positive elements of architecture. The concept of economy itself — a generalization of domestic economy, which is the administration of a household and the judicious use of its resources — was not a new one; but it played no significant part in architectural theory until the second half of the eighteenth century. Durand's immediate predecessors, practitioners and theorists alike, had become deeply concerned with questions of cost control — as witness the advice on the subject given by such authors as Pierre Patte and Nicolas Le Camus de Mézières.[91] But in the architectural culture of the Enlightenment the importance of economy went far beyond the financial: a piece of work might be economical in materials and in means of execution.

Thus interpreted, the principle of economy could be translated into spatial terms, through slender supports and simplicity of overall design. For example, churches with detached columns, or the stone bridges of Jean-Rodolphe Perronet, were economical in their use of materials, and their slender lines made this economy immediately apprehensible. The eventual construction bills for such undertakings as Soufflot's Sainte-Geneviève (now the Panthéon) or Perronet's Pont Louis XVI (now the Pont de la Concorde) demonstrated that economy in materials was not necessarily the same thing as financial economy. Despite the repeated lessons of experience, architectural thinkers continued to be haunted by the possibility of translating economy into visual terms.

This obsession was partly based on the concept of economy that had emerged in the life sciences in the seventeenth and eighteenth centuries. For scientists, the concept of animal economy referred both to the invisible and the visible: to the order of functions and circulations, hard to apprehend with the naked eye, and to the more readily apprehensible order of the conformation of organs.[92] It was in this dual perspective that Claude Perrault, for example, had studied the economy of living creatures in his *Mémoires pour servir à l'histoire naturelle des animaux* (Notes toward the Natural History of Animals; 1671–76) and in his *Essais de physique* (Essays in Physics; 1680–88).[93]

Durand's theoretical work seems to reflect this conception of harmony, with its conjunction of functional and morphological criteria. Economy as defined by the *Précis* relates to the principles of regularity, symmetry, and simplicity: "[T]he more symmetrical, regular, and simple a building is," Durand declares, "the less costly it becomes."[94] As proof of this, he argues the economy of materials permitted by elementary forms and volumes, such as the square and above all the circle, which make it possible to minimize the ratio between perimeter and enclosed area.

The argument seems disconcertingly naive. By thus giving precedence to the circle by virtue of its short perimeter, the author of the *Précis* appears to be transposing onto architecture, without qualifications, the *de maximis* and *de minimis* techniques worked out by scientists and engineers, first at the École du Génie, Mézières, and later at the École Polytechnique.[95] His real intention, however, is very different. For it was on those very principles of regularity, symmetry, and simplicity that Boullée and Ledoux had sought to establish a new, design-based practice of architecture. In choosing to have those principles sail under the colors of economy, Durand is laying a wager that he can devise a method of architectural composition that will be simultaneously autonomous, subject to purely geometric rules of association, and efficient. The comparison between the Panthéon in Paris, "so lacking in grandeur and in magnificence,"[96] and the rotunda that Durand puts forward to replace it is enlightening in this respect. Nothing is said about construction techniques or costs: the geometrical comparison is deemed to speak for itself. And so, though the *Précis* purports to be positivist, it actually inclines toward the very opposite, namely, utopianism. It is utopian to seek to free architecture from technical and economic constraints while simultaneously proclaiming their preeminence. After Durand, many other architects were to succumb to the same temptation, including the principal representatives of the modern movement, from Walter Gropius to Le Corbusier.

The relatively small space assigned to the technical and financial aspects of architecture is one of the most striking features of Durand's course of instruction. There is a marked contrast between the relatively rudimentary coverage of these matters and the emphasis on solidity, as the touchstone of fitness, and on economy. As we read the *Précis*, other tensions emerge. Durand almost entirely avoids direct references to natural objects, but some of them nevertheless creep into the theoretical discourse. The ideal of regularity, for instance, owes even more to the studies of Jean-Baptiste Romé de l'Isle and René-Just Haüy on crystalline structures than it does to any discussion of animal economy.[97] Durand is no doubt perfectly well aware of this background of natural objects and phenomena when he writes that his principles are "as simple as nature" and as fertile.[98] There is, of course, no inherent contradiction between avoiding the depiction of natural objects and deriving inspiration from such processes as crystallization. All the same, the reference to crystals is sometimes so literal as to be not far removed from imitation pure and simple, as in those plates in the *Précis* that show "roof combinations" and "ensembles of buildings resulting from various horizontal and vertical combinations."

Considering that Durand had given the world a number of projects for revolutionary monuments, his outright dismissal of the symbolic dimension is surprising, to put it mildly. The same goes for his denunciation of decoration, in view of the numerous examples of decorated buildings in his book. Durand's personal sensibility is such as to allow him to enjoy, as he freely admits, "the dreams of Piranesi, which are often eccentric but almost always sublime."[99] Again, the orders, which he dismisses as of no real interest, nonetheless form part of his syllabus. The paradox is partly resolved if we remember that the utilitarian role of architecture must involve some concessions to usage and taste; but it must be said that such concessions do somewhat impair the clarity of the message conveyed by the author of the *Précis*.

Of all the tensions that appear in Durand's writing, the most significant is between his assertion that architecture is justified by its social utility and his simultaneous attempt to turn the architectural project into a self-referential entity. How is architecture to meet constantly evolving needs while retaining its total autonomy? Revolutionary architecture reconciled these two imperatives by referring back to nature. Durand cannot do this, and so he needs a new answer. He never clearly supplies one, although the type is one notion that goes some way toward resolving the tension between the socialization and the autonomy of architectural production.

Anomalies of this kind are not, ultimately, too much of an embarrassment, since for Durand the conceptual foundations of architecture count for less than the exposition of his own method. The theory set out in the *Précis* is at its most truly positivist when it thus distances itself from the quest for the essence of architecture. Such a position recalls the way in which eighteenth-

35

century, post-Newtonian science gave up on the search for the ultimate truths of the universe to concentrate instead on phenomena. Durand's principle of utility operates in very much the same way as the law of universal gravitation: in that case, too, the reasons for the principle remain obscure, but it allows us to coordinate our observations relative to the courses of the heavenly bodies and the motion of falling objects.

Elements and Operations: The Triumph of Analysis

Durand's method stands in a straight line of descent from the analytical method defined by Locke, Condillac, and also Condorcet. Thus, the term *composition,* as used in the *Précis,* is less a reference to painting[100] than to the analytical method, the set of procedures that makes it possible to decompose objects and to set out their component parts in the "order in which genera-tion becomes easy." How could it be otherwise, with an architectural theorist who rejects the use of pictorial effects, washes, or perspective?[101]

In the last years of the eighteenth century, the analytical ideal of the Enlightenment was updated by the Ideologues, who attempted, in the wake of such thinkers as Antoine-Louis-Claude Destutt de Tracy, to draw from it the principles of a general theory of language (fig. 20).[102] There is no lack of linguistic reference in the *Précis*—as when its author likens the wealth and variety of the productions of architecture to that of the figures of speech.[103] Durand enlisted the help of a linguistic specialist, Jean-Baptiste Maudru, author of *Nouveau système de lecture applicable à toutes les langues* (New System of Reading Applicable to All Languages; 1799–1800), to see his first edition through the press.[104] All the same, his linguistic analogies remain on a superficial level—hardly surprising if we recall that, in rejecting the symbolic dimension, Durand has precluded himself from treating architecture as a system of signs analogous to a language. His approach in the *Précis* has nothing in common with the work of the Ideologues but its methodological framework.

The validity of such a framework rests on the hypothesis that the sciences and the arts are never anything other than combinations of elements. "In general, the elements of a whole are defined as the primitive and original parts from which we may suppose that that whole was formed," d'Alembert had written at the beginning of his long article "Élémens des sciences" in the *Encyclopédie.*[105] This conviction that the sciences and the arts may be con-sidered as combinations of elements was to inspire a number of intellectual endeavors; and, as we have seen, its influence extended to the speculative flights of revolutionary architecture. Without the starting point of an inven-tory of "primitive and original parts," it was difficult to progress "from the simple to the composite, from the known to the unknown," to quote Durand's account of his own method at the beginning of volume 2 of the *Précis.*[106]

Durand's list of the elements of buildings seems strangely meager by com-parison with the numerous avenues explored by the revolutionary architects.

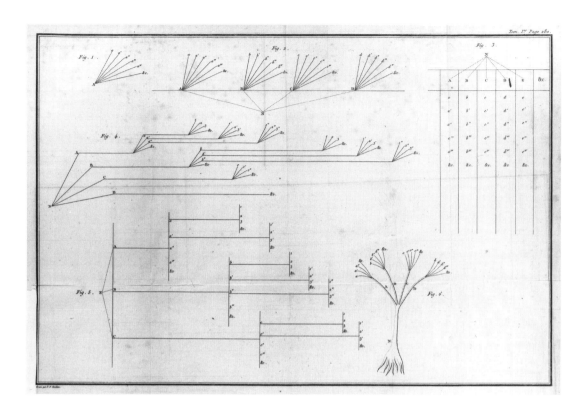

Fig. 20. P.-F. Tardieu, engraver
Analytical expression of complex ideas
From P.-F. Lancelin, *From "Poetry of Art" to Method à l'analyse des sciences,* 3d ed. (Paris: Bossange, Masson & Besson, 1801)

In the *Précis,* these elements are confined to the basic architectural ingredients: foundations, walls, detached supports, floors, vaults, roofs. There is no mention of the regular geometric solids, which Boullée listed at the beginning of his *Essai sur l'art* in accordance with the sensations that they were supposed to produce in the human mind. The functions of the dwelling, as analyzed by Le Camus de Mézières in his *Génie de l'architecture,* are also conspicuous by their absence. Durand seems to be deliberately confining himself to a positivist minimum of construction, an anatomy of building, in order to avoid the trap—into which the revolutionary architects had fallen—of the unbridgeable divide between the simple and the composite, between the elements of architecture and its actual productions.

But in that case why include the orders, under the heading detached supports? The author of the *Précis* has already made it perfectly clear that they are not essential. Here Durand seems to be regressing by comparison with Boullée, who discards them altogether in his *Essai sur l'art.* More generally, there is nothing genuinely "primitive" about the list of elements that Durand presents to his students. It is a list that refers to the architectural production of his own time and to its conventions.

The fact is that the adjectives *primitive* and *original* used by d'Alembert in referring to "primitive" elements are ambiguous from the start, in a way that needs to be disposed of. Contrary to what these adjectives might lead us to suppose, the elements of the sciences and arts have no existence prior to their discovery by humanity. Such elements represent only the results to date of a process of exploration and manipulation of the external world; and that process cannot possibly lead us to primitive entities of a kind that is either absolutely simple, like the elements in ancient Aristotelian physics, or indivisible, like the atoms of Epicurean tradition. D'Alembert, in "Élémens des sciences," deals with this by saying that a perfect intelligence would see no division within nature and would consequently distinguish neither elements nor combinations. "Partaking of the supreme intelligence, the human mind would see all its knowledge as united from a single, indivisible viewpoint," he adds, adopting a perspective that anticipates Pierre-Simon Laplace and his *Essai philosophique sur les probabilités* (1814).[107]

From this same viewpoint, the elements, or "simple substances," of Lavoisier's new chemistry—hydrogen, oxygen, nitrogen—are in fact simple only in relative terms, pending new information as to the complexity within them. Chaptal makes this clear in his *Élémens de chimie* (Elements of Chemistry; 1803):

> From the moment when chemistry believed itself far enough advanced to know the principles of substances, it supposed itself obliged to indicate the number, nature, and character of the elements; anything that resisted its methods of decomposition was deemed to be simple and elementary. If the elements are defined in this way as the end products of analysis, their number and nature will vary according to the progress and the revolutions that take place in chemistry: a reading of all the

chemists who have written on the subject will confirm this.... It is clearly dangerous to mistake the artist's terminology for the Creator's, and to assume that the
state of our knowledge is a state of perfection. The term *element* should therefore
be eliminated from chemical nomenclature, or at least regarded simply as an indication of the latest state of our analytical results.[108]

The elements of science are not founded on the rock of identity but on the
shifting sand of their relationship with humanity. In the fullest sense of the
term, they are experimental realities: realities that a d'Alembert—anticipat-
ing Comtian positivism—defines as positive by contrast with the uncertain
verities of the old metaphysics.

What such elements lack in firm identity they make up for in the ease with
which, thanks to them, we can describe the operations of nature and of humanity. To the scientists and technologists of the Enlightenment, those operations are more important than the identification of the elements that serve to
describe them—as the leading Ideologue, Pierre-Jean-Georges Cabanis, empha-
sizes in his *Rapports du physique et du moral de l'homme* (Relations between
the Physical and Moral Natures of Man; 1802):

> Everything is forever moving in nature; all substances are in continual flux. Their
> elements combine and decompose; they successively assume a thousand fugitive
> forms: and in their turn these metamorphoses, which are the necessary conse-
> quences of an action that never ceases, renew the causes of the universe and pre-
> serve its eternal youth. A moment's reflection will disclose that any movement
> entails or implies destruction and reproduction; that the properties of substances
> that are destroyed and reborn must change at every instant; that they cannot change
> without implanting new characteristics on the phenomena that relate to them; and,
> finally, that if we could clearly define all the conditions of the successive phases
> through which entities pass, the great enigma of their nature and existence might
> perhaps to a large degree be solved, even though the existence and nature of their
> component elements were to remain forever shrouded in an impenetrable veil.[109]

As the historian of science Jacques Roger has pointed out, this represents
a momentous epistemological shift. Already detectable in the work of Georges-
Louis Leclerc de Buffon, this shift was complete by the turn of the nineteenth
century. More and more decisively, the sciences turned away from the consideration of essentially static verities to the study of processes:

> If there is an order in the world, it is no longer an order of structures, the structures
> that are classified by taxonomists. It is an order of the "operations" of nature, an
> order of processes that permit life and its endless renewal, an order of the forces
> that animate the living world and of the laws that govern them.[110]

Inseparable from the analytical ideal, in which decomposition is followed
by rational composition, this emphasis on operations and processes allows us

once more to find analogies between Durand's theoretical work and the sciences and technologies of his day, most notably with descriptive geometry. At the École Polytechnique, descriptive geometry was taught through a reasoned succession of operations: projection, the construction of tangent straight lines and planes, the plotting of curves of intersection. Durand's proposition, with its horizontal and vertical combinations, its divisions of the square, and its serial compositions, is basically very close to this.

It now becomes easier to understand the arbitrary nature of the elements of architecture as presented in the *Précis*. They stand at the intersection of two principles: the first is utility, but a utility that pays respect to societal conventions; the second is the preeminence of those operations that initiate the architectural project. The elements therefore include some forms hallowed by usage, including the orders. This concession to the facts of architectural life at least brings with it a high degree of standardization, of which the treatment of the orders constitutes the best example.

Durand's system is closely modeled on that proposed by Claude Perrault in his *Ordonnance des cinq espèces de colonnes selon la méthode des anciens*— as are his supporting arguments. Perrault's distinction between "positive" and "arbitrary" beauty is reflected in Durand's distinction between those forms and proportions that "spring from the nature of materials" and those that "custom has in a sense made necessary to us."[111] The role assigned to custom or habit is virtually identical in the two writers. The objective is also the same: to replace the complexities of an obsolete tradition with forms and proportions that are "simpler and more definite." In both cases, the aim is to simplify the process of invention, although between the late seventeenth century and the early nineteenth the underlying political motive has changed: from the consolidation of an absolute monarchy to the establishment of a new postrevolutionary order.

Durand departs from Perrault in introducing a Greek Doric that takes account of the archaeological discoveries of the Enlightenment era, from the Temples of Paestum onward. He also goes no further than the Corinthian order, leaving out the Composite. However, the heights that he assigns to the columns follow an arithmetical progression like that in the *Ordonnance:* they measure respectively 6, 7, 8, 9, and 10 modules. This progression, along with the simplification of the details of each order, is the salient feature of the system set out in the *Précis*.[112]

Durand rounds off his simplified system with a collection of moldings, inspired by antique monuments, and a survey of the ordonnances prescribed by a number of authors. For the orders and their details, Durand seems to have adopted the eclectic approach taken by Le Roy in his *Ruines des plus beaux monuments de la Grèce:*

> In this connection, it would seem best to refer to all the fragments of the monuments of antiquity that can be collected in Greece, Asia Minor, or Syria, together with those that still remain in Rome; to the precepts of Vitruvius on the propor-

tions of the orders; and finally to the views of the most celebrated architects concerning such proportions: all of these elements may serve to compose the best orders possible.[113]

Essentially, the first part of the *Précis* is a catalog of stylized elements. Once more, the aim is not to survey all available examples in all their variants but to define a repertoire that affords sufficient combinations to answer human needs in society. To revert in part to the linguistic analogy, what counts is not the size of the vocabulary but the wealth of the syntax.[114]

The syntactical level begins with the parts of buildings: porches, vestibules, staircases, rooms, and courtyards. The manipulation of these represents the first stage in the study of composition. Here the square grid makes its appearance. This makes it possible to carry the standardization, initiated with the elements, one stage further, and to introduce the concepts of the alignment and the axis, which later emerge as crucial. Without being an absolute novelty—it had, for example, been used by the Italian engineer and architect Bernardo Vittone in his *Istruzioni elementari* (1760)[115]—the square grid takes on a new importance with Durand, who makes it into an instructional tool. He had his students do their composition work on squared paper—a practice entirely consistent with his professed disdain for illusionistic renderings, that is, perspective views or geometric drawings with too much wash. If "to project a building is to solve a problem," the student is far better off without the ambiguities that tend to attach themselves to issues of dimensioning or to the search for quasi-pictorial relief effects.

Like the elements of buildings, their parts bear no reference to use. Vestibules, halls, or rooms are studied strictly in relation to their morphological characteristics. Durand's generic approach to the parts of a building confutes the accusation of narrow functionalism so often aimed at him. This is not functionalism but geometricism.[116]

At this stage in the exposition of Durand's method, one of its most blatant limitations emerges. The combinatorial quality that Durand is looking for is negated by the intrusion of devices quite different from those that arise from the straightforward combination of elements. Thus, in the plate showing central rooms, the residual spaces generated by the building of a dome above a square space are enlivened by half-domes. Such devices often stem from the late-eighteenth-century theoretical projects that Durand had absorbed as a student. It is as if the architect's cultural background were surfacing in spite of him, in response to all those many problems that cannot be reduced to a combination of horizontal and vertical elements. Nourished by the antique and by its late-eighteenth-century interpreters, from Piranesi to Boullée, this cultural background often diverts him from his chosen method.

The student's apprenticeship in composition is nevertheless meant to be just as systematic as his study of the elements of buildings. It consists in mastering a series of operations of duplication or division. The square, for instance, must be divided into two, three, or four, as shown in the plate in the

1813 edition entitled "Ensembles d'édifices résultants de diverses combinai-sons horisontales et verticales" (Ensembles of Buildings Resulting from Vari-ous Horizontal and Vertical Combinations).

In techniques of composition, the floor plan counts for far more than the section or elevation: "As for the section, it is largely supplied by the plan," Durand declares, adding that "the elevation is all composed, just as soon as the plan and the section are composed."[117]

The plan is settled in a number of stages that are synthesized, from the 1813 edition of the *Précis* onward, in a section headed "Marche à suivre dans la com-position d'un projet quelconque" (Procedure to Be Followed in the Composi-tion of Any Project; fig. 21). An initial study of the purpose of the building, and of the *convenances* that apply to it, leads to an initial formula: whether the project should be in one piece or divided; which parts of it should be treated identically and which sharply distinguished. A system of primary and secondary axes gives substance to this formula. On the basis of this system, which is reminiscent of the reference plans used in descriptive geometry, the parts of the project take shape, followed by the constituent elements required.

In this process of defining the primary and secondary axes of the compo-sition, Durand once more reveals his debt to the innovative work on architec-tural form that had been done in the late eighteenth century. That work combined the primacy of the axes with considerations of function and conse-quent circulation, as best exemplified in the designs made by engineers for harbors and naval shipyards.[118] Under the First Empire, this functionalist approach was maintained in a number of major compositions entrusted to civil and military engineers, such as the new towns of Napoléonville (now Pontivy) and Napoléon-Vendée (now La Roche-sur-Yon), which were built to pacify and control Brittany and the Vendée, respectively.[119] This influence is less evident in the *Précis,* where the concern for regularity tends to prevail over any detailed scrutiny of functions and circulations. Durand's geometri-cism permits the adoption of a functionalist attitude, and it is quite compati-ble with the circulatory analysis that is typical of architecture and urban planning in the hands of engineers, but it does not presuppose any of this.

As Durand observes, the order of operations involved in composition is the exact reverse of those required in an architectural apprenticeship, since in composition the architect takes the definition of the whole as his starting point and ends up with the constituent elements of the building.[120] However, the one implies the other: analysis is inseparable from synthesis. Durand's method is analytical in its simultaneous manipulation of composition and decomposition, and also in its underlying hypothesis that teaching must always be the mirror image or symmetrical inversion of practice.

Such a method can also be considered analytical in a second sense. Analy-sis, as conducted by scientists and engineers, is not only designed to unravel the skein of operations that lead from simple to complex: it also has the pur-pose of arranging problems in a sequence to avoid confusion. In calling for the composition of elevations to be subordinated to that of the plan, Durand's

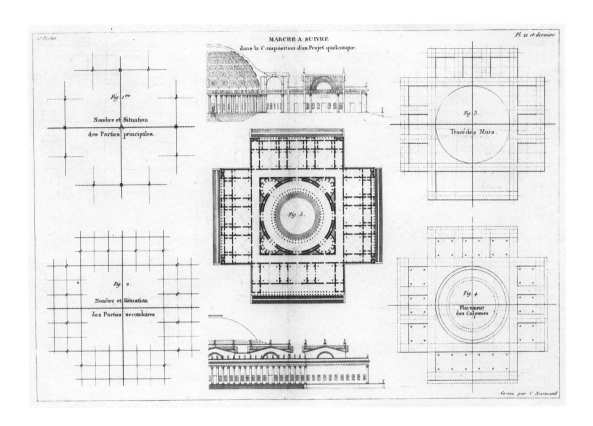

Fig. 21. Jean-Nicolas-Louis Durand, architect
"Marche à suivre dans la composition d'un projet quelconque"
(Procedure to Be Followed in the Composition of Any Project)
From Durand, *Précis des leçons d'architecture données à l'École Polytechnique,*
4th ed. (Paris: the author, 1825), vol. 2, plate 21
Photo: Getty Research Institute

method establishes the autonomy of each relative to the other. This potential autonomy is never exploited in the *Précis,* since Durand fights shy of eclecticism. The neoclassical style, to which his writings belong, is by no means so scrupulous in practice; and it is perfectly possible to imagine, given a redefinition of the morphology of the elements, that the compositional techniques of the *Précis* could be applied to Gothic, Moorish, or Chinese ordonnances. The variety of buildings presented in the *Recueil et parallèle des édifices de tous genres, anciens et modernes* is in any case an implicit invitation to eclecticism. The fruitfulness of Durand's method lies partly in this potential for wider application, which was to resurface at the École des Beaux-Arts.

Between the techniques of composition set out in the *Précis* and those that later made the fortune of the Beaux-Arts system, there is a kinship that is by no means confined to the primacy of the floor plan, or to the importance of defining the primary and secondary axes of the project: it also resides in the disconnection of plan from elevation, and of architectural form from construction.[121] In nineteenth-century France, this approach to the project was shared by architects and engineers. It allowed each to exercise his own competence within clearly defined limits, and occasions for conflict were accordingly reduced. Contrary to the repeated assertions of, for example, César Daly,[122] the conflict between nineteenth-century architects and engineers was more a myth than a reality. Composition, as presented by the professor of architecture at the École Polytechnique, was not only a project method but also the bearer of new forms of negotiation between architectural and structural specialists.[123]

Specific Forms of "Convenance": Types and Series
Focused as it is on the principles and "mechanics" of composition, volume 1 of the *Précis* has little to say as to the *convenances* relative to each kind of project. In his introduction, Durand justifies this choice by explaining that "to study, one after the other, the different classes of building in all of the circumstances that are liable to modify them" would be a "dauntingly long" process.[124] It would not only be long but liable to lead to misjudgment; as Durand adds: the architect must at all costs avoid embarking on a project with an a priori solution in mind.

This imperative partly explains the highly generalized character of the analyses of different classes of building that make up the greater part of volume 2 of the *Précis.* Durand seems anxious to prevent the reader from becoming too wedded to the examples that he presents. The origins of these examples are highly diverse. Some, such as the palace or the institute, are inspired by eighteenth-century compositions. Boullée, Percier, and Marie-Joseph Peyre are all drawn on. Others model themselves on more contemporary projects, such as the cavalry barracks designed by Détournelle in Year VIII (1799–1800). Durand also reuses some projects of his own: a simplified version of the Lathuille house appears in the chapter on private buildings.[125]

None of these project examples is, strictly speaking, a type. To grasp the content of Durand's typological approach, we need to move up a level or two, paying attention first of all to the system of classification of buildings that governs the organization of volume 2 of the *Précis*. This is based on the distinction between public and private, which may be likened to the distinction between classes—mammals, birds, reptiles, and the rest—in the life sciences.

Public buildings are subdivided, in turn, according to purpose. Temples or religious buildings constitute a first group. Then follow palaces, public treasuries, and more generally all governmental facilities (fig. 22). Then come buildings devoted to knowledge, from colleges to observatories, and those that contribute to economic life: markets, bourses, fairs (fig. 23). Theaters represent the world of entertainment; baths and hospitals that of hygiene and health. Prisons and barracks close the sequence.

The survey of private buildings is divided between town and country, with urban houses and apartments, on the one side, and villas, farms, and hostelries, on the other. On a second dimension of analysis, Durand describes the individual rooms within a dwelling, in a straight line of descent from eighteenth-century treatises on architectural planning. The analysis remains superficial, however.

The list of programs discussed in the *Précis* is far from being exhaustive. Factories, for example, are left out. Durand conjures up for his readers a kind of Arcadia, dotted with medium-sized towns and model villages. Though still just plausible when volume 2 first appeared in 1805, this picture was far less so by the late 1820s, when the effects of the Industrial Revolution were beginning to make themselves felt in France.

There is a hint of unreality at times, partly because of Durand's frequent references to antiquity. In a manual intended for budding engineers, there is something incongruous about his lengthy quotations from the letters of Pliny the Younger in the country house chapter. The typology that Durand has in mind is not a catalog of immediately applicable solutions but a system of classification that makes it possible to familiarize oneself with the various problems that may turn up in practice, but without any thought of covering them systematically. A number of obsolete programs are included, without any sense of unease at this violation of the principle of direct utility. For these programs serve to demonstrate the coherence of the system, in a way that recalls those hypothetical species, or "missing links," with which evolutionary theory attempts to fill the gaps in its knowledge of living things.

In relation to this system, the type defines itself as a kind of subsystem based on the association between functions, uses, and Durand's favorite axial schemes of spatial arrangement. The type derives its coherence and stability from a kind of internal economy, analogous to animal economy. Seen thus, it forms a matrix that serves to guide the conception without confining it to the imitation of a model. The projects presented in the *Précis* are not types: they are illustrations of the fruitful nature of the typological approach. This approach is in fact more clearly set out in the *Recueil et parallèle,* in which the juxtaposition of plans, sections, and elevations at the same scale makes it easier to apprehend the types from which they derive.

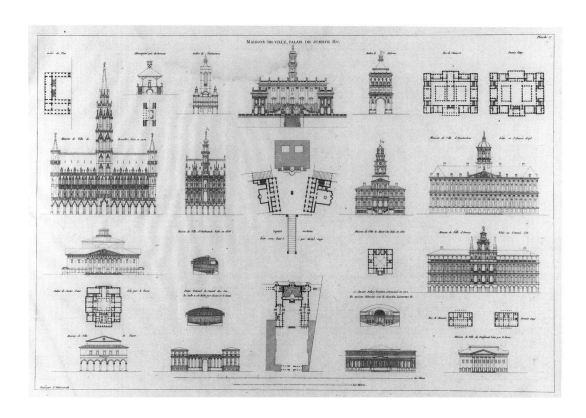

Fig. 22. Jean-Nicolas-Louis Durand and Jacques-Guillaume Legrand, architects
Charles-Nicolas Ransonnette, engraver
Town halls and courthouses
From Durand, *Recueil et parallèle des édifices de tout genre...*
(Paris: Gillé fils, Year IX [1800/1801])
Photo: Getty Research Institute

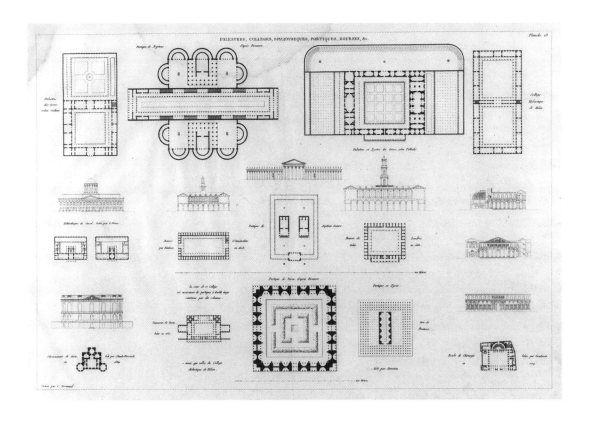

Fig. 23. Jean-Nicolas-Louis Durand and Jacques-Guillaume Legrand, architects
Charles-Pierre-Joseph Normand, engraver
Gymnasia, colleges, libraries, porticoes, commodity exchanges, and so on
From Durand, *Recueil et parallèle des édifices de tout genre...*
(Paris: Gillé fils, Year IX [1800/1801])
Photo: Getty Research Institute

Architectural types change from century to century. Some disappear; others are transformed; sometimes it is possible, or even desirable, to take a step backward. Thus, Durand suggests reverting to the type of the early Christian basilica, instead of perpetuating the errors for which he castigates Bramante and his successors.[126] The time dimension is one of the principal lessons taught by the *Recueil et parallèle*—though historical rigor is not exactly a high priority for its author, who blandly identifies a youthful project by the architect Pierre-Adrien Pâris as an "Indian Tomb,"[127] and who cheerfully accepts the "unauthentic" restorations of ancient Rome made by Palladio and Piranesi for the sake of "the fine solutions that these restorations present."[128] His aim is not so much to trace the factual evolution of architectural forms as to single out logical articulations and developments and to indicate sequences of which the typology of early-nineteenth-century architecture constitutes an interim product.

Durand was not the only writer to take a typological view of neoclassical architecture. A comparable approach is to be found in the *Études relatives à l'art des constructions* (1823–28) by the engineer and architect Louis Bruyère, who surveys the full range of public buildings of the Napoleonic period.[129] Typology is also the guiding principle of the collections of private architecture published by Louis-Ambroise Dubut and Jean-Charles Krafft.[130] With its borrowings from Greco-Roman antiquity, Palladio, and Italian vernacular architecture, with its somewhat mechanical compositions and with its stereotyped detailing, neoclassicism lends itself well to this kind of operation.

What makes the *Précis* and, above all, the *Recueil et parallèle* stand out among contemporary compilations is the system that drives them. As an element in a system, the architectural type defines itself at least as much by its differences from others as by its positive virtues. Here, again, the gulf that separates Durand's compositions from those of Quatremère de Quincy is striking. To Quatremère, writing in his *Dictionnaire de l'architecture* (1832), the type is a "preexistent germ," an "imaginative model," "a kind of nucleus around which the developments and variations of forms applicable to the object have coalesced and coordinated themselves."[131] As understood by Quatremère, the type derives from no general system: it is a primitive essence, an archetype.

Durand's systematic approach has often been likened to that of the life sciences, with the architectural type playing the same role as the species in botany or zoology. The Linnaean system of taxonomy abandons purely external criteria of differentiation, such as the number or shape of limbs, to concentrate on the layout and functional value of such major vital systems as reproduction. This suggests a path to be followed, in architecture, in order to distinguish the type from the model and typology itself from the mere recording of projects. Analogies also exist between the serial arrangements presented in the *Recueil et parallèle* and those devised by seventeenth- and eighteenth-century naturalists before the emergence of the concept of evolution.[132] In this respect, architecture may well have been ahead of botany and zoology, since the idea of the transformation of architectural types is less hard to accept than that of the mutability of plant and animal species.

In reality, the influence of the life sciences on Durand's approach is difficult to demonstrate with any precision. In the absence of direct interaction, it is perhaps best to refer back to the cultural frameworks that science and architecture had in common. These are frameworks of the kind that Michel Foucault tried to describe in *Les mots et les choses* (translated as *The Order of Things*), notably in relation to the overriding seventeenth- and eighteenth-century concern with the issue of representation and with the difficulty of matching the order of the world with the order of language; hence the importance attached to classification and tabulation in domains as disparate as natural history and grammar.[133] According to Foucault, the Enlightenment in its late phase clung to this framework in many respects, while at the same time a start was made on its reappraisal and replacement.

Foucault's perspective can be applied to the typological approach of a man like Durand, as it can to many of the scientific undertakings of his day. But we can also refer Durand's approach to a different cultural framework, by interpreting it as a continuation of the ideal of analysis that runs through all of his work, from his method of architectural composition onward. From the outset, the combinatorial nature of architecture enables us to limit the range of possible types and fit them into a system. The type is a complex device stabilized by function and usage, a condensation of architectural culture; it relates symmetrically to the element. The architect's apprenticeship begins with a catalog of the elements of buildings; the practice of design starts with a survey of established types, just as we comb a library for references before starting to write an academic treatise. There is something bookish in Durand's approach, with its rejection of the infinite variety of nature in favor of a twofold system of elements and types.

A Rationalist before His Time

Until the 1820s and 1830s, Durand's teaching tallied perfectly with the expectations of the École Polytechnique and its associated specialist schools, offering them a standardized design method. The effectiveness of his method may be gauged at the École des Ponts et Chaussées, where the students' compositions remained faithful to the principles laid down by Durand (figs. 24, 25), even though Mandar succeeded in inflecting them in the direction of a closer link between architectural and structural solutions. It was equally effective in the outside world, wherever state-employed engineers were required to build public facilities and housing, either in major projects such as the new towns of Napoléonville and Napoléon-Vendée or in rural areas where there were often no architects.

This unanimity between Durand and the professional world within which he developed his ideas had its source in a set of common values. First among these was utility. Bruyère, when he writes that a building is beautiful if its planning is appropriate to its use, is not far from the formulas used by the

Fig. 24. Unknown architect
Design for a public market for the architectural competition
of the École des Ponts et Chaussées, early nineteenth century
Paris, École Nationale des Ponts et Chaussées

Fig. 25. G. Girard de Caudemberg
Design for a hospice for the architectural competition of
the École des Ponts et Chaussées, 1815
Paris, École Nationale des Ponts et Chaussées

author of the *Précis*. Again, when Bruyère declares, "In any building, whatever embellishments the architect may use may be considered as the draperies of the sculpture, which must always serve to bring out the forms of the nude,"[134] he once more seems perfectly in step with Durand.

What nevertheless distinguishes Durand's objectives from those of the engineers whom he knew or trained is this: in his eyes, the imperatives of utility, fitness, and economy did not mean that architecture was in any way subordinate to engineering. On the contrary, the author of the *Précis* was constantly concerned to preserve the autonomy of the discipline of architecture. He would never have called, as Bruyère did, for the École des Beaux-Arts to be converted into a specialist school of the École Polytechnique — a change that would have amounted to handing over to the engineers a monopoly on architecture.[135]

From the 1830s onward, Durand's approach began to lose its relevance for the engineers, as can be seen from the policy followed by Léonce Reynaud, who was to all intents and purposes his successor at the École Polytechnique. Distancing himself from Durand's indifference to the decorative and symbolic aspects of architecture, Reynaud set out to restore "art" to its traditional prerogatives.[136] His *Traité d'architecture* (Treatise on Architecture; 1850–58), based on his own teaching, retained Durand's distinction between the elements and the composition of buildings, but this was now purely a matter of form. Nothing could be more remote from Durand's geometricism than the theory set out in Reynaud's *Traité d'architecture,* according to which art is "to be left all the latitude that is its due," for "what touches on the intimate essence of art is to be felt, not explained."[137]

"Is it not remarkable to find the cause of taste and imagination defended by a Polytechnician against the sophisms of a purportedly rational theory devised by an artist? This proves, at least, that the abuse of mathematics is not always the responsibility of mathematicians," remarked Fernand de Dartein, Reynaud's principal disciple and biographer.[138] Reynaud may have committed no abuse of mathematics, but his *Traité* allots an important position to science, as represented by Navier's work on the strength of materials and by Louis-Joseph Vicat's pioneering work on the chemistry of lime and cement. Science was now triumphant, and it became one of its major concerns to define the limits within which artistic genius might operate. A new kind of relationship was emerging between science and technology, on the one hand, and art and architecture, on the other. The quest for methodological frameworks applicable to both sides now gave way to the recognition of their differences and the exploration of the frontier between them. Instead of the Enlightenment dream of the union of art and science, there emerged the confrontation between the "two cultures," scientific and artistic.[139]

Durand's vision of scientific method was now finally superseded, though its insistence on the positive emerged triumphant in the work of Comte. Mathematical analysis, as revolutionized by Augustin-Louis Cauchy,[140] had little in common with Condillac's "complete decomposition of an object, and the distribution of its parts into an order in which its generation becomes easy." From physics to engineering, from chemistry to medicine, scientific and technological knowledge was now too complex to be seen in terms of combinations of finite numbers of elements.

Among architects, Durand's influence was also in decline. The romantics, led by Félix-Jacques Duban, Pierre-François-Henri Labrouste, Louis-Joseph Duc, and Léon Vaudoyer, turned their backs on the principles on which his teaching was founded.[141] Gottfried Semper mocked him for using squared paper.[142] His definition of utility now seemed unduly restrictive. As they came under the influence of utopian socialism, or of the great debates in the new life sciences of comparative anatomy and paleontology, architects dreamed of an organic architecture that would be impossible to reduce to any combinatorial formula.[143] The theoretical debate moved on, and the issues considered by Durand in the *Recueil et parallèle* and the *Précis* were left far behind.

Both nevertheless remained useful works of reference. For Durand had succeeded better than anyone else in formalizing the rules of architectural composition and the principles governing the employment of types. This was the nucleus of his teaching; but that nucleus was now left isolated, deprived of its justification, emptied of the polemical content that it had possessed in the immediate postrevolutionary period.

Here it is wise to qualify the analysis put forward by Henry-Russell Hitchcock, who saw Durand as the inspiration for a wide range of nineteenth-century northern European architecture.[144] Durand did of course have a number of German pupils, Leo von Klenze among them; but it would be wrong to overestimate his influence on their later careers.

Links nevertheless exist between Durand and the theoretical concerns of the second half of the nineteenth century. One of these is his ambition to make architecture rational. By replacing transcendental origins with an insistence on method, and by preferring clarity of argument to the seductions of form, the *Précis des leçons d'architecture données à l'École Polytechnique* earns a place among the earliest rationalist manifestos of the nineteenth century, though Eugène-Emmanuel Viollet-le-Duc and his successors were to dispense with its exclusively geometrical method.[145] Like Viollet-le-Duc after him, Durand was pursuing "a means of producing, even more than a product."[146]

Durand's rationalism, like Viollet-le-Duc's, anticipates some of the tensions within the modern movement. One of these is the difficulty, for architecture, of reconciling its desire for disciplinary autonomy with its eminently social nature. The curious status of architectural beauty in the *Précis*—whereby the quest for beauty can succeed only if it is in some sense involuntary—is reminiscent of the utterances of some twentieth-century engineers and architects who have set out in search of an art liberated from the desire to please. "So far from denying that architecture can give pleasure, we maintain that it cannot but give pleasure, where it is treated in accordance with its true principles."[147] Style apart, this sentence by Durand could without difficulty be put into the mouth of Jean Prouvé or Buckminster Fuller.

Finally, Durand's somewhat casual attitude to history may raise a smile, or it may be found disconcerting or even irritating. It is in fact entirely representative of the new and ambivalent relationship between theory and history that emerged with the demise of Vitruvianism. On the one hand, theory needed history to provide a foundation for its propositions. On the other, history had to be rewritten, simplified, stylized, if it was not to contradict the theoretical discourse. From his *Dictionnaire raisonné de l'architecture française* (Critical Dictionary of French Architecture; 1854–64) to his *Entretiens sur l'architecture* (Conversations on Architecture; 1863–72), Viollet-le-Duc himself was unable to escape from this vicious circle.

As a rationalist before his time, Durand thus prefigures a number of the ideals of the modern movement—the very modern movement that was to abolish his method of composition. The precise historical position of his theory is harder to define than it might seem. For such writers as Joseph Rykwert or Alberto Pérez-Gómez, it represents a revolution entirely for the worse: it marks the end of an architecture in touch with myth and history, the exhaustion of the poetics that sprang from the constant reinterpretation of Vitruvius.[148] The terseness of the plates of the *Précis* seems to bear out such a criticism. But this is to overlook the fact that Durand was opening up new paths for the architectural imagination even while he was rejecting others. He followed his former master, Boullée, in providing scope for a methodological examination of the nature of the architectural project. Most importantly, however, these critics overlook the sheer attractiveness of his theoretical work: it is both coherent and ambiguous, both introverted and open to the new questions that were being asked in its time. None of the plates in the *Précis* is absorbing in its own right. In sequence, nevertheless, there is a quasi-musical fascination about them. There is beauty in reason and in the systems to which it gives rise. Is reason really so cold and passionless? Perhaps Durand's undertaking is a madness, the very same madness that Walter Benjamin attributed to the nineteenth century and its capitalist and industrial modernity when he wrote that modernity was simply "a natural phenomenon whereby a new sleep, full of dreams, descended upon Europe, and with it a reactivation of mythical forces."[149] Perhaps the dreams and myths of contemporary architecture begin with Durand.

Notes

1. Jean-Nicolas-Louis Durand, *Précis des leçons d'architecture données à l'École Polytechnique*, 2 vols. (Paris: the author, 1802–5; rev. ed., Paris: the author, 1817–19; reprint of rev. ed., Nördlingen, A. Uhl, 1985). For the purposes of this introduction, I shall refer to the French text of the revised edition, of which a recent facsimile exists. Cross-references to the English text of the present translation (where these are possible, Durand having considerably modified his text in places) are given in brackets [thus]. Unless otherwise indicated below, all translations are by David Britt.

2. Jean-Nicolas-Louis Durand and Jacques-Guillaume Legrand, *Recueil et parallèle*

des édifices de tout genre, anciens et modernes, remarquables par leur beauté, par leur grandeur ou par leur singularité, et dessinés sur une même échelle (Paris: Gillé fils, 1799–1801; reprint of 1842 ed., Nördlingen, A. Uhl, 1986).

3. Bernard Huet, "Les trois fortunes de Durand," preface to Werner Szambien, *Jean-Nicolas-Louis Durand, 1760–1834: De l'imitation à la norme* (Paris: Picard, 1984), 6–11, 10: "*Le* Précis *est le premier traité d'architecture qui prenne pour objet l'Architecture même, l'Architecture sans référence à l'art de bâtir. Seul compte pour Durand l'acte instaurateur d'architecture que représente le projet.*"

4. Robert Krier, "Façades pour un palais," *Archives d'architecture moderne,* no. 11 (1977): 25–32; Livio Vacchini, "Letzte Etappe der 'Primarschule ai Saleggi' in Locarno TI," *Werk, Bauen und Wohnen,* no. 4 (1981): 17–21; Alberto Pérez-Gómez, "Durand and Functionalism," in *Architecture and the Crisis of Modern Science* (Cambridge: MIT Press, 1983; 2d ed., 1984), 297–326; Sergio Villari, *J. N. L. Durand, 1760–1834: Art and Science of Architecture,* trans. Eli Gottlieb (New York: Rizzoli, 1990).

5. Athanase Détournelle, "Architecture, second volume du *Précis,*" *Journal des arts, des sciences et de la littérature,* no. 410 (10 germinal an XIII, i.e., 30 March 1805): 25–30, esp. 27: "*manière trop énergique pour annoncer une vérité.*"

6. Here I take *neoclassical* in its French sense, which distinguishes the *style néoclassique* proper, contemporary with the First Empire and Restoration, from the antique-inspired work of the second half of the eighteenth century.

7. Durand was certainly not the only champion of this realignment. The increasingly theoretical character of the projects submitted for the Grands Prix de l'Académie d'Architecture during the second half of the eighteenth century reflects something of the same logic. The *Précis* nevertheless marks a turning point, by virtue of its emphasis on the questions of method raised by the idea of architectural design.

8. This was the "Monument destiné à rassembler les différentes académies" (Monumental Edifice to House the Different Academies), which won Percier the Grand Prix de l'Académie d'Architecture in 1786. There is a reproduction of this project in Jean-Marie Pérouse de Montclos, ed., "*Les Prix de Rome*": *Concours de l'Académie Royale d'Architecture au XVIIIᵉ siècle* (Paris: Berger-Levrault, École Nationale Supérieure des Beaux-Arts, 1984), 199–200. See also Joseph Rykwert, "The École des Beaux-Arts and the Classical Tradition," in Robin Middleton, ed., *The Beaux-Arts and Nineteenth-Century French Architecture* (Cambridge: MIT Press, 1982), 9–17, esp. 14.

9. The drawings for these two projects are now in the library of the École des Beaux-Arts, Paris. See our figures 1 and 2 for the 1779 project.

10. The *Précis* includes a number of allusions to Durand's observations in Italy, connected with, for example, the planning of fountains.

11. On this project see Szambien (note 3), 23–26.

12. These drawings are now in the Musée des Beaux-Arts, Rouen. Concerning them, see Werner Szambien, "Aux origines de l'enseignement de Durand: Les cent soixante-huit croquis des *Rudimenta operis magni et disciplinae,*" *Études de la revue du Louvre,* no. 1 (1980): 122–30.

13. On the Year II competitions, see Werner Szambien, *Les projets de l'an II: Concours d'architecture de la période révolutionnaire* (Paris: École Nationale Supérieure

des Beaux-Arts, 1986); *Les architectes de la liberté, 1789–1799,* exh. cat. (Paris: École Nationale Supérieure des Beaux-Arts, 1989).

14. Juste-Aurèle Meissonnier, *Paralèlle général des édifices les plus considérables depuis les Égyptiens, les Grecs, jusqu'à nos derniers Modernes, dessinés sur une même échelle* (Paris, ca. 1750; reprint, Bronx: B. Blom, 1969); Julien-David Le Roy, *Les ruines des plus beaux monuments de la Grèce* (Paris: H. L. Geurin & L. F. Delatour, 1758; 2d ed., Paris: L. F. Delatour, 1770). The plate in Le Roy's 1770 edition takes up a parallel devised by Le Roy himself in his *Histoire de la disposition et des formes différentes que les Chrétiens ont donnée à leurs temples depuis le règne de Constantin le Grand jusqu'à nous* (Paris: Desaint & Saillant, 1764). In 1764 Le Roy's (Christian) temples were not yet drawn to the same scale. Victor Louis, *Salle de spectacle de Bordeaux* (Paris: the author and Esprit, 1782). Among the precursors of Meissonnier, Le Roy, Louis, and Durand, one name must of course be mentioned: that of Johann Bernhard Fischer von Erlach, author of *Entwurff einer historischen Architectur* (Vienna: n.p., 1721).

15. On Durand's French and foreign pupils, see Szambien (see note 3), esp. 119–42; Werner Szambien and Simona Talenti, "Durand, Quaet-Faslem et Dartein; ou, L'influence européenne de Durand," *Bulletin de la Société des amis de la bibliothèque de l'École Polytechnique,* no. 16 (1996): 1–11.

16. See Szambien (note 3), esp. 19.

17. Jean-Nicolas-Louis Durand, *Choix des projets d'édifices publics et particuliers composés par MM. les élèves de l'École Polytechnique* (Paris: Gaucher, 1816); Jean-Nicolas-Louis Durand, *Partie graphique des cours d'architecture faits à l'École Royale polytechnique depuis sa réorganisation; précédée d'un sommaire des leçons relatives à ce nouveau travail* (Paris: the author and École Royale Polytechnique, 1821; reprint, Nördlingen, A. Uhl, 1985). Cross-references to the English text of the present translation are given in brackets [thus].

18. Antoine Picon, "Charles-François Mandar (1757–1844); ou, L'architecture dans tous ses détails," *Revue de l'art,* no. 109 (1995): 26–39, esp. 27: "*mérite classique.*"

19. Emil Kaufmann, *Von Ledoux bis Le Corbusier: Ursprung und Entwicklung der autonomen Architektur* (Vienna: Verlag Dr. Rolf Passer, 1933; French trans., Paris: L'Équerre, 1981); Emil Kaufmann, *Three Revolutionary Architects: Boullée, Ledoux, and Lequeu,* Transactions of the American Philosophical Society, n.s., vol. 42, pt. 3. (Philadelphia: American Philosophical Society, 1952). On Boullée, the standard work is still Jean-Marie Pérouse de Montclos, *Étienne-Louis Boullée, 1728–1799: De l'architecture classique à l'architecture révolutionnaire* (Paris: Arts et métiers graphiques, 1969); translated by James Emmons as *Étienne-Louis Boullée (1728–1799): Theoretician of Revolutionary Architecture* (New York: Braziller, 1974). Works on Ledoux include Michel Gallet, *Claude-Nicolas Ledoux, 1736–1806* (Paris: Picard, 1980); Anthony Vidler, *Claude-Nicolas Ledoux: Architecture and Social Reform at the End of the Ancien Régime* (Cambridge: MIT Press, 1990). Our knowledge of Ledoux's work has recently been increased by the rediscovery of a series of engravings that were not included in either of the two editions of his *Architecture* (see note 41). See Michel Gallet, ed., *Architecture de Ledoux: Inédits pour un tome III* (Paris: Éditions du Demi-Cercle, 1991).

20. Michel Gallet, *Les architectes parisiens du XVIIIᵉ siècle: Dictionnaire bio-*

graphique et critique (Paris: Mengès, 1995), 204: "*Théoricien d'une architecture indigente, Durand était lui-même issu d'un milieu voisin de la pauvreté.*"

21. On the Vitruvian tradition, see Hanno-Walter Kruft, *Geschichte der Architekturtheorie: Von der Antike bis zur Gegenwart* (Munich: C.H. Beck, 1985); Werner Szambien, *Symétrie, goût, caractère: Théorie et terminologie de l'architecture à l'âge classique, 1550–1800* (Paris: Picard, 1986); Georg Germann, *Einführung in die Geschichte der Architekturtheorie*, 2d rev. ed. (Darmstadt: Wissenschaftliche Buchgesellschaft, 1987).

22. Jacques-François Blondel, *Cours d'architecture; ou, Traité de la décoration, distribution et construction des bâtiments* (Paris: Desaint, 1771–77). For the course content, see Michel Gallet, in *Encyclopaedia Universalis* (Paris: Encyclopaedia Universalis, 1984–85), s.v. "Blondel (Jacques-François): 1705–1774"; Antoine Picon, "'Vers une architecture classique': Jacques-François Blondel et le *Cours d'architecture*," *Les cahiers de la recherche architecturale*, no. 18 (1985): 28–37.

23. Nicolas Le Camus de Mézières, *Le génie de l'architecture; ou, L'analogie de cet art avec nos sensations* (Paris: the author and B. Morin, 1780), 1; translated by David Britt as *The Genius of Architecture; or, The Analogy of That Art with Our Sensations*, ed. Robin Middleton (Santa Monica: The Getty Center for the History of Art and the Humanities, 1992), 69.

24. "I believe that a great change in architectural taste became sensible in France only after the death of Monsieur Blondel." Mathurin Crucy, letter to Baraguey, 1807, reproduced in *Mathurin Crucy, 1749–1826: Architecte nantais néo-classique*, exh. cat. (Nantes: Musée Dobree, 1986), 146–47.

25. On the general issues raised by the work of Emil Kaufmann and his notion of "revolutionary architecture," see, for example, Monique Mosser, "Situation d'Emil K.," in *De Ledoux à Le Corbusier: Origines de l'architecture moderne* (Arc-et-Senans: Fondation Claude-Nicolas Ledoux, 1987), 84–89. I still find it possible to apply the epithet *revolutionary* to Boullée and Ledoux, albeit in a far less literal sense than that adopted by Kaufmann. However, the triad of Boullée, Ledoux, and Lequeu, which he uses to illustrate his thesis, seems to me arbitrary in the extreme. Jean-Jacques Lequeu was a draftsman rather than an architect, and cannot possibly be set on a level with his two contemporaries.

26. On the importance of travel in the late-eighteenth-century renewal of architecture, see for example Werner Szambien, *Le musée d'architecture* (Paris: Picard, 1988).

27. On this concept of public facilities (*l'équipement*), see Bruno Fortier, "Logiques de l'équipement: Notes pour une histoire du projet," *Architecture–Mouvement–Continuité*, no. 45 (1978): 80–85.

28. See Monique Éleb-Vidal and Anne Debarre-Blanchard, *Architectures de la vie privée: Maisons et mentalités, XVIIe–XIXe siècles* (Brussels: Archives d'Architecture Moderne, 1989).

29. In the case of Paris, see J.-F. Cabestan, "L'architecture à Paris au XVIIIe siècle, distribution et innovation" (diss., Université de Paris I—Sorbonne, 1998).

30. Nicolas Le Camus de Mézières, *Le guide de ceux qui veulent bâtir: Ouvrage dans lequel on donne les renseignements nécessaires pour se conduire lors de la construction, & prévenir les fraudes qui peuvent s'y glisser* (Paris, 1780; 2d ed., Paris: the

author, B. Morin, and A. Jombert jeune, 1786; reprint of 2d ed., Minkoff: Geneva, 1972).

31. See Philippe Potié, *Philibert de l'Orme: Figures de la pensée constructive* (Marseilles: Parenthèses, 1996).

32. Philibert de l'Orme, *Nouvelles inventions pour bien bastir et à petits fraiz* (Paris: Federic Morel, 1561); reprinted, together with *Premier tome de l'architecture* (Paris: Federic Morel, 1567), in idem, *Traités d'architecture,* ed. Jean-Marie Pérouse de Montclos (Léonce Laget: Paris, 1988).

33. Denis Diderot, *Pensées sur l'interprétation de la nature* ([Paris]: n.p., 1754, 23: "*L'utile circonscrit tout. Ce sera l'utile qui dans quelques siècles donnera des bornes à la physique expérimentale, comme il est sur le point d'en donner à la géométrie.*" On the concept of utility in Enlightenment philosophy, see also Georges Gusdorf, *Les principes de la pensée au siècle des Lumières* (Paris: Payot, 1971), 428–43.

34. See Antoine Picon, *Architectes et ingénieurs au siècle des Lumières* (Marseilles: Parenthèses, 1988); translated by Martin Thom as *French Architects and Engineers in the Age of Enlightenment* (Cambridge: Cambridge Univ. Press, 1992).

35. On these dissertations, which were an integral part of the training of future Ponts et Chaussées engineers, see Antoine Picon, *L'invention de l'ingénieur moderne: L'École des Ponts et Chaussées, 1747–1851* (Paris: Presses de l'École Nationale des Ponts et Chaussées, 1992), 131–39, 734–35: "*Quelle est l'utilité des Ponts et Chaussées, relativement au commerce et à l'agriculture*"; ibid., "*l'utilité que l'on peut retirer pour l'État et pour la société de l'établissement fait depuis 1747 de l'École des Ponts et Chaussées.*"

36. Picon (see note 35), 734: "*l'esprit éclairé et le cœur bon.*"

37. Marc-Antoine Laugier, *Essai sur l'architecture* (Paris: Duchesne, 1753; 2d ed., Paris: Duchesne, 1755; reprint of 2d ed., Geneva: Minkoff, 1972), 8: "*Considérons l'homme dans sa première origine sans autre secours; sans autre guide que l'instinct naturel de ses besoins.*" On Laugier's theory, see Wolfgang Herrmann, *Laugier and Eighteenth Century French Theory* (London: A. Zwemmer, 1962; 2d ed., 1985). On the theme of the primitive shelter in general, see also Anthony Vidler, *The Writing of the Walls: Architectural Theory in the Enlightenment* (New York: Princeton Architectural Press, 1987).

38. In these churches, detached columns bearing an entablature took the place of the massive piers and arches of sixteenth- and seventeenth-century religious buildings. On this see, for example, Michael Petzet, *Soufflots Sainte-Geneviève und der französische Kirchenbau des 18. Jahrhunderts* (Berlin: Walter de Gruyter, 1961); *Soufflot et l'architecture des Lumières,* supplement to no. 6/7 of *Les Cahiers de la recherche architecturale* (Paris: Ministère de l'environment et du cadre de vie, 1980); Allan Braham, *The Architecture of the French Enlightenment* (London: Thames & Hudson, 1980).

39. This coexistence of Greek and Gothic models was perceived at a very early stage, well before the Abbé Laugier, by another theorist, the Abbé de Cordemoy. See Robin D. Middleton, "The Abbé de Cordemoy and the Graeco-Gothic Ideal: A Prelude to Romantic Classicism," parts 1 and 2, *Journal of the Warburg and Courtauld Institutes* 25, nos. 3–4 (1962): 278–320; 26 (1963): 90–123. On the eighteenth-century rediscovery of the structural qualities of the Gothic, see, more generally, Anne Coste,

L'architecture gothique: Lectures et interprétations d'un modèle (Saint-Étienne: Publications de l'Université de Saint-Étienne, 1997).

40. Étienne-Louis Boullée, *Architecture: Essai sur l'art,* ed. Jean-Marie Pérouse de Montclos (Paris: Hermann, 1968), 62–65.

41. Claude Nicolas Ledoux, *L'architecture considérée sous le rapport de l'art, des mœurs et de la législation* (Paris: author, 1804; reprint, Paris: Hermann, Éditeurs des Sciences et des Arts, 1997), 135: "*lettres alphabétiques des meilleurs auteurs.*" A second edition was published posthumously, with additional plates assembled by Daniel Ramée, as *L'architecture de C. N. Ledoux* (Paris, Lenoir, 1847; reprint, Princeton: Princeton Architectural Press, 1983).

42. Le Camus de Mézières (see note 23), 1: "*Personne n'a encore écrit sur l'analogie des proportions de l'architecture avec nos sensations.*"

43. Étienne Bonnot de Condillac, *Essai sur l'origine des connaissances humaines* (originally published 1746; Paris: Galilée, 1973), 139: "*à composer et à décomposer nos idées pour en faire différentes comparaisons, et pour découvrir, par ce moyen, les rapports qu'elles ont entre elles, et les nouvelles idées qu'elles peuvent produire.*"

44. Étienne Bonnot de Condillac, "Cours d'études pour l'instruction du prince de Parme," pt. 5, "De l'art de penser," in *Œuvres philosophiques de Condillac,* 3 vols. (Paris: Presses Universitaires de France, 1947), 1:769: "*la décomposition entière d'un objet, et la distribution des parties dans l'ordre où la génération devient facile.*"

45. I have devoted a number of articles to the spread of the analytical ideal of decomposition/recomposition. For example, on the approach followed in the accounts of craft activities in the *Encyclopédie:* Antoine Picon, "Gestes ouvriers, opérations et processus techniques: La vision du travail des encyclopédistes," *Recherches sur Diderot et sur* l'Encyclopédie, no. 13 (October 1992): 132–47. See also, more generally: Antoine Picon, "Towards a History of Technological Thought," in Robert Fox, ed., *Technological Change: Methods and Themes in the History of Technology* (Amsterdam: Harwood Academic Publishers, 1996), 37–49.

46. Joseph-Dominique Garat, "Analyse de l'entendement: Programme," in *Séances des Écoles Normales recueillies par des sténographes et revues par les professeurs,* 3 vols. (Paris: L. Reynier, n.d.), 1:138–69, esp. 148: "*méthode de l'esprit humain.*"

47. See Werner Szambien, "Notes sur le recueil d'architecture privée de Boullée (1792–1796)," *Gazette des Beaux-Arts* (March 1981): 111–24.

48. Boullée (see note 40), 73: "*Mettre du caractère dans un ouvrage, c'est employer avec justesse tous les moyens propres à ne nous faire éprouver d'autres sensations que celles qui doivent résulter du sujet.*"

49. On the concept of "speaking architecture," see Vidler (note 37).

50. Juan Bautista de Villalpando, *In Ezechielem explanationes et apparatus urbis ac templi Hierosolymitani,* 3 vols. (Rome: A. Zannetti, 1596–1604); René Ouvrard, *Architecture harmonique; ou, Application de la doctrine des proportions de la musique à l'architecture* (Paris: R.-J.-B. de La Caille, 1679). On this body of speculation, see Joseph Rykwert, *On Adam's House in Paradise: The Idea of the Primitive Hut in Architectural History* (New York: Museum of Modern Art, 1972).

51. Jacques-Bénigne Bossuet, *Introduction à la philosophie; ou, De la connaissance de Dieu, et de soi-mesme* (Paris: R.-M. d'Espilly, 1722), 37–38.

52. Boullée (see note 40), 49: "*Qu'est-ce que l'architecture? La définirai-je avec Vitruve l'art de bâtir? Non. Il y a dans cette définition une erreur grossière. Vitruve prend l'effet pour la cause. Il faut concevoir pour exécuter. Nos premiers pères n'ont bâti leurs cabanes qu'après en avoir conçu l'image. C'est cette production de l'esprit, c'est cette création qui constitue l'architecture.*"

53. Thus, Boullée grappled with the Pont Louis XVI, now the Pont de la Concorde, designed by the engineer Jean-Rodolphe Perronet; Ledoux includes drawings for a bridge at the beginning of *L'architecture.* Both sought to reconcile up-to-date engineering techniques with the evocation of a mythical source—the bridge of boats—by designing their piers in the form of boats. Boullée's project is reproduced in Pérouse de Montclos (see note 19), fig. 103. Ledoux's bridge project occupies plates 3 and 4 of *L'architecture* (see note 41).

54. Henri de Saint-Simon, *Lettres d'un habitant de Genève à ses contemporains,* written circa 1802, was the pioneer work of nineteenth-century *sociologisme.*

55. On the filiation of the École Polytechnique from the engineering schools of the ancien régime, see Bruno Belhoste, "Les origines de l'École Polytechnique: Des anciennes écoles d'ingénieurs à l'École Centrale des Travaux Publics," *Histoire de l'éducation,* no. 42 (1989): 13–53. On the history of the École Polytechnique in general, see Ambroise Fourcy, *Histoire de l'École Polytechnique* (Paris: the author and École Polytechnique, 1828; reprint, Paris: Belin, 1987); Terry Shinn, *L'École Polytechnique, 1794–1914* (Paris: Presses de la Fondation Nationale des Sciences Politiques, 1980); Bruno Belhoste, Amy Dahan Dalmedico, and Antoine Picon, eds., *La formation polytechnicienne, 1794–1994* (Paris: Dunod, 1994).

56. On the École du Génie, Mézières, and its teaching, see René Taton, "L'École Royale du Génie de Mézières," in idem, ed., *Enseignement et diffusion des sciences en France au XVIIIᵉ siècle* (Paris: Hermann, 1964), 559–615; also Bruno Belhoste, "Du dessin d'ingénieur à la géométrie descriptive: L'enseignement de Chastillon à l'École Royale du Génie de Mézières," *In Extenso,* no. 13 (1990): 103–28; Bruno Belhoste, Antoine Picon, and Joël Sakarovitch, "Les exercices dans les écoles d'ingénieurs sous l'Ancien Régime et la Révolution," *Histoire de l'éducation,* no. 46 (May 1990): 53–109.

57. See René Taton, *L'œuvre scientifique de Monge* (Paris: Presses Universitaires de France, 1951).

58. See Joël Sakarovitch, *Contribution à l'histoire de la géométrie descriptive: Origine et destin d'une discipline polymorphe,* documents assembled for accreditation to direct research at the École des Hautes Études en Sciences Sociales, Paris, 1997. The essentials of this work of synthesis were included in Joël Sakarovitch, *Épures d'architecture: De la coupe des pierres à la géométrie descriptive XVIᵉ–XIXᵉ siècles* (Basel: Birkhäuser, 1998).

59. Jean-Nicolas Hachette, *Notice sur la création de l'École Polytechnique* (Paris: Decourchant, 1828), 1–2: "*Il faut concevoir pour exécuter. Nos premiers pères n'ont bâti leurs cabanes qu'après en avoir conçu l'image. C'est cette production de l'esprit, c'est cette création qui constitue l'architecture.*"

60. A detailed analysis of the circumstances surrounding the creation of the École Polytechnique will be found in Belhoste (see note 55); Janis Langins, *La République*

avait besoin de savants: Les débuts de l'École Polytechnique: l'École Centrale des Travaux Publics et les cours révolutionnaires de l'an III (Paris: Belin, 1987).

61. On the mobilization of scientists under the French Revolution, see Nicole and Jean Dhombres, *Naissance d'un pouvoir: Sciences et savants en France (1793–1824)* (Paris: Payot, 1989).

62. Gaspard Monge, *Développemens sur l'enseignement adopté pour l'École Centrale des Travaux Publics,* reproduced in Langins (see note 60), 227–69.

63. In 1795, with France in full reaction against the excesses of the Terror, the École Centrale des Travaux Publics was compromised by the fact that it had been set up by the Comité de Salut Public. Its new name was designed to purge it of any suspicious links with the Robespierre régime.

64. *Textes de programmes de l'enseignement polytechnique de l'École Centrale des Travaux Publics,* reproduced in Langins (see note 60), 126–98.

65. Ibid., 142: "*susceptibles d'une définition rigoureuse.*"

66. Gaspard Monge, "Géométrie descriptive. Programme," in *Séances des Écoles Normales* (see note 46), 1:49–64, esp. 50–51: "*nécessaire à l'homme de génie qui conçoit un projet, aux à ceux qui doivent en diriger l'exécution, et enfin aux artistes qui doivent eux-mêmes en exécuter les différentes parties.*"

67. On stereotomy and its decline, see Jean-Marie Pérouse de Montclos, *L'architecture à la française XVIe, XVIIe, XVIIIe siècles* (Paris: Picard, 1982).

68. Britain, which dominated European mechanical engineering from the mid–eighteenth century onward, always remained disdainfully ignorant of the French engineers' descriptive geometry.

69. See Joël Sakarovitch, "La géométrie descriptive, une reine déchue," in Belhoste, Dahan Dalmedico, and Picon (see note 55), 77–93.

70. An excellent analysis of this evolutionary process and its causes will be found in Bruno Belhoste, "Un modèle à l'épreuve: L'École Polytechnique de 1794 au Second Empire," in Belhoste, Dahan Dalmedico, and Picon (see note 55), 9–30.

71. Fernand de Dartein, *Observations sur le cours d'architecture de l'École Polytechnique et sur le programme de ses leçons* (Paris: Imprimerie de Simon Raçon, 1874), 4.

72. Mandar's own principal publication reflects this emphasis on issues of construction: Charles-François Mandar, *Études d'architecture civile* (Paris: Carilian-Gœury, 1826).

73. Claude-Louis-Marie-Henri Navier, notes to the reprint of Bernard Forest de Bélidor, *La science des ingénieurs* (Paris: F. Didot, 1813), 497–98: "*ces maximes que donne ici Bélidor ont été consacrées et développées par M. Durand dans des leçons dont le souvenir sera toujours précieux aux élèves de l'École polytechnique.... M. Durand a su le premier fonder les principes de l'architecture sur des bases solides. Il n'en reconnaît d'autre que la convenance, c'est-à-dire qu'un parfait rapport établi entre la disposition d'un édifice et l'usage auquel il est destiné; en sorte que projeter un édifice, c'est résoudre un problème dont les données se trouvent dans les conditions de solidité, d'économie et d'utilité, auquel il est assujetti.*"

74. Durand, *Précis* (see note 1), 1:14: "*Quelle comparaison peut-on faire entre le corps de l'homme, dont la largeur varie à chaque hauteur différente et une espèce de cylindre dont le diamètre est par-tout le même?*" [Pt. 1, 81.]

75. Durand, *Précis* (see note 1), 1:16: "*produit informe des premiers essais de l'art.*" [Pt. 1, 83.]

76. See M. Mosser, "Le rocher et la colonne: Un thème d'iconographie architecturale au XVIIIᵉ siècle," *Revue de l'art,* nos. 58–59 (1982–83): 55–74.

77. Charles-François Viel de Saint-Maux, *Lettres sur l'architecture des Anciens, et celle des Modernes, dans lesquelles se trouve développé le génie symbolique qui présida aux monuments de l'antiquité* (Paris: n.p., 1787; reprint, Geneva: Minkoff, 1974). On the theories of Viel de Saint-Maux, see Jean-Rémy Mantion, "La solution symbolique: Les *Lettres sur l'architecture* de Viel de Saint-Maux (1787)," *VRBI,* no. 9 (1984): 46–58; Vidler (note 37), 45–50.

78. On Quatremère de Quincy, see for example the texts with which Léon Krier and Demetri Porphyrios preface their edition of Quatremère de Quincy, *De l'imitation* (Brussels: Archives d'Architecture Moderne, 1980); also Sylvia Lavin, *Quatremère de Quincy and the Invention of a Modern Language of Architecture* (Cambridge: MIT Press, 1992).

79. Durand, *Précis* (see note 1), 1:18: "*Soit que l'on consulte la raison, soit que l'on examine les monuments, il est évident que plaire n'a jamais pu être le but de l'architecture, ni la décoration architectonique être son objet.*" [Pt. 1, 84.]

80. Durand, *Précis* (see note 1), 1:6: "*Pour peu que nous observions la marche et le développement de l'intelligence et de la sensibilité, nous reconnaîtrons que dans tous les temps et dans tous les lieux, toutes les pensées de l'homme et toutes ses actions ont eu pour origine ces deux principes: l'amour du bien-être et l'aversion pour toute espèce de peine.*" This passage is quoted here as it appears in the 1813 edition of the work [cf. Pt. 1, 84.]

81. As Werner Szambien has noted, Durand's definition of utility presents close analogies to that of the eighteenth-century materialist thinkers.

82. On the history of the concept of *convenance* in French architectural theory, see Szambien (see note 21), 167–73.

83. Vitruvius, *Les dix livres d'architecture,* trans. Claude Perrault (Paris: J.-B. Coignard, 1673), 12 n. 3: "*l'usage et la fin utile et nécessaire pour laquelle un Édifice est fait, telle qu'est la Solidité, la Salubrité et la Commodité.*"

84. Claude Perrault, *Ordonnance des cinq espèces de colonnes selon la méthode des Anciens* (Paris: J.-B. Coignard, 1683); translated by Indra Kagis McEwen as *Ordonnance for the Five Kinds of Columns after the Method of the Ancients,* ed. Alberto Pérez-Gómez (Santa Monica: The Getty Center for the History of Art and the Humanities, 1993).

85. On Charles Perrault and his work for Colbert, see Antoine Picon, "Un moderne paradoxal," introduction to Charles Perrault, *Mémoires de ma vie* (Paris: Macula, 1993), 1–107.

86. On Claude Perrault's theories, see Wolfgang Herrmann, *The Theory of Claude Perrault* (London: A. Zwemmer, 1973); Antoine Picon, *Claude Perrault, 1613–1688; ou, La curiosité d'un classique* (Paris: Picard, 1988); Alberto Pérez-Gómez, introduction to Perrault, *Ordonnance for the Five Kinds of Columns* (see note 84), 1–44.

87. Boullée (see note 40), 51–53.

88. On the history of the term *positive* during the second half of the eighteenth century, see for example Keith Michael Baker, *Condorcet: From Natural Philosophy to Social Mathematics* (Chicago: Univ. of Chicago Press, 1975).

89. On the genesis of Comtian positivism, and the roles played in it by Comte and Saint-Simon, see Henri Gouhier, *La jeunesse d'Auguste Comte et la formation du positivisme,* 3 vols. (Paris: Vrin, 1933–41).

90. See A. Petit, "Heurs et malheurs du positivisme: Philosophie des sciences et politique scientifique chez Auguste Comte et ses premiers disciples (1820–1900)" (diss., Université de Paris I—Sorbonne, 1993); Mary Pickering, *Auguste Comte: An Intellectual Biography,* vol. 1 (Cambridge: Cambridge Univ. Press, 1993).

91. See Le Camus de Mézières (note 30); Pierre Patte, *Mémoires sur les objets les plus importants de l'architecture* (Paris: Rozet, 1769; reprint, Geneva: Minkoff, 1973).

92. The concept of economy as applied to the living organism is discussed in depth in Bernard Balan, *L'ordre et le temps: L'anatomie comparée et l'histoire des vivants au XIXe siècle* (Paris: Vrin, 1979).

93. Claude Perrault, *Mémoires pour servir à l'histoire naturelle des animaux* (Paris: Imprimerie Royale, 1671–76); Claude Perrault, *Essais de physique; ou, Recueil de plusieurs traitez touchant les choses naturelles* (Paris: J.-B. Coignard, 1680–88).

94. Durand, *Précis* (see note 1), 1:8: "*un édifice sera d'autant moins dispendieux qu'il sera plus symétrique, plus régulier et plus simple.*" [Pt. 1, 85.]

95. One of the best examples of the use of the *de maximis* and *de minimis* techniques is provided by the engineer Charles-Augustin Coulomb (of the Corps du Génie) in his "Essai sur une application des règles de maximis et minimis à quelques problèmes de statique, relatifs à l'architecture," in *Mémoires de mathématiques et de physique, présentés à l'Académie Royale des Sciences, par divers savans: Année 1773* (Paris: Imprimerie Royale, 1776), 343–82. On Coulomb and his use of *de maximis* and *de minimis,* from engineering to physics, see, for example, Charles Stewart Gillmor, *Coulomb and the Evolution of Physics and Engineering in Eighteenth-Century France* (Princeton: Princeton Univ. Press, 1971); Christine Blondel and Matthies Dörries, eds., *Restaging Coulomb: Usages, controverses et réplications autour de la balance de torsion,* Biblioteca di Nuncius, Studi e testi 15 (Florence: L. S. Olschki, 1994).

96. Durand, *Précis* (see note 1), 1:22: "*si peu grand, si peu magnifique.*" [Pt. 1, 87.]

97. See Jacques Guillerme, "Notes pour l'histoire de la régularité," *Revue d'esthétique,* no. 3 (1971): 383–94.

98. Durand, *Précis* (see note 1), 1:8: "*simples comme la nature.*" This passage does not appear in the first edition of the *Précis.*

99. Durand, *Partie graphique* (see note 17), 23: "*rêves quelquefois étranges, mais presque toujours sublimes, de Piranèse.*" [*Graphic Portion,* 198.] Durand was a silent partner in the company formed by Piranesi's sons to exploit the artist's works in Paris.

100. The article "Composition" in the *Encyclopédie* (see note 105) confines itself almost entirely to painting and music.

101. In this respect Durand departs from the approach of his former teacher, Boullée, who constantly refers to painting in his *Essai sur l'art.*

102. Antoine-Louis-Claude Destutt de Tracy, *Éléments d'idéologie* (Paris: Didot, 1801–3; 2d ed., Paris: Veuve Courcier, 1817; reprint of 2d ed., Paris: J. Vrin, 1970). On the Ideologues, consult François-Joseph Picavet, *Les Idéologues: Essai sur l'histoire des idées et des théories scientifiques, philosophiques, religieuses, etc. en France depuis 1789* (Paris: F. Alcan, 1891); Sergio Moravia, *Il pensiero degli Idéologues: Scienza e*

filosofia in Francia (1780–1815) (Florence: La Nuova Italia, 1974); Sergio Moravia, *Il tramonto dell'illuminismo: Filosofia e politica nella società francese (1770–1810)* (Bari: Laterza, 1968). The affinity between Durand's ideas and those of the Ideologues is the main theme of the book by Sergio Villari (see note 4).

103. Durand, *Précis* (see note 1), 30. This passage does not appear in the first edition of the work.

104. Szambien (see note 3), 91–92.

105. Jean Le Rond d'Alembert, "Élémens des sciences," in *Encyclopédie; ou, Dictionnaire raisonné des sciences, des arts et des métiers*, 35 vols. (Paris: Briasson, 1751–80), 5:491–97: "*On appelle en général éléments d'un tout, les parties primitives et originaires dont on peut supposer que ce tout est formé.*"

106. Durand, *Précis* (see note 1), 2:3–4: "*du simple au composé, du connu à l'inconnu.*" [Pt. 3, 132].

107. D'Alembert (see note 105), 491: "*L'esprit humain, participant alors de l'intelligence suprême, verrait toutes ses connaissances comme réunies sous un point de vue indivisible.*" This passage should be read in conjunction with that in which Laplace postulates an absolute intelligence for which the world is reduced to a single formula. Pierre-Simon Laplace, *Essai philosophique sur les probabilités* (Paris: Veuve Courcier, 1814), 2.

108. Jean-Antoine Chaptal, *Élémens de chimie* (Paris: Deterville, 1803), 54–55: "*Du moment que la chimie s'est crue assez avancée pour connaître les principes des corps, elle a prétendu devoir marquer elle-même le nombre, la nature et le caractère des éléments; et elle a regardé comme principe simple ou élémentaire tout ce qui se refusait à ses voies de décomposition. En prenant ainsi pour éléments le terme de l'analyse, leur nombre et leur nature doivent varier selon les révolutions et les progrès de la chimie: c'est ce dont on peut s'assurer en consultant tous les chimistes qui ont écrit sur cette matière…. Il faut convenir que c'est beaucoup hasarder que de prendre le terme de l'artiste pour celui de créateur, et de s'imaginer que l'état de nos connaissances est un état de perfection. La dénomination d'éléments devrait donc être effacée d'une nomenclature chimique, ou du moins on ne devrait la considérer que comme faite pour exprimer le dernier degré de nos résultats analytiques.*"

109. Pierre-Jean-Georges Cabanis, *Rapports du physique et du moral de l'homme* (Paris: Crapart, Caille et Ravier, 1802; 8th ed., Paris: J.-B. Baillière, 1844; reprint of 8th ed., Geneva: Slatkine, 1980), 181: "*Tout est sans cesse en mouvement dans la nature; tous les corps sont dans une continuelle fluctuation. Leurs éléments se combinent et se décomposent; ils revêtent successivement mille formes fugitives: et ces métamorphoses, suite nécessaire d'une action qui n'est jamais suspendue, en renouvellent à leur tour les causes et conservent l'éternelle jeunesse de l'univers. Pour peu qu'on y réfléchisse, il est aisé de sentir que tout mouvement entraîne ou suppose destruction et reproduction, que les conditions des corps qui se détruisent et renaissent doivent changer à chaque instant; qu'elles ne sauraient changer sans imprimer de nouveaux caractères aux phénomènes qui s'y rapportent; qu'enfin, si l'on pouvait marquer nettement toutes les circonstances de ces phases successives que parcourent les êtres divers, la grande énigme de leur nature et de leur existence se trouverait peut-être assez complètement résolue, quand même l'existence et la nature de leurs éléments devraient rester à jamais couvertes d'un voile impénétrable.*"

110. Jacques Roger, *Buffon: Un philosophe au jardin du roi* (Paris: Fayard, 1989), 130: "*s'il y a un ordre du monde, ce n'est pas un ordre des structures, de ces structures que classent les taxinomistes. C'est un ordre des 'opérations' de la nature, un ordre des processus qui permettent la vie et son perpétuel renouvellement, un ordre des forces qui animent le monde vivant et des lois qui les gouvernent.*" English translation (not used here) by Sarah Lucille Bonnefoi as *Buffon: A Life in Natural History*, ed. L. Pearce Williams (Ithaca: Cornell Univ. Press, 1997).

111. Durand, *Précis* (see note 1), 1:53: "*qui naissent de la nature des matériaux*"; ibid., "*dont l'habitude nous a fait en quelque sorte un besoin.*" [Pt. 1, 108.]

112. The system of the orders presented by Durand is discussed in depth in Szambien (see note 3), 74–80.

113. Le Roy, *Les ruines* (see note 14), part 2, "Discours sur la nature des principes de l'architecture civile," vi: "*Il paraît que ce que l'on peut faire de mieux sur cette partie est de regarder tous les fragments de monuments antiques que l'on peut recueillir dans la Grèce; tous ceux que l'on peut trouver dans l'Asie mineure ou dans la Syrie, ainsi que ceux qui restent encore à Rome; les préceptes de Vitruve sur les proportions des ordres; et enfin les sentiments des plus célèbres architectes sur ces proportions, comme autant d'éléments qui peuvent servir à composer les meilleurs ordres possibles.*"

114. Like Perrault, Durand was under the influence of a French cultural tradition that was quick to condemn the use of too extensive a vocabulary, whether in literature or in art.

115. See Pérez-Gómez (see note 4), 108–9.

116. In this respect, the title of Alberto Pérez-Gómez's chapter on the author of the *Précis*, "Durand and Functionalism" (see note 4), is unfortunate.

117. Durand, *Précis* (see note 1), 1:96: "*Pour l'élévation, elle se trouve toute composée dès que le plan et la coupe le sont.*" This passage does not appear in the first edition of the work.

118. See Alain Demangeon and Bruno Fortier, *Les vaisseaux et les villes* (Brussels: Mardaga, 1978); Paolo Morachiello and Georges Teyssot, *Nascita delle città di stato: Ingegneri e architetti sotto il consolato e l'impero* (Rome: Officina, 1983).

119. On these two new towns, see Morachiello and Teyssot (see note 118), 36–49, 147–67; Werner Szambien, "Napoléon, ville-modèle?" *303*, no. 12 (1987): 123–32.

120. Durand, *Précis* (see note 1), 2:92. This passage does not appear in the first edition of the work.

121. On the techniques of composition used at the École des Beaux-Arts, see for example Henri Bresler, "Dessiner l'architecture: Point de vue Beaux-Arts et changement de point de vue," in *Images et imaginaires d'architecture* (Paris: Éditions du Centre National d'Art et de Culture Georges Pompidou, 1984), 33–37; David Van Zanten, "Architectural Composition at the École des Beaux-Arts from Charles Percier to Charles Garnier," in Arthur Drexler, ed., *The Architecture of the École des Beaux-Arts*, exh. cat. (New York: Museum of Modern Art, 1977; 2d ed., London: Secker & Warburg, 1984), 111–323; Annie Jacques and Riichi Miyaké, *Les dessins d'architecture de l'École des Beaux-Arts* (Tokyo, 1987; French trans., Paris: Arthaud, 1988).

122. Daly, for example declared: "*Depuis le commencement du siècle, architectes et ingénieurs se regardent chez nous avec plus d'étonnement que de bienveillance. On*

croirait le dieu a + b et la déesse Fantaisie en train de se dévisager réciproquement." (Since the beginning of this century, architects and engineers in this country have looked on each other with rather more astonishment than benevolence. It looks very much as if the God of *a* + *b* and the Goddess of Imagination were trying to face each other down.") César Daly, *Ingénieurs et architectes (un toast et son commentaire), extrait de la Revue générale de l'architecture et des travaux publics* (Paris: Ducher & Cie, 1877), 4. Daly's motives are analyzed in Hélène Lipstadt, ed., "Architecte et ingénieur dans la presse: Polémique, débat, conflits," research report, I.E.R.A.U., Paris, 1980; see also Marc Saboya, *Presse et architecture au XIXᵉ siècle* (Paris: Picard, 1991).

123. On this cooperation between architects and engineers in the nineteenth century, see François Loyer and Antoine Picon, "L'architecte au XIXᵉ siècle," in Louis Callebat, ed., *Histoire de l'architecte* (Paris: Flammarion, 1998), 152–71.

124. Durand, *Précis* (see note 1), 1:27: *"étudier, l'une après l'autre, les diverses espèces d'édifices dans toutes les circonstances qui peuvent les modifier"*; ibid., *"d'une longueur effrayante."* This passage is quoted here as it appears in the 1813 edition of the work. [Cf. Pt. 1, 77.]

125. On Durand's sundry borrowings, see Werner Szambien, "Durand and the Continuity of Tradition," in Middleton, ed. (note 8), 19–33; Szambien (note 3).

126. Durand, *Précis* (see note 1), 2:41. [Pt. 3, 153.]

127. See Szambien (note 3), 290: *"tombeau indien."*

128. Durand, *Précis* (see note 1), 2:126: *"restaurations peu authentiques"*; ibid., *"des beaux partis que ces restaurations présentent."* ["Notice," 203–4.]

129. Louis Bruyère, *Études relatives à l'art des constructions* (Paris: Bance, 1823–28). Bruyère had the chance to put his architectural ideas into practice as *directeur des travaux* (director of works) for Paris from 1811 to 1820. On his career see Claude Dufour, "Louis Bruyère et la Direction des travaux de Paris" (thesis for the diploma of archivist and paleographer, École Nationale des Chartes, Paris, 1998).

130. Louis-Ambrose Dubut, *Architecture civile: Maisons de ville et de campagne de toutes formes et de tous genres* (Paris: J.-M. Eberhart, 1803; reprint, Munich: Walter Uhl, 1974); Jean-Charles Krafft, *Recueil des plus jolies maisons de Paris et de ses environs* (Paris: J.-L. Scherff, 1809).

131. Antoine-Chrysostôme Quatremère de Quincy, *Dictionnaire de l'architecture,* 1832, s.v. "Type," reproduced in Quatremère de Quincy, *De l'imitation* (see note 78), 58–60, esp. 58–59: *"germe préexistant"*; ibid., *"modèle imaginatif"*; ibid., *"une sorte de noyau autour duquel se sont agrégés, et auquel se sont coordonnés par la suite les développements et les variations de formes dont l'objet était susceptible."*

132. On the notions of type and series in seventeenth- and eighteenth-century natural science, see Balan (note 92), and also Henri Daudin, *De Linné à Lamarck: Méthodes de classification et idée de série en botanique et en zoologie, 1740–1790* (Paris: F. Alcan, 1926–27); Henri Daudin, *Cuvier et Lamarck: Les classes zoologiques et l'idée de série animale, 1790–1830* (Paris: F. Alcan, 1926).

133. Michel Foucault, *Les mots et les choses: Une archéologie des sciences humaines* (Paris: Gallimard, 1966); translated as *The Order of Things: An Archaeology of the Human Sciences* (New York: Pantheon, 1970). See also Michel Foucault, *L'archéologie du savoir* (Paris: Gallimard, 1969); translated by A. M. Sheridan Smith in

The Archaeology of Knowledge and the Discourse on Language (New York: Pantheon, 1972).

134. Louis Bruyère, manuscript notes on philosophy, architecture, and the fine arts, École Nationale des Ponts et Chaussées, Ms. 2023: "*dans tout édifice les embellissements que peut employer l'architecte peuvent être considérés comme les draperies dans la sculpture qui doivent toujours accuser le nu.*"

135. Bruyère (see note 129), 1:7.

136. On Reynaud's teaching, see Fernand de Dartein, *M. Léonce Reynaud: Sa vie et ses œuvres par l'un de ses élèves* (Paris: Dunod, 1885); Vincent Guigueno and Antoine Picon, "Entre rationalisme et éclectisme: L'enseignement d'architecture de Léonce Reynaud," *Bulletin de la Société des amis de la bibliothèque de l'École Polytechnique,* no. 16 (December 1996): 12–19.

137. Léonce Reynaud, *Traité d'architecture contenant des concepts générales sur les principes de la construction et sur l'histoire de l'art,* 2 vols. (Paris: Carilian-Gœury and Victor Dalmont, 1850–58), 1:vi: "*laisser à l'art toute la latitude qui lui appartient… ce qui touche à l'essence intime de l'art se sent et ne s'explique pas.*"

138. Dartein (see note 136), 72: "*N'est-il pas notable que les droits du goût et de l'imagination aient été défendus par un polytechnicien contre les sophismes d'une théorie soi-disant rationnelle conçue par un artiste? Cela prouve au moins que l'abus des mathématiques n'est pas toujours le fait des mathématiciens.*"

139. For a recent discussion of the "two cultures" issue, see, for example, the introduction by Caroline A. Jones and Peter Galison in idem, eds., *Picturing Science Producing Art* (New York: Routledge, 1998) 1–23.

140. See Bruno Belhoste, *Cauchy, 1789–1857: Un mathématicien légitimiste au XIXe siècle* (Paris: Belin, 1985); translated by Frank Ragland as *Augustin-Louis Cauchy: A Biography* (New York: Springer, 1991).

141. See for example David Van Zanten, *Designing Paris: The Architecture of Duban, Labrouste, Duc, and Vaudoyer* (Cambridge: MIT Press, 1987); Barry Bergdoll, *Léon Vaudoyer: Historicism in the Age of Industry* (New York: Architectural History Foundation; Cambridge: MIT Press, 1994).

142. Gottfried Semper, *Vorläufige Bemerkungen über bemalte Architectur und Plastik bei den Alten* (Altona: J. F. Hammerich, 1834); translated as "Preliminary Remarks on Polychrome Architecture and Sculpture in Antiquity," in Gottfried Semper, *The Four Elements of Architecture and Other Writings,* ed. and trans. Harry Francis Mallgrave and Wolfgang Herrmann (Cambridge: Cambridge Univ. Press, 1989), 45–73, esp. 46.

143. See Caroline Van Eck, *Organicism in Nineteenth-Century Architecture: An Inquiry into Its Theoretical and Philosophical Background* (Amsterdam: Architectura & Natura Press, 1994).

144. Henry-Russell Hitchcock, *Architecture: Nineteenth and Twentieth Centuries* (Harmondsworth: Penguin, 1958), 18–19.

145. Geometry—a geometry of natural origins—was of great importance to Viollet-le-Duc. But to him it was a morphogenetic system, rather than a combinatorial one as it was for Durand, and it involved mechanical, even constructional considerations that are absent from Durand's work. On Viollet-le-Duc's relationship to geometry, see

Françoise Véry, "Àpropos d'un dessin de Viollet-le-Duc," in Pierre A. Frey, ed., *E. Viollet-le-Duc et le massif du Mont-Blanc, 1868–1879* (Lausanne: Payot, 1988), 109–18; Martin Bressani, "Science, histoire et archéologie. Sources et généalogie de la pensée organiciste de Viollet-le-Duc" (diss., Université de Paris IV—Sorbonne, 1997).

146. Eugène-Emmanuel Viollet-le-Duc, *À Monsieur Adolphe Lance, rédacteur du journal L'Encylopédie d'architecture* (Paris: Bance, 1856), col. 11: *"un moyen de produire bien plus encore qu'une production."*

147. Durand, *Précis* (see note 1), 1:19: *"Nous sommes loins de penser que l'architecture ne puisse pas plaire; nous disons au contraire qu'il est impossible qu'elle ne plaise pas lorsqu'elle est traitée selon ses vrais principes."* [Pt. 1, 85.]

148. Rykwert (see note 8); Pérez-Gómez (see note 4).

149. Walter Benjamin, *Gesammelte Schriften*, 7 vols., ed. Rolf Tiedemann and Hermann Schweppenhäser (Frankfurt: Suhrkamp, 1972–89) V.1:494: *"Der Kapitalismus war eine Naturerscheinung, mit der ein neuer Traumschlaf über Europa kam und in ihm eine Reaktivierung der mythischen Kräfte."*

Précis
of the Lectures
on Architecture

Volume One

Preface

Whatever the object and the purpose of architecture, it is certain that of all the arts this is the most generally practiced and the most expensive.[1] There are few countries in which there are no private dwellings for individuals or public buildings for society at large. It is extremely costly to erect large buildings, and costly enough even for buildings of the least account. It follows that those who intend to devote themselves to architecture must possess the necessary knowledge and talents.

Architects are not alone in being required to erect buildings: so, frequently, are engineers, both civil and military. It might even be said, speaking of engineers, that they have more opportunities to carry out large undertakings than do architects proper. The latter may well build nothing but private houses all their lives; but the former, aside from being frequently called upon to do the same in those remote provinces where architects are rare, find themselves professionally required to construct hospitals, prisons, barracks, arsenals, magazines, bridges, harbors, lighthouses: a host of buildings of the first importance; and so knowledge and talent in architecture are at least as necessary for them as they are for architects.[2]

But youthful students embarking on the profession of engineering, whether civil or military, or on some other branch of the public service, have very little time to spare for such a study, whether at the École Polytechnique, or at the special schools to which they proceed on leaving it, or even when they have attained the rank of engineer.[3] For such students, therefore, it has been necessary to make their study of architecture, although extremely brief, nonetheless fruitful. To attain both of these ends as far as possible, we have found it necessary to proceed as follows.

Rather than be detained at every step by the need to criticize—at greater or lesser length—a multitude of particular faults that are encountered in buildings, we have given, in a brief introduction, an outline of the prejudices that give rise to such faults.

Having thus effaced any false preconceptions from our students' minds, and forearmed them against other similar ideas to which they might later be exposed, we have endeavored in the introduction to furnish them with accurate ideas as to the nature of the art: its purpose, means, and general principles. To make these ideas useful, we have made them general, so that they may generate all those specific ideas that, in our course of lectures, time has compelled us to pass over in silence. To avoid fatiguing the attention or over-charging the memory, we have sought, first, to make those general ideas as simple and as few as possible, and, second, to associate them with each other and with the specific ideas so that a first leads on to a second, and the second infallibly recalls to mind the first.

Having thus established general principles in the introduction, we have given an account of the elements of buildings in part I: engaged and detached supports, walls and the openings in them, foundations, floorings, vaults, roofs, terraces, and so on. These features have been considered with reference to the materials from which they may be constructed and to the forms and proportions that they may assume. In part II we have shown how these elements may be combined together, both horizontally and vertically; how to form these combinations into the various parts of a building, namely, porticoes, porches, vestibules, stairs both external and internal, rooms, courtyards, grottoes, fountains, and so on; and, finally, how to combine the parts: that is, to dispose them in relation to each other and to the composition of a building as a whole.

In the third and last part of these lectures, which will form the second volume of this work, all that has previously been said will be applied to the study and composition of as many buildings, public and private, as can be accommodated.

So much for the necessary knowledge; as will be seen, it can be quickly mastered. But knowledge, useful though it may be, does not make an architect. That requires a ready skill in the application of knowledge; and this skill is what we call talent. Talent comes only with repeated practice, and this requires the aid of drawing. But every drawing, however slight, takes time; and it may seem at first that, while knowledge demands little time, talent necessarily demands a great deal of it. We have accordingly turned our attention to the obstacle presented by drawing.

Some consider that drawing is the basis of architecture and of the other arts. However, drawing—serving as it does to depict the sundry objects that architecture employs—can no more be the basis of that art than lettering is the foundation of the sundry kinds of literature.[4] In the case of architecture, this supposed foundation amounts to no more than the art of drawing geometric figures with an added wash: an art that can afford nothing but a false idea of any building, since nothing in nature is geometric in form or in effect. Perspective alone might give a true idea of the effect of a building. Strange to relate, however, in an art that is alleged to be founded upon drawing, this is one kind of drawing that is not in use. Indeed, it is strictly forbidden, and an exclusive preference is accorded to geometric drawing—which is false, not to say absurd, if the intention is to represent the effect of a building, and dangerous in the extreme, whether architecture be considered for its usefulness or for the pleasure that it gives. Once confined to this kind of drawing, a young man who is ambitious for success will want to derive all the advantage he can from it. But often, and indeed almost invariably, a design that would make the greatest effect in execution has little or no effect as a geometric drawing.

What follows from this? That, in the attempt to produce an effect in the geometric elevation, the designer will add unnecessary parts and sometimes remove necessary ones. If anyone is so then unfortunate as to be misled by the charm of the drawing, the refinement of the line, or the purity of the tints into executing such a design, then not only does the mind of a rational observer remain unsatisfied but the architect's own eye is offended by effects and masses totally different from those that he expected. We shall not enlarge upon the ruinous consequences of the abuse of geometric drawing in architecture; suffice it to say that this kind of work does irreparable harm to young men whose talent has survived the obstacles set in their way by a senseless routine: they are robbed of much time that might more wisely have been used to expand their knowledge.

If it is dangerous for students of architecture to concentrate on drawing to the point of confusing it with architecture itself, it is far more so for those who intend to become engineers. As we are addressing the latter, it will by now be clear that we have been economical in our use of drawing. We have more or less reduced it to a single line, drawn to indicate the shape and arrangement of objects; and if we have had recourse to wash, this has simply been in order to distinguish solids from voids in our plans and sections. Justly economical with our students' time, we have therefore set aside very little of it for drawing.

But, some will argue, we make no claim that the foundation of the art is architectural drawing alone: it is drawing in general, and that of the figure in particular. Such men as Michelangelo and Bernini, for instance: were they not painters as well as architects? Did not their talents in drawing bring them their success in architecture? It is true that drawing imparts a facility in expressing one's ideas; and this is a great recommendation. But, for our own part, we do not regard it as essential; and, as for the architects just mentioned, even if we were to accept their superiority — which we do not — this would not persuade us to accept that they owe their reputations to their talents in drawing. Has it ever occurred to anybody to praise Palladio as a draftsman? And does anyone dispute that he was the greatest of architects?

We therefore recommend students to prepare themselves for the study of architecture through the exercise of drawing; but at the same time we advise them to abandon that exercise, rather than ever to confuse the one thing with the other.

Not only have we reduced drawing to its simplest terms, but we have also tried to place on a single sheet the largest possible number of objects, so that, most of the lines that represent them being shared, a considerable number can be drawn in no more time than it would have taken to draw any one of them separately.[5]

At all events, even if the principles we have laid down are not perfect; and even if the means we have used are not the most direct; we may still flatter ourselves that, by following the sequence we have indicated, the student will do in a few months what formerly required a matter of years.

If the public welcomes this first volume, it shall not wait long for the second.

In many places we have referred our readers to our *Recueil et parallèle*.[6] This has made it necessary to explain to them what this is, and to give them a clear idea of it; and such is the object of the "Notice" that concludes part II [see appendix, pp. 203–4].

Our preface would be incomplete if we were to leave the public in ignorance of the part that our friend Citizen Maudru has taken in bringing this volume to completion.[7]

We have hastened to complete this *Précis,* so that those of the students of the École Polytechnique who are to be examined on this part of the course might, by perusing our work, recall to mind the principal matters on which we have addressed them in our course. Besides, we exercise another function at the École, in addition to that of a professor; and this, making it difficult for us to devote ourselves to any sustained occupation, has left us even less at leisure to see this work speedily through the press.

In this situation, we have had recourse to the man of letters whose name we mention above; and what we have been unable to do, his zeal has performed.

Introduction

Architecture has as its object the composition and execution of buildings, both public and private.

These two kinds of building are subdivided into a great number of types, and each type in turn is capable of an infinity of modifications.

Public buildings comprise city gates, triumphal arches, bridges, squares, markets, schools, libraries, museums, town halls, basilicas, palaces, hospices, baths, fountains, theaters, prisons, barracks, arsenals, cemeteries, and so on.

Private buildings comprise private town houses, tenements, villas, and country houses; along with all their dependencies, workshops, factories, storehouses, and so on.

Differences in manners, customs, places, materials, and financial resources introduce a host of necessary variations into every class of building.

If, in order to learn architecture, it were necessary to study all the classes of building in succession, together with all the circumstances that are liable to modify them; then, even supposing such a study possible, it would be not only lengthy but highly imperfect. Nothing would be gained but isolated notions that, far from corroborating each other, would often conflict; and the more of them there were, the more confusion they would create.

If, instead of pursuing such a course, we were to return to the first principles of the art—that is to say, to the pursuit of certain ideas that are few in number but general in application, and from which all the particular ideas would necessarily derive; then the labor would not only be very much curtailed but rendered more fruitful; for we should have a safe and rapid way to compose and execute buildings of all kinds, in all places, and at all times.

But the principles of any art, or of any science, are none other than the results of observation. To discover them, one must observe; and to observe with profit requires method.

In all courses of architecture, the art is divided into three distinct parts: decoration, distribution, and construction. At first sight, this division appears simple, natural, and fruitful. But, to make it so in fact, the ideas that it suggests would have to be applicable to all buildings; they would have to be entirely general, affording elevated vantage points from which to embrace the art as a whole before descending to survey the whole range of particulars. Now, of the three ideas expressed by the words *decoration, distribution,* and *construction,* only one is applicable to all buildings. In the sense normally assigned to the word *decoration,* most buildings are incapable of it. By *distribution,* nothing more is meant than the art of disposing, in accordance with our present-day customs, the different parts that make up a building intended for habitation: for no one speaks of the distribution of a temple, a theater, a courthouse, and so on. The word *construction,* which expresses the combination of the various mechanical arts that architecture employs, such as masonry, carpentry, joinery, locksmith's work, and so on, is thus the only one that affords an idea general enough to apply to all buildings.

But since architecture is not only the art of executing but also of composing all buildings, public and private, and since no one can execute any building without first conceiving it, the idea of construction needs to be accompanied by another general idea, which would be the source of all those particular ideas that must guide us in the composition of all buildings.[8] As this method fails to supply any such general idea, it is consequently defective.

The first defect of this method

Not only is this method defective, in that it affords an incomplete idea of architecture, it is positively dangerous, for the ideas it affords are utterly false, as will soon be apparent.

The second defect

What is more, even if this method were to afford a sound and comprehensive view of architecture, its practical shortcomings would in themselves be reason enough to reject it. To divide architecture into three entirely independent arts, which may and indeed must be studied separately, is to ensure that the aspiring architect will develop a predilection for one of those arts, devote himself to it, neglect the two others, often fail to concern himself with them at all, and consequently acquire only a portion of the knowledge that he needs.

The third defect

However, it remains impossible to embrace at one time all the particular ideas comprised within the general idea of architecture. A division is indeed necessary; but—far from pitting particular ideas against each other in mutual opposition, as often happens—it must be a division that binds them together through the simple and natural order in which it presents them to the mind.

To succeed in anything, one must have a tangible and rational aim. Otherwise, success would be purely a matter of chance. But if the aim itself is a chimerical one, then the further one proceeds, the further one departs from the true aim; and this is something that we observe all too often.

The right way to study architecture

Nor is it enough to have a tangible aim in view: one must have the means to attain it. And so, our first concern must be with the aim to be pursued in the composition and execution of buildings, both private and public, and the means to be employed.

From this, once established, we shall naturally deduce the general principles of architecture; and once these are known, it will only remain for us to apply them, (1) to the objects that architecture uses, that is, the elements of buildings; (2) to the combination of these elements, in other words, composition in general; and (3) to the alliance of these combinations in the composition of a specific building.

Such are the objects of our study and the order in which we shall examine them.

The idea of architecture
conveyed by most
writers on the subject
Most architects take the view that architecture is not so much the art of making useful buildings as that of decorating them. Its principal object, accordingly, is to please the eye and thereby arouse delightful sensations: an object that, like the other arts, it can attain only through imitation. It must take as its model the forms of the earliest huts erected by men and the proportions of the human body. And, as the orders of architecture invented by the Greeks, imitated by the Romans, and adopted by most of the nations of Europe are an imitation of the human body and of the hut, it follows that they constitute the essence of architecture. It follows that the ornaments formed by the orders are so beautiful that in matters of decoration no expense is ever to be spared.

These ideas considered
But no one can decorate without money; and it follows that the more one decorates, the more one spends. It is therefore natural to consider whether it is true that architectural decoration, as conceived by architects, gives all the pleasure that it is expected to give; or at least, whether the pleasure justifies the expense.

If architecture is to please through imitation, it must, like the other arts, imitate nature. Let us consider whether the first hut made by man is a natural object; whether the human body can serve as a model for the orders; and, finally, whether the orders constitute an imitation of the hut and of the human body.

*Laugier's description
of the hut*
Let us first of all form an idea of the hut and the orders in question. Here is what Laugier says on the subject of the hut:[9]

Let us consider man at his origins, without aid or guide other than the natural instinct to satisfy his needs. He requires a place to rest. Beside a quiet stream, he notices a stretch of grass; its nascent verdure delights his eyes; its downy softness invites him; he comes; and, reclining at his ease on that carpet of flowers, he thinks only of enjoying the gifts of nature in peace; he lacks for nothing; he desires nothing. But soon the burning heat of the sun compels him to look for shelter; he sees a forest that offers him its cool shade; he hastens to conceal himself beneath its dense foliage, and he is content. In time, it happens that a host of vapors, dense clouds obscure the air, and a fearful deluge of rain falls on that delightful forest. Ill sheltered by the leaves, man has no defense against the unwelcome moisture that soaks him through. A cave presents itself; he slips inside; finding himself in the dry, he congratulates himself on his discovery; but new discomforts make him uneasy in this refuge: he finds himself in darkness, breathing foul air, and he comes out determined to remedy the negligence of nature through his own efforts. Man wants a dwelling that will shelter him without smothering him. A few branches, broken off in the forest, supply what he needs. He chooses four of the strongest, sets them upright, and arranges them in a square. He lays four others across their tops; and on these he raises more branches on a slope, so as to meet in a point at either end. This sort of roof is covered with leaves, close-packed enough to keep out both the sun and the rain; and man has a home. He will, it is true, suffer the effects of cold and heat in his house, while it is open on every side; but then he will fill in the spaces between his pillars, and he will be secure.

"The little hut that I have just described," continues Laugier,

> is the model from which architecture in all its magnificence has been derived; it is by approximating to the simplicity of this first model that the elementary faults of execution are avoided and the true perfections captured. The upright pieces of wood gave us the idea of columns. The horizontal pieces above them gave us the idea of entablatures. And, finally, the inclined pieces that form the roof gave us the idea of pediments. All the masters of the art have acknowledged this.

Columns, entablatures, and pediments, united to form what are known as the *orders of architecture:* these are the essential portions of the art, which constitute its beauties; and walls, doors, windows, vaults, arcades, and all the other parts that necessity alone compels us to add, are no more than indulgences, to be tolerated at best. Such is the conclusion drawn by the author whom we have just quoted.

What is usually understood by the term order

From the nature of the hut, let us pass to that of the orders and read what Vitruvius has to tell us on the subject:[10]

Greek orders

> Dorus, king of the Peloponnese, built a temple to Juno at Argos, and it so happened that it was in the manner that we call *Doric;* later, in a number of other cities, others were built in this same order, no rule yet being established for the proportions of architecture. At that time the Athenians sent several colonies to Asia Minor under the command of Ion; and they gave the name of Ionia to the country where he settled. The first temples they built there were Doric, the principal one being dedicated to Apollo. But, not knowing how to proportion their columns, they looked for a way to make them strong enough to support the load of the building, and at the same time pleasing to the eye. To this end, they took the measure of a man's foot, which is the sixth part of his height, and on this they patterned their columns, so as to give them a height of six diameters. And so the Doric column was used in those buildings that possessed the proportions, the strength, and the beauty of a man's body.
>
> Some time later, they built a temple to Diana and sought for a new manner that would achieve beauty by the same method. They imitated the delicacy of a woman's body; they raised their columns upon a base formed like twisted cords, to serve as the shoe; they carved volutes on the capital to represent the locks of hair that hang to left and right; they placed on the brow of their column a cyma and echinus to imitate the rest of the hair, gathered and tied behind a woman's head; in the flutings, they imitated the folds of their dresses. This order, invented by the Ionians, took the name of *Ionic.*
>
> The *Corinthian* represents the delicacy of a girl, whose age makes her figure more slender and better suited to those ornaments that serve to enhance its natural beauty. The invention of its capital is due to the following accident. A Corinthian maiden of marriageable age died, and her nurse placed on her tomb a basket containing certain little vases that she had loved when she was alive; and, lest they be immediately spoiled by the weather, she laid a tile on the basket. By chance, this

Doric, imitated from the human body

Ionic, imitated from the body of a woman

Corinthian, imitated from the body of a girl

had been set down on an acanthus root; when the leaves began to sprout, the basket, which was over the center of the root, caused the stalks of the plant to grow up over its sides. Where they met the corners of the tiles, they were forced to turn over and to curl into the form of volutes. Callimachus, a sculptor and architect, saw this object with pleasure and imitated its forms in the capitals of the columns that he afterwards executed at Corinth: establishing on this model the proportions of the Corinthian order.

Roman orders

Tuscan

A number of Greek colonies brought to Etruria, which is now Tuscany, the knowledge of the Doric order, which was the only one then used in Greece. This order long continued to be built there in the same way as in the country of its origin; but in the end a number of changes were made: the column was extended and given a base, the capital was changed, and the entablature was simplified. The order thus modified was adopted by the Romans under the name of the *Tuscan* order.

Composite

Long after, the Romans, who had adopted the three Greek orders, conceived the notion of adding the Ionic volutes to the Corinthian capital; and this combination caused those columns in which it appeared to be given the name of *Composite*.

Such are the five orders, which are regarded as the essence of architecture and the source of all the beauties of which decoration is capable, because they are supposed to have been imitated from the forms of the hut and from the proportions of the human body. Let us consider whether they are in fact such an imitation.

Are the proportions of the orders imitated from those of the human body?

Let us begin with the Doric order, which the Greeks, it is said, defined by the proportion of six diameters, because a man's foot is one-sixth of his height. First of all, a man's foot is not one-sixth but one-eighth of his height. What is more, in all Greek buildings, the proportions of Doric columns are endlessly varied (see the *Recueil et parallèle,* plate 63); and, within this infinite variety, the exact proportion of six to one is not found in a single case. If any Greek architect ever did see fit to assign this proportion to the Doric order, it would appear that the Greeks took no notice; otherwise, it would be found, if not in all their buildings, at least in those of the age of Pericles: buildings that are justly regarded as masterpieces.

They are not, and can never have been

The same variety is observed in the proportions of the other orders, supposedly imitated from the body of a woman and from that of a girl (see *Recueil et parallèle,* plate 64). It is therefore untrue that the human body served as a model for the orders.

But even supposing that the same order always has the same proportions in the same circumstances; that the Greeks consistently followed the system attributed to them; and that the length of a man's foot is one-sixth of his height: does it then follow that the proportions of the orders are an imitation of those of the human body? What comparison is there between a man's body, which varies in width at different heights, and a kind of cylinder with a constant diameter throughout? What resemblance can there be between these two objects, even if one were to suppose them to have the same base and the same height? Clearly, the proportions of the human body did not serve, and can never have served, as a model for those of the orders.

The forms of the orders were no more imitated from a hut than their proportions were derived from the human body. Columns possess either a base and a capital or, at least, a capital; for a column consisting of a plain cylinder would never be recognized as a column at all. There is no trace of any of this in the trunks of trees or in the posts that support the hut. It would be vain to argue that planks or boards were subsequently laid on the posts to broaden the upper part and make it more capable of carrying the entablature; seeing that for an equal length a piece of wood made up of longitudinal fibers is less likely to break than a piece of stone composed of an aggregation of little grains. If one of these objects had served as a model for the other, it would be more natural to suppose the wooden boards to have been imitated from the stone capitals than to suppose the latter to have been imitated from the former.

The entablature is no more a close imitation of the upper parts of the hut than the columns are imitations of its supports. In a square building, where mutules or modillions—said to represent the ends of the sloping pieces of the roof of the hut—are employed, they are used all around; it would be absurd to do otherwise. In the hut, however, they appear only along the sides; the same applies to the triglyphs. Besides, in the hut, the ends of the beams or joists, which the triglyphs are said to imitate, are smooth. Triglyphs are channeled, and owe their very name to the two whole and two half channels that are seen in them. If, therefore, the architects who invented the orders were seeking to imitate the hut, they imitated it extremely badly. However, it appears from more than one passage in Vitruvius that the Greeks, far from slavishly imitating the hut, were at pains to conceal those parts of their buildings that might most have resembled the parts of the hut. Here is what that author has to say on the subject of triglyphs:

> Long after columns came to be made of stone, entablatures continued to be made of wood. The Greek architects, finding the smooth ends of the joists unsightly where they rested on the architrave or main beam, added small boards to form what we call the femurs of the triglyphs and coated them with wax. As this wax, unlike the rest of the entablature, was impervious to rainwater, the water ran down the channels thus formed and gathered below in drops, which were subsequently imitated in stone entablatures.

In the entablatures of the Ionic and Corinthian orders, the Greeks went still further: they eliminated all reference to the hut (see *Recueil et parallèle*, plates 65 and 66); and yet, by a strange contradiction, the adherents of the hut theory consider these last-named orders to be the most beautiful.

It is evident, therefore, that the Greek orders were not an imitation of the hut at all; and that, if they had been, this imitation would have been utterly imperfect and consequently incapable of producing the effect that was intended.

Are the forms of the orders imitated from those of a hut?

The triglyphs of the Doric order, made to conceal from view the ends of the joists

The smooth friezes of the Ionic and Corinthian orders

The forms of the orders are not imitated from those of a hut, or only imperfectly so

Is the hut a natural
object?

Furthermore, is not such a model even more defective than the copy? What is a hut, open to every wind, laboriously built by man to shelter himself, and yet sheltering him not at all? Can such a hut be regarded as a natural object? Surely this is no more than the inchoate production of the first falterings of art? Might it not be that the instinct that directed man in this construction was so crude that it does not merit the name of art, and might it not be for this reason that it is regarded as a product of nature?

Imitation is not a means
proper to architecture

Now, if a hut is not a natural object; and if the human body can never have served as a model for architecture; and if, even on a contrary assumption, the orders are not an imitation of either; the necessary conclusion must be that these orders are not the essence of architecture; that the pleasure to be expected from their use, and from the decoration that derives therefrom, is nil; that such decoration is itself a chimera; and that the expense that it entails is folly.

From this it follows that, if the principal aim of architecture is to please, it must either imitate to better effect, or choose other models to imitate, or adopt other means than imitation.

Inquiry as to the true aim
of architecture

But is it true that the principal aim of architecture is to please and that decoration is its principal concern? In the passage by Laugier, quoted above, it will be seen that the author, for all his curious prejudices, is forced to acknowledge that this art owes its origins to necessity alone and that it has no other goal than public and private utility. How could he ever have imagined otherwise, even if we suppose that the builder of the hut, the alleged prototype of all architecture, was capable of conceiving the idea of decoration? Surely, the idea of his needs, and of the means proper to satisfy them, would have presented itself first, and would indeed have banished all other ideas? Is it reasonable to suppose that, left alone to defend himself from the inclement weather and from the fury of wild beasts, needing to provide himself with many advantages that he had always lacked, the builder of the shelter gave a moment's thought to making it an object to delight his eye? Is it any more reasonable to suppose that men in society, with a host of new ideas and, consequently, a host of new needs to satisfy, adopted decoration as the principal concern of architecture?

Some writers, who have sustained and elaborated the hut theory with all conceivable ingenuity, will object that we have been speaking of mere building; that in this respect architecture is no more than a manual trade; and that it never merited the name of art until the nations, having attained the height of wealth and luxury, undertook to adorn the buildings that they had erected. But here we appeal to these authors themselves. Was it after the Romans attained the height of wealth and luxury, covering their buildings with moldings, entablatures, and so forth, that they produced their best architecture? The Greeks were far less wealthy; and is not their architecture, in which such objects are so few in number, preferable to the architecture of the Romans? These same authors readily admit as much; indeed, they go so far as to say that the Greek is the only architecture worthy of the name. Now, Greek architecture, which they admire, and which deserves to be generally admired, never took pleasure as its aim or decoration as its object. Of course, care and purity are apparent in its execution; but is not care essential for solidity? In some buildings, sculptural ornaments are to be found; but the others are, for the most part, totally devoid of them, and are none the less highly esteemed. Is it not clear that such ornaments are not essential in architecture? And when architecture does use them, do they not show that it cannot aspire to give pleasure by virtue of the intrinsic beauty of its proportions and its forms? And even if some forms are found that do not directly spring from need, do not the differences that appear in them, from one building to the next, prove that the Greeks attached no importance whatever to architectural decoration?

Whether we consult reason or examine the monuments, it is evident that pleasure can never have been the aim of architecture; nor can architectural decoration have been its object. Public and private utility, the happiness and the protection of individuals and of society: such is the aim of architecture. Whether it be accorded or denied the name of art, it will nonetheless deserve to be practiced, and the means to its end will deserve to be examined; and this we shall now do.

The aim of architecture

We shall find, on looking into the matter, that, in all ages and in all places, all of men's thoughts and actions have sprung from two principles alone: love of comfort and dislike of all exertion. Accordingly, whether building their own private dwellings in isolation, or erecting public buildings in society, men inevitably sought (1) to derive from their buildings the greatest possible advantage, consequently making them as fit as possible for their purpose; and (2) to build them in the way that would in early times be the least laborious and later—when money had become the price of labor—the least costly.

The means that it must employ

Thus, fitness and economy are the means that architecture must naturally employ, and are the sources from which it must derive its principles: the only principles that can guide us in the study and exercise of the art.

Fitness and economy

First, if a building is to be fit for its purpose, it must be solid, salubrious, and commodious.[11]

General principles relative to fitness

It will be solid: if the materials employed in its construction are of good quality and intelligently disposed; if the building rests on good foundations; if its principal supports are sufficient in number, placed perpendicularly for greater strength, and equally spaced so that each may support an equal portion of the load.

Solidity

It will be salubrious: if it is situated in a wholesome place; if the floor or pavement is raised above the soil and protected from humidity; if there are walls to fill the intervals between the supports that form its skeleton, and to protect the internal parts from heat and from cold; if those walls are pierced by openings permeable to air and light; if all the openings in the internal walls correspond to each other and to the external openings, thus promoting the renewal of the air; if a covering shelters it from rain and sun in such a way that the edge of this covering, projecting beyond the walls, throws the water

Salubrity

away from them; and if its exposure is to the south in cold countries, or to the north in hot countries.

Commodity

Finally, it will be commodious: if the number and size of all its parts, their form, situation, and arrangement, are in the closest possible relation to its purpose.

So much for fitness; now for economy.

General principles
relative to economy

Symmetry
Regularity
Simplicity

If a given area demands less length of perimeter when bounded by the four sides of a square than when bounded by those of a parallelogram, and less still when bounded by the circumference of a circle; if the square form is superior in symmetry, in regularity, and in simplicity to that of the parallelogram, and inferior to that of a circle: it will be readily supposed that the more symmetrical, regular, and simple a building is, the less costly it becomes. It is hardly necessary to add that, since economy demands the utmost simplicity in all necessary things, it absolutely forbids all that is unnecessary.

Such are the general principles that must have guided reasonable men, everywhere and in every age, when they came to erect buildings; and such are the principles that governed the design of the most universally and justly admired of ancient buildings, as will later become apparent.

May not architecture
blend the pleasurable
with the useful?

It will be argued that, since there are buildings that are rightly admired, or rightly despised, it follows that there must be beauties and defects in architecture; that it must pursue the former and avoid the latter; and thus that it is capable of giving pleasure; that, if such is not its principal aim, it must at least attempt to blend the agreeable with the useful.

It is impossible for the
productions of this art
not to give pleasure

So far from denying that architecture can give pleasure, we maintain that it cannot but give pleasure, where it is treated in accordance with its true principles. Has not nature associated pleasure with the satisfaction of our needs, and are not our keenest pleasures the satisfactions of our most pressing needs? Such an art as architecture, which immediately satisfies so many of our needs, which places us in a position to satisfy all the others with ease, which defends us against the seasons, and which leads us to enjoy all the gifts of nature: an art, indeed, to which all the other arts owe their very existence: how could it fail to give us pleasure?

Beauties observed in
architecture

They present themselves
naturally, when we
concentrate on
disposition

Certainly, the grandeur, magnificence, variety, effect, and character that are observed in buildings are all beauties, all causes of the pleasure that we derive from looking at them. But where is the need to run after such things, if a building is disposed in a manner fitted to its intended use? Will it not differ sensibly from another building intended for some other use? Will it not naturally possess a character—and, what is more, a character of its own? If all of the parts of the building, being intended for different uses, are disposed as they should be, will they not inevitably differ? Will not the building afford variety? And if the same building is disposed in the most economical, that is to say, the simplest manner, will it not appear as grand and as magnificent as it is possible to be? Undoubtedly, it will, because the eye will embrace the greatest number of its parts at one glance. Again, where is the need to chase after all those partial beauties?

Far from being necessary, indeed, such a pursuit is harmful even to decoration itself. For if, smitten with the effect of certain beautiful features in one building, you attempt to transfer them to another, where they are out of place; or if, where such beauties are naturally present, you seek to amplify them further than the nature of the building permits: is it not plain that they will disappear; and, worse still, that they will be transformed into faults? The Medici Venus and the Farnese Hercules are admirable figures. But if anyone, on the grounds that one head is more graceful or has more character than the other, were to set that of Venus on Hercules's body, and vice versa, would not those masterpieces of art become masterpieces of absurdity? And if, because the individual parts of those statues are admirable, the sculptor had sought to enhance the beauty of the whole by increasing their number, and had given his figures four arms, four legs, and so on, would they not be downright monstrous?

They disappear when we concentrate on architectural decoration

From all of this, it follows that one must neither strive to make architecture give pleasure—seeing that it is impossible for it not to give pleasure—nor seek to endow buildings with variety, effect, and character, since these are qualities that they cannot be without.

It is unnecessary and even dangerous for architecture to seek to please

Disposition must therefore be the architect's sole concern—even if he were a lover of architectural decoration, even if he wished only to please—since decoration cannot be called beautiful or give true pleasure, except as the necessary effect of the most fitting and the most economical disposition.

Disposition is the principal object of architecture

Thus, all of the architect's talent comes down to the solution of two problems: (1) in the case of private buildings, how to make the building as fit for its purpose as possible for a given sum; (2) in the case of public buildings, where fitness must be assumed, how to build at the least possible expense.

Architecture consists in the solution of two problems

It will thus be seen that in architecture there is no incompatibility, and no mere compatibility, between beauty and economy: for economy is one of the principal causes of beauty.

One example will serve to cast light on these ideas and present these principles with the greatest certitude. The building now known as the Panthéon Français was first intended as a temple.[12] The purpose envisaged in buildings of this kind, whatever the form of worship for which they are intended, is not only to assemble the multitudes but to capture their imagination through the senses. Grandeur and magnificence are the aptest means to this end. It might consequently appear that decoration ought to be, if not the sole aim, at least the principal concern in the composition of such a building; and that expense must be no object. We shall see, however, that if, in the building in question, all idea of decoration had been set aside in order to dispose it in the fittest and most economical way, the result would have been a building far more likely to produce the desired effect. The Panthéon Français is 110 meters long by 80 wide. It is made up of a portico and four limbs united by a dome, the whole forming a Greek cross. The perimeter of the walls is 612 meters. There are 206 columns, distributed as follows: 22 in the portico, 136 in the limbs, and 48 in the dome, which has 32 outside and 16 inside.

Plate 1

Who would not expect such a building as this, of such dimensions, and with so prodigious a number of columns, to present the grandest and most magnificent spectacle? And yet it does nothing of the sort. Inside, the building is only 3,672 [square] meters in true area. The apparent area is even less, since the cruciform shape adopted by the architect allows hardly more than half of it to be seen on entry.

The quantity of columns no more succeeds in conveying an idea of magnificence than the dimensions convey an idea of grandeur. Of the twenty-two columns of the portico, only six or eight are clearly visible. Those of the dome are three-quarters masked by the portico. Once inside, no more than sixteen are clearly seen, and those sixteen mask all the others. Of the columns inside the dome, only half are visible; and even then one is forced to make an effort. And yet this building, so lacking in grandeur and in magnificence, cost nearly seventeen million to build.

If, instead of pursuing the forms that the architect considered most apt to produce effect and movement, he had used those that economy naturally suggests for the disposition of a building that is formed of a single room, in other words a circle; if he had arranged his columns concentric to this circle, so as to reduce the span of the vault on the inside, and to form a spacious portico on the outside capable of receiving a vast crowd from every direction: then what would have been the grandeur, the magnificence, of such a building! Its area, no part of which would have been concealed from the eye, would have been 4,292 [square] meters; the exterior would have presented, from every angle, 32 columns to the view, while the interior would have offered a multitude of them. These are two very different buildings. And wherein lies the difference? In the former, there was an effort to create something beautiful, and it was supposed that the only way to do so was to spend lavishly; whereas, in the latter, the only consideration was to dispose the building in the fittest and most economical way. And, indeed, the latter, though grander and more magnificent than the former, incorporates only 112 columns; its walls are only 248 meters in circumference; and it would cost just half as much. That is to say that, for the cost of the other, two buildings might have been built, not like the one that exists but like the one that here replaces it; or else one single building, twice the size of the one just proposed.

This example, although the least favorable to the system that we propose, nevertheless suffices to make known the truth of our principles and the consequences, for the wealth and the comfort both of private individuals and of society at large, that stem from an ignorance of those principles, or from the failure to observe them.

Recapitulation   Let us recapitulate in a few words what we have found to be true of the nature of architecture, its object, its purpose, its means, and its general principles.

Architecture is an art of a kind unique to itself, and its object is the composition and execution of buildings, both public and private.

Its purpose, in composing and in executing such buildings, is to satisfy a great number of our needs, and to place us in a position to satisfy all the others.

The means that it employs to this end are fitness and economy.

Fitness includes solidity, salubrity, and commodity.

Economy comprises symmetry, regularity, and simplicity.

Solidity consists in the selection and use of materials, and in the number and disposition of supports.

Salubrity depends on the situation, on the exposure, on the elevation of the ground, on the walls, on the openings in them, and on the covering.

Commodity springs from the relation between the form of a building, its magnitude, and the number of its parts, on the one hand, and its purpose, on the other.

The most symmetrical, most regular, and simplest forms, such as the circle, the square, and the slightly elongated parallelogram, are the forms most suited to economy, since they enclose a given area with a smaller perimeter than other forms; and these forms are consequently to be preferred.

Decoration is not the architect's business; unless what is meant by decoration is the art of applying painting, sculpture, and inscriptions to buildings. This kind of decoration, however, is no more than an accessory.

The orders, as objects of imitation, have nothing to contribute, because they resemble nothing in nature.

Disposition must be the architect's sole concern; and this is so, even if his only end is to give pleasure. Character, effect, variety—in a word, all those beauties that are found in buildings or that men seek to introduce into architectural decoration—naturally emerge from any disposition that embraces fitness and economy.

But before disposing any edifice, before combining and assembling its parts, the parts must first be known. And they, in their turn, are combinations of other parts that may be called the elements of buildings, such as walls, openings, supports both engaged and detached, raised foundations, floors, vaults, coverings, and so on. First of all, therefore, these elements must be known.

PART I

Elements of Buildings

Section One. Qualities of Materials

The objects that architecture employs are built with materials of different kinds and consequently possess dimensions, relations, proportions, and forms. We shall consider them under all of these separate aspects.

Materials used in buildings

First, let us consider materials, which are the substance, so to speak, of the objects concerned.[13]

Three kinds of material

These may be arranged in three classes:

Those that are hard and laborious to work, which are for this reason very expensive.

Those that are softer and easier to work and therefore cheaper.

Finally, those that serve only to join together the other materials.

The materials of the first kind are granites, porphyries, jaspers, marbles, and hard stones.

Those of the second kind are soft stones, rubble, brick, tile, slate, and timber.

Those of the third kind are plaster, lime, sand, ballast; the various mortars prepared by mixing these; iron, copper, and lead.

First kind divided into two classes

Materials of the first kind are divided into two classes.

Those of one class are found in masses in quarries, such as granite, porphyry, jasper, marble, and some sandstones; and the others, such as limestones, appear in beds.

Marbles in general

Although the composition of granite, porphyry, and jasper differs from that of marble, all these materials, being in general hard and colored, are classified in the trade as marble.

Granite, porphyry, jasper

Granite exists in various colors: red, pink, green, gray, russet. The colors of porphyry vary similarly: red, brown, green, and gray. Jasper, likewise, may be black or purple, red or gray or green.

Marbles proper

A distinction is drawn between two varieties of marble, antique and modern. *Antique* marble is that from quarries now lost and known to us only through some of the works of the ancients; *modern* is that from quarries still extant and in use today.

Veined marbles and breccias

Among the various antique and modern marbles, a further distinction is made between *veined* marbles, which present veins in one or more colors, and *breccia* marbles, which offer a mass of pebbles or shells encrusted in a sort of paste.

Antique marbles

The antique marbles are as follows: red and green *porphyry; lapis,* which is a dark blue; *serpentine,* which is a brownish green; *alabaster; blanc antique; African* marble, spotted with red and veined with white and green; *noir antique,* spotted with white; *brocatelle,* with shades of yellow, red, and gray; *jasper,* greenish with red spots; *vert antique, jaune antique,* and so on.

The modern marbles are: *white marble,* found at Carrara and the most esteemed; that of the former province of Languedoc, which is the least esteemed, being of a dirty vermilion with prominent white veins and spots; the marble of the former province of Bourbonnais, of a dirty red, veined with gray and yellow; *sérancolin,* which is gray and yellow, spotted with blood-red; *griotte,* which is flesh-colored; *vert campan,* mingled with red, white, and green; *vert d'Egypte,* of a dark green, spotted with tow-gray; *vert de mer,* lighter than *vert campan; violet breccia,* and the other breccias; *veined white; bleu turquin,* dark blue; *rance;* and so on.

Marbles in general have the advantage of being hard, of presenting a combination of the most beautiful colors to the eye, and of taking a perfect polish.

Marbles that are rejected as defective include the following: those that are excessively hard and difficult to work; those that are *fibrous,* having fissures that run through them, as do rance and *sérancolin;* those that are *terreous,* having soft parts that have to be filled with mastic, like most of the breccias; those that are *dull,* failing to take a polish; those that are *soft,* like sandstone, incapable of taking a sharp arris.

The various marbles are imitated by a composition known as *stucco,* which, although comparatively hard, is affected by changes in humidity; it is consequently little used except in interiors.

Marble is costly, and for this reason is not commonly used except as a revetment or an incrustation. It is seldom used in blocks, except for columns, vases, basins, figures, and so on, or in perpend.

The various colors of marble call for some care in their combination. Veinless white marbles must be reserved for sculpture; veined whites for the backgrounds; and the variegated sorts for columns, friezes, and inlay panels. Avoid combinations of colors that contrast too sharply, and even more those of colors that are too similar.

In Paris, sandstone is hardly used except for paving; it exists in hard and soft varieties. The color of the latter is grayish. For jointing sandstone use a mortar composed of lime and cement. Where sandstone is used for building, zigzag cavities must be cut in its courses, to prevent the mortar from drying too quickly.

Limestones are always found in beds, but some are hard and some are soft. We shall not give a detailed account of the limestones of every region, but restrict ourselves to those that are most used in Paris and in its environs.

The finest of the hard limestones is *lias.* There are a number of quarries around the Faubourg Saint-Jacques, at Saint-Cloud, and at Saint-Leu. It is found in thicknesses varying from 18 cm (7 in.) to 27 cm (10 in.). There are two kinds, the "free," *franc,* or *doux,* and the "false" or *férault.* The latter is the harder and is used by preference for exteriors. The chapel at Versailles is built

	Modern marbles
	Qualities of marble
	Defects of marble
	Stucco
	Use of marble
	Combinations of marbles
	Sandstone
	Limestones
	Hard limestones
	Lias

of it. For the sake of economy, lias is often used in place of marble: vestibules, antechambers, and dining rooms are paved with it; chimneypieces and architraves are made of it; all those works, in fact, that require a hard, fine stone.

Arcueil and Bagneux stone

The second variety of hard limestone, and the most frequently used, is that of *Arcueil* and *Bagneux*. These stones are classified by depth into high and low. The former will measure anything between 48 cm (18 in.) and 80 cm (2½ ft.); the latter from 32 cm (1 ft.) to 48 cm (18 in.). It is used to make steps, architraves, door and window sills, and shelves.

Tonnerre stone

Tonnerre limestone is highly esteemed for its fine, close grain. As solid as lias, it is softer, whiter, and will measure approximately 48 cm (18 in.). It is commonly used for sculpture. The Grenelle Fountain is entirely built of it.

Vergelée stone

Vergelée limestone, which is quarried at Saint-Leu, is rustic and full of little holes. It is excellent for building under water.

Soft limestones
Saint-Leu stone

Of all the soft limestones, that of Saint-Leu is the most commonly used. It measures from 64 cm to 1.28 m (2 to 4 ft.). It may be used to advantage for elevated parts; but not in damp positions, nor under heavy loads.

Conflans stone

Another soft limestone that is used is that of Conflans-Sainte-Honorine, near Saint-Germain; its grain is very fine. The entablature of the porch of the Panthéon Français is made of this stone.

Chalk and gypsum are of little value. The latter is so apt to dissolve in water, and to crumble under any burden, that its use in building is forbidden by law.

Slate

Slate is a black, gray, or greenish stone that is easily split. There are two kinds, hard and soft. The hard is used to make paving stones and tables; the soft, which is sold in whatever thickness may be required, is used to roof buildings. There are several sizes: the largest roofing slate is 32 by 20 cm (12 by 8 in.), and the smallest is 20 by 10 cm (8 by 4 in.). Anjou slate is the best.

All these varieties of stone, and a host of others, are used only in dressed form. There are others that are used just as they come out of the quarry, such as rubble and burrstone.

Rubble

Rubble consists of large blocks of stone that are too irregular to be dressed. They most often come from the quarry roof and are used in foundations.

Burrstone

Burrstone is also used in foundations, because the mortar readily adheres to its cavities; it can also be used to advantage in the lower parts of buildings. Its reddish color, which contrasts with the yellowish white of the other stones, can introduce a natural element of variety into the appearance of a structure.

Qualities of stone

In general, for stone to be good, it must be *clean*, that is to say, without fissures, soft veins, and shells; it must *harden* on exposure to air; it must be *sound*, that is to say, neither as hard as the stones that form the quarry roof nor as poor in quality as those that adhere to the floor. It must also have a fine and even grain.

Defects of stone

Fissures, shells, and soft veins are defects in stone: fibers, because, being harder than the rest, they make the stone liable to split; shells, because once the stone is dressed, its face is not smooth enough; and soft veins, because they crumble under load.

When stones are taken from the quarry, their layers or beds are covered with a friable layer known as *bousin,* which must be cleaned off, as it is liable to crumble to dust under the action of rain and humidity in the same way as soft veins.

Those materials that are quarried in masses may be placed in any direction; but those that are formed in beds must be laid in the same direction as in the quarry; that is to say, along their courses. Experience has shown that they hold better in this position than in any other. For stone is like a book: laid flat, it can support enormous loads; but upright it yields to the least pressure that separates the pages.

This is not to deny that stones have very often been placed vertically. The Goths were in the habit of making their columns in this way; and the same applies to the columns of the garden front of Versailles, and of the courtyard of the Louvre. Wherever columns are used without necessity, merely for decoration, as in the examples that we have just cited, it is of little consequence how the stone is placed; but in a rational building, where the columns must serve to carry loads, it is highly important to bed the stones correctly.

Besides the names that stones derive from the places where they are found, they assume other names either from the place that they occupy in buildings, or from the state in which they are before being laid, or even before arriving at the building site.[14]

Pierre d'échantillon is stone dressed in accordance with measurements sent by the mason to the quarryman;

pierres de haut ou de bas appareil are dressed stones of greater and lesser height, respectively;

pierre brute, stone that has yet to be cleaned off;

pierre en chantier, stone fixed in place by the stonecutter before being dressed;

pierre débitée, stone sawn, with a toothed saw in the case of hard stone, an untoothed saw for soft stone;

pierre faite, stone that is entirely dressed and ready to be laid;

pierre fichée, with the inside of its joints filled with mortar or plaster;

pierres de parpain, those that pass through a wall and appear on both faces;

pierre d'attente, a stone that projects from the end of a wall; and

pierres perdues, those stones that are cast into rivers when work is to be constructed there, and when the depth or the nature of the soil does not allow the driving of piles.

Rubble is taken either from the quarry waste or from a thin vein broken up to use in this form. Its main quality is to be well squared and lie well, because then it has more bed and consumes less mortar.

Rubble must be cleaned off, or else the friable layer would prevent adhesion; it must also be bedded.

Coursed rubble, reduced to a uniform depth, is called *picked* rubble, because the face is often picked with the point of the hammer. This is how it is used in carefully finished work. In less-finished work it is used more or less as it comes from the quarry. Then it is plastered, to compensate for the unevenness of the courses.

Brick

Brick is a kind of artificial stone, made from clay, kneaded and tempered to produce a ductile paste that is shaped in molds. It is then dried in clamps and burnt in a kiln fired by wood or by coal.

Qualities and defects of brick

For a brick to be sound, the clay used for its making must be moist, strong, and free of stones and gravel; it must be sufficiently tempered with a beater and adequately and evenly burnt.

An essential precaution is that bricks must be allowed to cool slowly; otherwise they are liable to spall and crumble when exposed to frost and to loads.

How to judge its quality

Brick is sound when it resists frost, when it gives a clear note on being struck, and when the grain is fine and close.

The dimensions of a brick are 20 cm (8 in.) in length, 10 cm (4 in.) in width, and 5 cm (2 in.) in depth. Its color is a yellowish red or brown.

Use of brick

The best brick comes from Burgundy, but there are few places where it cannot be obtained. It can perfectly well substitute for stone in places where the latter is scarce; it is far more resistant to fire and to humidity. Its lightness makes it valuable in a large number of structures, and for vaults above all. Few materials combine so many advantages. Chimney funnels, fireplaces, ovens, kilns, and so on, are almost always made of brick.

Tiles

Tiles are of the same composition as brick, and should have the same qualities, except that they are burnt harder. They are made in two sizes. The Burgundy tile, which is the better of the two, and which is called the *grand moule* tile, is 34 by 23 cm (13 by 8½ in.); the *petit moule* tile, which comes from the neighborhood of Paris, is 27 by 16 cm (10 by 6 in.).

In Italy, in Holland, in Flanders, and in part of Germany, tiles, instead of being flat, are hollowed out in an S-shape.

The disadvantage of tiles lies in their weight, which forces roofs to be more steeply pitched than if they were covered with slates.

Quarry tiles

In addition to bricks and roof tiles, burnt clay is also used to make floor tiles, with which buildings are paved.

Timber: Three classes

Timber, as used in building, is classified into the woods used for *carpentry,* for *joinery,* and for *veneering.*

Carpentry timber

The woods most commonly used for carpentry are oak and pine. Elm, beech, hornbeam, walnut, lime, and so on, are also used. But none of these bears comparison with oak or even with pine.

Oak

Oak is the wood that best resists weathering, lasts longest when sunk in water or driven into the earth, and can offer the largest pieces in length and squared thickness.

Pine

Pine has the advantage of being lighter than oak and of lasting longer under a coat of plaster.

Joinery timber

For joinery and for carving, the woods commonly used are soft oak, pine, aspen, and so on.

Veneer timber

The woods used for veneers are ebony, mahogany, Oriental woods, palisander, and others, which are sold in sheets, and which take a high polish.

The advantages of wood over stone are that it is less brittle and easier to work. It is more convenient to transport, may be placed under tension as well as compression, and can be placed in any direction; but it has the disadvantage of being vulnerable to fire.

Advantages of timber

Wood must not be used too green, otherwise it would bend too easily and decay very quickly.

Precautions to take

If obliged to use it when it is still slightly green, soak it in water for a time to dissolve all the sap; this is the best way to protect it from decay.

Great care must be taken to remove all the alburnum. This constitutes the outer layers, which have yet to take on a good consistency. They are removed if the timber was not stripped of its bark before felling; otherwise, they may be left.

Alburnum

Also to be rejected are whitewood, which easily decays; *quaggy* wood, with shakes caused by frost; dead wood, which is good only for burning; knotty or brash timber, which is liable to snap; wood that warps because it is not sufficiently seasoned.

Names relative to defects in timber

Aside from the terms that indicate the faults in wood, there are others that designate the ways in which it may be worked. There is *exposed* wood, which is not concealed by plaster; *planed* wood, smoothed with a jackplane in structural carpentry and with a trueing plane in finish joinery; *unhewn* wood, from which only the four wane surfaces have been removed to square it up; and *sawn* wood, as it comes from the sawmill, in rafters, joists, and planks.

Names relative to its uses

Wood is one of the materials most used in building. It constitutes, if not the whole, a large part of the whole. In floors and roofs it is almost invariably employed.

The use of wood

Wood varies in strength. Oak, for example, is one of the strongest; and poplar, one of the weakest. In every variety, strength is in inverse proportion to length, in direct proportion to width and to the square of thickness. Other things being equal, this strength varies according to position: for a piece of wood laid horizontally across two supports will break more easily than if it were placed on a slope; and in the latter case it would break more readily than if it were upright.

Among the agents that serve to join these various materials, one of the most commonly used is plaster.

Agents used to join various materials

To be sound, plaster must be well burnt, rich, white, easy to work, and adhesive.

Plaster

Its qualities

As far as possible, plaster should be used straight from the kiln and never exposed to the open air, to humidity, or to sun. The sun heats it, rain waterlogs it, and air spoils it.

Its defects

Plaster has a host of uses; its action is rapid and, what is more, self-sufficient. In this it differs from lime, which needs the presence of another agent to harden it.

When it should be used

But it is not to be employed indiscriminately; for, while it is perfectly suitable for application to ceilings, chimney breasts, and internal and external walls, it is highly unsuitable for damp locations, for the foundations of buildings, and for jointing ashlar walls. It bonds well with iron but not with wood, unless the wood is studded with nails.

How it should be used

Plaster is used: (1) straight from the kiln, and roughly pulverized with a ram; this is how it is used in the construction of rough rubble walls, or for roughing in timber partitions; (2) riddled, for filling, jointing, and laying coats; and (3) sieved, for floating, for moldings, and for sculpture.

Roughing in is daubing with mortar or with plaster. *Filling* is repairing old walls; *jointing* is throwing on plaster with a trowel and pressing it by hand into the joints of a wall; a *laying* coat is plaster applied with a broom, without passing a trowel or a hand over it; and a *setting* coat is a uniform coat of plaster laid on a wall or wooden partition.

These various manners of using plaster demand differing ways of mixing it. A stiff mix is used for rough work, sealing, and setting; a wetter mix for moldings run with a mold; and it is used highly dilute for casting, for screeding, and for pointing stonework.

In all these cases, care must be taken to mix plaster only as it is needed; otherwise it sets and can no longer be used.

It is mostly quarried at Montmartre; it is also found at Meudon, at Triel, and so on.

Mortar is a compound of lime with sand or with cement. Before we enter into the details of its composition, a word is in order on the ingredients that are used in it.

Lime

All marbles, and all those stones whose composition bears an analogy to that of marbles, are proper for the making of lime; but the heaviest, the hardest, and the whitest are the best. The ancients always made their lime with marble.

Lime is burnt in kilns fired with wood or coal.[15] When it has been burnt it should be sonorous, and emit quantities of steam when moistened. After it comes out of the kiln, it is essential to transport it only in well-sealed barrels, to exclude moisture. It is no less necessary to slake it soon after burning; for, if it is kept in the solid state for too long, even away from the air, it loses some of its virtue.

Rainwater, spring water, and river water are the only waters suitable for slaking lime; even so, the water must be exposed to the air for several days; for if the water is too cold the lime coagulates.

Lime is slaked in a trough next to the pit where it is intended to be kept. It is tossed into the trough after being crushed and stirred with paddles while the water is poured in by measure and with care; for too much water drowns it.

When it is diluted, the pipe leading from the trough to the pit is unstopped, with a grid in the conduit to catch foreign bodies. When the lime has flowed out, the conduit is stopped, and the operation is repeated as often as necessary.

When the pit is full, it is left open for five or six days, and sprinkled with water to fill the cracks; and when it has ceased to crack, it is covered with 32 or 64 cm (1 or 2 ft.) of sand, to prevent contact with the air. It may thus be kept for a long time without losing its virtue.

There are two varieties of sand: river sand, which is yellow, red, or white; and pit sand, from sandpits or quarries. Sand

Sand is good if it leaves no earthy residue when rubbed between the hands, and if water in which it has been placed and stirred remains perfectly clear.

Cement is none other than crushed bricks or, preferably, tiles. Ballast

Mortar, as we have said above, is a mixture of lime with sand or cement. A Mortar good mortar is made with a mixture of one-third lime to two-thirds sand. But, if the lime is not of the best quality, use a little more; the same applies to the sand.

If the lime is freshly slaked, there is no need to add water to make the mixture: one has only to temper it by beating with wooden beaters. In any case, use as little water as possible.

Mortar in which brick dust is substituted for sand is used especially for work under water.

Plaster hardens at once; mortar takes time to set, but it then becomes infinitely harder.

To join different materials together, use is additionally made of iron, of copper, and of lead.

Iron, to be sound, must be soft and have a fine grain; it must contain no Iron hair cracks or flaws. The best comes from the former province of Berry.

It is essential to use only as much as is necessary; otherwise, far from making the joint, it would often obstruct it.

Iron members used for joining are generally classified as rough hardware. Such are ties, anchors, lintels, plates, bolts, cramps, fireplace hoods, firebacks, and so on.

There are others that serve for security, and these are called finish hardware. Such are locks, hinges, pegs, latches, draw bolts, and so on.

Sometimes, however, rough hardware appears in devices intended for security, as in window bars, gratings, beam locks, and so on.

The name of *flat bar* is given to iron 13 to 18 cm (5 to 7 in.) wide by 13 to 18 mm (6 to 8 lines) thick; *square bar* is 2 to 5 cm (1 to 2 in.) square in section; *round bar,* which is used to make rods, is 1 to 2 cm (9 to 10 lines) in diameter; then there is square dowel, 12 to 22 mm (5 to 9 lines) in thickness; and *bullnose,* all those forms that have the arrises rounded off. For various purposes, iron is also used in thin plates as much as 2 meters (6 ft.) long.

Lead is used not only to join other materials but to make downspouts and Lead water pipes. It is also sometimes used to roof buildings.

For this last purpose, two kinds of lead are used: cast and milled. Where the thickness is equal, the former is to be preferred, as its flaws are not concealed by compression.

The best lead is obtained from England or from Germany.

Copper is another metal that is used either to fasten stones or to roof Copper buildings. In the former case, the ancients preferred it to iron because of its greater durability.

Such are the principal materials employed in the construction of buildings. The little that we have said will suffice not only to give an idea of their good and bad qualities and their use in general, but also to convey the variety that their dimensions, their different colors, their regularities or irregularities should contribute to buildings: when, that is, these materials are intelligently combined.

Section Two. Uses of Materials

Foundations
Plate 2

To ensure that the various elements of buildings are solid, the materials must be of good quality, intelligently employed, and set on sound foundations; and these can be sound only if they are built as they should be, and on good soil.

The quality of the soil may be established by sounding or by sinking shafts.

If the soil is bad, then art must come to the aid of nature.

Qualities of the soil

The soils on which buildings can be solidly based are rock, gravel mixed with earth, stony soils, and loam.

The bad soils are quicksand, clay, and all disturbed, imported, or marshy soils.

Precautions to be taken
in laying good
foundations

Where the soil lacks the necessary consistency, and it is necessary to dig down too far to find solid ground, and where the building is not very heavy, and the soil is capable of being evenly compressed, a timber grating is laid down, on which the foundations are raised as uniformly as possible, so that the whole mass takes an equal load.

Where holes or cavities are found in any part of the plot, these are filled, if they are not of any size; otherwise, stone pillars are raised from the solid ground, and on these pillars arches are built, capable of supporting the walls.

Where water is encountered, piles are driven down to support the grating.

The first course of the foundations must consist of good large rubble stones, on which is laid a course of coarse rubble, hard and well cleaned off, on a bed of mortar, lime, and sand. The wall is built in this way as far as 8 cm (3 in.) above the cellar floor. At this height a base course of hard stones is laid to the full thickness of the wall, and on this, leaving the footing to project 8 cm (3 in.) on either side, the cellar or basement wall is raised to the height of 8 cm (3 in.) above ground: all this being laid with a mortar of lime and sand, not with plaster.

Four classes of wall
Plate 2

There are several distinct varieties of walls: *enclosing* walls, *retaining* walls, *exterior* walls, and *partition* walls.

Walls are sometimes built entirely of ashlar and sometimes entirely of rubble or brick; more often, they are built partly of stone and partly of rubble, burrstone, or brick.

Whatever the use and the material of a wall, the courses must always be horizontal and all the joints perpendicular, coinciding neither on the face or in the thickness, but always corresponding to the center of the stones above and below. It would be desirable to have all the courses of an equal height; they must be constructed with setbacks on a course of stone, itself set back on cellar or foundation walls. The whole may be jointed with plaster, but lime and sand mortar is much better.

Enclosing and partition walls must be perpendicular.

Retaining walls must have a batter, on the outside, proportional to their height and to the nature of the soil that they support. When of ordinary height, the batter is one in six.

Exterior walls may be perpendicular, or receding at each story, or with a slight batter on the outside. Of these three methods, the two latter are the most proper to contain the thrust of the floors or vaults.

It must not be supposed that all the parts of any wall bear an equal stress: there are some parts that bear all the load of the floors, vaults, and roofs, or are liable to be disturbed by various shocks; others are nothing but infilling. It is therefore natural to give the former parts greater strength, either by making the material harder or by making the walls thicker, and sometimes both. Thus, in walls entirely built of ashlar or rubble, the thickness will be greater at the ends, at the corners where they meet, at the points where the cross walls join them, at the door and window piers, beneath the principal members of the roof and of the suspended floors, and beneath the imposts of the vaults. Ashlar piers will descend to the lowest part of the foundations and will pass up into the vaults in the form of arches.

Engaged supports, piers, or quoins

In walls that are built partly in ashlar and partly in rubble or in other materials of the same kind, these same parts, and these alone, will be built in ashlar, and the filling between them will be brick, rubble, or burrstone. In such a case, the piers may either be thicker than the wall or of the same thickness.

In all cases, the ashlar piers must be made up of alternating short and long stones, so as to form a perfect bond with the materials of the infilling. Where the piers stand proud of the wall, in some cases they project to their full depth, and in others their projection does not exceed that of their shortest stone; in the latter case they take the name of *pilasters*.

Piers of these various kinds normally project only by a few inches. But when they have great forces to contend with, they have a projection equal to their width; then their outer face is sometimes not perpendicular but battered: in which case they are called *buttresses* or *counterforts*.

Vertical piers of ashlar are not the only reinforcements that are used to consolidate a wall: string courses are placed where the principal members of suspended floors are built into the wall; at the springing line of the vaults; at those places where walls cease to be continuous, as at window sills; and finally at the tops of walls. The first named are known as *plinths*; the last, those that appear at the top of external walls, are known as *cornices*.

String courses

These string courses are composed of stones longer and harder than the rest, tied together by cramps; by their weight, they hold in place the lighter materials on which they rest, prevent them from falling apart, tie together the ashlar piers, and prevent any kind of movement.

The thickness of the walls is relative to their height. External walls are commonly made 64 cm (2 ft.) thick; cross walls and enclosure walls, 48 cm (18 in.).

Stone, rubble, and so on, are not the only materials that are used in the construction of exterior and partition walls. Wood is also used; in the first

Timber-framed walls and partitions

case it is called *timber framing,* and in the second it is called *studding.* Both consist of *corner posts, wall plates, framing posts, angled braces,* or *stays* inserted to support the wall plates; *sills* or cross pieces beneath windows; *cripples* or pieces of unequal length; *lintels,* which form the tops of windows and doors; and finally those struts or posts that are shorter than the others and serve as infilling.

The plates are tenoned into the corner posts, and the framing posts into the plates.

Posts at the end of the wall are *corner posts;* those that flank the doors and windows are called *studs.*

Three kinds of partition

Three kinds of partition are distinguished by the ways in which they are filled: *simple, solid,* or *hollow.*

Partitions with visible studs are nailed into the sides of the timbers and filled in with nogging or rough plaster. They are plastered flush with the timbers, which remain visible.

In solid partitions, after filling, laths are attached on both sides, every 8 cm (3 in.), and plaster is applied to the laths to cover the whole surface.

Finally, in hollow partitions the laths are placed close together, with no filling, and plastered like the foregoing.

Exterior timber framing may be constructed like simple or solid partitions but never like hollow ones.

Since we have recommended placing a plinth or base course of stones below all walls built of rubble, and so on, it will be clear that this precaution is even more necessary beneath timber-framed walls and partitions, to protect them from decay.

Light partitions

Timber-framed walls and partitions are normally built to a thickness of 16 to 18 cm (6 to 7 in.).

As well as timber framing, there are joinery and plaster partitions. The former are 8 cm (3 in.) thick, and the latter 3 to 5 cm (1½ to 2 in.).

There are two kinds of joinery partition. One kind is made with planks assembled in an openwork disposition, in grooved heads and sills, and held together by cross rails. They are lathed, either solid or hollow, and are plastered flush with the heads, sills, and cross rails.

The others are made of tongued and grooved boards, assembled vertically, in grooved heads and sills, and are only 1 cm (1 in. [*sic*]) thick.

Plaster partitions are made from large stretchers that are cast in a mold and laid one upon the other.

Detached supports

As well as engaged supports or piers, built at those places in a wall that have to support some weight or resist a force, there are detached supports, which are used to support floors, ceilings, and sometimes vaults. These are known as *posts* or as *pillars,* according to whether they are made of wood or of stone. When built in accordance with certain proportions, they are called *pilasters* if they are square in plan, and *columns* if they are circular. When they receive the impost of an arch, are square, and are of stouter proportions than pilasters, they are known as *piers* or *abutments.*

Pillars, pilasters, columns, and piers are built in courses or drums if they are made of stone. They are made in one piece only if the material used is wood or marble. Care is taken to make the drums all equal in height, so that the compression is equal; try also to ensure that each drum is made in one piece.

Columns and pilasters normally rest on a continuous wall of the same height as the elevation of the floor of the building above the natural grade. This wall, which is known as the *dado,* is built, like all the other walls, on a wider base course of hard stone, the *plinth,* which is designed to protect it from humidity. It is crowned with a projecting course of stones to throw off the water, which falls on the pavement of the portico formed by the columns. This stone projection is called the *cornice,* and this whole assemblage of plinth, dado, and cornice is known as the *pedestal.*

What they rest on

Sometimes, to attach the column to its pedestal in what is supposed to be a more solid fashion, the column itself is placed on a kind of footing, called a *base;* and on the column, to lessen the span of those members that have to link the columns together, there are invariably one or more projecting stones, known by the name of *capital.*

These objects are regarded as belonging to the column; they form part of it. The column may therefore be said to consist of three parts: the base; the column proper, known as the *shaft;* and the capital. But this is not always the case: for sometimes the column consists of two parts only, a shaft and a capital.

Columns are linked together, either by wooden or marble members, or else by flat arches composed of several stones shaped to converge towards the center. Whatever material is used, the part that rests directly on the capital is known as the *architrave.* On this, in order to join the columns to the wall, there is placed a second architrave, which is commonly known as the *frieze.* The space between the columns and the wall is spanned either by a soffit, or by a stone slab, or by a flat arch; in all cases, this is continued so as to project beyond the frieze. The *cornice,* which rests on this projection, throws the water from the roof away from the base of the building.

The parts that they support

The architrave, frieze, and cornice, taken together, constitute the *entablature;* and the assemblage of pedestal, column, and entablature, when certain proportions are observed, forms what is known, however improperly, as an order of *architecture.* Clearly, to model an order of architecture on a hut is, if not absurd, entirely unnecessary; for nature and good sense would supply all the parts that are ascribed to the orders and regarded as essential.

Where the architraves are composed of several arch stones, an iron dowel is inserted in the center of each column.[16] This dowel continues to the top of the architrave or cornice. At this height, the dowels are connected by iron ties, which pass from the axis of one column to that of the next, and also from the axes of the columns to the axis of the wall, in which they are anchored. In the latter case, where the dowels rise to the level of the cornice, the iron ties are reinforced for safety's sake by others placed diagonally. Where the dowels do not pass through the entire height of the column, they must at least run down through one-eighth of it.

If two rows of columns are superimposed, the lower row must be made of hard stone and the upper row of soft stone.

Openings   Door and window jambs are connected by lintels, and so on, in the same way as columns are by architraves.

When jambs and lintels have a continuous projection, it is called a *bandelet* or *chambranle*.

To prevent the water that is driven by the wind against the part of the wall above the doors and windows from falling upon the sill or the window breast, there is sometimes a cornice above the chambranle.

When the columns or piers are far apart, and when the spans are too great for lintels, the supports are joined by arches.

The name of *imposts* is given to the projecting stones that terminate the jambs and receive the thrust of the arches; and that of *archivolts* to the moldings that run around the arches.

Niches   Other openings in the thickness of walls, aside from doors and windows, are those known as *niches,* which are recesses designed to accommodate statues, and so on. As these niches do not pass through the whole thickness of the wall, their jambs have no need to be reinforced by piers; and so they ought never to have a chambranle.

Chimneys   Chimneys are built against the walls or carried up within their thickness. They are always built against the wall if it is a party wall; sometimes they are embedded in partition walls. They are composed of two jambs, a mantel, which joins them, and a flue, which gives passage to the smoke.

They are built in large, intermediate, and small sizes. The large commonly open to a width of 1.92 m (6 ft.) by 96 cm (3 ft.); and the small, 80 by 80 cm (2½ by 2½ ft.). The depth in both cases is approximately 64 cm (2 ft.). The jambs and mantel of the largest are 18 to 20 cm (7 to 8 in.) wide, and of the smallest 8 to 10 cm (3 to 4 in.). The flues must be no less than 72 cm (2 feet 3 in.) by 24 cm (9 in.) wide. Their withes are 8 to 10 cm (3 to 4 in.) thick.

The whole is built either of brick or of ashlar or of plaster.

Care must be taken to avoid resting a hearth on any floor timber. A *hearth cavity* must be left in these, 8 cm (3 in.) wider than the outer face of the chimney by 96 cm (3 ft.) in length, measured from the chimney back, or—which is the same thing—from the *back plate*.

These hearth cavities are filled with a mixture of plaster and plaster waste, supported by two iron bands curved at each end. Sometimes this is crossed by a third band, built into the wall. On the plaster, a marble or ashlar hearthstone is laid; or else the floor tiles are continued as far as the chimney back.

At the back of the fireplace is a cast-iron back plate, or a wall of tiles or bricks. The mantel is supported by an iron bar, bent at both ends, which rests on the jambs and is built into the wall. The whole is faced with a stone or marble chimneypiece and a mantel. The flue is supported by a flat bar, which rests on the piers.

When there are several fireplaces together, one above the other or back to back, the flues must be diverted. But this must not be done if they are embedded in the thickness of the wall, because of the cantilevers that would be created; and even where they are back to back, the flues must be so diverted as to slope as little as possible, to avoid overburdening the walls.

Floors are constructed in bays, in order to avoid an excessive span for most of the timbers of which they are built. These bays are formed of a certain number of joists, laid on edge at regular intervals, and supported on girders that are built 32 cm (1 ft.) into the walls and rest on string courses of stone. Sometimes, to reduce the dimensions of the girders, plates or smaller timbers are fixed to their sides, and the joists rest on or fit into these; similar plates are attached to the walls, in order to avoid weakening the walls by building into them the ends of so many joists. These plates are built into the walls, in the same way as the girders, and supported at intervals along their lengths by iron brackets. Where they butt at one of these brackets, they are fixed to it by bolts and bridle irons.

Binders are sometimes designed only to support the header joists in front of hearths, and the iron bands that support the hearthstone; in which case one end rests in the wall and the other on the beams or wall plates. Sometimes they also serve to replace the girders, and in that case they are built into the walls just as those are. But they do not bear the weight of the common joists throughout their length: their ends support plates laid along the walls or across the fireplace openings, and the common joists are tenoned into these.

Where the external walls are entirely built of rubble, a course of corbels is laid at each floor level, 13 cm (5 in.) deep, on which the joists rest.

Where floors are of a certain width of span, they may be stiffened and reinforced by block bridging, using pieces of wood known as keys, which are forced from below into slots previously made in the joists.

At the end of every girder, there must be an iron stay or band, with a tie some 96 cm (3 ft.) long, to prevent movement.

All those timbers that pass close to chimney flues must be 8 cm (3 in.) away from them.

Apart from the various timbers that we have mentioned, others are used, particularly in those floorings that are built immediately below the roofs. We shall say a word on the subject when we come to roofs.

Floors were formerly made open, with all the timbers visible below, and plaster in the intervals only. Such floors are no longer made except in buildings to which no importance is attached. Since ideas of architectural decoration have gained currency, the appearance of the members that make up a floor and proclaim its solidity has been regarded as ignoble; by preference, they are masked with plaster ceilings, which, while increasing the expense, cause the floors above to rot and often compel them to be remade shortly after building, to avoid still worse consequences. What a difference, moreover, between the appalling, frigid, monotonous sight of these plaster ceilings and the reassuring, animated, and varied sight of those majestic old open floors, whose joists, and the beams that marked every bay, were constructed with the utmost care and protected from humidity and from insects by the application of the most beautiful colors! It is enough to compare our modern ceilings with those that still exist in some ancient mansions to recognize how much, in this department of architecture, the pursuit of beauty has led in the opposite direction.[17]

Be that as it may, we shall now make known the way in which ceilings are made.

As soon as the timbers of a floor are finished, it is lathed above and below, while taking care that the laths do not touch each other. On the upper laths, a plaster screed is laid, 8 cm (3 in.) thick, on which the floor tiles are bedded; below, the floor is ceiled.

In order to improve the solidity of such ceilings, the intervals between the joists are sometimes filled with plaster pugging; and this is how this is done. After lathing below, with laths well spaced, the sides of the joists are studded with nails; then, with a plank held beneath the laths, the space between the joists is plastered to create a semicylindrical channel. The pugging unites with the plaster of the ceiling below to prevent cracks.

If it is desired to floor with parquet instead of tiles, rough floorboards are laid on the plaster screed. Even better, the plaster can be dispensed with, and the boards are laid on close-fitted lathing. If the joists are well assembled, the parquet may even be laid directly on them.

Brick floorings or shallow vaults

Ordinary floorings are hardly more than 32 cm (1 ft.) thick altogether, when tiled, or 40 cm (15 in.) when parqueted. For entresols, floors can be made to a thickness of no more than 16 cm (6 in.).

In the construction of floors, brick may be used in place of timber, creating a kind of shallow vault, which has the advantages that it costs less than a wooden floor, lasts longer, and resists fire.

In order to build such a floor, start by making a light centering of nailed or jointed woodwork, 6 cm (2½ in.) thick, with the same curvature as the intended vault. On this, fix close-fitted boards, and support the centering on horizontal timbers built into the walls; where the vault is to be of any length, these in turn are supported by vertical props. The vault is then begun at one end of the room. Two workmen posted at opposite sides of the centering lay the first course of bricks, bedded flat, in the recess left for the purpose in the walls; and they carry on in this way until they meet in the center and close the vault. They then repeat the same operation until the centering has been entirely covered. Then they line this vault with a second course of brickwork, carefully breaking the joints.

The centering thus being covered, it is slid along the horizontal timbers that support it; and the operation is repeated until the other end of the room is reached.

This form of vaulting produces a kind of barrel vault. Others are made in the manner of a cloister vault. In these, the centering cannot be mobile but must occupy the entire area of the ceiling. The bricks are laid from all four sides at once. When the first two courses have been laid all around, the lining bricks are added at once; and in this way the work continues until the vault is closed.

All such vaults are jointed with plaster.

The reins of the former kind of vault are filled with rubble, and a screed is laid over the top. In the reins of the latter, counterforts are constructed at intervals of 1.60 m (5 ft.) and at the corners of the vault; the rest is filled with well-dried earth, and tiles are laid.

Sometimes vaults are made with a single tier of bricks; in which case they are laid on edge. In every case, such vaults are plastered beneath. Walls of a thickness of 64 cm (2 ft.) suffice for a vault spanning 6.48 to 8.10 m (20 to 25 ft.); but care must be taken to limit the rise to one-sixth of the span, and to limit the separation of the walls by using parallel ties, for a barrel vault, and cross ties, for a cloister vault.

Across the face of chimney flues, an iron lintel should be inserted to resist the thrust of the vault.

The thickness of these vaults, at the crown, is only 10 to 13 cm (4 to 5 in.).

Apart from the shallow vaults just mentioned, there are others with a greater rise, which are substituted for shallow vaults and flat ceilings when the width is too great; just as curved arches are substituted for flat arches when the span becomes too great for these.

These are the *barrel* vault, in the shape of a hollow semicylinder; the *rising* vault, which differs from the barrel vault only in being on a slope; the *groin* vault and the *cloister* vault, which result from the interpenetration of two semicylinders; the *cul de four* vault, which is hemispherical; the *niche,* or half of the *cul de four; pendentive vaults,* the product of the interpenetration of two semicylinders and a hemisphere; and the *annular* vault, generated by the movement of a semicircle around a point.

The groin vault and the cloister vault differ in that the groins project in the former and recede in the latter; and that the latter is supported all around, whereas the former rests on four points only.

There exist other forms of vaulting, such as *squinches, splays, skew vaults, surbased vaults,* and so on. But we shall not discuss them, as these structures are to be used, if at all, only in restoration work.[18]

What has been said of the construction of walls may be applied to that of vaults; except that, in walls, the stones take the form of a parallelepiped; in vaults, they take the form of a wedge. In walls, the beds are horizontal; and in vaults, they are aligned toward a center.

From the form and disposition of these stones, known as *voussoirs,* there results an action of thrust that tends to push the supports of the vaults apart, and thus to break them down. The supports must therefore be stout enough to resist this force; and, as semicircular vaults, the only ones that we adopt, tend to break between the impost and the central voussoir, known as the *keystone,* the body that resists the thrust must extend to this height. If it cannot be made thick enough, it must rise even higher, thus acquiring a perpendicular force that will compensate for its lack of horizontal force.

The lower the rise of a vault, or the greater its diameter and thickness, or the taller its supports, the greater resistance must be opposed to its thrust.

Aside from these considerations relative to the thrust occasioned by the form of the voussoirs—considerations common to all vaults—there are others that relate to the nature and construction of every particular form of vaulting. The barrel vault exerts its thrust laterally, against the walls that support its impost; the cloister vault exerts its thrust on the walls around its base; the groin vault has a diagonal thrust, which is the resultant of the lateral thrusts of the two barrel vaults of which it is composed; the *cul de four* has only a slight thrust from center to circumference; the pendentive vault bears almost exclusively on the tunnel vaults that penetrate it; and so on. These, in each case, are therefore the places where the resistance has to be applied.

Although the barrel vault naturally exerts a continuous action on the walls that support it, it is possible, through the action of *lunettes* or relieving arches, to concentrate this thrust on specific points, to be chosen at will. These points will then be reinforced; and the rest of the wall may be made as thin as desired, being now no more than infilling.

When there is a row of arcades or of barrel vaults, every pier may be given either sufficient strength to contain the vault that it supports or else no more strength than is necessary to resist the compressive force. In the latter case, the thrust of all the vaults is transferred to the supports at the end of the row, and these will need to have sufficient strength to resist all the individual thrusts.

We possess no treatise that specifies accurately, for every case, the resistance required to counter the thrust of any vault. But soon we shall have, on this subject, an excellent work, long and impatiently awaited by artists, from the pen of Citizen Rondelet, who is as well versed in theory as he is in practice.[19]

If vaults are intended to support great loads, and must therefore be made to a great thickness, then stone is the material to be preferred. But where they have only their own weight to bear, they can be built of rubble, of brick, or even of terracotta, as the ancients often did with advantage.

Where vaults are very thick, there is no need to make this thickness the same throughout; it would suffice to make separate arches, at specific intervals, and to connect these arches by string courses of horizontal voussoirs, spaced at the same distances as the arches. The remaining voids would be filled with flat, thin stones. These square reinforcements would naturally form what are called *caissons*.

In the construction of vaults, it is wise to use as little iron as possible; this metal is too weak to ensure their solidity.[20] It would be best not to use it at all; but when there is no avoiding its use, try at least to make it stretch rather than bear.

In southern lands, vaults have no need to be covered by a roof; but in other countries, this precaution is essential for their conservation.

Roofs   Roofs commonly have two gutters and sometimes four. Where they have only one, they are known as *shed* roofs. Their ends are called *hips*, if they have the same slope as their sides; and *gables*, if they are terminated by an upper continuation of the wall. Finally, when the cornice of the building continues along the two inclined sides of the gable, the latter takes on the name of *pediment.*

The pitch of roofs must be greater or less, according to the climate in which they are built and according to the material used to cover them.

In the north, where snow falls abundantly and lies long on the roofs, they slope more steeply than in countries where such inconveniences are unknown.

Tiled roofs must also be steeper than those hung with slate. In any case, roofs must not have a pitch of more than one in three or less than one in six.

The false ideas of beauty and decoration that have crept into architecture are responsible for those enormous roofs to whose construction such sums have been devoted, only to hasten the ruin of the buildings that they cover and to afflict the eye that contemplates them. It is those same ideas that are responsible for that absurd class of roof, the upper part of which is almost as flat as a terrace and the lower part almost as steep as a wall: a kind that, displeasing though it is, has nevertheless played its part in immortalizing the name of Mansard.

When a building is very wide, and its roof would consequently become too tall, it is divided into two, three, or even more roofs, which are then only one-half, or one-third, of the height of the single roof.

Roof structures are made either of timber, or of brick, or of stone.

Timber roofs are made in bays, like floors. These bays are supported by *trusses,* each composed of two principal *rafters* inclined according to the slope of the roof; a *tie beam,* into which their lower ends are tenoned, and which holds them together; a *collar beam,* tenoned into the principals, parallel to the tie beam, to prevent them from bending; a *king post,* also tenoned into the principals, which prevents the collar beam from bending; *braces,* which reinforce the collar beam; and finally *struts,* tenoned into the king post, to stiffen the principals. The trusses are joined together by a ridge, which fits into the top of the king posts, and by an under-ridgeboard which fits into the collar beams.

The trusses thus disposed, one or several rows of purlins are placed on the principal rafters and supported by battens and gussets; and on these purlins are placed the common rafters, the upper [sic] ends of which are tenoned into a wall plate resting on the top of the wall; their upper ends rest on the ridge.

Where roofs are hipped, *half trusses* are situated at the corners and centers of the hipped ends; and those at the corners are known as *hip trusses.*

Inside the roof, with the tie beam serving as a floor beam, the hipped roof requires a half tie beam, one end of which fits into the tie beam and the other rests on the wall; in such a roof there are also *gussets,* fitted into the tie beams; *furrings* or diagonal pieces, fitted into the gussets, which serve to tie together the hip trusses; and, finally, *tailpieces,* which fit into the furrings.

Once the framework of the roof is completed, it is lathed; and on the laths is laid the tile or slate covering.

The plank trusses invented by Philibert de l'Orme have great advantages over common roof trusses; and if their use has not become universal, custom alone is to blame.[21] They place a far smaller load on buildings, needing no tie

Plank roofs

beams or any of the timbers that obstruct the space, and this represents a great economy. They give the garrets and upper floors of buildings the greatest possible space, which makes it possible either to give greater height to the story below or to build lodgings, which would not be possible with a conventional timber roof. Another advantage of these roofs, which have the internal form of a vault but which exert no outward thrust, is that they can span considerable widths.

Brick roofs   The roof is formed of trusses, approximately one meter apart. Each truss is composed of two layers of planks, between 97 and 129 cm (3 to 4 ft.) long, assembled with breaking joints, that is, with the end of one corresponding to the center of another. These trusses are joined together by keys, each pinned tightly on either side of the rib.

Brick roofs, apart from the advantages that they share with these plank roofs, have the further advantage of being immune to fires.

Their construction is more or less the same as that of the first type of shallow vault. On a mobile centering, with a semicircular curvature, two tiers of brickwork are bedded flat, with breaking joints; and over the vault thus formed, three little triangular masses of tiles are set to mark the pitch of the roof; then the whole is plastered, and the slates are nailed to the plaster. Although these roofs have almost no thrust, it is best to tie the supporting walls together with several iron rods.

Most stone roofs resemble those of which we have just spoken, differing only in the materials, the vault consisting of stone instead of brick, and the covering consisting of flagstones instead of slates. Sometimes, however, stone roofs are built to resemble plank roofs rather than brick ones. These roofs are built in bays formed of flagstones laid with breaking joints, and supported by arches that perform the function of trusses; the arches are linked by lintels. The vertical joints of the flagstones, which correspond directly to the central axis of each arch, are covered by semicylindrical stone rolls that fit into each other; and the span of the flagstones is supported by iron bars, built into the arches. What we have now to say on the subject of roof terraces will complete the explanation that we have just given of stone roofs.

Terraced roofs   The object of roof terraces is to afford the opportunity to walk on the tops of buildings, to enjoy the surrounding view, and to breathe fresh air.

Terraces, like other roofs, have a slope sufficient to allow the water to run off; but this slope is much less; and for this reason, the construction of terraces requires more care than that of brick or stone roofs, especially in northern countries.

Terraces are constructed either of sheets of lead, soldered together, or of flagstones. If necessary, the former may be laid on timber flooring covered by a plaster screed; but the latter must always lie over vaults.

The joints between the stones must always be placed in line with each other, and directly above a little channel chased into the vault; so that, should water enter, it runs off into the gutter constructed below the lowest slab. For greater safety, the edges of the joints are to be made convex.

Stone roofs and terraces are laid in mortar and jointed with mastic.

We shall not enlarge any further on the ways of employing materials in the construction of the elements of buildings. Those who desire more detail may consult the works of Patte, from whom we have borrowed much on the subject.[22] What we have said on this topic will suffice to give a general idea to those who are studying architecture, and to save them from committing the gross and palpable errors that are all too evident in those designs in which decoration is the sole concern; it will, moreover, make it sufficiently clear that decoration—if, by that word, we mean anything beyond the application of painting and sculpture to buildings—is largely to be produced by making the construction evident.[23]

To be sure of this, we have only to look at the imposing remains of the buildings of antiquity; at the splendid fabrics, in every part of Italy, in which stone, brick, marble, and so on, show themselves as they are, and where they should be; and even at the figures of plate 2, although the intention there is merely to show the disposition of materials in relation to their nature, and to the uses of the things they serve to build. This will surely banish the temptation to abandon this natural and satisfying form of decoration and to replace it, at great additional cost, either with the appearance of an imaginary construction—which, not being the real construction of the building, falsifies the latter, and detracts from its character instead of enhancing it—by an arbitrary decoration made up of an assemblage of unnecessary objects that can never give pleasure but only fatigue the eye, outrage common sense, and displease in every way.

Section Three. Forms and Proportions

In our consideration of materials and of their use in the construction of the elements of buildings, it must have become apparent that, while nature offers some ready to be used, most of the others have to be worked, either to make them suitable for building in general or to fit them to the uses to which the different elements of buildings are to be put. Thus, timber is deprived of its alburnum, and stone is cleaned off; ashlar and rubble are squared to bed them in the construction of walls and cut into wedges in order to construct vaults. We have observed, also, that the union of these materials naturally gives rise to forms and proportions: nor could this be otherwise, seeing that matter necessarily possesses forms and that forms have their inherent relations and proportions. It is in the light of these last two facts that we must now consider the elements of buildings.

Forms and proportions may be divided into three categories: those that spring from the nature of materials, and from the uses of the things they serve to build; those that custom has in a sense made necessary to us, such as the forms and proportions of the buildings of antiquity; and, finally, those simpler and more definite forms and proportions that earn our preference through the ease with which we apprehend them.[24]

Of these, only those in the first category are essential; but they are not so firmly defined by the nature of things that we cannot add to them or subtract from them, so that there is no reason not to combine them with those of the second class, derived from ancient buildings. Since these vary considerably in the Greek buildings, which were imitated by the Romans, who were imitated in their turn by the modern peoples of Europe, one is at liberty to select the simplest: which, being the most economical, are the best suited to satisfy both the eye and the mind.[25]

The importance of forms and proportions appears most clearly in the orders. Here, as we have seen, the principal forms derive from the use of some of the elements of buildings; as we shall see, the principal proportions have the same origin and no more depend on the proportions of the human body than the forms of the orders depend on those of the hut.

General proportions
of the orders
Plate 4

In private buildings of the lowest class, expense is always a consideration; and here, if fitness demands detached supports, they will necessarily be made of the cheapest—which is to say, the least firm—materials. To reduce their number, they will be placed as far apart as possible: an economy that enables the other requirements of fitness to be observed. Solidity, however, must not be too much impaired; and so these supports will be made very short, in order to increase their strength; for the same reason, they may perhaps be made square instead of round.

Whether as columns or as pilasters, these supports thus widely spaced will, to avoid failure, require a higher architrave than if they were close together. The frieze—being intended to join the columns to the wall, just as the architrave joins the columns to each other—will be of the same height as the architrave. As for the cornice, to make it solid, it must have a projection equal to its height; and both dimensions must be proportionate to the height of the building that it protects against water from the roof. In this first case, the building is not very tall; and so the height of the cornice may be less than that of the frieze or of the architrave.

By contrast, in the most important public buildings—where none of the requirements of fitness may be neglected at any cost, and where durability is a condition imposed not only by fitness but also by economy, seeing that there is no economy in erecting such buildings over and over again—the materials employed will be such as offer the greatest resistance; and in a given space there will be as many supports as possible. These will accordingly be more elegant in form; and, for ease of passage between closely packed supports, they will be made cylindrical. The narrowness of the spaces between them will naturally lead to architraves and friezes that are less high; and, as the building itself will be tall, the cornice will need more projection in order to throw the water further off and will consequently be deeper than the frieze or the architrave.

Columns can, and according to circumstances must, be made short in some cases and long in others. But there are certain limits that must not be transgressed. Too long, the columns would lack solidity; to make them too short would be to fall into the opposite excess. Experience, that is to say, observation of the proportions of columns in those antique buildings that are held in highest esteem, will serve to determine their proportions. The shortest columns seen in such buildings are those of the Greek Doric order; but, as we have already said, their proportions vary in every case. In some, as in one temple whose ruins may be seen at Corinth, they are only four diameters high. In others, they are as much as nine diameters high, as in the temple at Cori; but as this last example is the only one in which the columns are so elongated, a height of six diameters will give us a kind of proportional mean, to which we shall adhere for the proportions of the shortest columns, especially since this proportion comes closest to that of the majority of Greek Doric columns.

The longest columns are those of the Corinthian order, but their proportions are not always the same. Some, like those of the Tower of the Winds and the Colosseum, are eight and a half diameters high; others, like those of the Lantern of Demosthenes and of the Temple of Vesta in Rome, are nearly eleven. Most, however, are approximately ten diameters high; and this more exact proportion is the one that we shall assign to the tallest columns.

Between the private buildings of the lowest class and the public buildings of the highest, there are a host of intermediate classes; and so, between these two orders of columns, it would be possible to interpose a host of others. But for simplicity of study, and in order to depart as little as possible from the received systems, we shall limit ourselves to three intermediate orders, defined as follows: first, between the column height of six diameters and that of ten, we shall set a column height of eight, the proportion of the Doric order of the Theater of Marcellus, which is the most highly esteemed Roman Doric; then, between this and the Greek Doric, we shall have columns of seven diameters, which is the proportion of the most widely adopted Tuscan, that of Vignola; and finally, between the Roman Doric and the Corinthian, there will be a column nine diameters tall, a proportion that corresponds, more or less, to the mean of all the various Ionic orders, both Roman and Greek, and to the near-unanimous practice of the moderns. And so the columns will grow in the following ratio: Doric, six; Tuscan, seven; Roman Doric, eight; Ionic, nine; and Corinthian, ten.[26]

All columns must taper by one-sixth, a cone being firmer on its base than a cylinder. As for the capitals and bases, they should increase in height in proportion to the columns; but these proportions are more a matter of custom than of necessity, and they have little importance in construction. Accordingly, to avoid interference with established custom, we shall assign one module, or one half-diameter, to all bases, and also to the capitals of the first three orders; one module and a half to the Ionic capital; and two and one-third modules to the Corinthian capital.

The more massive the columns, the more widely spaced they may be; conversely, the more slender, the closer they must be. The least possible interval between columns, as used in antiquity, is one and a half diameters. We shall retain this proportion for the Corinthian; we shall increase it by one half-diameter, for every one diameter by which the columns taper, in the following proportion; Corinthian, 1½; Ionic, 2; Doric, 2½; Tuscan, 3; Greek Doric, 3½.

As the height of the architrave and the frieze must vary in accordance with their greater or lesser span, we shall assign them one module and a half in the Greek Doric order, and one module and a quarter in the Corinthian. As for the cornice, as its projection and height must vary in accordance with the height of the orders, it will measure one module in the first order and one module and a half in the fifth order. The proportions of the various parts of the entablature being thus fixed for the two extreme cases, it will be an easy matter to find those that correspond to these same parts in the intervening orders. The sum of all those parts, in all the orders, will be two diameters or four modules: a precise proportion, easy to remember, and nevertheless in keeping with the degree of strength or lightness in the columns, since it will measure one-third in the first order, one-fifth in the last, one-quarter in the third, and so on. This proportion is close to that found in the majority of Greek and Roman orders; or at least in the Greek Doric and the Corinthian.

Pedestals may be relatively high or low. But, in order to depart as little as we can from the orders adopted by the ancients and from the principal systems of ordonnance—and, above all, to simplify the study of the matter as much as possible—we shall make our pedestals just one module higher than the entablature: that is to say, two diameters and a half or five modules. The plinth will be one module high, and the cornice half a module.

Such are the forms and proportions indicated for the principal parts of the orders, first, by the nature of things; second, by the respect that we owe to habits acquired through seeing the orders of the ancients and those imitated from them; and, third, by the care that must be taken to avoid fatiguing the eye with indeterminate proportions.

If our system is neither as complete nor as consistent as might be desired, at least it is preferable in both respects to all systems hitherto devised. It also has the advantage that it rests on a more solid foundation than the imitation of the hut and of the human body. It is not offensive to good sense, and presents none of those absurdities that can only inspire a distaste for architecture in any mind accustomed to rational thought. Simple and natural, it is as easy to remember as it is to grasp. But even were it far better than it is, if it is wrongly applied, and if these forms and proportions are used in any building to clothe unnecessary objects, then the result will not only be bad architecture but bad decoration. And in the absence of all these forms, a building that presents all that is needed and nothing but what is needed, and in which all is disposed in the most fitting and most economical manner, will satisfy both the mind and the eye.

Details of the orders in general or moldings
Plate 5

Just as, in general, an order comprises three parts, a pedestal, a column, and an entablature; and as we then distinguish within the pedestal a plinth, a dado, and a cornice; within the column a base, a shaft, and a capital; and within the entablature an architrave, a frieze, and a cornice: similarly, each one of these parts in its turn includes several others, which are themselves composed of other, even smaller parts.

The first cornices were probably no more than squared stone blocks.

111

Corbeled out from the wall, such a block was too heavy; and so the idea arose of beveling it. But as this made it too weak, a projection was made in the center; and the cornice then came to have three parts, distinguished by the names of *upper cyma, corona,* and *lower cyma.* Later, and when cornices of great size were made, the single stone was sometimes replaced by several stones, and this gave rise to new divisions. Hence those coronas or larmiers, within the height of which projecting stones were inserted to support the overhang: these stones were called *mutules* in the Doric order and *modillions* in the Corinthian. Other forms included those of *dentils,* cut at intervals into the corona; *intermediary cymas;* and so on. In buildings in which the orders do not appear, a strongly projecting corona has on occasion been supported by other projecting stones, larger than modillions, known as *consoles.*

Each one of these parts is divided in turn into several others, endowed with various geometric forms. An idea of these may be gained from plate 5. They have been used not only in the members of cornices but in the cymas of architraves, and in various members of capitals and bases, and so on. As these look like nothing in particular, and as they nevertheless entail expense—each molding surmounted by a fillet counting as 32 cm (1 ft.) of wall, even if it is only 5 cm (2 in.) high—we shall merely suggest that they be used very sparingly; and that the available funds be saved for painting and sculpture, which are more likely to give pleasure than moldings, because they always represent something.

Any assemblage of moldings is known as a *profile;* and profiling is an art to which the advocates of architectural decoration attach great importance. We do not. The use of moldings having nevertheless been consecrated by custom, care must be taken in combining them to avoid offending the eye. The only way to succeed is to give a pronounced movement to each profile, to combine rectilinear and curved moldings, and to contrast the thinnest with the thickest. The Greeks in their Doric and Ionic orders, and the Romans in their Corinthian, offer good examples of profiles. By contrast, some very bad examples have been set by the Greeks in their Corinthian, and by the Romans in their Doric and Ionic.

The art of profiling may be acquired by comparing the profiles of the Greeks and the Romans—as may readily be done by inspecting plates 65, 69, and 70 of the *Recueil et parallèle*—and then drawing, freehand, a large number of profiles.

The profiles of the various orders owe their value solely to habit, which is the reason why we have made no attempt to invent any new ones. Those that we offer have all been taken from antique buildings or from the authors most commonly followed. But there are considerable variations in the profiles of every order, and so we have assumed the liberty of making a choice. We have consequently selected the simplest, because these are the least laborious and the most economical. Sometimes we have even ventured to simplify them still more, although only where a precedent is to be found elsewhere. Thus, in the profile of the first order—which is approximately that of the Parthenon, at Athens—we have placed the triglyph directly above the column; and this, the

The art of profiling

Profiles of the different orders

Plate 6

greatest change that we have made, is because the triglyphs are so placed in all the Roman Dorics.

In the profile of the second order, which is Vignola's Tuscan, we have merely eliminated a few fillets and beads.

In the profile of the third order—which, with some slight alterations, is Vignola's Doric—we have eliminated the dentils and the flat mutules of the soffit of the corona; for this we have the authority of Serlio, Barbaro, Cataneo, Viola, Bullant, and Philibert de l'Orme.

In the profile of the fourth order, which is that of Serlio, we have simply omitted the dentil molding of the corona and the three fascias of the architrave. Precedents exist for all these omissions: for the former in the Ionic entablature of the Colosseum, in Leon Battista Alberti, in Jean Bullant, and in Philibert de l'Orme; and for the latter in the fine Ionic entablature of the Temple of the Ilyssus. Finally, the profile of the fifth order is identical with the Corinthian entablature of the attic story of the Roman Pantheon.

There are many Corinthian entablatures that incorporate modillions, but there are also many that do not, such as those of the Temple of Vesta at Tivoli, of the small altars in the Pantheon, and of the Temple of Antoninus and Faustina. The modillions do not spoil these entablatures, but in our view they should be reserved for giant orders. (See plate 70 [of the *Recueil et parallèle*].)

We were tempted to omit the triglyphs in the Doric order. A number of the monuments of antiquity, such as the Temple of Agraule in Athens, the baths of Paulus Aemilius, the Colosseum, and the amphitheater at Nîmes, in all of which they are absent, would have authorized the omission. But so many still regard them as an essential attribute of this order that we have allowed them to remain.

For the same reason, we retain the forms and the proportions of the Ionic and Corinthian capitals. On completion of the magnificent work on Egypt now undertaken by a number of intrepid scholars, it may well transpire that the naturalness, the simplicity, the elegance, and the nobility of certain Egyptian capitals will entirely displace the flimsy, incurved *abacus* of the Corinthian capital; the *wood shavings,* known as *volutes,* that are supposed to support it; and the bolsters of the Ionic capital, which make it so irregular and in many circumstances so awkward to use.[27]

Details specific to certain orders
Plate 7
As for the other capitals and pedestals, we have followed the same method as in the entablatures: and to spare our readers the trouble of referring to other books, we have given, on plate 7, the development of the capitals, columns, and pilasters of the Ionic and Corinthian orders; a number of examples of cornices for the interiors of apartments; and, finally, the outline of the Ionic volute.

Where engaged pilasters and columns appear together in the same building, because the former do not taper, the capital is made to project less far from the face of the pilaster than from that of the column, so that the projection of the pilaster capital, relative to the entablature, does not differ too markedly from that of the column capital.

Cornices within apartments differ to varying degrees from those of the orders; and may resemble them in all but slight details, if the apartment walls are reasonably high. But where they are too low, which cannot always be avoided, the cornices must be made with little height and much projection, in order to make the ceiling of the room appear to be higher. Moreover, the light indoors is far less bright than out of doors; and, once money has been spent on moldings, they might as well be visible. Profile them, therefore, in such a way that they meet, not at right angles but at acute angles, with a narrow interval between, to give a line of black that will make them stand out.

As for the Ionic volute, here is the way to trace it:

First draw, at a distance of one module from the axis of the column, a vertical line, known as the *cathetus,* which will pass through the center of the eye of the volute; and along this line, from the underside of the talon of the abacus, measure twenty-one parts and one-third of a module for the total height of the volute. Still moving in the same direction, take twelve of these parts, and you will have the center of the eye, the diameter of which is two and two-thirds parts. In this circle inscribe a square, one angle of which coincides with the intersection of the cathetus and the circle; and divide into six equal parts each of the two lines that pass through the center, perpendicular to and contained between the sides of the square. This yields points *1, 2, 3, 4,…,* and *12,* which are the centers of the outline of the volute. Use them as follows:

From point *1,* erect a vertical line to intersect the crown of the volute at *A.* From the same point *1,* and with a radius equal to *1A,* describe an arc of a circle, which will intersect at *B* the continuation of the line that passes through points *1* and *2.* Taking point *2* as center, and with a new radius *2B,* describe a second arc of a circle, which will terminate at *C,* on the continuation of the line that passes through points *2* and *3.* Taking point *3,* and thereafter points *4, 5,…,* to *12,* as centers, describe new arcs, each of which will have as its radius the distance from the end of the preceding arc to the center of the one that follows; taking care to observe that in every case the centers of two consecutive arcs and their junction are in a single straight line, so that they meet without forming an angle.

The width of the fillet, which is one-quarter of the height remaining below the curve of the first revolution, will easily be found by dividing into four each of the parts that served to indicate the centers for the first volute; this will yield twelve new points, to be used as above.

As we have said, when detached supports, whether columns, pilasters, or piers, stand far apart, they are spanned with arches instead of lintels. The kind of opening that results from this disposition is known as an *arcade.*   Arcades Plate 8

Arcades may be continuous, or they may be discontinuous—that is to say, separated by intercolumniations, by doors, by windows, or by niches. If continuous, the distances between the interaxes of the supports are equal; if discontinuous, they are not.[28]

Where the arches of discontinuous arcades bear on columns, the interaxes will relate to each other according to the proportions of the columns. If the columns are to be Greek Doric or Tuscan, locate their axes by dividing the distance between the axes of adjacent arcades into three parts. But if the columns are Ionic or Corinthian, divide the same distance by eight: three-eighths for each half-arch, and two-eighths for the interaxis.

Where the arcades are continuous, if the arches rest on piers, divide into three the space between the [axes of adjacent] arcades. In this way, the pier will be one-half the width of the arcade.

Suppose the arcades to be separated by windows or by niches: in this case, first divide the interaxis [of the openings] by four, and then the two middle quarters by three; this will give the width of the piers and of the window or niche.

If the arcades are separated by doors, divide the interaxis by five. The piers will be one-half as wide as the opening, and the width of the door will equal that of the piers.

Where the arcades are continuous, the arches must always rest directly on the columns; where discontinuous, the arches rest on an architrave.

The relation between the width and height of arcades varies according to the uses to which they are put. In a market hall, a customhouse, and so on, they may be as high as they are wide. In certain other buildings, they may be half as high again as they are wide. As for the arcades that form ordinary porticoes, make them twice as high as they are wide; that is to say, the center of the arch will be at three-quarters of the height of the opening.

Where arcades are composed of arches resting on columns, this proportion may be achieved as follows: mark off, along the axis of the opening, three times the distance between this axis and the axis of the column; then divide this height into a number of parts equal to the number of modules contained in the desired column alone, or in the column and architrave together, plus three. By subtracting three modules from this height, you will have that of the center of the arch. The rest speaks for itself.

The mere look of the construction of arches is the best decoration of such a feature. However, an archivolt may be added on occasion; and this is quite often done. There is only one case in which it must be avoided at all costs, and that is when arcades are both continuous and supported by columns: for in such a case, infallibly, the archivolts would either intersect or become too narrow.

Doors, windows
Plate 9

If the arches rest on piers, whether they are encircled by an archivolt or not, an impost must always be included to support the springing of the arch. The profile of an impost or of an archivolt is the same as that of an architrave, and the width of one or the other is approximately one-ninth of the opening.

Door and window openings may be arched, when very wide; or they may have square terminations, when they are of no more than ordinary width. On principal floors, they are made twice as high as wide, as are the openings of arcades. On subsidiary floors, they are made half as high again, or exactly as high, as they are wide; or only two-thirds as high. Where the spacing of the windows is narrow, the latter are no more than holes pierced in the wall. If the spacing is wide, the windows are surrounded by a chambranle, equal in width to one-sixth of the opening; its profile, like those of the imposts and archivolts, is that of an architrave. Where two rows of windows are separated by a considerable space, a frieze and a cornice are erected above the chambranle, each to a height equal to the width of the chambranle itself. Sometimes, the two ends of the cornice are supported by consoles, one-half as wide as the chambranle itself.

The cornice is sometimes surmounted by a pediment, to throw off the water to either side. In the case of a door, this becomes a necessity. The height of the pediment is between one-quarter and one-fifth of its base. Sometimes the chambranles are replaced by pilasters and an entablature. Doors and windows may also be flanked by columns, to afford better protection from the rain by giving more projection to the entablature.

Where the last row of windows is very close to the cornice that terminates the whole building, no cornice must be placed above the windows. Nor should any be placed above internal doors; for in both cases cornices are entirely unnecessary.

The only difference between doors and windows is that doors extend to the floor of the building, whereas windows rest on a breast crowned by a plinth. If the space between two rows of windows is considerable, a second plinth may be placed at the level of the upper floor; otherwise, one plinth is enough.

Where the wall is of an ordinary thickness, this is divided into three parts, one for the reveal and two for the embrasure.

If the various kinds of window that we offer, in which all is natural and simple, are compared with those windows that are burdened at great expense with moldings, modillions, crossettes, flanges, and so on—of which, unfortunately, Italy supplies all too many examples—it will be seen how much harm the mania of decoration can do to decoration itself.

To gain an exact idea of the various compartments of paving, it will suffice to inspect the plate that represents them. And as for the compartments of walls, one need only see them, on the same plate, to be convinced that the true decoration of a wall resides in the appearance of its construction. We shall add only that, where it is desired to bevel the joints in order to prevent the edges of the stones from chipping, this must be done in such a way as to have only obtuse angles, as shown in the figure. Any other method is defective. The head joints are less subject to chipping than the bed joints; and here, if desired, the beveling may be omitted. *Plate 10 / Compartments: / Of paving / Of walls*

In order to make apartments healthier, they are often paneled all around in wood; sometimes this is done to the full height of the walls, and sometimes to elbow height only. In both cases, the paneling is composed of pilasters, frames, and panels. The panels are fitted into the frames, and these are then fitted between the pilasters, which are themselves made up of frames and panels. A plinth is placed at the foot and a cyma at elbow height. *Of paneling*

It is customary to frame the panels with moldings 5 cm (2½ in.) wide for large panels and 3 cm (1½ in.) wide for the pilasters, separated by an interval of 6 cm (3 in.). These borders may be dispensed with, and we have examples to prove it.

The panels may be ornamented either with historical subjects or with landscapes or with arabesques. For the last-named, see, in the *Recueil et parallèle,* those of the Baths of Titus, plate 78, and those by Raphael, plates 85 and 86. It will be of value, also, to inspect the interesting productions of Percier and Fontaine; those of Normand and Lafitte, which are to appear shortly; and a number of the interiors decorated by our best architects.

Of vaults

The caissons that result from the construction of vaults are naturally square, and it would be best to restrict oneself to that form. However, antiquity supplies so many examples of caissons in the form of octagons, hexagons, lozenges, and so on, that we feel no need to disallow them. (See plate 76 of the *Recueil et parallèle.*) We shall therefore merely express the wish that, whenever the construction of a vault does not naturally create caissons, they may be replaced, either with important mythological or historical subjects, as in several palaces in Italy and in France, or with less grave subjects, as in the fragments of painting that are admired in Rome, in the Baths of Titus, at Herculaneum, and so on. (See plate 77 of the *Recueil et parallèle.*) For the rest, whatever their shapes, caissons may be made with one, two, or three steps, with or without moldings; for there exist examples of fine steps without moldings.

We shall conclude the little we have to say on forms and proportions with the observation that, however rational the three classes discussed above, they are not likely to contribute to the pleasure of the eye—or, consequently, to decoration itself, which has that pleasure as its object. To convey a certain degree of pleasure, they must be accurately perceived by the eye; they must thus exist in the same plane; and that plane must be perpendicular to the line of sight. For, if the plane were horizontal or oblique, the forms and proportions embodied in it would shift according to the point of view. Now, it is very rare for the forms and proportions of any building to be located in a plane that will allow the eye to perceive them fully and assess them judiciously.

On this subject, we shall cite Citizen Le Roy, and we do so all the more gladly because most students of architecture owe a great part of their talents both to the instruction that he has imparted and to the encouragement of all kinds that he has so generously bestowed.[29] In his excellent discourse on the theory of architecture, having given an arresting description of the magnificent effect of peristyles when their columns are set away from the wall, he goes on to say:

> The beauty that results from such peristyles is so general that it would still be perceived if the pillars that compose them, instead of presenting to the beholder the aspect of superb Corinthian columns, were to exhibit nothing but tree trunks, cut off between the roots and the spring of the branches; or if the columns were imitated from those of the Egyptians or of the Chinese; or even if those pillars

represented no more than a confused mass of diminutive Gothic columns, or the massive square piers of our porticoes.

This goes to show how slight is the influence exerted by forms and proportions on the pleasure that we feel on looking at a building; and any lingering doubts may be dispelled by referring to the *Recueil et parallèle*, which shows some buildings that afford the greatest pleasure despite bizarre forms and imprecise proportions, and others that are supremely displeasing, even though they display all the forms and proportions of the antique. The reason is that in the former cases the objects clad in these forms are disposed in a simple and fitting way, and that in the latter cases they are superfluous or badly disposed.

From this comparison we shall draw the following conclusions. In composition, neither forms nor proportions are to be envisaged with pleasure in mind; and those of the first of our three classes, although the most important, will receive scant attention, even with utility in view; for they arise naturally from the use of the objects concerned and from the nature of the materials used to construct such objects. The forms and proportions of the second class will be regarded as a purely local matter, employed solely to avoid offending against our customs: so that if one were building in Persia or in China or in Japan, one would avoid them, because to act otherwise would be to transgress against the customs of the country and even the materials that are in use there. The forms and proportions of the third kind will be employed, for the reason that in a host of situations they promote economy, and that they always ease the study and the practice of architecture. Our sole concern will be with disposition; for when it is fitting, and when it is economical, it will attain the purpose that architecture sets for itself, and will thereby become the source of the pleasurable sensation that buildings convey to us.

Disposition must therefore be our sole concern in the remainder of this work; and ought to be so, even if—we repeat—even if architecture were to take pleasure as its principal object.

PART II

Composition in General

Section One. Combination of the Elements of Buildings

The first part of our lectures concerned the elements of buildings, the principal parts of architecture having been discussed in the introduction. In this second part we shall tell how those elements may be combined; how such combinations may be used to form the parts of buildings; and how such parts may be united to form a whole. In a word, we shall discuss disposition, in accordance with the principles expounded in our introduction.

The elements of buildings may be placed side by side or one above the other. In the composition of a building, both kinds of combination must be kept simultaneously present in the mind; but for ease of study they can, and indeed must, be considered separately.[30] We shall therefore distinguish between two kinds of disposition: horizontal, as represented by plans; and vertical, as represented by sections and elevations.

Columns, as has already been said, must be equally spaced within any given building; but their spacing must vary in accordance with circumstances. In private buildings of the least importance, to limit the expense, the number of columns must be reduced, and they must be spaced as widely as possible; whereas in the most considerable public buildings, for greater durability, they must be as densely arrayed as possible. In any building, columns must be employed only where they serve to form porticoes or galleries; it follows that their distance from the wall must be at least as great as the distance between them. Such a disposition suffices where the columns are widely spaced and short, but where they are very tall and very closely spaced, it ceases to be appropriate; for the resulting tall, shallow portico would offer no protection from sun and rain. In such a case, the relation between columns and wall must change, if the portico is to serve the purpose for which it is built; and the columns will accordingly be set not one but two, or even three, interaxes away from the wall. And then there will be a precise relation between the depth of the portico and its height.

Equally, the nature of the construction of the upper part of porticoes, or of galleries, may call for new combinations. Where a portico with a depth of two or three interaxes is spanned by timber flooring, the upper part may be supported by a wall and a single row of columns; but where that same portico is spanned by a vault, it will become necessary to contain the thrust, either by setting a second row of columns in front of the first, if the vault is cylindrical,

Plate 1
Horizontal combinations:
Of columns

or by setting columns at all the intersections of the axes, if it is constructed on the principle of the flat arch.

When pilasters are detached, they are disposed like columns; but when they are engaged, they must be placed only at the ends of walls, at the corners of buildings, and at the intersection of one wall with another. As partition walls are always further apart than columns, the intervals between pilasters must for this reason be much wider than those between columns. In buildings where both pilasters and columns are employed, the axes of the pilasters must not be less than three interaxes apart.

Of pilasters

The exterior walls, which are designed to close off the building, must pass directly from one corner to the other, the straight line being the shortest distance between two points; and the partition walls, which not only divide the interior into several parts but also link the outside walls with each other, must, as far as fitness permits, run to the whole length or width of the building. Where there is no avoiding an interruption, they must at least be continuous along the top, either through beams or through arches. For the same reason, if there are columns on the exterior of a building, every wall must correspond to one of them.

Of walls

Windows and doors not only serve to establish communication between the various parts of a building and to afford the pleasure of seeing exterior objects, but they also admit air and light: they must therefore correspond to each other as much as possible. Site them, therefore, on common axes, which may be determined by bisecting the interaxes of the walls or of the columns.

Of windows and doors

Where columns appear on the outside of the building, windows or doors may be placed either in all the intercolumniations or in every other one. The former arrangement is suitable where the columns are widely spaced, and the latter where they are closely spaced. The same applies to niches.

Such is the simple and natural manner in which columns, walls, and so on, were disposed in the finest buildings of Egypt, of Greece, and of Rome; in the most interesting productions of Palladio, Scamozzi, Serlio, and others; and, finally, in the buildings constructed or designed by the best architects of the present day.

In the majority of modern buildings, we see columns placed back to back, engaged, coupled, or even joined; pilasters canted, truncated, splayed, and so on; walls that constantly project and recede from their natural alignment: and all this in honor of decoration. What a world of difference between such combinations and those just mentioned! The grand effect of the latter may well be imagined—as may the pitiable effect of the former.

It will be seen, from what we have said concerning horizontal disposition, that this aspect of composition is an entirely simple matter. Once we have set out parallel and equidistant axes, and drawn other axes at identical intervals to intersect them at right angles, the walls are set down on the axes, as many interaxes apart as is considered appropriate, and the columns, pilasters, and so on, are placed on the intersections of those same axes; then the interaxes are bisected to create new axes that serve to define the positions of the doors, windows, arcades, and so on.

Vertical combinations

Vertical combinations are just as simple as the horizontal combinations just discussed; for, without exception, the vertical are naturally derived from the horizontal. But, since any given horizontal disposition is capable of giving rise to several vertical dispositions, the latter are infinitely more numerous. They would take too long to describe, or even to enumerate. We shall therefore refer the reader to the plates, which, although far from representing them all, nevertheless show a considerable number and convey more than could ever be said in words.

Plate 2

At the foot of plate 2, plans have been drawn to represent a number of horizontal combinations; and above these plans are sections drawn to show vertical combinations that correspond to the horizontal ones below. Finally, above the sections are elevations to show the variety of architectural decorations that naturally arises from these horizontal and vertical dispositions.

In the related plates that follow, we have omitted to draw the horizontal and vertical dispositions, because they may be deduced without a figure. But it must clearly be understood that the plans and the sections have been done, and that these elevations are not arbitrary compositions. Otherwise, there would be a danger of succumbing to the attraction of one or another of these decorative ensembles and composing in the manner of those who, because they see nothing in architecture but decoration, start a project with the facade and then make shift to fit their plan and section to the elevation: a way of composing that runs counter not only to the aim of architecture but to the very aim that an architect has in mind when he sets out to decorate. All buildings and designs devised in such a spirit are more or less alike, and despite their great number they offer no more than three or four different combinations; whereas those composed in a natural order—that is to say, in which the plan is considered first, then the section, and in which the elevation is no more than the result of these two—offer such variety that the same decorative effect is never found twice. For conclusive evidence of this, see only the elevations shown on plates 2, 3, 4, 5, 6, 7, and 8.

Plate 3

In some of the elevations on plate 3, something has been added to the visible reflections of the internal disposition: and this addition, because it consists of sculpture, must and does enhance the beauty of the decorative effect—which would infallibly have suffered if, instead of representing some natural object, the architect had added any of those so-called architectural members that have neither use nor meaning.

The same plate contains a number of vertical combinations of columns. The upper columns must be less tall than those below: sometimes by one-quarter of the height of the latter, sometimes by one diameter only. The same applies to pilasters.

It is unnecessary to add that the orders must be separated from each other only by a plinth or stylobate placed upon an architrave. From all that we have said, it will be apparent that in such a case a cornice, being unnecessary, can only displease.

Plate 5

From plate 5, which offers a number of examples of the use of buttresses or counterforts, it will be seen how the appearance of useful objects, far from impairing the decoration, helps to lend it character, and consequently how absurd it is to seek to decorate a building by masking such objects: above all— as often happens—by masking them at great expense.

The same principle is found once more on plates 6, 7, and 8. Observe how essential it is, for the sake of architectural decoration itself, to concentrate entirely on the disposition; what variety of effect is produced, both horizontal and vertical; and, finally, in how many different but always agreeable ways buildings may stand out against the sky—when, instead of chasing after the forms of the parts, and the masses of the whole, the architect limits himself to the principles of fitness and economy.

Plates 6, 7, 8

Section Two. The Parts of Buildings

The principal parts of buildings are porches, vestibules, stairs, rooms of all kinds, and courtyards.

Porches and vestibules are made to serve as the entrances to buildings and to precede the other rooms that compose them.

Porches are vestibules that are open, either through their intercolumnia-tions or through arcades or through both. They may either be applied to the exterior of buildings or form part of their depth. In the former case they may be open to the front and on both sides, or only on the front; and in the latter case they form an opening. The manner of covering determines whether or not columns are situated at all the intersections of the axes.

Porches
Plates 9, 10

A porch may run to the entire width of the building or occupy only a part of the width; and the same goes for its height.

Vestibules differ from porches in that they are normally enclosed by walls, in which the doors form simple openings: access to them is rarely through intercolumniations.

Vestibules
Plate 11

Vestibules, like porches, are almost always wider than they are deep. Sometimes, even so, fitness demands that they be made square or even longer than they are wide. Whatever its shape, a vestibule may be divided into three equal or unequal parts by rows of columns that serve to reduce the span of the ceiling or the span, and consequently the height, of the vault.

Another way to reduce the number of columns is to use a groin vault in place of a barrel vault.

The vestibule leads to a staircase, which serves to communicate between the various stories of a building. Where this is intended to serve a number of stories, and space is limited, it turns back upon itself; if it merely leads from the ground level to the floor above, and if space permits, it may be made straight; but, in either case, to make it less fatiguing, there must be at least one landing between one floor and the next. The rise of the steps is generally one-half of their width or tread. If a staircase leads to a large number of rooms on a single floor, it is surrounded by galleries. Sometimes it consists of a single flight and sometimes of two. Each of these simple stair forms may be combined with another of the same kind; in which case a vestibule is placed between the two.

Stairs
Plate 12

Some of these arrangements require columns, either to support the landings or to support the impost of the vaults. For the rest, the plate will convey a clear idea of the different ways in which this part of a building may be disposed.

Rooms

Plates 13, 14, 15

Rooms may be made square, round, or semicircular; they may be wider than they are long, or greater in length than in width: this latter case is the most frequent, and sometimes such rooms end in a semicircle. All are covered either by ceilings or by vaults of various kinds.

Rooms of modest dimensions consist merely of walls and ceilings or vaults; but more extensive rooms are divided by columns or of rows of columns, just as in vestibules and for the same reason. The difference is that in vestibules the divisions may either be equal or unequal; whereas in rooms the central portion must always be wider than the flanking aisles.

In order to add to the floor space of a room—as sometimes needs to be done—a second gallery may be placed above the first, along two or three sides, or even all around. If the room is not too large, the columns of the upper gallery may be omitted, and the gallery will become a sort of tribune. Then the remaining columns will no longer lend any support to the ceiling or vault, which in this case will rest upon the walls; but they will retain a real function, that of supporting the tribune floor.

When a room contains two rows of columns, one above the other, it must always have a ceiling; a vault would make it too tall and would overload the columns, which in such cases can only be of a very modest diameter.

When a room of this kind is no longer than it is wide, then, whether it is square or round in form, the ceiling must take the form of a cone. The reason is that in any given building such a room is always wider than any oblong room; and that, if the ceiling were flat, its span would be disturbing.

Circular rooms, when vaulted, must be lit from a horizontal opening at the crown of the vault. It is possible to light most other rooms in the same way, although in such cases vertical openings would be preferable: if covered by a ceiling, they are lit by ordinary windows made in the walls; if vaulted, they may be lit by large semicircular openings in the upper part of one or both end walls. If these do not suffice, or if no openings can be made in those places, they are placed on the sides, transforming the barrel vault into a groin vault.

The height of a vaulted room on a rectangular plan is approximately half as great again as the width between its columns, if any. In round, vaulted rooms, the height is approximately equal to the width. This also applies to rooms with ceilings, where length exceeds width. In square rooms, the height is less than the width. In any given building, rooms whose length is equal to their width must generally be lower, in relation to width, than rooms that are longer than they are wide. For the rest, from the little that we have said of the proportions of rooms, it will be apparent that those we indicate are intended only for ease of study. We offer only points of departure, to be left or approached in the course of composition, according to specific requirements, or to the demands of the design as a whole.

In interiors, slender columns are generally preferable to massive ones; but the latter may be used, for instance, when it is desired to limit the number of columns. In a room with two rows of columns no more than three interaxes apart, if the columns were Corinthian, then either the intercolumniation would be too wide or the room excessively tall. Conversely, should the nave—that is, the central part of the room—be five interaxes wide, then short columns would have to be avoided, because the room would then appear too low.

Where the nave is five interaxes wide, no columns—not even the tallest, complete with architrave—can reach as high as the springing line of the vault. However, they can be made to do so with the aid of a stylobate, which will serve to reinforce the architrave and make it better able to support the weight of the vault; this is much greater in such a case than where the nave is only three interaxes wide.

Accordingly, in vestibules, or in any rooms no more than three interaxes wide, the springing line of the vault will rest on the architrave; but it will move upward to the top of the stylobate, if the width between the rows is five interaxes or more.

There are many who invariably put complete entablatures on their interior columns, and who would consider anything else a violation of the holiest rules of what they are pleased to call architecture. The truth is that nothing is more offensive to good sense than an interior cornice that serves only to conceal a part of the vault. There is, however, one case in which it may be employed: that is, where an order supports a ceiling; for in such a case the cornice, by its projection, will help to reduce the span of the ceiling.

The architectural decoration of rooms, like that of the external portions of buildings, springs naturally from their disposition and from their construction. If more is wanted, this can only consist in painting, sculpture, or inscriptions. Fitness often requires that this be done. All that has neither use nor meaning, far from adding to their beauty, can only detract from it.

Courtyards, like rooms, may be square or circular, longer than they are wide, or wider than they are long; they may be surrounded by plain walls or by porticoes, and often by both. Some porticoes continue all around; others occupy only one side, or two, or three; sometimes the portico appears only on the ground floor, supporting either the rooms of the upper floor or a terrace placed before such rooms; and sometimes it supports a second portico. Porticoes may consist of colonnades or of arcades of various kinds. *Courtyards / Plate 16*

From what has just been said, it is clear that, where disposition becomes the sole concern, this part of a building—like all the parts of which we have already spoken—may present an infinite variety of forms.

Aside from what may be called the *principal* parts of buildings, there are others that might be called *accessory* parts, such as external flights of stairs, grottoes, fountains, pergolas, and vine arbors.

External stairs have the purpose of communicating between different levels of ground. As space is rarely a difficulty, they are most often built in a single straight flight, whether approached directly or climbing alongside a terrace wall. When this arrangement is not possible, the flight may be bent *External stairs / Plates 17, 18* back upon itself or arranged on a circular plan. In the latter case it becomes known as a horseshoe stair.

Grottoes
Plates 17, 18

Very often, the substructures of such stairs are used to make grottoes for the sake of coolness. In most of the parts of buildings that have been discussed hitherto, circular forms are rare; in grottoes, however, such forms are necessarily frequent. Grottoes are mostly built into the earth, which presses on their walls for most of their height; and walls built on a circular plan resist this force far better than those built in straight lines.

Niches of varying sizes are made in the walls for the same reason: the stonework of the niches resists the pressure of the earth even more firmly, because it is built much closer to its own center than is that of the main wall of the grotto.

Grottoes are not always located at the foot of a flight of stairs; but as they are ordinarily built into higher ground, it is rare to find them without stairs nearby.

The position of grottoes naturally supplies them with more or less abundant water, which is used to create nappes, cascades, jets, and fountains that render such places still cooler and more pleasant.

Fountains
Plate 18

Fountains are not to be found in grottoes alone; they are set up in the centers and at the ends of courtyards, in public squares, and so on. They freshen the air, which they purify; and they are consequently highly useful. They are also highly necessary for many of the purposes of life. Their appearance can only contribute greatly to the beauty of any decoration.

This being so, one might expect to come across them at every turn; and yet nothing could be further from the truth, especially in France. At the very least, one might expect to see water flowing in torrents in those few buildings that are specially constructed for its collection and distribution. Nothing of the kind: at a number of celebrated fountains, rivers appear only in the guise of marble allegorical figures; what is worse, we find an accumulation of columns and pilasters, accompanied by all that is commonly known by the name of architecture, with never a drop of water beyond what issues from a narrow spout or even a post. Such is the effect of the mania for supposedly architectural decoration: to deprive us of a multitude of precious advantages.

In this respect, at least, matters are different in Italy. Not only do entire rivers flow in public squares: there is not a single house, however small, without a fountain at the end of its courtyard and in front of its vestibule. Hence the lively satisfaction with which we walk the streets of Rome.[31] Italy is truly the place to learn how to make fountains—and, we may add, architecture in general. Unfortunately, in that beautiful country, as elsewhere—and perhaps more than elsewhere—buildings present a multitude of details that have neither use nor meaning. What is worse, some of those who go to Italy to study architecture, while justly enamored of the charm that springs solely from the disposition of the buildings, extend their admiration from the disposition to the details. Eventually, swayed by the prejudices current in architecture, they persuade themselves that the buildings owe all their beauty to such details.

What is the consequence? When they come to compose for themselves, they neglect the true beauties in favor of the imaginary ones, with which they proceed to fill their own productions.

Those vine arbors, those pergolas where it is such delight to walk, and which at so little expense go so far to decorate—and which do, indeed, completely and pleasingly decorate—so many houses in Italy, inspire thoughts akin to those we have expressed on the subject of fountains. When reason places in our hands, as it were, a host of architectural decorations that are constantly varied and always new; when all the arts urge upon us their imitations of nature; when, finally, nature itself presents to us a host of objects well suited to captivate us in every way: is it not strange that, neglecting so many great and easily procured advantages, men should devote so much arduous and fruitless effort to chasing after a vain phantom of decoration?

Section Three. Buildings as a Whole

All the parts that enter into the composition of buildings are now known to us; and we have seen how to combine the elements that make up those parts.[32] We have now to unite the parts to form a whole.

As we saw in discussing combinations in general, the general principles of architecture require that walls, columns, doors, and windows, whether in the length or breadth of a building, should be placed on common axes. It naturally follows that the rooms formed by such walls and columns, and opened by such doors and windows, are necessarily also placed on common axes. Along those axes, they may be combined in a thousand different ways. And so, referring the reader to plates 22 and 23, we shall merely say a word on the different combinations that may be applied to these axes within the ensemble of a building.

Four axes may be so disposed as to form a square. One or two of the four may be omitted; and this will produce two new dispositions.

There is nothing to prevent our dividing a square in two with a new axis, either in one direction or the other, or sometimes in both directions at once.

From these divisions of the square, new plans arise; and if some of the axes are omitted, this in its turn will give rise to different plans.

If the simple division of a square into two produces so many simple dispositions, it will be apparent how many new dispositions will result from the division of the square into three, four, and so on; from the divisions of the parallelogram and of the circle; and, finally, from the combinations of the circle with the square and parallelogram. To be convinced of this, it is enough to look at the plate that shows the most important of these divisions, and combine each of the different horizontal dispositions with all the varieties of vertical disposition that one can devise; for there is no telling how many different compositions this host of combinations can produce.

We shall conclude part II by inviting students to pursue, in their study of architecture, the progression that we have mapped out for them: a progression that is the same as is followed in other branches of human knowledge. In

Pergolas, vine arbors
Plate 19

Combinations of the parts of buildings

Ensembles of buildings
Plate 20

literature, for example, the student begins with the parts of speech; and in music, before singing any air, he sings solfège. Is it not extraordinary that, in studying architecture, one commonly composes without having studied all of the objects that one is to assemble? By contrast, if students apply themselves to the plan that we have laid before them, they will become familiar with the forms and the proportions of the elements, and, still more important, with the various combinations of those same elements. Then, when they come to compose, the forms, proportions, and combinations best suited to the matter in hand will spontaneously come to mind at the appropriate places; and they will produce, with far less labor, designs more satisfactory to taste and to reason.

Confident though we are of the soundness of our principles, it remains possible that other and truer ones may be found. In that case, we invite students to choose, on mature reflection, those that they consider the best. In any case, we shall have attained our main purpose if we succeed in making them reflect on so important an art as architecture.

It may at first seem that we have been too forthright in condemning certain views expressed in works no less notable for the excellence of their contents than for the knowledge and talents of their authors. But, if such opinions had appeared only in mediocre writings, we should never have drawn attention to them. To us, they appear all the more dangerous in association with a multitude of good things; for the latter might all too easily procure the adoption of the former. Our criticism is therefore all the more pardonable in that it tends not so much to injure those authors' reputations as to afford them their due meed of praise.

As for the topic of drawing, which we have omitted, this is an omission that no one ought to regret, whatever his ideas on architecture. Even supposing that architecture had to be associated with other arts to ensure its survival, this would certainly not be achieved through geometrical drawings. These false images, far from setting architecture on a level with the noble art of painting, would at best associate it with certain trifling occupations that are the province of caprice alone. Instead, let drawings be done in perspective; and such true and satisfying images will indeed, up to a point, bring architecture close to the other arts. Better still, in view of architecture's importance for humanity, let it be treated in accordance with its true principles. Then, perhaps, far from needing to advance it to equality with any other art, we shall find no other that can justly be placed on a level with it.

Précis
of the Lectures
on Architecture

Volume Two

Preliminary Discourse

Because engineers are more often than ever called on to erect important buildings, the students of the École Polytechnique cannot be too earnestly recommended to study architecture; and at the same time they must be given the means of doing so with success.

Students leave the École with enough knowledge to appreciate the merits of a building and to make all the necessary drawings to put it into execution; and their compositions, rapid though they are, often contain happy ideas and rarely those gross errors that are all too often found even in the most famous buildings. This is no mean achievement, in view of the brief time that they devote to this study; but it is certainly not an adequate preparation for the important functions that most of them will soon be called on to assume.

Architecture is at one and the same time a science and an art. As a science, it demands knowledge; as an art, it requires talents.[33] Talent is accuracy and facility in the application of knowledge; and such accuracy and facility can be acquired only through sustained practice and repeated application. In the sciences, you may know a thing perfectly well after considering it once only; but in the arts it can be well done only after it has been done many times over.

A project can be well conceived only if it is conceived all at once; and this can be done only through long familiarity with all the parts that must enter into its composition; otherwise attention is distracted by details and drawn away from the whole, and the imagination cools, producing nothing but poor and feeble ideas, and often losing the capacity to produce anything whatever.

We therefore once more urge students to study architecture as much as possible in the various specialized schools to which they will proceed after they leave the École Polytechnique;[34] we exhort them not to rest on their knowledge, or even on whatever beginnings of talent they may possess, but to return often to every one of the objects on which they have worked, in order to make them as familiar as possible; and to approach them methodically, which is the only way to work with profit.

Despite the brief time that students are able to devote to architecture at the École Polytechnique, the course of study seems to have been to their advantage; and we trust that it will remain so when, in their other schools, they have more time to devote to the study of this art. We therefore think it best to begin the précis of the third part of our course, which forms the subject of this second volume, by recalling to their attention the sequence pursued, together with the principal ideas of our course.

The course is divided into three parts.

In part I we discussed the elements of buildings, which are walls, doors, windows, and arches; engaged and detached supports, known as pilasters, columns, and piers; floors, ceilings, vaults, roofs, and terraces. We examined the various materials that may enter into their construction; the ways in which they are to be employed; and, finally, the forms and the proportions that can be applied to each element.

Having reviewed all those objects that can enter into the composition of buildings, in part II we examined how to combine them and how to dispose them in relation to each other, both horizontally and vertically. Once familiar with these various combinations, we used them to form the different parts of buildings, namely, porticoes, porches, vestibules, stairs, rooms of various kinds, courtyards, and so on. Finally, going on to combine the different parts of buildings, we came to the composition of the whole in general.

In part III we concerned ourselves in a more specific manner with the composition of every kind of building in particular. First we looked at the approaches to cities, their entrances, and the streets, bridges, and public squares that connect their different parts; then we reviewed the principal public buildings necessary for government, education, subsistence, commerce, health, pleasure, security, and so on; finally, we turned our attention to those meant for habitation, such as private town houses, tenement houses, country houses, farms, inns, and so on.

This sequence, as will be seen, is no different from the course that is followed in all the sciences and in all the arts: it consists in a progression from the simple to the composite, from the known to the unknown; one idea always prepares the mind for that which follows, and the latter always recalls that which precedes it. We do not believe that in the study of architecture it is possible to follow any other sequence—still less to dispense with one altogether, as do many architects, who say that rules and methods are the shackles of genius. Far from sharing any such opinion, we consider that they ease its emergence and ensure its progress; moreover, reason may dispense with genius, but genius can only go astray unless led and illuminated by reason.

Advantageous though this method seems to us for speed of study, we should never have considered it adequate for success, without the more general remarks that we have prefixed to our successive particular observations; if, before considering the elements of buildings, the composition of their parts, and buildings as a whole—architecture, in a word—we had not known what architecture is, why we practice it, and how to practice it.

We therefore deemed it necessary to address ourselves, first of all, to the nature of the art, the purpose toward which it tends, and the means that it must embrace; in order to extract some general principles on which all of the particular principles might securely rest.

In examining these different objects, we observed:

That architecture, of all the arts, was the one whose productions exacted the most trouble and the most expense, and that it was, nevertheless, the art most generally practiced in every age.

That men are naturally as hostile to all forms of exertion as they are desirous of comfort; and that they would never have practiced architecture so generally and so constantly as they do, if it had not been of great advantage to them.

That, of all the arts, this is indeed the one that offers us the most immediate, the most important, and the most numerous benefits; that it is to architecture that the human race owes its survival, society its existence, and all the other arts their birth and their development; that it is to architecture, in consequence, that man owes the sum total of happiness and esteem that nature has permitted him to enjoy.

That if, instead of all these inestimable benefits, architecture had offered no more than the frivolous advantage of delighting the eye, it would soon have been eclipsed by painting and sculpture, two arts whose productions, made to please not only the eyes but the soul, are also incomparably easier to learn.

That, in consequence, the purpose of architecture cannot be pleasure but utility.

That, even if pleasure had been the purpose of architecture, this could never have been attained through imitation, a resource proper to the other arts. For, if any pleasure is to result from imitation, the object imitated must be an object of nature, beyond which we know nothing, and beyond which, in consequence, nothing can interest us. The imitation of the object must, furthermore, be perfect. Now, of the two models held up for imitation by architecture, one (the hut), being anything but a natural object, and not even deserving consideration as an object of art, must not be imitated in its forms; the other (the human body), bearing no formal analogy to any architectural body, cannot be imitated in its proportions.

That, even supposing any analogy to exist between these two species of body, it would remain supremely absurd, in seeking to give pleasure through imitation, to do so by means of analogy—that is to say, at a distance—as architects profess to do, in place of a positive and direct imitation such as is made by painters and sculptors.

Pursuing our observations, we saw that, if the means adopted in any art are to be effective, they must bear some relation to the nature of the art in question, and to our own predispositions; that architecture is necessary for our existence and for our happiness, but that it sets a high price on its benefits; that we are lovers of comfort and haters of exertion; that consequently, in constructing buildings, it is our nature to do so with the least possible exertion or expense; and that, to this end, the buildings that we erect must be disposed in the fittest and most economical manner possible.

That fitness and economy were thus the means proper to architecture, as imitation was not.

That, for a building to be perfectly fit for its purpose, it must be solid, salubrious, and commodious.

That, to make it as inexpensive as possible, it must be as symmetrical, as regular, and as simple as possible.

That, when a building has all that it needs, and nothing but what it must have; and when everything necessary is disposed in the most economical—which is to say, the simplest—manner, then that building has the kind and degree of beauty appropriate to it; and that to seek to add anything but the ornaments of painting and sculpture is to weaken and sometimes to obliterate its style, its character, and, in a word, all the beauties that are desired for it.

That, from whatever point of view architecture is considered, no one should seek to please by means of a purported architectural decoration based entirely on the use of certain forms and certain proportions—which, being themselves founded on nothing but a fictitious imitation, are incapable of giving any pleasure.

That, in all cases, disposition must be the architect's sole concern: since, if the disposition is as fit for its purpose and as economical as it can be, it will naturally give rise to an architectural decoration of a different kind, one that is truly calculated to please because it shows us a true image of the satisfaction of our own needs: a satisfaction to which nature has attached all our truest pleasures.

At every subsequent step in the study of architecture, we became more firmly persuaded of the truth and importance of these observations.

In examining the different materials and their applications, we saw that they differ in dimensions, in form, and in color; and that, if fit to their use, they naturally provide buildings, and the parts of every building, with the effect, variety, and character for which they are fit.

That some materials were hard, difficult to work, and consequently costly, and others soft, easy to work, and consequently cheaper; that it was natural to employ the former for the construction of the most important public buildings, in which fitness must be absolute, whatever the cost; that it was also natural to make use of the latter in private buildings of the lowest class, in which one is always limited by expense and should aim only to satisfy the requirements of fitness as well as possible within the stipulated cost; and that between these two classes of building there were a host of others, in which it was natural to use materials of both kinds together.

That all the parts of a building were not under an equal stress, so that firm materials might be reserved for those parts that make up its skeleton, such as the corners of buildings and the jambs of doors, of windows, and of arcades, the piers that receive the springs of vaults or the ends of beams, the piers that must be placed to coincide with the junctions of partitions and exterior walls, the various detached supports, and finally the string courses, which, by tying all the parts together, consolidate their strength; soft materials being kept for those parts that are merely infilling; and that from this disposition of materials there sprang a host of different forms of architectural decoration, all equally satisfying to the eye and to the mind.

That it was consequently absurd and futile to seek to decorate buildings by chimerical and extravagant means, while sure and simple means are offered to us by nature and by common sense, as part of the very construction itself.

Passing from the study of materials and of their uses to the forms and proportions of the different elements of buildings, we perceived that, while the imitation of the hut and of the human body offered no satisfaction in any respect, the uses of such elements, and the nature of the materials that can be used in them, pointed clearly enough to the principles that we must observe.

We saw that an engaged support must be square in plan, the better to connect with the adjacent infilling; that a detached support must generally be cylindrical, the form most proper to facilitate the circulation of people; that detached supports must be raised above the ground for the sake of salubrity; that they must be joined together at the top by an architrave; that they must also be joined to the wall by a second architrave, improperly known as the *frieze;* that these two architraves, together with the empty space between them, must be surmounted by a cornice with a projection sufficient to throw the rainwater away from the base of the building; that columns must widen at the top into a capital to ensure the solidity of the architrave by reducing its span; and so on.

That in the simplest buildings, constructed with materials of little strength, the supports of whatever kind must be short, to maintain sufficient solidity; that in the most important buildings, constructed with more resistant materials, they may be more elegant in proportion; that between the two extremes it is possible to insert as many mean proportions as there are buildings between the former and the latter.

That in the former class of buildings economy required the supports to be spaced as widely as possible, in order to reduce the number used within a given space; that in the latter class fitness demanded that they be brought as close together as possible, to ensure and to prolong the stability of the building.

That in the former case the architraves that span the supports must, to obviate fractures, be higher from top to bottom than they are where the supports are closer together; that the secondary architrave, or frieze, must in all cases be equal in height to the architrave proper, since both fulfill similar functions; that the cornice must be more or less prominent according to the height of the building; and, finally, that the height of the cornice must be equal to its projection; because if the height were less than the projection it would lack solidity, and if the projection were less than the height it would not serve its purpose.

Having thus reviewed the essential forms and proportions of architecture — which must naturally have been employed in every age — we examined those of the buildings of antiquity, as they have been generally adopted in Europe and transformed by custom into a kind of need. We observed that the forms and proportions of such buildings constantly varied; that columns of the same order never repeated the same proportions, and that columns of different orders often had similar proportions; that some columns ascribed to the *Doric order,* such as those of the Temple of Cori, had taller proportions than certain other columns known to us as *Corinthian,* such as those of the Tower of the Winds at Athens or the Colosseum at Rome (see plates 64 and 68 of the *Recueil et parallèle*), and so on; and that there were some Ionic columns of the same proportions as the latter, and consequently less tall than those of Cori, such as those of a temple situated on the banks of the Ilissus (see plate 64 of the *Recueil et parallèle*); and so on. We concluded by agreeing with a celebrated professor, Monsieur Le Roy, that the Greeks did not recognize those distinct orders in which the moderns see the essence of architecture and the principle of all beauty in decoration; and that those nations saw nothing in what we call the *orders* but supports and parts supported: useful objects, which they proportioned, not in imitation of anything whatever, but in accordance with the eternal principles of fitness.

That the study of the buildings of the Greeks—enlightened as they were in matters architectural—could not fail to be of the greatest advantage to us; that it might compensate to us for the loss of many centuries of experience; and finally that it might serve to remedy the imprecision of such ideas of form and proportion in the elements of buildings as we might have derived from the unaided contemplation of nature.

It was, in fact, a comparative study of all the buildings of antiquity that taught us the limits that must not be exceeded in the proportions between supports and parts supported. We perceived that the shortest support must not be less than six diameters high, nor the tallest more than ten; that the heaviest entablature must not be more than one-third as high as the column, and the lightest no less than one-fifth; and that the widest intercolumniation must not be more than three and a half diameters, or the narrowest less than one and a half; between which systems as many others may be inserted as may be judged necessary, all of which will yield accurate relations between the supporting parts and the parts supported.

Passing from the general proportions of ancient buildings to their proportions of detail, we found far less wisdom in most of the latter than in the former. We were convinced, nevertheless, that a comparative study of antique details would still be of use to us, since it would show us which of those details to adopt, which to reject, and which merely to tolerate; and that to this end it was important to study the antique with the eyes of reason, rather than to stifle reason—as is all too often done—by an appeal to antique authority.

That the best antidote to the blind admiration and servile imitation of those antique details that reason condemns is to be found in the antique itself, since at every turn it offers us details of the same nature treated in diametrically opposite ways; and that it is therefore easy to reconcile reason with our acquired custom of admiring and employing antique details.

That, although the example of some antique buildings has led us to put bases under our columns, in defiance of utility, commodity, and economy, there exist not only a host of Doric but even some Corinthian precedents that reason may take as its authority for dispensing with them.

That, although the delicate and beautiful workmanship of some Ionic columns has induced us to adopt this form in spite of its lack of fitness and oddity, the perfect fitness of the Greek Doric capital, the almost universal use made of it in Greece, and several examples of its use on columns of Ionic proportions, will be sufficient authority to reject forever so absurd a form of capital as the Ionic.

That, while the grace of the overall form, and the elegance of the proportions, of the Corinthian capital have in a sense compelled us to copy it, with its flimsy, incurved abacus, and its volutes in the shape of wood shavings, the example of the Corinthian columns of the tomb of Mylassa and of the Tower of the Winds, where the abaci are square and no volutes are to be seen, and the still more numerous examples of those superb Egyptian capitals composed according to the same system, are quite sufficient authority for ridding the Corinthian capital of all that has neither use nor meaning and restoring to it all that it lacks to serve its purpose to perfection.

That, although triglyphs, which serve no purpose and look like nothing in particular, or at least nothing rational, are almost always to be found in Greek and Roman Doric buildings, there are nevertheless some in which triglyphs have been omitted, such as the Chapel of Agraule at Athens, the baths of Paulus Aemilius and Colosseum at Rome, and the amphitheater at Nîmes; and that, as the Greeks recognized no distinction between the orders, and never used triglyphs in Ionic and Corinthian friezes—where they would have been needed if they ever were needed in the frieze of the Doric—we have every reason to banish them forever, without doing violence either to our own customs or to the just respect that we owe to antiquity.

Having thus distinguished those antique details that are to be adopted from those that are to be rejected, we surveyed those that may be tolerated: that is, moldings and their combinations. We observed that moldings, which serve no purpose and resemble nothing, deserved our attention only by virtue of our acquired custom of using them; that, this being so, we ought to employ them with the greatest possible restraint; that, since their use cannot give us any real pleasure, we should be content to ensure that it causes us no displeasure; that to this end, following the examples of the Greeks in their Doric and Ionic orders, and of the Romans in their Corinthian orders, those combinations of moldings known as *profiles* should each possess a pronounced movement, with rectilinear moldings intelligently combined with curved moldings, and the thinnest moldings set against the thickest.

All our observations on matters of form and proportion brought us to the conclusion that, however rational might be those that originate in the nature of things, we should not expect to derive any great pleasure from their use: for, to make this pleasure strongly felt, both the form and the proportion would need to manifest themselves in the most evident way, and the eye would need to be able to grasp their relations with the greatest accuracy; and this would require all of them to present themselves in a single vertical plane: a thing that never happens and never can happen. What applies to essential forms must apply even more to those that have no merit beyond our customary respect for them: a merit that would be nothing of the sort to the nations of Asia and of Africa. In applying these latter proportions, we should therefore seek not so much to satisfy the eye as to avoid offending it; in employing the former, we must keep in view only the fitness and the economy that they can contribute to buildings—convinced, as we must be, whatever our view of architecture, that its beauties derive less from the forms and proportions of the objects employed than from their disposition.

Passing on from the elements of buildings to their combination, we saw that in any building the columns must always be equally spaced, in order to support an equal portion of the load; that they must stand clear of the wall by one intercolumniation at least, since otherwise they would serve no purpose; that this relation between walls and columns, well suited to minor buildings in which the supports are made as short and as widely spaced as possible, would not be fit for buildings of great importance, employing taller and more closely spaced supports, as the resulting porticoes would become too narrow for use and for their height; that, for fitness's sake, the space of one interaxis between the axis of the wall and that of the columns must be increased to two and sometimes three.

That the nature of the construction of the upper part of porticoes gave rise to other combinations; that, if a portico with a width of several interaxes were to have a vault instead of a flat soffit, a single row of columns would not suffice to resist the thrust of the vault, and a second row must be placed on the adjacent axis; and that, if this vault, instead of being cylindrical, were to consist of flat arches, columns would have to be placed at every intersection of the axes.

That, pilasters being no more than engaged supports, piers of stone that form part of the skeleton of a building, their place was at the corners of the building, at the points of intersection of the external and partition walls, and at the ends of the side walls of porches, as we saw in dealing with the use of materials; and that, as the walls of any building are further apart than are the columns or other detached supports, the interval between any two pilasters must never be less than three interaxes.

That, since the exterior walls are intended to enclose a building, and since a straight line is the shortest distance between two points, such walls should always pass directly from corner to corner of the building, or of any of its parts, without break or projection; that partition walls, being designed not only to divide buildings but also to tie the outside walls together, must run to the whole length or breadth of the building; and that, where there is no avoiding an interruption, continuity must at least be maintained along the top of the walls, by means of arches or beams; and accordingly that, if there are any columns on the outside of a building, every partition wall must correspond to one of them.

That doors and windows, to give free passage to air and light, must be aligned with each other along new axes intermediate to those of the walls or columns.

We next saw that all possible vertical combinations sprang from this small number of horizontal combinations; and that the union of these two kinds of combination quite naturally gave rise to a host of different forms of architectural decoration—all of them equally satisfying, because precisely matched to the disposition and construction of the building.

That, in giving graphic expression to an architectural idea, one should begin with the plan, which represents the horizontal disposition of the parts intended to enter into the composition of a building or part of a building; then continue with the section, which explains their vertical disposition; and finish with the elevation; and that to begin with the elevation, as some architects do, and then subordinate the section and the plan to it, would be to deduce the cause from the effect, a notion whose absurdity speaks for itself.

That, the elusive idea once captured quickly in a croquis, the next step, in order to render it with the greatest ease and precision in a working drawing, was to establish those axes whose positions and intersections would define the positions of walls, columns, and so on; that, these features being fixed on the plan, their height must be defined in the section, and from it their width or thickness in plan, small dimensions always being subordinated to large; and finally that, with the plan and section firmly settled, the elevation was no more than their projection.

That, by proceeding in this manner, one would run no risk of straying into those expensive, unnecessary, bizarre combinations, inspired by decorative prejudice, that are so often observed in the majority of our French buildings, with an effect that is as weak, monotonous, and displeasing as that of simple, natural combinations—as used by the ancients and by Palladio—is grand, varied, and satisfying.

Once familiar with the various horizontal and vertical combinations of the elements of buildings, and with the methods of showing them in drawings, and once steeped in the general principles of architecture, we found no difficulty in applying these combinations to the forms of the different parts of buildings.

In studying them, we perceived that columns must be used only in order to reduce either the excessive span of ceilings or the excessive diameter—and thus excessive height—of vaults; that, in an interior, columns that serve no purpose are no more pleasing, even to the eye, than columns used unnecessarily on exteriors.

That, whenever vaults bear on columns, it is sometimes in the interests of fitness—and always in the interests of economy—to replace barrel vaults with groin vaults, since barrel vaults require columns along their whole length, and groin vaults need them only at the corners; that barrel vaults permit rooms to be lit only from the ends, whereas groin vaults enable them to be lit both from the ends and from the sides.

That, to increase the area of floor in a room without increasing its dimensions, one can and must employ two rows of columns, one above the other, whatever the decorative prejudice against such an arrangement.

That, just as it is absurd, where fitness requires two rows of columns on the exterior, to separate them with a complete entablature (the cornice being made only to throw off the water from the roof), it is even more absurd to do so in an interior, where all the parts are sheltered; and that cornices in such places are consequently not to be admitted, except where they reduce the span of a ceiling and thus in a sense perform the office of a capital.

Passing from the composition of the various parts of buildings to that of the whole, we saw that, since walls, columns, doors, windows, and so on, are necessarily sited on common axes, both in breadth and in depth, the rooms composed of such elements ought similarly to share common axes.[35]

That the shared axis of a number of rooms must never be the same as that of their columns but always identical with that of their doors or windows.

That these new axes, which might be known as *principal axes,* might be combined in a thousand entirely different but equally simple ways; that one might apply all the elementary combinations in turn to each of the numerous general dispositions that result from such combinations, and consequently obtain, by a kind of supercombination, a host of different plans; and finally that, by adapting all the possible vertical combinations to each of these plans in turn, one would arrive at an incalculable number of architectural compositions.

We concluded our remarks on composition in general by observing that there is a near-infinite variety of classes of building; that each is susceptible of an infinity of modifications; that the particular requirements of any one building might be varied by places, times, persons, sites, costs, and so on; that to seek to learn architecture by successively studying all classes of building in all the circumstances that can modify them would be an impossibility; that, even if a lifetime were long enough, such a mode of study would remain as fruitless as it would be laborious, since, as all buildings differ in their uses, the more precise the ideas derived from the design of any one, the less applicable they would be to another; and that, consequently, every new design would demand a new study. Such a manner of studying architecture is not only unprofitable and arduous but harmful, whatever view we may take of that art: after studying a number of projects, one would infallibly be lulled by indolence or by vanity into certain associations of ideas that would then reproduce themselves in all of one's subsequent projects, even where least appropriate. We see all too many instances of this.

That if—instead of devoting one's time to the production of designs— one were to first look at the principles of the art, and then familiarize oneself with the mechanism of composition, it would be possible to execute with facility, and even with success, the design of any building whatever, even without having previously done any other; and that one would merely have to inquire as to the particular requirements of the building in question, since one would already possess every possible means of worthily filling the commission.

That the study of the principles and of the mechanism of composition was thus well suited to develop genius and enrich imagination—just as any study of a succession of projects, when not preceded by general study, was calculated to cramp the one and impoverish the other.

And so, in part III of this course, of which we shall now give the précis, we have endeavored, in examining various kinds of building, not so much to explain the particular requirements of each as to develop the general principles applicable to all kinds and all classes of building, and thus to familiarize the student with the mechanics of composition.

Examination of the Principal Kinds of Building

Section One. The Principal Parts of Cities

Just as walls, columns, and so on, are the elements of which buildings are composed, buildings are the elements of which cities are composed.[36]

As the general dispositions of cities may vary in a thousand ways, according to circumstances; as one seldom gets the chance to build a whole city; and as the principles to be followed in their composition are the same as in the composition of each building; we shall say nothing of the cities as wholes. Before examining the different buildings that form such wholes, we shall merely glance at their approaches, their entrances, and those parts of them that serve to establish communication between all the others.

The Approaches to Cities

How should the approaches to a city be decorated?

This is a question that might well be put to the students as a test. The answer would be simple, if cities were laid out as they should be, and if those buildings that ought never to be included within them, such as hospitals, cemeteries, and so on, were relegated to the countryside beyond their walls. Glimpsed through the single or double lines of trees that would be planted along the roads to shelter travelers from the sun's heat, such buildings would stand out against the sky, or against woods or mountains, and would naturally afford the most varied, the most magnificent, the most interesting views. For the best way to decorate the approaches to a city—or to decorate any building whatever—is to give no thought to their decoration, but to envisage only the fitness of their disposition.

To this principle Athens, Rome, Palmyra, Sicyon, Puteoli, Taormina, and so on, owed the magnificence of their approaches; a host of interesting monuments, scattered among the trees, gave the Ceramicus and the Appian Way all their nobility and all their charm; and a disposition of this kind prompts the delightful sensations that are still felt to this day at that locality in the kingdom of Naples, known as the *Elysian Fields,* which is situated on the shores of the Lake of Acheron.

The beauty of a highway would not in the least require the wayside funerary monuments to be as colossal as the pyramids of Egypt, or as majestic as the tombs of Hadrian, of Augustus, or of Septimius Severus. It is, of course, impossible to withhold our admiration at the sight of such astonishing manifestations of human patience and industry; but when we reflect on their lack of use or meaning, on the number of useful buildings that might have been built at the same cost, and on the magnificence that might have been added to each city as a whole by a greater number of edifices—we are left with nothing but regret at the spectacle of human ability so often ill employed.

The monuments of this kind among the Greeks were not by any means so large or so magnificent as those just mentioned: the tomb of Themistocles, on a promontory near Piraeus, consisted of a single stone; that of Epaminondas, in the plain of Mantinea, was a single column, on which his shield was suspended. The monuments erected at Thermopylae by the Amphictyons in honor of the three hundred Spartans and of other Greek troops were nothing but cippi, adorned only with inscriptions such as the following: "Here four thousand Greeks of the Peloponnese fought against three million Persians. Go, traveler, and tell Lacedaemon that we lie here because we obeyed her sacred laws." It will be clear that in spite of their extreme simplicity—or rather because of it—these monuments must have promoted feelings as delightful as those evoked by the others are distasteful.

Among the tombs placed along the highways, some would be those of private individuals; others would belong to families. The latter might be square towers, like the tombs of Palmyra; or rotundas, like that of Plautia and Metella; or pyramids, like the tomb of Cestius: all forms are equally suited to this kind of monument, except those that lack simplicity. To gain an idea of the variety of forms of which tombs are susceptible, see plate 1 of the present work and plates 19, 20, and 74 of the *Recueil et parallèle*.

City Gates

How should city gates be decorated? To commemorate their victories for posterity, the Romans erected triumphal arches. Their example has been followed by most of the nations of Europe. If, instead of being set up inside cities, such monuments were to be sited at the entrances to them, where they would be more conspicuous than anywhere else, those entrances would be magnificently decorated, at no expense, and in the noblest and most momentous way.

A triumphal arch may have a single opening, like those of Hadrian at Athens; of Augustus at Rimini, Susa, and Pola; of Aurelian, Gallian, and Titus at Rome; of Trajan at Ancona and Benevento; and of Gavius at Verona. Or it may have three, like those of Marius at Orange, of Julian at Reims, and of Constantine and Septimius Severus at Rome. Some, like those at Verona, Autun, and Xaintes, have only two; such a disposition is not to be condemned in structures that are city gates rather than triumphal arches, because it makes it possible to enter and to leave with the minimum of obstruction, but it would be out of place in any monument through which triumphal processions are likely to pass, because on meeting the pier between the two openings they would be obliged to turn aside to right or left.

In almost every one of the monuments mentioned above, the principal faces incorporate four columns, applied to the wall, perched on thin pedestals, and supporting nothing but entablatures whose profiles break around each column in turn. Notwithstanding the great number of existing precedents, and the even greater number of copies that have been made of them, we shall continue to believe that such arrangements, which would be intolerable in any other kind of structure, are even more so in a triumphal arch, a monument whose every part must combine to exalt and inspire the beholder's soul by evoking the image of some glorious action. No one will ever persuade us that unnecessary and frigid columns have the power to convey anything whatever to the mind, let alone speak more eloquently on a triumphal arch than the inscriptions and sculptures whose places they usurp.

In every other respect, we believe that these monuments of antiquity cannot be too closely studied. (See plate 21 of the *Recueil et parallèle;* see also the first plate of the present work.)

Streets

How should the streets of a city be decorated?

If, to shorten the journey, to avoid congestion and the accidents that frequently result from it, and to promote the renewal of the air, the streets were made to intersect at right angles; if, to spare those who pass along them the inconveniences of mud, rain, and sun, they were lined with porticoes; if those porticoes, being designed for the same purpose, were made uniform in disposition throughout a given city; and if, finally, those houses to which they give access were disposed in the manner best suited to the fortune and condition of their occupants, and varied in mass accordingly: then such a city would afford the most delightful and theatrical scene.

It was in such a way that the streets of Alexandria and Antinopolis, built by Hadrian, and those of other antique cities, were planned; the same is true to this day of the streets of Turin, Bologna, and other Italian cities; and no one passes along such streets, or recalls passing along them, without a sense of delight.

Bridges

How should bridges be decorated?

If their composition incorporates all that is necessary; if nothing unnecessary is introduced; if the necessary is handled in the simplest way; in short, if the same principles of fitness and economy are observed in the composition of bridges as ought to be followed in that of buildings of all kinds; then bridges will possess all the beauty of which they are capable. To convince oneself of this, one has only to compare the bridge at Neuilly with the bridge formerly named for Louis XVI.[37] In the building of the latter, there was a pursuit of what is called *decoration;* the sole concern in the former was with construction; and yet the look of the Neuilly bridge is as satisfying as that of the Louis XVI bridge is awkward and displeasing.

Most bridges, like those of which we have just spoken, are unroofed; but in cities, especially, to shelter those who cross them from the discomforts of rain and sun, they are sometimes covered with galleries and porticoes, either

145

completely—as at Alessandria, in Italy, or at Bassano on the Brenta—or the footways only, as on the Aliverdikan bridge at Ispahan or the old triumphal bridge at Rome. Open bridges may be lit at night by lanterns set on columns directly over the piers—as on the Aelian bridge, now Ponte Sant'Angelo. In those cities where there is occasion to erect several triumphal arches, after some have been set up at the gates, others may be placed on the bridges: either a single one above the central arch, as on the triumphal bridge of ancient Rome or Augustus's open bridge at Rimini, or else one at either end, as with the bridge at Saint Chamas in Provence. It will be clear how many different varieties of architectural decoration must naturally result from these different dispositions. Accessory decoration—that is to say, the use of sculpture—may naturally reinforce the effect of any of these forms of architectural decoration: trophies may fittingly be placed above each pier, and it would be equally appropriate to range statues along the parapets.

In almost all the bridges of antiquity, the arches were semicircular; in the majority of modern bridges they are based on arcs of circles. This latter form is infinitely more suitable, since it offers a far freer passage to the waters than does the former.

The arches of the old covered bridge of Pavia, built by Duke Galeazzo Visconti, are ogival: a better shape than any other to ensure the safety of a vault, but not of a bridge, since, as the water rises, the piers present a greater surface to it, and offer greater purchase to the current to overthrow them. To avoid the drawbacks of this shape, while at the same time retaining its advantages, the ingenious architect made each arch with an extrados, leaving a void in each pier between one arch and the next—so that, as the rising water finds less space to pass beneath the arches, it finds more space to pass through the triangular voids in the piers.

This bridge, as will be seen, bears no formal analogy with the bridges of antiquity; but the effect created by its disposition is no less satisfying or less magnificent for all that; which goes to prove that forms and proportions have less influence on the beauty of decoration than do fitness and simplicity of disposition.

On the subject of bridges, see plates 22 and 23 of the *Recueil et parallèle*.

Public Squares

Just as the architectural decoration of streets derives from the porticoes and private buildings that line them, that of squares derives from the porticoes and public buildings that surround them. The magnificent squares of antiquity would supply the proof of this, if only they still existed. Unfortunately, time has left us barely a vestige of them; we can form an idea of them only from the descriptions given by Plato, Xenophon, Demosthenes, Aeschines, Pausanias, and Herodotus.

According to these writers, the ancient public squares were surrounded by buildings erected for the worship of the gods or for the service of the state. On that of Athens stood the Metroon, or temple precinct sacred to the Mother of the Gods; the Temple of Aeacus; the Leocorion, a temple built in honor of the daughters of Leos, who sacrificed themselves to avert the plague; the palace where the Senate assembled; the rotunda, surrounded by trees, where the officiating Prytanes came to take their meals every day and sometimes to offer sacrifices for the prosperity of the people; the tribunal of the First Archon, surrounded by the ten statues that gave their names to the ten tribes of Athens; the precinct set aside for popular assemblies; the camp of those Scythians whom the republic employed to maintain order; and finally the markets from which came the provisions necessary for the subsistence of a great people.

In the public square of Halicarnassus, which was built by Mausolus, king of Caria, on a sloping site that stretched down to the sea, could be seen on one side the palace of the king; on the other the Temple of Venus and that of Mercury, built beside the spring of Salmacis; and at the foot, various markets stretched along the shore. At the landward end rose the citadel and the Temple of Mars, where stood a colossal statue. In the center of the square, all eyes were drawn to the tomb of Mausolus in the form of a pyramid, crowned by a chariot and decorated on every side with the masterworks of such artists as Bryaxis, Scopas, Leochares, Timotheus, and Pythius.

In most of the public squares in Greece, splendid buildings were fronted by magnificent porticoes, their walls covered with inscriptions, paintings, statues, and bas-reliefs by the most celebrated artists. In one of the Athenian porticoes, known as the Poecile, the walls were hung with shields captured from the Lacedaemonians and from other nations. There, the capture of Troy; the aid that the Athenians gave to the Heraclids; and their battles against the Lacedaemonians at Oenoe, against the Persians at Marathon, and against the Amazons at Athens itself, all were depicted by Polygnotus, Micon, Panaenus, and other celebrated painters.

The square at Athens, and those of several other cities, were beautified by the shade of a forest of plane trees, beneath which stood a host of altars, together with statues, granted to those kings or private individuals who had deserved well of the Republic; cippi; and columns inscribed with the principal laws of the state.

Nothing was more magnificent than the forum or marketplace of Trajan, built by Apollodorus of Damascus. Pausanias, Aulus Gellius, and Ammianus report that its buildings were of striking grandeur and magnificence: a basilica in which the consuls gave audience to the people; a superb temple in honor of Trajan; a library surrounded by a peristyle in which were bronze statues of all the celebrated men of letters; triumphal arches, magnificent fountains, whole streets adorned with statues; and finally the beautiful column that was set up after Trajan's conquest of the Dacians.

If one wished to describe some of our modern squares, it might be done in a manner not only less vague than the above but complete in every detail, since we have them before our eyes. The Place Vendôme, for example, might be described as follows. This square, laid out in the reign of Louis XIV, an age in which all the arts, eclipsed for twenty centuries, had at last regained the splendor that they had possessed under Augustus: this square consists, in plan, of a parallelogram of so many toises long by so many wide. The corners of this parallelogram are canted; it is surrounded on every side, except at its two entrances, by various private buildings, all restricted to a uniform height and decorative scheme. This scheme consists of a Corinthian order of pilasters raised on a basement, whose height is two-thirds of that of the order. The basement in turn is decorated with a blind arcade, which frames the windows that light both the first floor and the entresol; the piers of this arcade are adorned with quoins, and its keystones with masks. The order that stands on this basement rises through two stories. It is crowned by an entablature whose height is between one-quarter and one-fifth; its profile is that of Vignola; above it is a high roof hung with slates and pierced with dormers variously ornamented. All the windows in the square are basket-arched. To lend movement and effect to the decoration, each of the blocks on the long sides of the square has a frontispiece formed by four engaged columns with an entablature crowned by a pediment, in the tympanum of which there is a cartouche supported by genies. In the center of the square the statue of the monarch formerly stood.

How arid an impression is left in the mind by such a description of one of the finest of modern squares, precise though it is! What delightful and sublime emotions, by contrast, are conveyed by the preceding descriptions of the public squares of the ancient world, for all their vagueness! Where does the difference lie? In the modern square, there is nothing but decoration; in the ancient ones, the objects arranged are of the greatest interest and importance.

We shall perhaps be told that, if our squares lack the beauty of those of the ancients, this is because our customs are different, and our abilities inadequate; and that in that case, for want of a true decoration, it is reasonable to supply the deficiency at least with an image of decoration. An examination of the former Place de Louis XV—which of all our squares seems to reveal the greatest aspiration toward economy, since it has buildings only along one side—will serve to answer these objections.

The city of Paris expressed the desire to erect a statue to Louis XV. It was customary to lay out a square for every new statue. The city of Paris, observing that, if it were to erect a few more statues, there would soon be nothing left of it but a single great square, concluded in its wisdom that this square must be built outside its precincts. The architect, considering with equal logic that a public square in open country should be less magnificent, and less costly, than squares within cities, thought fit to erect buildings on one side only. True, such an arrangement did not amount to a square; but he soon found a way to make one. He enclosed a considerable extent of land with wide, deep moats. This would have made the Place de Louis XV inaccessible; but the architect remedied this slight difficulty by constructing six stone bridges, each with three arches, by means of which communication was reestablished between the field now known as a *square* and the surrounding land. These moats were then lined with a thick wall; and—architecture being not so much the making of a wall, or of anything else, as its decoration—a sum approximately equal to one-third of the cost of the walls and bridges was spent on embellishing the whole with returns, platforms, projections, recesses, balustrades, and so on. See plate 2, figure 1.

In spite of all this decorative luxury, the square produces no effect when one passes through it; it follows that all the money spent on it has been wasted, even from the point of view of decoration.

In the composition of this square, if, instead of forms, proportions, and all those childish trifles that are supposed to decorate and beautify, the prime concern had been disposition, fitness for purpose, and—in a word—everything that truly deserves the name of architecture; and if any notice had been taken of the facts that the square was situated between two much-frequented promenades, that often, even on the finest day, the serenity of the skies was troubled by storms, which forced promenaders to seek shelter, and that a public square is frequently the scene of the most brilliant festivities and the most solemn ceremonies; if, in consequence, the square had been surrounded with spacious porticoes, which would have offered a covered walk in inclement weather and convenient places for an entire population on festive occasions; and if, to freshen the air, an abundance of fountains, and so on, had been placed there: what a magnificent sight the square would then have afforded, with its great porticoes outlined against the trees on one side, against the river on another, and against the public buildings erected on the side nearest to the city! See the same plate, figure 2.

And such a square—so commodious and so majestic, so worthy in every respect to stand comparison with those erected by the Greeks and Romans—such a square would have cost less than the one that exists. The cost of the interior walls of the moats, added to one-third of that of the exterior walls, would have sufficed to build the four rows of columns necessary to give the porticoes an adequate width; the cost of the remaining two-thirds of the exterior wall, and of the unnecessary projections on the perimeter of the square, would have sufficed for the construction of the soffits or ceilings of the portico; the expense of the bridges would have sufficed to adorn the square with fountains; the portico roofs, all around the square, might have been adorned with numerous and interesting statues whose execution would have encouraged sculpture and developed the germ of a multitude of talents in that art. The square once completed in this way, there would still remain the cost of excavation and removal of earth, an enormous sum, more than sufficient to cover with a portico the bridge that leads into the square. See the same plate, figure 3.

It is thus evident that, if our squares are so far from possessing the majesty of those of the ancients, this difference is not a result of any requirements of fitness specific to us—since porticoes are even more necessary in so rainy a climate as ours than they are beneath the clear skies of Greece—nor yet of our lack of finances, since the square of ours that was built with the greatest economy cost far more than another that would equal the magnificence of those of

Greece and Rome: the difference stems solely from the mania for decoration that compels us to spend enormous sums without profit or pleasure; a pernicious and hateful mania that renders us unable to build a host of buildings of the greatest importance from which, collectively, our cities would derive the greatest splendor and the most precious advantages.

Although the majority of the plans of public squares contained in plates 13, 14, 16, and 46 of the *Recueil et parallèle* are far from exact, they are the work of celebrated architects, steeped in the spirit of the ancients, and we believe that they may be studied with profit.

Section Two. Public Buildings

Temples

The need to erect a sacred building will seldom occur, as these exist everywhere in excessive quantities.[38] In view of this, and of the little time that students have to devote to the study of architecture, it might seem appropriate not to concern ourselves here with buildings of this kind; but, since our purpose is not so much to teach the student how to make such and such a building as to set out the principles that ought to direct the composition of any building; since the study of the buildings of antiquity, and their comparison with those of modern times, is the most direct way to this end; and since, of all the buildings of antiquity, temples are those that we still possess in greatest numbers, we take the view that it is worth dwelling on the subject for a moment.

The majority of ancient temples, whether in the environs of Athens, Corinth, Rome, and so on, or within the walls of those celebrated cities, were not so much places of public worship as monuments designed to call to mind some virtue whose practice might be useful to the fatherland. Such was the principal object of the Temple of Honor, to which the Temple of Virtue served as a vestibule, and which Marcellus, vanquisher of Hannibal, erected after his victories, so that troops setting out to war might remember that glory could be attained only through courage, and honor acquired only by virtue. Such, too, was the object of the Temple of Concord erected by the tribune Flavius after he had had the good fortune to reconcile the classes within the Republic. The Temple of Beneficence erected by Marcus Aurelius had no other purpose than to teach his successors that this must be the foremost virtue of any prince.

Such temples contained nothing but the statue of the deity to which whey were dedicated, the tripods necessary for burning incense, and the tables on which to lay the offerings. In most cases, only the priest or the priestess was permitted to enter, and so they had no need to be of any great size.

Most consisted of a single rectangular room, of fairly modest dimensions, fronted by a simple porch of four or six columns, reached by means of steps that ran to its full width.

Even in the temples of those deities to whom full sacrificial honors were paid, such as the temples of Jupiter Olympius at Athens, of Jupiter Capitolinus at Rome, and of the Sun at Baalbek and at Palmyra, the *cella*—the sanctuary, the main body of the temple—was scarcely any larger than the above; and this was entirely right, in view of its function and the number of objects that it was intended to hold. These latter buildings were greatly extended by the addition of enclosures for sacrifices, either in front of each temple or all around it; of porticoes, to accommodate the crowds attracted by that portion of the cult; and of peristyles, sometimes double, sometimes single, that were built around the *cella* for the ministers of the gods.

Despite all the new elements that entered into the composition of these great temples, such buildings were not so immense as is commonly supposed; nor did they exist in great numbers.

It will be seen, from the small size of the temples of antiquity in general, from the small number of elements of which they were composed, and from the simplicity with which those few elements were arranged, how strictly the ancients observed the laws of fitness and economy, even in those very buildings in which decoration would seem foreordained to play the greatest part. At the same time, it is well known how noble and stately those temples were. In some of them, the architectural decoration that resulted from their disposition was greatly reinforced by objects well suited to enhance their splendor. What could be more majestic than those sacred groves that shaded the forecourts of the temples of Jupiter and Juno, near Olympia, or that of the Temple of Aesculapius at Epidaurus, or that of Jupiter Olympius at Athens, and so on? What more magnificent than the host of altars, tripods, statues, chariots, and other votive monuments that filled those groves? What more apt to speak to the soul than the sublime paintings with which the walls of the temples and of their enclosures were sometimes covered, or the superb bas-reliefs that adorned their friezes and pediments? And what more stately than the figures of the gods raised on the rooftops of their respective temples?

And yet it will be seen that all these things, which contributed so much to the decoration, were not what is called *architecture*—that is, objects with neither use nor meaning—but the productions of Nature herself, or else the masterpieces of the fine arts; and what is more, they owed their presence to a sense of fitness. Most temples were devoid of all such ornaments; and even so, such was the effect created by their disposition that we are roused to the liveliest admiration at the mere sight of their ruins.

If decoration was of no concern in the buildings of which we have just spoken, it might be said that it was of even less concern in the temples of the early Christians, known as *basilicas* on account of their resemblance to the buildings of that name in which the ancients used to administer justice. The basilica of Saint John Lateran, the old basilica of Saint Peter on the Vatican, and that of Saint Paul on the road to Ostia, all founded by Constantine after the defeat of Maxentius, were constructed entirely from the debris of antique temples and other buildings. In their interiors there were hardly two columns that did not differ in material, in dimensions, or in proportions; to get the tops of the capitals on a level, sometimes the bases were omitted, and sometimes they were raised on plinths. The roof timbers—far from being covered by a magnificent ceiling, as they are at Saint Mary Major—remained visible. Even so, despite the bareness that prevailed in these buildings as a whole, and despite the lack of symmetry in their details, their interiors were no less noble and no less majestic than the exteriors of the antique temples. Why so? Because their disposition was no less simple, no less economical, and no less fit for its purpose.

Catholic worship, consisting as it does largely in numerous, frequent, and lengthy assemblies, called for a building with a spacious, well-enclosed, and well-lit interior; nothing could better fill these requirements than a basilica. The Church of Saint Paul outside the Walls; that of Saint Peter, which no longer exists, but which was precisely similar; and that of Saint John Lateran, which has been entirely disfigured in the attempt to modernize it, may give us an idea of the disposition and the effect of them all.

The width of the church is divided by four rows of columns, which support walls on which rest the roofs of the central nave and four side aisles; the nave is wider and taller than the aisles to either side, and these in turn are taller than the two outer aisles, which run along the exterior walls. This arrangement ensures that the nave and all the aisles are directly and perfectly lit by windows in the walls that form their upper parts.

Toward the end of the church, the nave and side aisles, which run from east to west, intersect a transverse nave, which runs from south to north; and in the side of this, facing back along the principal nave, there is an apse or large semicircular niche to contain the seats of the priests and the bishop. This basilica, like all the others, is fronted by a porch, to prepare the mind for the respect that must be shown on entering.

Such is the disposition of the basilica of Saint Paul; the view shown us by Piranesi adequately conveys the magnificence of its effect.

Those churches that are improperly called *Gothic* show no greater symmetry in their details than do the earliest Christian basilicas. Indeed, those details are even less calculated to please, in that they bear no resemblance to the antique details in which so much of the essence of architecture is commonly supposed to reside. What, therefore, is the source of those sublime and profound sensations that we feel in walking through temples of this kind? After what we have just said, surely no one will suppose that it lies in what is known as *decoration*.

It is, nevertheless, by decorating—that is to say, by piling up the useless upon the useless, the meaningless upon the meaningless, at enormous expense, and by sacrificing every requirement of fitness to decorative absurdity—that the moderns have presumed to excel the ancients in the composition of their temples. We shall see whether they have succeeded.

A porch is well known to be an essential part of a temple. Modern churches almost never have one. And yet, porchless though they may be, the portals of such churches seldom lack the columns with which porches might have been built. Instead of the four, six, or eight, at most, that would have been required for that useful feature, we often observe as many as twenty or thirty, crowded against the walls for the sole purpose of decorating them. If, however, we compare the facade of the smallest antique temple with the most celebrated of our modern portals, that of Saint Gervais, it is easy to see how the effect of the former is satisfying and noble, and that of the latter paltry and wearisome.

Since modern churches are designed for exactly the same purpose as the basilicas of the early Christians, all that was needed was to imitate their disposition; but when Bramante, who was a man of merit, came to compose the new Church of Saint Peter, the craving for novelty led him to imitate instead the composition of the Temple of Peace—although that building was not so much a temple as a treasury, built by Vespasian to house the spoils of Judaea. Later, the desire to surpass the ancients, by assembling in a single building the beauties of several, induced the same architect to crown his imitation of the Temple of Peace with a second edifice in imitation of the Pantheon.

To beautify their edifice to the ultimate degree, Bramante's successors covered its piers and walls with attached columns, pilasters, projecting entablatures, pediments of all kinds, and so on. Thus decorated, it became the model for the most considerable churches in Europe.

It is easy to see how much less fit for their purpose such buildings are than the basilicas. In the latter, walls and columns occupy only one-tenth of the total area; in modern churches, walls and supports occupy more than one-fifth. Given two churches of equal dimensions, the internal area of the one composed on the modern system is thus smaller than that of the other by one-ninth or more. In modern churches, the supports, although considerably fewer than the columns in the basilicas, occupy more space. Such churches therefore offer less freedom of movement.

By comparison, such churches are lacking not only in fitness but in solidity. The facts speak for themselves. The basilicas have stood since Constantine's day. Saint Peter's, built much later, would be a mere heap of ruins today, had it not been for the immense labor of repair that is continually in progress and the rings of iron that have had to be placed around the dome.[39]

Deficient in fitness and in solidity, such buildings are also far more costly. This is easily verified: they contain twice the mass of the basilicas, and for that reason alone must cost twice as much. If you then consider the horrendous expense involved in the construction of the domes, and in all those objects devoid of use or meaning, which are known by the name of *architecture,* and with which such buildings are filled, you may safely conclude that the total expense must be ten times greater.

What greater sacrifice could have been made in the cause of what is known as *architectural decoration?* And what does it gain? Let us not compare our churches, in point of beauty, with the temples of the ancients. Let us only compare them with the basilicas; or even, if you will, with those churches known as *Gothic.*[40] Does the sensation of entering a modern church even remotely resemble that which we feel in the latter?

How could it be otherwise? Of any two interiors of equal size, the one that presents more divisions will appear the larger; and the one that presents more objects at one glance will appear the more magnificent. The modern churches—whose naves present to the eye only a small number of dismal arcades and massive piers, while the basilicas and even the Gothic churches offer a host of convenient passages and elegant supports—are thus far less well suited than the latter to strike our souls with a powerful impression of magnificence and immensity.

As for their domes—those portions of our churches that only the eye can enter—these are buildings set upon buildings in the oddest and most precarious manner, since they rest on the nave arches at only four points, and for the rest of their circumference they are cantilevered throughout. If their object, as has been claimed, is to proclaim from afar the opulence and the magnificence of a city, they do so with very little success: for, at the sight of such costly and unnecessary constructions, any rational person will conclude that the city that contains them must be lacking in a host of essential buildings whose appearance would infallibly have contributed to its magnificence and its beauty.

We have seen that the ancients, the early Christians, and the more modern Christians who built the Gothic churches, did not chase after decoration, made no effort to please, and sought only to dispose their sacred buildings in the fittest and most economical way; and that these buildings produce the grandest effects: whereas the moderns, by contrast, have aimed only at decoration, to which they have sacrificed everything else, and that nevertheless the effect of their temples is nil, if not downright unpleasing. Are not these observations apt to convince anyone of the truth of the principles that we have set out and of the importance of their application from whatever point of view?

For buildings of this kind, see plates 1 to 15 of the *Recueil et parallèle*.

Palaces

A palace is a building designed, on the one hand, to accommodate a prince, and on the other, to receive those persons who come to seek a public or private audience with him. As such audiences cannot be granted to everybody at once, and as those who seek them deserve respect, it is necessary, aside from apartments for the prince and his family, and lodgings for his suite and other subordinates, to incorporate porticoes, vestibules, galleries, and halls, in which everyone may, at any season, wait in comfort and dignity to be summoned into the presence. Such are the principal requirements of a palace. It will be seen that magnificence must be a natural consequence of the disposition of such a building.

The palaces of the Escorial, of Versailles, of the Tuileries, and a number of others, are of vast extent; immense sums have been lavished on covering their exteriors with what is generally known by the name of *architecture*. According to the ideas commonly held on this subject, we should expect to find them beautiful in the extreme; however, nothing could appear more mean and trivial. The majority of palaces in Italy, on the contrary, are extremely small, are composed of far fewer objects, and so have cost infinitely less; and yet nothing could be more noble. Why should this be? Because in the former the disposition of the whole, and the requirements of fitness, were totally neglected for the sake of decoration, and in the latter fitness and disposition were, at least initially, the principal objects of consideration.

The limits of this précis do not permit a close and detailed examination of the palaces mentioned, for which we refer the reader to plates 43, 45, 46, 47, 53, and so on, up to 60 inclusive, of our *Recueil et parallèle*. Here we shall restrict ourselves to a few observations on the celebrated Palace of the Louvre. These will answer our main purpose in discussing this kind of building.

In a palace such as the Louvre, where the state apartments are on the second story, it was perhaps a requirement of fitness that this story should have—as indeed it has—a colonnade, from which a princely occupant might have enjoyed the festivities held in the square in front of the building. Now, since the Louvre is generally admired, by all those who consider architecture solely as the art of amusing the eyes, for the sake of the colonnade that appears on its facade, is it not clear that it would have earned twice the admiration if, beneath the existing colonnade, another colonnade had met the eye?

The buildings that surround the courtyard of the Louvre are one room deep. This is an inconvenient arrangement, because, in order to reach the rooms at the ends, one has to pass through all the others, or else constantly go up and down the stairs that obstruct communication within the apartments. If there had been a colonnade all around the courtyard, both on the first and second stories, as there is in most Italian palaces, would it not have eliminated all these inconveniences, and added considerably to the beauty of the decoration? Can anyone deny that real colonnades offer a more striking spectacle than the imperfect and confused images of colonnades that form the architectural decoration of the courtyard of the Louvre?

The colonnade of the Louvre is interrupted in the center by an immense frontispiece, the lower part of which incorporates the entrance to the palace: an entrance universally judged unworthy of such a building. If this unnecessary and inconvenient projection did not exist, and if the colonnade extended, as it naturally ought to do, from one end pavilion to the other, would not the colonnade make an infinitely more impressive effect? If, from the second colonnade that ought to have been placed on the lower floor, there had been access through five intercolumniations to a vast vestibule; if a matching row of intercolumniations had led from the vestibule to the porticoes of the courtyard; if grand staircases to right and left of the vestibule had led up to the principal floor: would not the entrance to the Louvre have possessed all the majesty that it now lacks?

Clearly, fitness would have made the building far more beautiful than it now is; no less clearly, economy, far from opposing such an effect, would have gone far to augment it. No calculations are needed to satisfy oneself that the expense of the frontispiece, the pediments, and countless unnecessary or contrived features abhorred alike by economy and by taste, would have been more than enough to build the essential features that the building lacks, and that would infallibly have given it all the beauty of which it was capable.

The design for a palace that will be found on plates 3 and 4 of the present work is assumed to be built in the countryside.[41] In such a case, the land available is not so restricted as it is in town, and it becomes possible, as it were, to spread oneself at will. We therefore thought best to give the palace one story only: partly in order to ensure that there should be no lodgings above the apartments of the prince and partly to make it easier, from all the apartments on the first story, to enjoy the promenades afforded by the gardens.

It will be observed that this building requires some rooms of considerable size, the height of which must in consequence be greater than that of a number of others, whose area is less; and that the differences in height naturally give rise to a certain movement in the elevation of the building. Again, since fitness demands colonnades in certain parts of the plan, and would condemn them in others, this distinction effortlessly supplies the elevations with projections, recessions, ornamental parts, and smooth parts, thus giving the building all the variety of which it is capable.

As for the general plan of our palace, our aim in giving it has merely been to show that, by bringing together buildings that bear a relation to each other, and by forming them into a whole, it is possible, without increasing the expense, to increase the magnificence of the scenes that architecture displays.

Public Treasuries

Buildings of this kind, designed, on the one hand, to house a great part of the wealth of a nation, and on the other, to distribute it through various channels, require a disposition that is, first, as secure as possible, and second, best suited to facilitate and distinguish its various operations. The design that we offer, plate 5, seemed to us to fill both these purposes perfectly. As for security, the treasury proper, placed at the center of the entire building, is doubly defended by the walls of the rooms that surround it. It is further defended by the enclosure walls, which have no windows and a small number of gates that may be made as stout as desired; guardrooms, both internal and external, are placed at all of the entrances. This disposition also promotes the ease and distinctness of the operations. From the treasury, the sums required for daily payments may easily be transferred to the counting houses at its corners; from the two vestibules that precede it, there is easy access to all four counting houses; from the rooms set aside for administration, placed to either side of the treasury and between the counting houses, the closest supervision may be maintained everywhere; and, finally, the offices to which those seeking payment must apply for the necessary documents, being relegated to the outer walls, are separated from the main building in which the treasury and the counting houses are situated. Consequently, no confusion or obstruction could arise in the working of the institution.

An inspection of the design will convey an idea of the effect that this building would produce.

Courthouses

Among the ancients, those buildings in which justice was administered were called *basilicas;* they consisted of a single vast hall, divided in various ways by rows of columns, as may be seen on plate 15 of the *Recueil et parallèle.* Among the moderns, the buildings known as courthouses are considerably larger. They must include several courtrooms; a large hall that serves as a lobby, and in which the attorneys and the litigants walk while discussing their business; chambers for the judges; clerks' offices; places of refreshment; guardrooms; and sometimes prisons.[42]

In such a building, where large numbers of persons always gather, the exits must be numerous and conspicuous. Moreover, the rooms set aside for the administration of justice must be so disposed that no extraneous noise can distract the litigants or the judges. In the design for a courthouse that we give as plate 6, all these requirements of fitness are perfectly fulfilled. At the same time, they are fulfilled in the simplest manner possible. And so, as will be seen, the architectural decoration has all the character, all the style, all the variety, and all the effect that this kind of building requires.

Justices of the Peace

A single courtroom, preceded by a lobby, accompanied by the justice's lodging and a number of subsidiary rooms, the whole surrounded by a little precinct to exclude the noise: this is all that a building of this kind requires. By its nature, such a building will clearly be far smaller than a courthouse; and yet it may be seen, even from the design that we offer on plate 7, that, being intended for an analogous purpose, it might, if treated in the same spirit, have quite as much dignity.

Town and City Halls

The size of these buildings varies in accordance with the size of the towns in which they are built. We offer as an example a town hall for a place of modest size, in order to show, as with the preceding design, that, although in architecture, as in everything, magnitude is one of the qualities that strike us the most forcibly, a building in which it must necessarily be absent may still be beautiful, providing that the requirements of fitness are fulfilled as they ought to be.

Aside from a hall for municipal assemblies, and a number of offices, a building of this kind, whatever its size, requires porticoes to accommodate those who have business there. These porticoes must also afford easy access to every part of the building. It will readily be seen that the design shown on plate 7 combines all these advantages, and that in execution, despite its small size, the building would present an imposing appearance.

The most celebrated city halls are those of Amsterdam, Antwerp, Maastricht, Oudenaarde, and Brussels. The first three are decorated with orders of architecture. The two others are Gothic; nevertheless, their aspect far more clearly proclaims a public building: which goes to confirm what we have said and proved more than once, that it is the disposition of the building, rather than its forms and proportions, that governs the beauty of its decorative effect.

These buildings may be seen on plate 17 of the *Recueil et parallèle*.

Colleges

These buildings, designed for the instruction of the young, were known to the Greeks as *gymnasiums*. Their gymnasiums were spacious buildings, each with its own gardens and consecrated grove. First one entered a square court, with porticoes and buildings all around. On three sides were spacious halls, furnished with seats, in which philosophers, rhetoricians, and so on, assembled their disciples. On the fourth side were rooms for baths and for other purposes. The portico exposed to the south was a double one, so that the winter winds would not drive the rain into its inner part.

From this square court one passed into others, lined with porticoes along their longer sides and shaded with plane trees. One of the porticoes was called the *xystus*. Along its center ran a sort of sunken path, about four meters wide by a little less than half a meter in depth. It was there, sheltered from the weather, and separated from the spectators who stood on the edge of the dip, that the young students exercised themselves in wrestling. The buildings also included a stadium for races.

It will readily be seen that the disposition of the gymnasiums was as commodious, as salubrious, and so on, as that of the Paris colleges is the very opposite. It will no less readily be imagined that the appearance of the former, with its nobility, its variety, and its pleasantness, was as apt to elevate the spirits of the young as the gloomy and repulsive aspect of the latter is calculated to do the opposite.

The same spirit that directed the Greeks in the composition of their gymnasiums may be found in that of the numerous colleges in the cities of Cambridge and Oxford. As well as spacious courts, rooms for various kinds of study, chapels, libraries, refectories, dormitories, and so on, there are theaters, porticoes giving shelter for the performance of various exercises, and gardens refreshed by fountains: in short, all that may tend to promote health and the development of all the faculties. And, in consequence, these buildings are generally admired, despite the Gothic style in which most of them are built.

Although considerably smaller than the colleges in England, and differing in several respects in their use, the Roman College, and that of the Sapienza, at Rome, the University of Turin, the Helvetic College in Milan, and a number of other colleges in Italy are deservedly no less celebrated; treated in accordance with the same principles, they necessarily convey the same sensations. The plans of several of these buildings will be found on plate 18 of the *Recueil et parallèle*.

In composing the design for a college that will be found on plate 8, we have tried to absorb the spirit of the ancients and to turn to good account all the interesting features offered by the modern buildings of this kind. We shall not discuss this design in any great detail but merely observe that the buildings intended for the exercises of the mind are ranged around the principal court and thus remote in every direction from the surrounding streets, so that they would invariably enjoy all the calm necessary for study; that, as the subsidiary courts are placed at the corners of the rear part, the work of the kitchens, refectories, and so on, would be done with the greatest ease and without causing the least obstruction or disturbance in the other parts; and, finally, that the view from the study court across the gardens, through the vestibules that would lead to them, would endow that court with an air of life and gaiety that is more necessary than might be supposed in places devoted to the labors of the mind.

Buildings for Assemblies of Scholars, Men of Letters, and Artists
In Greece, as in Rome, there were in general no places exclusively set aside for this purpose. Scholars and philosophers conversed either in public squares, or in the porticoes that surrounded them, or in the exedrae of the gymnasiums, of the palaestrae, or of the baths. In Athens, however, it seems that scholars of various kinds gathered by preference at the Academy, a place named for Academus, the Athenian citizen who had presented it to the philosophers as a place in which to assemble and confer. This was not a building, however: it was a wide, walled expanse of ground, with walks shaded by trees, and with streams that flowed in the shade past statues and altars of the gods.

In the beautiful climate of Greece, no place could have been better suited for such gatherings. But under the rainy skies of France there must be closed and covered buildings for meetings of scholars, or of men of letters, or of artists. These various classes were formerly separated under the name of academies. Now, for some years past, they have been united, to their mutual advantage, under the name of the institute. The building of which we give the design on plate 9 would be intended for an interesting union of this kind.[43]

An inspection of this magnificent plan will suffice to show how precisely and how simply all the requirements of fitness are satisfied, and the superb effect that would result from its execution. The institute is divided into three classes; one wing is assigned to each; each class is divided into several sections; and each wing contains a number of rooms, each with its separate entrance. As the various classes and sections need to communicate among themselves, and to congregate in the central hall on days of public assembly, there is an internal gallery to make this possible. Finally, the public requires access to the building on certain days; and a wing, similar in external appearance to the others, contains vestibules to afford a suitably dignified approach to the assembly hall that lies at the center.

Libraries
The names of the libraries of Jerusalem, Luxor, Alexandria, and so on, are all that remain to us of those magnificent buildings. We know only that above the door of the library set up by Ozymandias, king of Egypt, in the immense building that was to serve as his tomb, the following words were written: *The*

Soul's Remedy—a fine inscription, since repeated by Muratori in the library at Modena. Most of the libraries now extant were not originally built for the purpose, and have little to reveal to us about the composition of buildings of this kind. That of the Vatican, one of the most famous, has nothing remarkable to offer but the rows of Etruscan vases that adorn it. The Medici library in Florence, and that of Saint Mark in Venice, were indeed expressly built for the purpose, the former by Michelangelo and the latter by Sansovino; but they owe their fame largely to the names of their architects. Special mention is due to the Oxford library, which is circular in plan; and to that of Sainte-Geneviève in Paris, which is arranged in the form of a cross with a central dome and decorated—as, according to Pliny, were most of the ancient libraries—with busts of great men. But even these give no more than a very incomplete idea of this kind of building.

A library may be considered, on the one hand, as a public treasury enshrining that most precious of deposits, the knowledge of humanity, and on the other as a temple consecrated to study. Such a building must therefore be so disposed that the greatest security and the greatest calm may prevail. The design for a library on plate 10 has been composed accordingly.

An enclosure, at the corners of which are placed the librarians' lodgings, the guardrooms, and all those other parts where fires may be required, isolates the library proper from all other buildings. The construction, which is entirely in stone, completes its defense against the danger of fire. The general disposition shelters it from any external threat; the specific disposition of its reading rooms, all converging upon the position of the librarians at the center, would assure order and facilitate internal supervision. The lighting of the rooms from above, leaving the greatest possible surface for the bookshelves, would at the same time favor the necessary mental composure. Finally, the porticoes surrounding the principal portion of the building, and the trees that shade the outer court, would offer both shaded and unshaded walks in which to reflect or converse with pleasure and in tranquillity.[44]

Museums

In great cities, there may be several museums, some to hold the rarest productions of nature, others to contain the masterpieces of the arts. In lesser places, a single museum can serve these separate purposes simultaneously; and, for still greater economy, it might also incorporate the library. But whatever the extent of such buildings, whatever classes of objects they may be meant to hold, they are built to conserve and to impart a precious treasure, and they must therefore be composed in the same spirit as libraries. Our general remarks on the latter may thus be applied here also. The only difference that affects the disposition is that, since libraries hold only objects of a single kind and are designed throughout for a single use, they need no more than a single entrance; indeed, security requires it; but museums, even those exclusively designed to hold the productions of the arts, contain objects of different kinds and are made up of parts intended for different kinds of study. To maintain the calm that must prevail in all their parts, they must afford, aside from the principal entrance, as many separate entrances as they contain distinct departments. We shall perhaps be told that these multiple openings would impair security; but the design, plate 11, shows how, through common vestibules, each part would retain free access without any need for a large number of doors to the outside.

Observatories

These buildings, designed for astronomical observations, must be sited on an eminence and built to a considerable height to afford a wide horizon from the terraces that surmount them. On these terraces, in turn, a tower must stand to hold the astronomical instruments. The body of the building must enclose meeting rooms for the scholars, a library, a cabinet of physics, lodgings for the director, for the various scientists, and for the artificers attached to the establishment, another for the janitor, laboratories, workshops, stores, and so on. The Paris observatory, built by Perrault in the reign of Louis XIV, offers a fine model of the genre.[45] See the *Recueil et parallèle,* plate 18. An idea for an observatory will also be found in the present volume, plate 12; it will be seen that, in both, the construction itself is decoration enough.

Lighthouses

A lighthouse is simply a tall tower built by the sea. Lights are lit in the upper part to guide vessels at night. Such a building commonly stands on a platform on which are smaller buildings to house the keepers whose task it is to light and maintain the lights.

The most famous is that known as the *Cordouan Tower,* built at the mouth of the Gironde by Louis de Foix in 1584; see plate 25 of the *Recueil et parallèle.* This building is decorated with three or four orders of architecture. The design for a lighthouse that we give here, plate 12, offers nothing to the eye but the appearance of its construction. If these two buildings are compared, it will be seen that the latter has the character appropriate to this kind of building, whereas the other has none.

Market Halls and Marketplaces

Among the ancients, marketplaces were often identical with the public squares themselves, as with the Forum Boarium and the forums of Augustus, Trajan, Nerva, and so on. Sometimes they occupied only a part of the square; but in every case they afforded wide, airy spaces, planted with trees, surrounded by porticoes, and refreshed and cleansed by numerous fountains.

Nothing could be less like those ancient markets than those of modern times. Most are held in the streets, which they obstruct and foul. The vendors and their wares are exposed to the weather and mingled with carriages. Even those markets that are expressly built for the purpose are so mean, so ill situated, so difficult to access—in a word, so neglected—that in any city they are as much a blemish as the ancient markets were an ornament.

All modern markets do not deserve these reproaches, however. Some are exemplary in a number of respects: for example, the market halls of Amiens and Brussels; the fish market at Marseilles, a work of the celebrated Puget; the market of Florence; or that of Catania in Sicily: plans of all these will be found on plate 14 of the *Recueil et parallèle*.

Although the word *market* is used indiscriminately to denote those places where goods, and principally victuals, are sold, a distinction must be made here between two kinds of structure. Those markets intended for the sale of fish, vegetables, flowers, and all livestock—merchandise attended by some degree of odor—must be very well aired and therefore uncovered, at least in part. In all such cases, the markets must be open. Markets intended for the sale of grain, wine, cloth, and so on—articles liable to be damaged by air, sun, or rain—must be covered and enclosed.

The most celebrated covered market is the Halle au Blé (grain market) of Paris.[46] It deserves its fame in several respects; and it would deserve it even more, if there had been less pretension in it. This is apparent from a comparison between it and the design for a market hall that we give on plate 13, which is entirely free of pretension; this design shows a stairway leading from the lower part, intended for everyday sales, to the upper floors, where grain and flour is to be stored. This stairway is so designed that four persons at a time can ascend or descend without obstructing each other, thus avoiding all confusion and congestion.

Slaughterhouses

This kind of building, set aside for the sale of meat, was known to the Romans by the name of *macellum*. A medal struck by Nero and the plans found on the Capitol are the only documents that can give us an idea of the way in which these buildings were treated by the ancients; a faint idea, given the imperfect manner in which buildings are represented on medals and the present decayed state of the plans. Faint though it is, however, it suffices to convey the spirit in which the ancients composed such buildings. They certainly had no desire to make them ostentatious; and yet we find in their disposition the dignity that always ought to be present in buildings designed for public purposes. Colonnades and porticoes were included; for fitness required them.

An important feature that may be observed in the butcheries of the ancient world is that the slaughterhouses—instead of forming part of them, as they often do with us—were completely separate. In the design for a butchery on plate 14, this part is absent. Cleanliness, salubrity, and even the safety of the inhabitants absolutely require that such places be relegated to the remotest suburbs.

Bourses

These buildings, also known as *exchanges,* are places where merchants, brokers, and bankers assemble to trade in money and in public bonds. Among the ancients their purpose was served by the basilicas, which combined all their functions and united all that had to do with commerce and with men of business. Among the moderns, the bourse is sometimes an open square, surrounded with porticoes and planted with trees, like the London exchange designed by Inigo Jones, or that of Amsterdam, by Danckerts: structures that deserve examination for the simplicity of their plans and the fine decorative effect that results from this: see plate 18 of the *Recueil et parallèle*. Most often, exchanges are buildings with a first story made up of several porticoes, vestibules, guardrooms, halls, and offices, such as that which we offer, plate 14.

Customhouses

These buildings are set up to collect certain duties on the various goods that arrive in a country or in a city, and to hold some of these goods until the owner comes to collect them. On the first story, therefore, there must be guardrooms at the entrance, offices with a view of all that goes on in the courtyard, and sheds in which to examine the bales under cover. On the second story there must be rooms for the administration, a lodging for the custodian, and storerooms to hold those goods that require to remain in customs for any length of time. The safekeeping of such goods requires the building to be vaulted throughout. This form of construction, and the requirements of fitness, which would demand large openings on the first story and far smaller openings on the second story, would naturally create the decorative form of this kind of building: as may be seen on plate 14.

Fairgrounds

Fairs are a kind of market, to which, at certain times of year, merchants from out of town bring their goods free of duty. Merchants also attend from the city at or near to which the fair is held, to offer for sale articles of adornment and feminine dress. Among the crowds that gather in such places, there are many persons with money and leisure; and so these fairs naturally incorporate shows of all kinds, gaming houses, cafés, restaurateurs, and so on. They may therefore be regarded as places devoted equally to commerce and to pleasure.

It follows that an establishment of this kind must contain three distinct sections. First, places to sell in bulk such purely useful merchandise as livestock, leather, iron, wool, and so on; second, places to sell fancy items, such as trinkets, jewelry, goldsmith's work, fashionable dresses, and so on; and, finally, places of entertainment, such as pleasure gardens, theaters, billiard rooms, and so on. For the convenience of the merchants, who are mostly far from home, there should be lodgings for them above the booths; and, for the safety of their goods, all the covered portions of the building should be vaulted. Care should also be taken to incorporate in the design of fairground buildings—as in that of all markets—guardrooms and places where the magistrate in charge may officiate to settle any disputes that may arise. It need hardly be said that all the parts of the fairground left open should be planted with trees and adorned with fountains, and so on.

In the design for a fair that we give as plate 15, the circular form has been preferred as the most conducive to promenading of the kind favored in such buildings; the use of this form having no adverse effects in the present case because, the diameter of the circle being very large, and the divisions of the circumference very numerous, the booths formed by these divisions would not appear markedly irregular in shape, despite the convergence of their walls toward the center.

The bazaars, or covered streets, lined with shops and lit by magnificent domes, that are seen in great numbers in the cities of Turkey, of Persia, and throughout the Orient, may in more than one respect serve as a model for the composition of fairs. The plans of several of these bazaars will be found on plate 14 of the *Recueil et parallèle*.

Theaters

The Romans, who loved shows to the point of madness, had several kinds, including those of the theater, the circus, and the amphitheater. Their theatrical performances offered the twofold advantage of delighting both the mind and the senses, using pleasure as a means to convey the precepts of wisdom to the soul; such performances—which, far from deadening the sensibilities, carried them to an extreme—were such as to excite the liveliest interest. The performances in the circus, consisting of foot, horse, and chariot races, preceded by sacrifices, and heralded by pageants or processions in which appeared the images of the gods, choirs to sing their praises, spoils taken from the enemy, and finally the magistrates who were to preside at the games: these performances, too, were calculated to inspire the noblest and most cheerful ideas. As for the performances of the amphitheater, which consisted in fights between gladiators and wild beasts, they did no more credit to the humanity and sensibility of the Romans than did the horrid battles that were sometimes fought between galleys in the watery—and soon the bloody—arena of the naumachia.

Whatever the nature of the shows of antiquity, it remains true that the buildings in which they took place—being built for the entertainment of a great nation, and being solidly constructed and nobly disposed, as they ought to be—all inevitably possessed *character* in general; that every one of those buildings, designed for a particular kind of show, and having, as it ought to have, a particular form, naturally offered a different *character;* and finally that, all being disposed in the manner most fitting to the specific purpose for which they were built, it was impossible that even one of them should lack a *character* all its own. See plates 37, 39, 40, and 41 of the *Recueil et parallèle*.

Theatrical performances being the only kind of spectacle customary among modern nations, we shall say no more on the subject of amphitheaters, naumachiae, and circuses. We shall speak only of theaters, which are no less well attended among us than among the ancients.

Designed as they are solely for pleasure, such buildings must be so disposed that the expected pleasure is enjoyed to the full, with no trace of disturbance or disquiet. The theaters of the ancients fulfilled all of these conditions to perfection; an array of tiers, arranged in a semicircle and crowned by a superb colonnade, offered numerous seats from which all could see and hear equally well; facing them, an immense proscenium offered, by its great width, the scope to give the decorations all possible power of illusion, and the performances all imaginable splendor; vast and numerous stairways, placed beneath the tiers, with which they communicated by means of vomitoria, permitted an audience of thirty thousand—such as these theatrical spectacles often attracted—to depart, as it were, all at once. Finally, the construction of these buildings, which was in stone or even in marble, removed all fear of fire.

In ancient theaters, no effort was spared to combine all possible advantages; in modern theaters, it would seem that the aim has been to combine all the possible disadvantages. In most of them, a quarter or more of the spectators see nothing, or see very little; the space of the stage, or theater proper, although often deeper than it need be, is always so restricted in width that the decorator has no scope to give full rein to his genius or to confront the eye with the spectacle of immensity. Finally, these buildings, so constructed that a single spark would send them up in flames, nevertheless offer so few exits, and the stairs are so few, so narrow, and so difficult to find, that after the performance some time always passes before the crowds can disperse. What a danger such places are! And what pleasure can they possibly afford?

The disposition of the ancient theaters being as fitting and simple as that of our theaters is the opposite, it necessarily follows that the former had a character of majesty and grandeur that the latter entirely lack. They may be compared on plates 37 and 38 of the *Recueil et parallèle*.

The design for a theater on plate 16 differs essentially from the theaters of the ancients only in that, instead of being covered simply by an awning, as those were when they were not totally uncovered, it has an iron-framed roof: a form of covering that would by no means be impracticable, as our largest theaters never house even one-sixth of the audiences for which those of the ancients were built, and therefore need not have anything like the same size.[47]

Baths

The use of baths is as essential to health as it is to cleanliness; it is, besides, endlessly pleasurable. And so, private baths apart, most of the nations of antiquity, like all the modern nations of the East, possessed a host of public buildings designed for this purpose. In the city of Rome, alone, there were as many as eighty, some of which occupied an area of more than thirty acres. Apart from the hot baths, which gave these immense buildings their name of *thermae,* there were a host of rooms set aside for various bodily exercises, intellectual diversions, and popular amusements. Of all those magnificent buildings, the baths of Titus, of Diocletian, and of Caracalla are the only ones of which any vestige remains. In the *Recueil et parallèle,* from plate 30 to plate 36, may be seen the restorations that Palladio has given us. Alongside will be found those that we have made for our own purposes. A comparison will readily show that, if the Roman baths—composed as they were with great dignity and nobility—had been handled with greater simplicity throughout, they would have gained in magnificence.

The baths of which we give a design, plate 17, are supposed to be set in extensive gardens, beside a river. They are separated into two parts, one for men, the other for women. In each are open and covered baths, both public and private; in the center of the whole is an immense lake for boating, jousts, and fireworks. On all sides are cafés, restaurateurs, and so on.

Suppose these to be not ordinary baths but baths of mineral water: since those who resort to them, either for their health or for their pleasure, often come from far afield and intend to stay for some time, it would be necessary to incorporate in the general composition of such an establishment, besides the features relative to the baths, a temple, a theater, ballrooms, concert rooms, gaming rooms, kitchens, stables, carriage houses, and other subordinate offices.

Hospitals

These are of several kinds. Some are intended to house the poor, as at the General Hospital; or criminals, as at Bicêtre; or women of ill fame, foundlings, and lunatics, as at the Salpêtrière; others to receive the sick, of both sexes, as at the Hôtel-Dieu, the Charité, the Incurables, and so on. We shall concern ourselves only with the last-named category; and even here we shall not enter into all the details, which would demand a volume. We shall limit ourselves, as with the other kinds of building, to an indication of the principal requirements of fitness and of the spirit in which such buildings are to be composed.[48]

Of all buildings, hospitals are those that must be the most salubrious; and of all buildings, they are generally those that are the least salubrious. In most of them, all the wards, which meet either at the corners of a square or at the center of a cross, form hotbeds of infection, deadly not only to those who resort to such places to relieve their ills but to the inhabitants of the cities within which the hospitals are most unwisely built. Such is the neglect and barbarity with which these buildings are treated in all their other parts, and such is the dismal aspect of the whole, that even the poorest wretch will balk at being taken to a place that seems less a refuge than an abyss, opening its jaws to engulf suffering humanity. Almost the only hospitals to merit any praise are those of Milan in Italy and of Plymouth in England.

The Milan hospital, one of the most celebrated in Italy, was built with great magnificence at the expense of Cottoni, a rich citizen of the town. It affords the pleasing sight of spacious and numerous porticoes, supported by marble columns, which, by establishing communication between the separate parts of the building, ease and safeguard the care of the sick, and provide convalescent patients with commodious and pleasant walks, such as will hasten their complete recovery. We applaud the humanity that prompted the architect's genius in the arrangement of these several parts; but at the same time we regret that the wards are no better arranged than in most other hospitals from the essential aspect of salubrity.

Of all hospitals, that of Plymouth, built with equal care by Rovehead in 1756, is the best disposed. It offers fifteen pavilions, separated from each other, and linked at ground level by a colonnade that borders a square court. Of these fifteen pavilions, ten are for the patients, the five others for service. The disposition of this building is clearly far superior to that of the Milan hospital; but it is nevertheless far from perfect. Each pavilion contains a pair of intercommunicating rooms on each floor, and in consequence the air cannot circulate freely throughout.

The hospitals of La Roquette and Saint Anne, outside Paris, composed by Monsieur Poyet in accordance with the program laid down by the Academy of Sciences, were begun in 1788 and almost immediately abandoned. They would have been models of their kind, if only they had been completed. These hospitals combine all the advantages of those of Milan and of Plymouth, without any of the disadvantages. The conception will be found on plate 18. Every ward, whether for men, on one side, or for women, on the other, is allotted to a particular kind of disease. Each of these wards is ten meters wide by approximately nine meters high. Behind the beds, which are arranged in two rows in each ward, there is a corridor one meter wide, which serves to insulate them from the wall, to keep the service separate, and also to mask a privy, in the window recess corresponding to each bed, which would have been emptied unseen into the latrines at either end of each corridor.

Above these corridors, which are only a little more than two meters high, each wall has a row of windows that would light the rooms perfectly and renew the air readily. At appropriate distances, there are openings at the crown of the brick vault that spans the wards.

At one end of each ward are the stairs that lead up from the portico to the wards; at the other end are the service rooms.

Below the wards, on the vaulted first floor, would be kitchens, pantries, pharmacies, dispensaries, and other accessory offices such as baths, lodgings, and refectories for nurses, physicians, and surgeons, and so on. In the intervals between the various wings are gardens planted with trees. The laundries, vapor baths, oil store, candle manufactory, butcher's, bakehouses, woodsheds—in a word, all those places intended to hold a quantity of combustibles—are located far away from the wards, along the boundary walls of the hospitals.

Hospices disposed so perfectly, in keeping with the importance of their function, would leave no one in dread of having to turn to them for succor. Their appearance in itself—noble and pleasing, if not magnificent—would enhance the effect of the remedies dispensed there. On entering a building that expressed such respect for humanity, and for suffering humanity in particular, the weight of shame—often a more intolerable burden than misfortune itself—would be lifted from the patient's shoulders.

These last-named hospitals may be compared with those that we have cited on plates 29 and 30 of the *Recueil et parallèle*.

Prisons

In large cities, there ought to be special prisons for every class of inmate. Humanity, justice, and above all morality forbid that criminals should be held within the same walls as men imprisoned for debt or for some youthful indiscretion. Far from reforming the latter—which is the purpose for which they are detained—this would expose them to the near-certain danger of turning as wicked as the villains they would meet and of becoming more of a nuisance to society than before. In lesser cities, where there can often be only one prison, that prison must at least be so designed that different classes of prisoner do not communicate. In all cases, the women must be kept entirely separate from the men.

In any prison, all possible care must be taken to render the place salubrious. The loss of liberty, however brief, is affliction enough, without adding diseases and the death that they all too often bring in their train—especially since some who lose their liberty have done nothing to deserve it.

If the justice due to prisoners demands attention to these concerns, the interests of society absolutely require it. Who has not heard of the disease known as *jail fever* and of its fateful effects! The examples cited by John Howard are enough in themselves to make us tremble. All those present at the Assizes held at Oxford prison in 1577 were dead within forty hours. The same happened at Launton in 1730. Twenty-five years later, at Axminster, a small town in Devonshire, an acquitted prisoner infected his family and the whole town. In London, in 1750, three judges, the Lord Mayor, and countless other persons were stricken by this same disease and died.

In the design for a prison, which we give on plate 19, and which is supposed to be for a large city, the endeavor has been to unite a maximum of salubrity with a maximum of security.[49] Thanks to the enclosure wall that separates the prison from the neighboring houses, it would be surrounded by a considerable mass of air; the grounds would be extensive, planted with trees, refreshed by abundant springs; since no cell would be at ground level, which is entirely taken up with porticoes, all would be free of humidity. The infirmaries, located in pavilions taller than the rest of the building and open on every side, would cause no harm to the other parts. The prisoners, who would never congregate except in the yards or workshops at certain times of day, and who would be shut away for the rest of the time, each in a cell with its window facing onto the yard, could never conspire to escape; if any plot were nevertheless laid, it would inevitably fail, in view of the position of the four guardhouses placed at ground level, from which anything could be seen as it were at a glance, either outside or inside, either in the grounds or beneath the porticoes.

Barracks

This kind of building, intended to house the military, was known to the ancients by the name of *castrum,* that is to say, *camp.* The Romans built them in great numbers, both in Rome and in the various provinces subject to their rule; but of all those buildings, only one, the camp at Pompeii, buried beneath the ashes of Vesuvius in Titus's time, along with all the other buildings of that city and of Herculaneum, and discovered only at the end of the last century, is well enough preserved to give us some idea of their general arrangement.

The building was in the shape of an elongated square. The yard, or place of arms, was surrounded by a covered gallery supported by columns without bases. This gallery gave access to the rooms occupied by the soldiers, and simultaneously served as a walkway; beyond the far portion of it was a superb theater.

The very considerable remains of the same kind that are still to be seen at Baiae, and at the Villa of Hadrian (the ruins known as *The Hundred Chambers*), add nothing to the general idea of such buildings that emerges from the above description of the soldiers' camp of Pompeii; but the restoration of the Praetorian camp in Rome, given by Pirro Ligorio, may perhaps supply the deficiency. True, all that remains of that building is one corner of its enclosure wall. But it may well be that more existed in the lifetime of that author; and, steeped as he was in the study of antiquity, there was no need for the building to be very complete for him to form an accurate idea of it. What is more, there is such a resemblance between the arrangement of the principal parts of the Praetorian camp and of the camp at Pompeii, a building that Pirro Ligorio cannot have known and consequently cannot have imitated, that this in itself suffices to dispel any doubt as to the accuracy of his restoration.

The building, which is as extensive as that of Pompeii is small, is composed of two enclosures: one for the soldiers, the other for their officers. Along the front of the lodging chambers are galleries serving for communication and as promenades. Each enclosure offers two stories of chambers and galleries. At intervals, the outer enclosure is interrupted by square towers, higher than the wall, which contain stairs leading to the rooms and galleries on the upper floor and to the terraces on the roof, and a number of rooms that probably served as kitchens, latrines, and so on. Outside the second enclosure are exedrae: open or covered locations in which the old soldiers forgathered to mull over their battles and their victories. In the center of this second enclosure stands a magnificent temple dedicated to Augustus, in which the council assembled.

Whether this structure was truly arranged in this way, or differently, a knowledge of this fine restoration cannot fail to be of inestimable value for any study of architecture in general; in particular, it gives a far more exact and satisfying idea of a building designed to accommodate soldiers than anyone could ever gain from the largest and most celebrated of our own barracks, the Hôtel des Invalides. If we except the principal court, which is surrounded by fairly appropriate colonnades, this whole vast building has nothing to show, in place of the airy and spacious galleries of the Praetorian Camp, and even those of Pompeii, but narrow, endless corridors, each confined between two rows of rooms, lit only from the ends, and consequently dark, foul, incommodious, and even dangerous. What a difference between these two arrangements! What a difference, too, between the gloomy and oppressive aspect of the Hôtel des Invalides and the aspect of the ancient camp, so fitted by its nobility to elevate the soul and to sustain the courage of the warriors. See all these buildings, plates 26 and 27 of the *Recueil et parallèle*.

The barrack design on plate 20 was composed in Year VIII by an adjutant of military engineers in charge of quartering troops in Paris.[50] Being designed for cavalry, it is necessarily quite different in disposition from the ancient buildings mentioned above, which were intended for infantry. But it will readily be seen that these barracks are carried out in the same spirit. Although different, their appearance would be no less imposing, and no less noble.

It would always be desirable for barracks, prisons, and hospitals to be placed on the banks of a river, into which would discharge the drain collecting ordure from their several parts.

Section Three. Private Buildings

Private buildings differ from public buildings only as one public building differs from another: that is to say, by virtue of the uses to which they are put. In the composition of private buildings, architecture has the same aim as in that of public buildings: utility. Its means to that end are also the same: fitness and economy. All are formed of similar elements. All must consequently be treated in accordance with the same principles; and the mechanisms of composition must not differ. In the teaching of architecture, the topic of distribution is invariably distinguished, separated, even isolated from those of decoration and construction—a distinction that, as we have shown in our introduction, is hardly conducive to the education of good decorators, good "distributors," or good constructors, let alone good architects. Distribution is no more or less than the art of designing private buildings in the same way as public buildings: that is to say, with the greatest possible fitness and economy. Once imbued with the true principles of architecture and familiarized with the various combinations of the elements of buildings—in other words, with the mechanics of composition—the student who turns to private buildings need do no more than study the requirements of fitness. After a thorough study of architectural principles, the more applications one is able to make of them, the better those requirements will be satisfied. This exercise must be all the more heartily recommended because, although the requirements of private buildings intended as dwellings are more uniform than those of public buildings intended for differing uses, within every individual private building the requirements are far more varied, and the means of satisfying them usually more limited. We therefore think it necessary, not only to specify the general requirements of buildings of this kind but also to draw our students' attention for a moment to the principal categories of private building.

Private Town Houses

Most private houses built in towns present a number of compositional difficulties rarely encountered in country buildings of the same kind. The latter are generally built on more extensive and more open sites. Consequently, we are at liberty to isolate such buildings, to light them from every side, to separate subordinate structures from the principal block, and to arrange the whole in the simplest manner. In cities, on the other hand, private houses are generally built on restricted sites that are almost always confined between two party walls and often highly irregular. In such houses, nevertheless, the requirements of fitness, which differ little from those of country houses, must be equally well observed. It will be seen that, in order to overcome all these obstacles, no attempt should be made to arrange the whole of such a building in the way that is simplest in itself, and that all that should be done is to arrange it in the simplest way relative to the situation. Such new forms of disposition can vary endlessly; it will suffice to mention the most important.

General Dispositions of Town Houses

According to requirements, and to the dimensions of the site, a private town house may consist only of a single *corps de logis* (block), overlooking the street on one side and the inner court on the other; or of one block facing the street and another at the far end of the inner court. The composition may include one wing or sometimes two; finally, the court may be surrounded by buildings on all sides.

Instead of facing onto the street, the principal block may be built between court and garden: and this disposition, in turn, may be combined with any of those mentioned. Finally, a house may have only one court, if the site is small; or it may have two, if it is of moderate extent; or three or even more, if the site is large.

Divisions of Different Blocks

The depth of a block may be one room, one and a half, or two rooms. It is one room deep, if in its thickness it includes only a single room; one and a half rooms deep, when it contains one large and one small room; two rooms deep, when its thickness is made up of two large rooms; and finally three rooms deep, when it is made up of three. Principal blocks may be divided in any of these ways; wings, however, are seldom more than one or one and a half rooms deep, being almost invariably built against party walls, in which no windows can be made except those borrowed lights known as *customary lights,* and often not even those. For all this, see plate 21.

Apartments

A block may consist of a single apartment or several. An ordinary apartment, according to our customs, must contain five rooms at least: an antechamber serving as a dining room, a salon or parlor, a bedchamber, a cabinet, and a closet. There are some in which fitness demands a vestibule; several antechambers, some to hold servants, both those of the house and those from elsewhere, and others to receive persons who come to call on the master; a private dining room accompanied by a servery; a salon; a bedchamber; several cabinets, followed by a back cabinet and a muniment room; closets of ease and closets for linen and clothes; a dressing room, boudoir, and suite of rooms for the bath, often comprising a small antechamber, a bedroom, a vapor bath, and so on, as well as the bathroom itself. Finally, there are more considerable apartments still, which require, besides all the rooms of which we have just spoken, several salons, a gallery, a theater, a concert room, a ballroom, billiard and gaming rooms, and cabinets of natural history, of paintings, of antiques, and so on.

Such are the rooms that enter into the composition of apartments; and such, approximately, is the order in which they most usually succeed each other.

Any apartment must be free of access, that is to say, so arranged that, in order to leave it, either through the vestibule or through one of the antechambers, one is not compelled to retrace one's steps and pass again through most of the rooms that one has already traversed. The bedchambers, cabinets, and closets are the rooms that have most need of separate access. Mostly, the closets themselves serve this purpose.

When, on a single story, a block includes several interconnected apartments, such as those of husband and wife, the whole must be arranged so that the vestibule, antechambers, and even salon are common to both apartments.

When a block is made up of several stories, a staircase is necessary to pass from one to another. When not inside the vestibule itself, the staircase must face it or rise to the right of it. Place it on the left only when it is impossible to do otherwise.

The east is the best exposure for those rooms that are most constantly occupied. The north is the worst.

The Dependencies of Apartments

In private houses that can have no more than a single block, the servants are housed in the garrets, and the stables, carriage houses, kitchens, and pantries are on the first floor. Sometimes, indeed, the latter are housed on a basement floor, on a level with the cellars. In those houses where it is possible to build wings or other structures either facing the street or at the far end of the court, these various offices, or at least those that emit undesirable noises or smells, are housed there. Finally, in even more considerable houses, the kitchens and other offices are relegated to a yard of their own, and the stables and carriage houses to another, to keep the principal court always clean and free of obstruction.

At the entrance to the principal court, a lodging is set aside for the porter. The granaries for fodder, and the lodgings of coachmen, grooms, and so on, are placed above the stables and carriage houses; the cooks, pantrymen, and most of the other domestics are housed above the kitchens. As for the lady's maids and valets de chambre, they are lodged in entresols built in the main block above the closets and other small rooms.

The kitchens are commonly accompanied by a larder, laundry, wood store, and servants' hall, and sometimes by a roasting chamber, pastry kitchen, and so on. The best exposure for the kitchens is to the north.

The pantry must be accompanied by a room where desserts are prepared, a fruitery, and a number of other rooms for confectionery, silver, and porcelain. The pantries must have an easterly exposure.

The stables may be single or double. A single stable must be four meters wide; a double stable, a little more than seven; and if it is long, the width must not be less than nine or ten meters. The space occupied by each horse is approximately one meter and a quarter wide. The light in stables should fall on the hindquarters of the horses. Where this is absolutely impossible, the window sills must be at least three and one-third meters above the stable floor. In great houses there are several stables, some for carriage horses, others for saddle horses, for sick horses, and finally for the horses of visitors to the house. Whatever their use, stables must as far as possible have an easterly exposure.

Carriage houses, on the contrary, must face north. They may be single or double. The former must be three meters wide; the latter five and one-quarter. Where the shafts are not raised, carriage houses are seven meters deep, and where they are raised, five meters; all must be four meters high.

Stables and carriage houses must be accompanied by a harness room, a saddle room, and a manure yard leading straight to the street. Finally, latrines for the servants.

We shall say no more concerning private town houses. Plates 22, 23, 24, 27, and 28,[51] which show a considerable number of such houses, arranged in differing ways, are better suited to familiarize students with this kind of building than anything that we could add.

Irregular Plots
Often the plots on which private houses are to be built in towns are irregular. Irregularity in the component parts of a house would not only be offensive to the eye but highly inconvenient for use. To avoid such inconvenience, build as many parts as the site permits in a regular form, and correct the irregularity of the rest either by using canted corners or by making them circular in plan. See plate 25.

Tenements
Tenement houses are intended to accommodate several individuals or several families. A landlord, who often has a private house of his own, builds such houses only in order to derive revenue from them. In order to maintain this revenue, as far as possible, at all times and in all circumstances, such houses must be so arranged that all the rooms in each of the apartments that they contain may be let either together or separately, as desired. The two designs on plate 25, and the second on plate 26, offer this advantage; the design next to the latter does not.

Country Houses
If happiness is anywhere to be found, it is surely in a country house, agreeably sited, far from the cares of business, the tumult of the cities, and the vices of overpopulous communities. In such peaceable dwellings the sweetest repose may be enjoyed, and the joys of study savored without distraction; there, the

delights of friendship are unconstrained; the soul is exalted by the magnificent spectacle of nature.

The Greeks and the Romans, keenly though they craved and appreciated all enjoyments, and great though their passion was for spectacles of every kind, preferred the simple pastimes of the countryside to the most gorgeous shows and brilliant festivities of their capital cities. Accordingly, their country houses were as spacious and elaborate as their town houses were modest and restrained. That of Herodes Atticus, on Mount Pentelicus, from the brow of which streams rushed down to wind their way through forests before losing themselves in the river Cephisus; the Arpinas of Cicero, built where the river Tiber forms a little island, and commanding a view of the loveliest natural cascades; or his Tusculanum, formerly the house of Sulla, adorned with portraits of a multitude of great men and with the rarest masterpieces of Greek sculpture; the Hadrian's Villa at Tivoli, in which he built full-sized copies of all the buildings he had seen on his travels: all these were places of enchantment. Some have entirely disappeared; others are no more than a few piles of ruins. The descriptions that Pliny has left us of his Laurentinum, and of his house in Tuscany, are the only remaining monuments that can convey to us something of the spirit in which the country houses of the ancients were composed.[52] But these rich vestiges are well suited to guide us in the composition of our own.

Pliny to Apollinaris

Nothing could be more beautiful than the landscape in which it is set. Picture an immense amphitheater, such as the hand of Nature alone could form. A wide and extensive plain is surrounded by mountains, their summits crowned with lofty and ancient forests that abound in game of more than one kind. The second region is one of coppiced woodland, extending over the flank of the mountain, and interspersed with hills whose rich soil is the equal of the most fertile plains. The harvests there, though late, are none the less golden, nor less abundant. Lower down, and in every direction, vineyards extend along the slopes into the far distance, bounded on the downhill side by bushes. Cultivated fields and pastures stretch to the horizon.

The meadows are carpeted with flowers, teeming with clover and other herbs, always fresh and always reborn. Unfailing streams maintain a perpetual abundance. These great quantities of water nevertheless create no swamps, thanks to the lie of the land, which discharges into the Tiber all the water that it does not absorb.

The view over the whole country from the mountain top would delight you. The variety of views, the diversity of the locations on every side, so charm the eye as to suggest not natural landscapes but paintings in which all has been deliberately composed for the delight of the beholder.

Although my house stands at the foot of the hill, it enjoys this beautiful view as if it stood on its brow. It is reached by a slope so gentle and imperceptible that one finds oneself high up without ever being aware of climbing. The Apennines are behind it, in the far distance. Even on the finest days, the prevailing winds blow from the mountains, but so tamed and spent by distance that there is nothing rough or impetuous in them. Its principal exposure is to the south. In summer toward the middle of the day, and in winter a little earlier, it seems to play host to the sun, which it receives into a wide and proportionately long portico.

My house is composed of many blocks; I even have an atrium, or vestibule, in the manner of the ancients. In front of the portico is a parterre, intersected by several walks and box hedges. It ends in a gentle rise, on which the box trees are clipped into a number of animal shapes. All around is a walk, bordered with a green hedge. From there one passes to a shaded promenade, laid out in the form of a circus. Then follows the lawn, as beautiful by nature as the rest is by art; then the fields, the orchards, and the adjacent pastures.

To return to the main block: the end of the portico leads to a banqueting chamber; its doors face one way, affording a view over the further part of the parterres, and its windows face the other, across the pastures and cultivated fields. The windows also reveal the edge of the parterre and the tops of the trees that surround the hippodrome. Near the middle of the portico is an apartment built around a small courtyard shaded by four plane trees, in the center of which is a marble pool with fountains that maintain, like a gentle dew, the freshness and greenness of the grass and trees on which they fall. This apartment is made up of a bedchamber, sheltered from the light and insulated from all noise; a salon for friends, which is in daily use; a portico that opens onto the little courtyard, with the same view as the foregoing; and another bedchamber that enjoys the shade and the greenery of one of the plane trees. This room is finished with marble to elbow height. The rest of the walls are adorned with paintings, no less beautiful than the marble, of foliage in which birds of every color disport themselves. Below is a pool, into which water falls from a basin around which a number of jets commingle to create a pleasant murmur.

From one corner of the portico, one passes into a large room that faces the dining room; it overlooks the parterre on one side and the pastures on the other. Its windows immediately overlook a canal into which a cascade falls amid clouds of foam, its whiteness merging with the brilliance of the marble that receives it, a delight to eye and ear.

The room of which I have just spoken is excellent in winter, because the sunlight pours into it from every side. If the sky is overcast, the fire is lit in the adjoining baths, and its influence replaces that of the sun.

Then comes the disrobing chamber for the baths. It gives access to the cold room, where there is a huge bath of black marble. In the center, a pool is hollowed out, and into this, if one wishes, one may step down to bathe in greater warmth and comfort. Next to the cold room is the warm room, which is greatly heated by the sun, though less so than the hot room, which is very prominently placed. Above the disrobing chamber is the ball court, where one may take various kinds of exercise. Near the bath is a stair that leads to the underground gallery, by way of three cabinets, of which the first has a view over the plane-tree court, the second takes its light from the lawn side, and the third overlooks the vineyards. At the end of the gallery is a bedchamber that affords a view over the hippodrome, the vineyards, and the mountains. It is adjoined by another room, which is very much exposed to the sun, especially in winter. At this point begins an apartment that connects the hippodrome to the rest of the house. Such is the facade and its aspect.

On one flank, facing south, is a lofty gallery from which the vineyards seem so close that one might almost touch them. Toward its center is a banqueting chamber that receives the wholesome breeze from the Apennines. It looks out over the vineyards in two directions, from its windows on one side and from its doors on the other. But across the gallery, on the side that has no windows, there is a service stair that is highly convenient for attendance at table. At the end is a chamber that commands, thanks to the gallery, a view as pleasant as that of the vineyards. Under the gallery already mentioned, you will find another, below ground, which is like a veritable grotto. Air from outside cannot reach it or affect its temperature. After these galleries, and starting at the end of the banqueting chamber, there begins a portico where the sun shines until noon, thus making winter mornings as agreeable as summer evenings. This leads to two small apartments, consisting of three and four rooms, respectively, which receive sun and shade by turns as the sun travels round.

From this charming facade there is a distant view of the hippodrome. It is open in the center, and the eye on entering at once discovers its full extent. It is bounded by plane trees, entwined with ivy and interspersed with laurel. The hippodrome is straight, but at either end it curves round in a semicircle. Shrubs cut to the shape of turning posts alternate with fruit trees all along the straights. The regular planting is thus interspersed with trees that seem to grow naturally and at random; their happy negligence corrects the monotony of art.

At the end, a trellis supported by four columns of Carystian marble shades a rustic banqueting chamber with white marble tables and couches. From beneath the couches, water issues in a number of jets, as if pressed out by the weight of the guests; it is received in a polished marble basin, which it fills without ever over-flowing, by means of an unseen outlet pipe. When a dinner is held here, the more substantial dishes and the main course are ranged along the edges of the pool. The lighter delicacies are served on the water, where they float on dishes shaped like boats or birds. Opposite, a fountain springs, constantly receiving and returning the same water. After rising, the water falls back upon itself, and, on reaching the out-lets pierced for the purpose, it pours down, only to rise again into the air. The rus-tic salon and the room of which I have just spoken are opposite to each other, and each is an adornment to the outlook from the other. The latter room is very beauti-ful and is resplendent with the finest marbles. The doors and windows all around are crowned with greenery. Adjacent is another small apartment that seems to insert itself into that same room, and nevertheless forms a part of it: and here there is a bed. Although there are several windows, the light is moderated, and almost obscured, by the dense foliage of a vine that climbs the outside wall as high as the roof. You might imagine yourself reclining in the shade of a grove, with the addi-tional advantage of shelter from the rain. This room also has its fountain, whose waters vanish at their source; and here, as in the preceding room, marble seats are an invitation to rest after a walk. Close to each seat is a little basin. All along the hippodrome you will find streams whose water, obedient to the hand of art, winds murmuring through its channels and serves to maintain the greenery by irrigation, either on one side, or on the other, or everywhere at once.

Pliny to Gallus

My house is spacious and commodious, without being too costly to maintain. First one comes to a vestibule and atrium, which is neither sumptuous nor too simple; then a courtyard, small but charming, adorned with circular porticoes. This gives excellent shelter from bad weather; you are protected by glazed windows, and also by the overhanging eaves. From the center of these porticoes you pass into a large and cheerful courtyard, and on into a beautiful banqueting chamber overlooking the sea, whose waves gently lap the foot of the wall. On every side, this room is pierced with doors, and with windows equal in size to doors; so that, looking ahead and to either side, one might be looking out upon three different seas. To the front is the great court, then the small court with its porticoes, then the porticoes of the atrium, and the forests and mountains in the distance. To the left of this room, and set back a little, is a large chamber, followed by another similar one, with openings on both sides to receive the first and last glimpses of the sun. This room, too, enjoys a view of the sea: less close, admittedly, but calmer. This chamber and the dining room form an angle in which the sunlight is concentrated and its heat redoubled.

This spot is much frequented in winter by the members of my household, who turn it into a gymnasium. The place of exercise knows no breath of wind, beyond those breezes that fleetingly cloud the sky but do nothing to disturb its tranquillity. Bookcases, built into the thickness of the walls, contain a choice collection of my favorite books. From there, you pass to a number of bedchambers, along a corridor with a suspended flagstone floor. Through the underground passage below, the fire that is maintained there circulates and communicates a temperate heat to every part. The rest of the chambers in this wing are for the use of freedmen and slaves; and most are presentable enough to serve as guest rooms for my friends.

The other wing is composed of one very fine chamber, and of a second that can be used as a moderately sized reception room. The latter is brilliantly lit by the rays of the sun and the reflection from the sea. There follows an antechamber that gives access to a large and lofty room, well sealed, sheltered, and as cool in summer as it is warm in winter. From here you pass to the cold bath. This is a large and spacious room. On either side, and facing each other, are two large, circular pools where one may swim, if desired, without going any further. Close by are the sweating room, [the room] in which to perfume oneself, and the warm room. There follow two other rooms, elegant rather than rich, and adjacent to them [the vapor bath].[53] The warm room is so well sited that one can swim in it and see the sea. Close to it is the ball court, exposed to the full heat of the setting sun. At one side rises a tower, which contains two cabinets on the first floor, two similar ones on the floor above, and above those a reception room from which can be seen the vast expanse of the sea on one side and on the other the whole length of the coast and the charming houses that adorn it. Another, similar tower contains a chamber with openings to east and west, and above it an ample storehouse and a granary that occupy the space above a large banqueting chamber, where the sound of a rough sea can be heard, but attenuated by distance.

This room has a view over the gardens and the rides all around. The rides are bordered with box and rosemary. A young vine arbor shades the part between the rides and the orchard. A salon enjoys this view, which is little less delightful than that of the sea, from which it is remote. Behind this room are two pavilions whose windows overlook the vestibule of the house and the kitchen garden. On this side is the *cryptoporticus* or subterranean gallery, a work that has all the beauty and magnificence of public buildings. It is pierced with windows on both sides, but more toward the sea than toward the garden. When the weather is calm and serene, all of them are opened. If there is a wind from one side, the windows on the other are opened. A fragrant bed of violets fronts this gallery, which traps, reflects, and intensifies the heat of the sun, while sheltering the flowers from northerly winds. The gallery is thus as warm in front as it is cool behind. It breaks the force of the wind from Africa, so that on every side it offers shelter from a different wind. Such is the pleasure that it affords in winter; but in summer the pleasure is even greater. Until noon it shades the parterre, and in the afternoon the rides and other parts of the garden that lead to it; the shadow can be seen to grow and shrink as the days lengthen and shorten. However, the gallery never receives the heat of the sun when it is at its greatest, that is to say, when it is directly above the roof. Then the windows are opened and receive on every side the breath of zephyrs that renew the air and stir pleasantly to keep it healthful.

At the end of the parterre and of the gallery is the garden pavilion; this is a small detached building in which I take great delight. There is one room that the sun from every side turns into a stove; it overlooks the parterre on one side and the sea on the other. Its entrance leads to a neighboring bedchamber, and one of its windows opens into the gallery.[54] A private cabinet, elegantly adorned, adjoins this room on the side near the sea, in such a way that, by means of glazed doors and curtains that can be drawn back, sometimes the cabinet forms part of the room and sometimes it is closed off. There is space for a couch and two chairs. From the side where the couch stands against the wall, there is a view of the houses along the coast. At the foot of the couch you see the sea, and at the head you see the neighboring forests. There are as many views as there are windows, and they may be combined and divided at will.

From there you pass into the night chamber, which is dedicated to sleep. Nothing could be more tranquil than this room. The voices of slaves can never reach it. There, neither the roar of the sea, nor the whistling of the winds, nor the din of thunderstorms can be heard. Neither the lightning flash nor the light of day can ever enter, unless the windows are opened. The source of this profound tranquillity is that between the wall of this chamber and that of the garden are the men's quarters,[55] with a large courtyard that dissipates all the noise from outside. Beneath this room I have installed a tiny stove room, which communicates as much heat as is desired through a small opening. Finally, there is an antechamber and another chamber, both well exposed to the sun, which they receive—albeit obliquely—from dawn to noon.

When I withdraw to the place that I have just described to you, I imagine myself a hundred leagues away from my home. I take particular pleasure in it at the season of Saturnalia. While the whole house resounds to the sound of merrymaking and to the joyous cries that license elicits from my servants, there I withdraw to savor the delights of study, without disturbing their enjoyment, and without being disturbed by them....

On plate 44 of the *Recueil et parallèle* will be found a plan of the Laurentinum by Scamozzi. On that same plate, and on plates 43, 45, and 46 of the same work, will be found an assortment of plans of Greek and Roman houses. The differences that are apparent, even between those that ought to be the most similar, do nothing to predispose us in favor of their accuracy. At all events, the talents of the architects to whom we are indebted for these plans, and the simplicity that reigns therein—a simplicity to be pursued by every imaginable means—are reason enough to study them. As for the country houses of modern Italy, and the delightful gardens that accompany them, the plans of which will be found on plate 52 (*bis*) of the *Recueil et parallèle,* a glance at them will show that they stand in no need of recommendation.

As for the designs for country houses that we give in this volume, on plates 27, 29, 30, and 31, our principal aim in providing them has been to show in how many different ways private houses may be disposed, according to circumstance, without doing violence to our customs.

Farmhouses or Rustic Houses

The cultivation of the soil calls for buildings to accommodate the farmer, his family, and various animals; to keep the implements of agriculture and the various produce of the soil and of the livestock; and so on.

Nothing could be less commodious or less salubrious than the majority of our farmhouses. They present nothing but an accumulation of buildings, scattered dunghills, and foul ponds. Accordingly, such places are often sources of spreading infections.

The size and disposition of any farmhouse must be in keeping with the climate, with the extent of the land, and with the nature of its produce. These vary so widely that we must limit ourselves to some general ideas.

The best situation for a farmhouse would be slightly elevated, without any stagnant water, untroubled by the fear of flood, and free of habitual fogs, and so on.

To avoid the danger of fire as much as possible, the residence of the farmer or yeoman should be kept separate from all the other buildings; and these should themselves be detached from each other. To facilitate supervision, the whole ought to be so arranged that every one of the rooms in the principal building commands a view over all the subordinate buildings. Those that serve related purposes should be close to each other, and those whose uses are essentially different should be separated. Ponds and dunghills, which commonly obstruct and befoul the yards in which they are placed, ought to be placed in a special enclosure sited to the north of the farmyard. All those buildings intended to house animals ought to be so placed as to have direct access to this dung enclosure. See plate 32.

If farmhouses—those peaceable dwellings, where the most interesting concerns and the sweetest occupations are conducted in the bosom of Nature—were only sited and arranged as they ought to be, what a delight they would be to look upon! Given the unpardonable negligence with which most farmhouses have been treated, only an absurd extreme of elaboration could ever deprive us of that pleasure. Neither one extreme nor the other is to be found in the houses of this kind built by Palladio on the charming banks of the Brenta, near Vicenza, or yet in a host of buildings designed for the same purpose, in every part of Italy, under the name of *fabricche*. With their simple and pleasing forms, all are a delight to the eye. See plates 49, 50, and 51 of the *Recueil et parallèle,* and plates 5, 6, 8, and 19 of part II of the present work.

Inns
Such places, built to accommodate travelers, are nothing more, in most parts of Europe, than private buildings that mostly offer no more order, convenience, or cleanliness than do the majority of our farmhouses. In the Orient, on the other hand, those same places, known as *caravansaries,* are public buildings, set up and maintained with the greatest care by the government. Simple in their disposition, as will be seen from plate 30 of the *Recueil et parallèle,* these buildings are universally reputed by travelers to be as splendid in appearance as our own inns are notoriously ignoble and repellent. And yet nothing would be easier than to make them agreeable. They have only to be designed with the fitness and the simplicity that they demand. See only the sketch that we give, plate 32.

The Procedure to Be Followed in the Composition of Any Project
The foregoing comparative examination of a considerable number of buildings, both ancient and modern, together with more than fifty designs (all simple in the extreme, and yet all quite different), should have conveyed an adequate idea of the requirements of fitness, as they affect the principal kinds of building, and should have cast light on the principles that govern the treatment of all buildings. To accomplish the purpose that we set ourselves here in part II, it remains only to recall to students the procedure that is to be followed in the composition of any design whatever.

To combine the different elements, then to proceed to the different parts of buildings, and from those parts to the whole: such is the natural sequence that should be observed in learning to compose. By contrast, when you come to compose for yourself, you must begin with the whole, proceed to the parts, and finish with the details.

Above all, make sure that you understand the use and the requirements of the building that you have to design; steep yourself in the spirit in which it must be conceived; examine which, of the various qualities that may appear in a design, deserve most particular attention: whether it be solidity, as in light-houses; salubrity, as in hospitals; commodity, as in private houses; security, as in prisons; cleanliness, as in meat and other markets; calm and tranquillity, as in places set apart for study; cheerfulness and gaiety, as in those set apart for pleasure; and so on. After this, consider whether the building is to present, in plan, a single mass; whether this mass is to be solid or pierced by one or several courtyards; whether the different blocks are to be contiguous or separate; whether the building is to front the street or be separated from it by an enclosure wall; if all the blocks are to have the same number of stories or not; and so on.

Passing from the whole to the individual parts, consider which rooms are principal and which are subordinate; which rooms must be adjacent to or remote from certain other rooms: and establish their position and size in consequence. Then see whether the rooms are to be covered by a ceiling or a vault; what kind of vault is to be chosen; whether the span of the ceilings or vaults needs to be reduced by the use of columns; and so on.

Once these observations are made, and a croquis drawn accordingly, the number of interaxes in each room must be determined and noted in figures on the sketch; add all the interaxes together to find the number of divisions into which the site is to be divided. This total number once found, look to see whether each of these interaxes is not too wide or too narrow, relative to the scale; and, if this is so, reduce or increase the number of interaxes, whether in all of the parts or only in some of them.

The greater or lesser number of interaxes in each room determines the order to be employed there; examine whether the center of the vaults should be level with the top of the architrave, or higher, and so on.

A sketch once made in this way, there remain to be determined in the finished or working drawing only the various profiles, and the painted or sculptured ornaments, that you see fit to employ.

It is easy to see with what facility and with what success any building might be composed, if the architect, imbued with principles derived from nature, would only follow the course indicated by reason, both in studying the art and in composing buildings — for both these are neither more or less than an uninterrupted succession of observations and reasonings.

Graphic Portion of the Lectures on Architecture

How to Acquire in a Short Time True Architectural Talents

Architecture is both a science and an art. As a science, it demands knowledge; as an art, it requires talent. To become perfectly acquainted with a science, it is enough to listen, to understand, and to remember; but to possess an art, what is known must be applied; and the degree of talent, or the greater or lesser facility in applying one's knowledge, depends on the number of applications that one has already made.

Formerly at the École Polytechnique, the graphic work required of students of architecture amounted to four drawings, which had as their subjects: (1) the orders; (2) doors and windows; (3) a room; and, finally, (4) a staircase. Such work, which offered to their minds so limited a range of ideas, and uninteresting ideas at that, entirely occupied the little time that they were given in the course of a year for the purpose of preparing themselves for the competitions; it was far better suited, by the fatigue and ennui that it visited upon them, to turn them against architecture altogether than to cause them to acquire any talents in that direction.

This is not to deny that there always were some students who left the École with promising talents; but it is clear that this advantage sprang solely from the excess of zeal that led them to devote their time, with the future in mind, to the little that circumstances permitted us to show them of the art of composition.

Since the reorganization,[56] a decision of the governing council of the École has abolished the requirement of making these four drawings and replaced it with that of making a drawn record, in the classroom, of all the lectures given in the amphitheater. The four drawings were thus replaced by a fairly large number of sketches relative to the mechanism of composition; and the progress made by architecture in the École in every successive year demonstrates the advantage that the students have derived from this new form of working.

This happy change in the graphic portion of the course has necessarily led to another change in the oral portion. Obliged to make the lectures conform with this novel mode of working, we have omitted from them all that did not lead us directly and promptly to composition, and we have compressed all related matters in order to leave all possible scope for the work of drawing.

For the rest, we have remained faithful to our principles, and have extended our manner of teaching to the graphic portion of the course. Just as in the oral portion we have proceeded by breaking down the general idea of architecture into special ideas, and those into particular ideas, in the graphic portion we have broken down the general ideas of buildings into those of their parts, and these in turn into those of their primary elements; then, by working back from the elements to the ensemble of the buildings—that is to say, by analyzing them—we have succeeded in forming a precise idea of them, just as we had first succeeded in forming a precise idea of architecture itself by analyzing the general idea expressed by that word.

Although our ideas on architecture have not changed, and although we expounded them in the first volume of our précis, we cannot forbear to recapitulate them here in summary form, since the graphic portion not only connects with them but necessarily derives from them; it could have had no other principle.

Summary of the Oral Portion
of the Lectures

Lecture One. General Ideas

For any art to be practiced with success, it must be practiced with relish, with love; and this presupposes some notion of what it is. You cannot love what you do not know, as a poet said. It is necessary to know why it is practiced, and how in general it should be practiced: to know, in other words, the end that it sets itself and the means that it employs to that end.

Of all the arts, architecture is the one whose productions are the most costly; at the same time, however, it is the art that is most constantly and generally practiced. It follows that this must be an art of great usefulness to man, a creature who is as averse to all exertion as he is studious of his own well-being. It is to architecture that man owes his survival, society its existence, and the arts their birth and development. In a word, utility—and the greatest utility possible, both public and private—is the sole purpose of architecture.

Architecture is made for man and by man. By his very nature, when he erects buildings, he must seek to enjoy all the consequent advantages at the least possible cost in exertion and expense, and thus to arrange them in the fittest and most economical way. Fitness and economy: such are the means that architecture must naturally employ.

For a building to be fit for use, it must be stable, salubrious, and commodious.

To make it stable, the materials must be distributed intelligently; the principal supports must be equally spaced, so that each may support an equal portion of the load; and the closest bond must exist between all the parts.

To make it salubrious, the foundations must stand above the ground; and, where openings are made in the walls that have been built to protect the interior from heat and cold, they must be so placed as to allow free passage to air and light.

To make it commodious, the number, the size, and the respective positions of all its parts must relate closely to its purpose.

So much for fitness; now for economy.

For a building to be as economical as possible, it must be made as symmetrical, as regular, and as simple as possible.

The architect's sole concern must therefore be to dispose his buildings as fitly and economically as possible. All his talent consists in resolving two problems: (1) in the case of private buildings, where cost is a given requirement, to make the building as fit as possible for its purpose; and (2) in the case of public buildings, where fitness is a given requirement, to make the building as inexpensive as possible.

When the composition of a building incorporates all that is necessary and nothing but what is necessary, and when those necessities are disposed in the simplest arrangement, it is impossible for it to lack the kind and degree of beauty that it requires. The architect, therefore, will never concern himself with so-called architectural ornament, which, serving no purpose and resembling nothing, entails an expense as huge as it is absurd; and if he desires to add to the natural beauty of a building that is fitly and simply arranged, this will be done only by means of accessory decoration, which is none other than the employment of the productions of the other arts.

The Way to Represent One's Ideas in Architecture to Oneself and to Communicate Them to Others

Drawing is the promptest and most accurate means that can be used. There are three kinds: (1) croquis; (2) sketches; (3) working drawings. Whatever kind of drawing is used, three figures must be drawn in order to give a complete idea of a building: (1) the plan, which represents its horizontal arrangement; (2) the section, which conveys its vertical arrangement or its construction; (3) and, finally, the elevation, that is to say the exterior, which is not and cannot be anything other than the outcome of the other two.

If these three figures can be drawn one above the other on a single sheet of paper, much time will be gained, as all the vertical lines are common to all and may be ruled at the same time. At all events, begin by drawing a line in the center of the paper; intersect it at right angles with another; on either side, parallel to those two principal axes, draw the axial lines of the walls, with half the thickness of the wall on either side; similarly, half of each opening will be on either side of its axial line.

This refers only to finished drawings and sketches; croquis are done entirely freehand, without a rule or a compass, and without any recourse to axial lines, unless they serve as signs to mark the position of the walls.

Lecture Two. The Elements of a Building

Any building as a whole is not and cannot be other than the result of the assembly and combination of a greater or lesser number of parts. One can assemble, or combine, only what one has to hand. In order to compose an architectural ensemble, of whatever kind, it is necessary, first and foremost, to become perfectly acquainted with all the parts that may enter into the composition of all buildings; and, to this end, to examine them, to compare them, to observe the ways in which they agree or differ, and to distinguish what is specific to each from what is common to all. Furthermore, as these parts themselves are no more than an assemblage, a combination of elements, we must begin by examining and becoming acquainted with those elements.

The elements are not numerous. They comprise: (1) walls, the piers and string courses incorporated in them, and the various openings that appear in them; (2) detached supports and the horizontal members which they support and which link them together; (3) floors and roofs; and, finally, (4) vaults.

Walls, Piers, String Courses, and Various Kinds of Opening
All buildings may be reduced to three classes: (1) the most important; (2) the least important; (3) those in between.

All buildings are constructed with materials which, although numerous, fall into two categories: (1) those that are more durable but more costly; (2) those that are less durable and cheaper.

The former will be used in the most important buildings, and the latter in the least important; in ordinary buildings, both will be used.

There are four places in every building that are subject to more strain than the others, and these must be reinforced: (1) the corners; (2) the junctions between walls; (3) those parts of the walls that receive the thrust of the vaults, or the weight of the floor beams; and, finally, (4) the points at which the walls cease to be continuous. In buildings of the first and third classes, the walls are reinforced at these points by increasing their thickness; and in buildings of the intermediate class, the stronger materials are employed here, and the weaker materials are used to fill in.

The reinforced parts, which are known as piers, are linked horizontally by string courses, which are placed: (1) at the foot of the building; (2) at ground level; (3) level with the window sills; and, finally, (4) at the top of the building.

In general, the height of doors and windows is twice their width; that of an architrave is one-sixth; those of the frieze and cornice likewise, so that these three parts, taken together, amount to one-half of the opening.

The height of pediments, which are not and must not be anything but the termination gables of a roof, is between one-fifth and one-sixth of their base.

Lecture Three

Detached Supports and the Horizontal Members That Connect Them
In addition to the engaged supports, which, with the string courses that connect them, form the skeleton of a building, there are detached supports: these are known as columns when they are circular in plan and as pilasters when they are square.

They are connected with each other by an architrave, and with the wall by a second architrave known as the frieze; the whole is crowned by a cornice. The combination of these three members is called the entablature, and the combination of the entablature and the column is known as an order.

Pilasters have parallel sides; columns taper by one-sixth. Both are crowned by a capital whose projection supports the architrave.

In the least important buildings, those in which the height of each story is equal to two interaxes at most, this height is divided into sixteen parts, twelve for the column and four for the entablature. Each of these fractional units is known as a module; and the diameter of any column is always two modules.

In the most important buildings, in which the height of each story is equal to four-and-a-half interaxes, this height will be divided into twenty-four parts, twenty for the column and four for the entablature.

As any number of intermediate classes of building may be imagined between the most and the least important, any number of differently proportioned orders may also be imagined; but it will suffice here to insert one, between the two just described: or, rather, to define the height for ordinary buildings as three interaxes. This height is to be divided into twenty parts, sixteen for the column and four for the entablature. This will give a common order, which, together with the two others, will suffice for the purposes of the present study.

To ease our labor, it is worth remarking that, although the height of the entablature is sometimes one-third, sometimes one-quarter, and sometimes one-fifth of the height of the column, it always stands in the same relation to the diameter of the column, that is, four modules or two diameters.

As for the three parts of the entablature, the two lower parts are always to be equal in height; the highest part is to be equal to the two others in the common order, less in the first, and more in the third.

Lecture Four

Floors and Roofs

In floors and roofs, as in walls, it will be observed that there are some parts that compose the skeleton of the building, and that all such parts are vertically aligned. In flooring, these parts are the beams or binding joists, on which lie the common joists that fill the bays; and in roofs they are the trusses, linked by purlins on which the rafters are set.

In small roofs, the trusses are reduced to one tie beam and two principal rafters; in roofs of intermediate size, a king post is added; and the largest are made up of tie beam, collar beam, king post, two queen posts, and two principal rafters.

Lecture Five

Vaults

The only forms of vault that are to be used, because they alone are regular and simple, are: the straight or descending barrel vault; the circular barrel vault, or annular vault; the groin vault, formed by the intersection of two semicylinders; the cloister vault, the four groins of which are reentrant, not projecting like those of the foregoing; the dome or spherical vault; the pendentive vault, combining a groin vault with a spherical vault of a diameter equal to the diagonal of the groin vault.

All vaults, in general, exert two forces: one vertical, which is that of weight; the other horizontal, which is called thrust.

The barrel vault exerts its two forces against the two walls that support it; the cloister vault exerts them uniformly upon the walls all around; the groin and pendentive vaults only on the four corner supports; finally, the spherical vault rests, with no outward thrust, on the whole circumference of its base.

Any vault might be constructed in semicircular strips, starting out from one column and resting on the column on the other side of the opening; these vertical strips would be tied together by horizontal strips, likewise equally spaced. All that would remain would be to fill the square cells left between the strips or bands with very thin stone plates. Vaults of this kind, which would be very inexpensive, and which would exert very little thrust, would naturally present to the eye the recesses that are known as caissons.

How to Draw Caissons

With a barrel vault supported by walls or columns three interaxes apart, the vault, in its final form, will contain only five caissons; if the span between the supports is five interaxes, there will be seven caissons. In all cases, the caissons will not be exactly square; in the vault three interaxes wide they will be slightly longer than they are high, and in the other they will be slightly higher than they are long; but, by cheating a little on the width of the ribs, this fault will be concealed from the eye.

To draw the caissons of a barrel vault, however sectioned, it will suffice to consult figures AA and BB of plate 2. As for the caissons of spherical vaults, this is what must be done. From the center of the dome, in the plan, describe a circle tangential to the columns; in the vertical section, draw a horizontal line at the height at which you wish the caissons to terminate. Take the radius of the vault at this point; on the plan, with the compasses open at this width, describe another circle. In the space between this circle and the first, draw tangents from the center to the diameters of the columns; project the points where these lines intersect the first circle onto the line marking the lower limit of the caissons in the sectional drawing; project the points where these lines intersect the second circle onto the line marking the upper limit of the caissons. All that remains is to join each lower point to the corresponding upper point, by a curve whose center will be found by trial and error along the base of the vault, and you will have the projection of the vertical ribs.

As for the horizontal ribs or bands: these must reduce in width, as do the caissons themselves, towards the top of the vault, and so it will be necessary to draw the development of half of the vault separately, as in figure CC; along the base of this developed figure, and on either side of its axis, add a half width of caisson and a whole width of rib, and from these four points draw lines to the point that marks the apex of the figure; with an equilateral set square, draw the diagonal of each caisson and each rib in turn, and this will yield their gradual diminution. All that remains is to curve the development to some degree round the profile of the vault, and to draw the horizontal lines in the section.

Lecture Six

General Combinations of the Elements

The unit to which we shall refer all quantities in architecture will be the inter-axis: that is to say, the distance between the axes of two columns.

All columns disposed in rows must be equally spaced; they will be separated from the axis of the wall against which they are placed, most frequently by one interaxis, sometimes by two or even three; and, if they appear inside a building, they will always correspond to some of those placed outside.

Pilasters should not be used except in those places where the wall must be strengthened.

The external walls, being designed to enclose the building, should pass in a straight line from one corner to another; and the cross walls, being intended not only to divide the building but also to tie the outer walls together, should also travel in a straight line from one of those walls to another. If some good reason prevents this, the link will be maintained through foundations, beams, and the transverse arches of the vaults.

Doors and windows must correspond in every direction. To this end, they will be aligned on common axes; as will walls and columns, whenever these appear in conjunction.

The drawing of this small number of simple combinations is itself a simple matter. First describe a number of equidistant parallel axes and intersect them at right angles with other axes spaced exactly like the first; then, at whatever intervals may be judged necessary, set the walls on the axes and the columns, pilasters, and so forth, on the intersections of those same axes; then bisect each interaxis to create the new axes of doors, windows, arcades, and so on.

By means of these few simple combinations of a small number of elements, it will be easy to pass on to the composition of the parts of the building.

Lecture Seven

Composition of the Parts of Buildings by Combining Their Elements

The parts of a building are hardly more numerous than the elements. They are as follows: (1) porticoes, (2) porches, (3) vestibules, (4) staircases, (5) rooms, (6) galleries, and (7) courtyards. All this has been discussed in some detail in the first volume of the *Précis*; here we shall take the most general view.

All the parts of buildings are no more or less than spaces surrounded by walls; often covered, sometimes uncovered; sometimes covered by vaults and terraces, sometimes by ceilings and roofs. The most conspicuous features of some of these parts will be columns designed to diminish the span of ceilings or the diameter, and consequently the thrust, of vaults. Such parts may be square, rectangular, circular, or semicircular; they may be small or large; some are only one, two, or three interaxes wide, and others five, seven, or more; only the latter require the use of columns, and we shall consider these, as being the only ones whose study can be profitable to us.

Such parts may appertain to public or to private buildings; public buildings may well consist of a single story, and may be spanned by vaults of varying widths, or by vaults of uniform diameter; private buildings will most often consist of several stories, and will almost always be spanned by flooring and by pitched roofs.

This is the order in which we shall examine them; and the examination will be a profitable one, if we first observe in what ways these objects resemble each other, and in what ways they differ.

Where columns are introduced into certain parts of buildings in order to relieve the pressure of the vaults, and to increase the resistance offered to them, the form of the vaults is a matter of some consequence: if, for example, a cloister vault is employed in a square room, five interaxes wide, then twelve columns will be needed to support the vault. If a barrel vault is used instead, only eight will be needed; and if this is transformed into a groin vault, only four will be needed, in place of the twelve that would have been necessary in the first case: plate 3, figures A, B, C, D.

In a room of the same shape, but seven interaxes wide, the cloister vault would require twenty columns, the barrel vault twelve, and the groin vault still only four. This example shows the importance of forethought in architecture, since in the first of these two rooms there is a saving of eight columns out of twelve, and in the second a saving of sixteen out of twenty. In the former case the saving is one-third, and in the latter it is four-fifths: all achieved by choosing the groin vault.

What applies to square rooms will also apply to oblong rooms, of which it should be remarked in passing that the square room is the unit used in drawing.

If by any chance the length of a rectangular room, measured in interaxes, were not such as to allow three bays of groin vaulting, one such bay might still be used in the center. In this way, at least four columns would be saved in a room five interaxes wide, and eight would be saved in a room seven interaxes wide: plate 3, figures F and G.

If, for a given size of vault, the weight and thrust are increased, the columns may be converted into pilasters, each tied to the walls of the room by a short length of wall: figure H. If even more strength is required, the void may be filled to create a single solid pier: figure 1 [*recte:* I].

The height of the springing line of the vault above the floor of the room will equal three interaxes in rooms five interaxes wide, and four and a half in rooms seven interaxes wide. In the former case, divide this height into five, four for the column and one for the entablature; and in the latter, divide this height into six, of which five will be for the column. By the use of these proportions, if two five-interaxis rooms are placed flanking one seven-interaxis room, that principal room will be no less well lit and aired than if it were completely isolated: plate 3.

Sometimes, at the ends of rooms, the weight of the vault is supported by the walls, figure K, instead of by columns, as in figure L. The arrangement in figure K cannot be used unless the room in question leads into another in which the vault is borne by columns, figure M. In rooms that do not lead into other rooms, the vault should be supported by columns one interaxis away from the wall, as in figure 4 [*recte:* D].

Once the student has grasped what we have said in general concerning the parts of buildings, and familiarized himself with all of the figures on plate 3, he will have at his disposal a kind of graphic formula with which, in all of the succeeding ensembles of public buildings spanned by vaults of differing sizes, he will be enabled to design the plan and section of every constituent part without any effort, in the briefest time, with the most perfect understanding, and with the greatest benefit to himself.

Lecture Eight

Composition of the Ensemble of a Building by Combining Its Parts
What we have said of the combination of the elements of buildings naturally leads us on to what little we shall have to say concerning the combination of their parts.

As the walls must keep to a single axis in whichever direction, it follows that, if—in length, in depth, or in both—the building contains several rooms, these will inevitably be situated on common axes; as they must.

It may be supposed, in view of all this, that the composition of the ensemble of a building can hardly afford very much variety; but this is a misconception that will soon be dispelled if one only reflects in how many different ways the principal axes of buildings—that is to say, those on which their component parts are placed—can be combined together, thus providing different compositions, not only on plots that differ in shape and size but even on those that precisely agree both in size and in shape.

Let us take as an example the simplest of forms, the square. Divide this into two, three, or four, and we shall have a multitude of different arrangements; if we eliminate, in each one of these arrangements, some of the axes by means of which the divisions have been made, the number of new arrangements thus obtained will approach infinity. See plate 3, figures N and O.

In the latest editions of the first volume of our *Précis*, we have gone so far as to say that one of the best ways to determine the composition of the ensemble of a building is to carry out most of these dispositions by setting down the successive parts of buildings on the axes that indicate them; by such means, indeed, it would be possible in every case to satisfy the three requirements that are common to all places and all times: solidity, salubrity, and commodity: *at least, in general, the last-named.*

This method, given the generality of its application, indubitably offers great advantages; it might, however, have the defect of failing to provide sufficiently for those requirements of fitness and of commodity that are specific to each individual building. As it is our object to satisfy both general and specific requirements perfectly, we have thought it far better to set ourselves programs of a sort, admittedly abstract (for it would be still more dangerous to set ourselves any that were not, as we shall presently see), but designed to instill the habit of satisfying both specific and general requirements at the same time. We shall therefore hypothesize specific requirements of number, form, situation, and size. By this means, our method will have all the advantages, while escaping the numerous and ruinous disadvantages, of an exclusive study of specific projects.

Method to Be Adopted When Composing or Copying

In learning to compose, therefore, the following method is to be adopted: conceive an ensemble formed of a certain number of parts, similar or dissimilar, placed in a certain relation one to another; then, having a clear idea of all these parts, and of the relations that unite them, you will necessarily have a clear idea of the ensemble. Then consign your ideas to paper by means of a croquis, in the order in which they have been conceived; that is, begin by expressing the principal ones, then those that are subordinate, and finally those that are subordinate to the latter. In this croquis, positional relations are to be expressed by signs and relations of size by numbers.

But the more you have thought in the past, the more rightly you think; thought costs effort, when the habit has yet to be acquired; and even a first idea could never be conceived without the stimulus of some external cause. And so we have not insisted that our students devise their own programs, and certainly not at the beginning. We have set these before them in graphic form, as shown in the series of sketches that are given here. These drawings at once draw their attention to the ensemble and to the parts that combine to make such ensembles. These drawings aid and encourage them to think in architectural terms and ultimately lead them to acquire the beneficial habit of doing so. It will be seen that, for this end to be attained, it is not enough to copy slavishly.

One example will give an idea of the method that we show them of putting their work to the best possible use.

In plate 4 an ensemble has been specified consisting of a courtyard—which, by its size and its relative position, ought to be the first thing that presents itself to the imagination, after one has ceased to look at the model—together with four rectangular rooms and four square rooms at the corners. With this abstract proposition clearly in mind, set down your mental image of the model in an initial croquis, which, by means of signs placed in an appropriate relation to each other, will fix the idea and allow its author to examine it and to judge whether it is truly what he intended; if it is satisfied, he can then realize it by indicating the axes of the walls that are to enclose the ensemble and the parts of the building. The number, shape, and situation of these parts being once indicated, a second croquis is made in order to gain an idea of the relative sizes.

This second croquis need not necessarily embrace the whole extent of the building. The study of one corner may suffice to determine these new relations throughout all the parts: by observing a single corner room, which we will suppose to be five interaxes wide, it will be seen, as we have said, that all the rooms will be of the same width; and that, just as in this room the introduction of four columns reduces the diameter of the vault from five to three interaxes, the same will have to be done in all the rectangular rooms, none of which can have fewer than three bays. All that is necessary is to mark the scale on this new croquis, from which one may pass at will to a sketch and even, if this is considered necessary, to a finished drawing. As for the vertical sections, not only of this ensemble but of all those similar ones that follow, we have given a formula, in our discussion of the parts of the building, that will make it unnecessary even to look at the sections that we give of each ensemble. As for the elevations, which are and must be nothing but the natural and necessary consequences of the plan and the section, it will be even easier to devise them without consulting the model. In general, the less slavishly the student copies these models, the more rapidly he will progress in the mechanics of composition.

It would be too long and tedious to speak successively of the numerous compositions offered in the thirty-four plates contained in this volume. We shall limit ourselves to a number of specific observations that we consider necessary. The plates themselves, and the table of contents that precedes them, will suffice to identify these compositions and the order in which they appear.

For example, plate 4 contains two ensembles that essentially differ only in that in the first the vault bears on two columns, whereas in the second it bears only on one. In both, the supports are equally distributed throughout the building; this is the best arrangement, though the location does not always allow it. An example is given in the second figure of plate 5. In the greater part of this composition, use is made of the single-column system, in view of the presumed smallness of the site; but in the central and corner portions a double-column system is used, in consequence of the need to oppose adequate resistance to the thrust of the three intermediate bays.

The essential feature of both these plates is contained in the central figures of both, which show how to set ideas down on paper in the form of a croquis.

On plate 8 it should be noticed that the rooms and galleries, which, for most of their length, are only five interaxes wide, have an additional width of two interaxes in the central and corner portions.

In the examples cited hitherto, parts with a width of five interaxes have been combined only with other parts of equal width; in the examples that follow, widths of five interaxes are combined with others of seven; and the same combinations subsequently appear in conjunction with large semicircular and centrally planned rooms.

Among the last-named combinations, there are some in which the columns support raised tribunes instead of vaults.

If all that precedes has enabled us, without excessive expenditure of time or effort, to familiarize ourselves with the overall composition of those vaulted public buildings in which most of the parts serve different purposes and must be differently constructed and arranged, we shall find it even easier to compose those in which all the parts, being designed for similar or analo-gous uses, must all be arranged and constructed in the same manner. One dif-ference that may be observed between these two kinds of building is that, in the former, the height of the springing line of the vault above the floor of the building is equal to the number of interaxes between the columns that sup-port the vault; whereas in the latter this height is mostly no more than half the number of interaxes. Plate 16 offers a graphic formula relative to this kind of building. As for its applications, we have supposed that the two on plate 17 might suffice.

We shall say little more on those buildings, whether public or private, that consist of two stories spanned by floorings and roofs.

Plate 18 presents the graphic formula applicable to all those with stories two interaxes high. Plate 19 presents a corresponding formula for those with stories three or four and a half interaxes high. In both of these formulas, the orders are either equal in height to the stories or else diminished by the height of the plinth on which they rest. The former manner is the better, being the simpler and the more natural; the latter, which is used only in order to give more height to the second story, would be supremely bad in those buildings with columns both outside and inside on that story, where it would compel us either to employ columns of different heights on one and the same story, or else to hoist those inside onto dadoes or pedestals to make them level with those outside.

Stories with a height of two interaxes are the only ones in which columns can be linked by arches. In order to have simple ratios between all the parts of this system, divide the height of the story into five parts: three for the column, one for the height of the arch, and one for the solid mass of wall above.

In buildings with stories two interaxes high, there may be openings in all the interaxes; in stories three interaxes high, the same may be done, although it would perhaps be better to alternate them; in stories four and a half inter-axes high, the openings must be even further apart, unless they are niches.

Plate 20 offers four ensembles of the same shape and size—the width and height of the rooms remaining two interaxes throughout—but differing markedly in appearance both within and without, the rooms being differently combined with the porticoes and stairs.

The same variety is observed in the ensembles shown in plates 21 and 22: here the width of the rooms, which is equal to the height of the stories, is three interaxes. In these two plates, and in the two that follow, it will be observed that rooms without columns are combined with others in which there are columns, and which consequently measure five interaxes. Finally, these same successive plates show all the possible arrangements and combinations of staircases with other rooms.

In the ensembles shown in plate 23, the stories are three interaxes high, and the porticoes two interaxes wide. In plates 24 and 25, the height of the stories is the same, but the porticoes and the rooms in general are three inter-axes wide. In these two last plates there is a disparity of size such as is scarcely ever found except in public buildings; at the same time, it will be seen how simply these disparities are managed, and the finesse with which the court-yards and the porticoes are matched to each other.

To complete our work, after considering buildings as wholes resulting from an assemblage of parts, we have considered the buildings themselves as elements within larger and far more magnificent compositions, formed by the assembly and combination of the buildings themselves, in greater or lesser number. In the composition of these new ensembles, we have summoned to our aid all that the ancient historians have handed down to us concerning the grandest and noblest achievements of the Egyptians, the Greeks, and the Romans in architecture, and also the dreams of Piranesi, which are often eccentric but almost always sublime. Having exercised the student's judgment in the preceding sketches, we trusted that these would serve to awaken his imagination—a faculty no less necessary to the architect, but one that he can receive from nature alone; for instruction can do no more than stimulate.

In the first volume of the précis of our lectures, after setting out our own ideas on architecture, we gave an account of those that are commonly held in relation to this art, so a comparison might be made and a judgment arrived at. Similarly, having set out in this volume the method that we think most proper to allow students to acquire in a brief time some genuine talents in this mag-nificent art, we shall say something of the method that is most commonly fol-lowed, so that a choice may be made between the two.

Often, after no preliminary study but that of drawing, a number of designs are copied; then a certain number are composed and studied; and that is what is normally described as learning architecture. By such means it is supposed that adequate talents in this art may be acquired; and sometimes as many as twelve or fifteen years are devoted to this activity. Even assuming the most protracted study and the most persevering toil, the three months' study that each design demands will mean that, in fifteen years, only sixty will have been studied.

Unfortunately, architecture is not the art of making a certain number of designs; it is the art of making all possible designs, public and private; and of doing so, furthermore, in all the circumstances that may occur to modify them. There is no other art, perhaps, that embraces so large a number of objects; and if one were to spend one's whole life in such an exercise, and suc-ceed, by untold exertions, in preparing a thousand designs, it is clear that one's study would remain incomplete; for, if one were commissioned to pre-pare the thousand-and-first, one would have to start all over again, having done no more than study individual designs, instead of learning the art that teaches us to make them all.

This highly incomplete manner of learning is also highly imperfect; for, as all designs pertain to architecture, it is impossible to make even one without a thorough knowledge of that art; and how could anyone ever succeed by copy-ing designs without understanding each one of them, without dissecting and analyzing the buildings that one copies? There are, it is true, some elements that are impossible to miss; and the false ideas of architecture that now pre-vail—that is to say the ideas of architectural ornament—single them out all too readily: all those columns, pilasters, pedestals, entablatures, pediments, attics, projections, and recessions that present themselves to view in the ele-vation of a design; this is all that is noticed, and with this one composes.

The attention devoted to these various features might not be totally wasted, because some of them, after all, do indeed figure among the elements of build-ings; but for this to be the case, two things would be necessary: first, they must be considered as objects of use, and not of ornament; second, the study of architecture must not be limited to them alone. But how could this latter condition ever be satisfied, while in almost every elevation, which is regarded as the most interesting portion of a design, little else meets the eye; and while, far from displaying to the eye and to the mind a number of the essential parts of a building, the architect constantly affects to cloak them and make them disappear, by surrounding them with costly and useless walls, in order to con-ceal those parts whose appearance might have endowed the exterior of the building with variety, effect, character, and all the beauties that are pursued at so much vain expense through the decoration of those mere boxes—or rather those pits, those sepulchers—that engulf a multitude of the essential parts of any building: parts which, if seen, would have completely satisfied both mind and eye by offering a spectacle that is natural and true?*

How is anyone to acquire a true knowledge of architecture, or any true tal-ent, by copying such things, and above all by copying them in the way in which they are copied? How is anyone to create compositions of his own, without accurate knowledge of the objects with which he is to compose? How is anyone to devise an ensemble of any kind, even tolerably well, without any notion as to its constituent parts, and in ignorance of the general way in which those parts are to be combined?

We shall be told that, in the designs that are copied, the elevations are always accompanied by plans and sections, in which the parts of the building necessarily appear; but these are clearly not the parts of any design that most interest men full of the idea of ornament; besides, in copying ten or so designs, one does not encounter a half, or even a quarter, of those parts of buildings that it is essential to know.

Meanwhile, after having devoted more or less time to this kind of work, one passes on to composition. What can such productions be like? Designs made up of bits and pieces; designs that incorporate a multitude of costly and unnecessary items, and often none of those most urgently called for by the requirements of the program.

What subsequent profit can anyone derive from the long and painful elab-oration of more or less unformed and undigested designs? And it is in this deplorable occupation that a host of young men, many of them most fortu-nately endowed by nature; men who, if only they had adopted an appropriate

*See the new Church of Sainte-Geneviève.

course of study, would surely have commended themselves by their talents not only to their contemporaries but to posterity: it is, I say, in this ruinous occupation that they irremediably waste the finest years of their youth, the most precious portion of their lives.

We have seen that this method was incomplete; it will be realized that, worse than imperfect, it is disastrous: that it is absurd to profess a knowledge of architecture on the strength of having copied, composed, and elaborated a few designs, since architecture is the art of making all designs. It must, at the same time, be recognized that in every respect it would be better to study the art in a comprehensive, natural, simple, and rational manner—which is, after all, the manner that is universally adopted in the acquisition of all other branches of human knowledge. Having learned architecture in this way, one would no longer need to study every design in isolation and at arduous length: one would make them all, and make them well, because one could never fall short of the general requirements of fitness, and because the special requirements of any individual building would be easily dealt with as soon as recognized.

Even so, it may be asked, does not architecture, by common consent, boast a number of men of the greatest merit? No one is more convinced of this than we ourselves, and we have taken every opportunity to demonstrate our conviction by paying homage to their talents. We shall go further, and say that such men exist, not only among architects but among those young men who intend to practice architecture; but they certainly do not owe their merit to any lack of method and still less to the practice of a bad method: they can but owe it to personal disposition and to that felicitous education by circumstance, from which one often derives more profit, the less one is aware of receiving it.

Again, it may be asked: Have all those who have pursued your method become able architects? Alas, no! But after what we have said, it is easy to see why: if imagination without good instruction amounts to very little, even the best instruction is nothing without aptitude, imagination, zeal, and application.

For the rest, even supposing our method no better in itself than any other, it would still surpass all others by virtue of its brevity. It does not require twelve or fifteen years of work; and, even supposing little to be gained by pursuing it, at least one would not be left deploring the loss of a long span of time, which of all commodities is the most precious and, when lost, the most sorely missed.

We shall end by expressing our ardent and heartfelt wish that, in an art that brings such great and manifold benefits to humanity and to society when well understood, and such disasters when ill understood, knowledge and talent may grow, disseminate themselves, and even become general; and that they may no longer remain the sole prerogative of those who practice architecture as a profession.

And why should our wish not become reality? For does not any sound education include the study of music, of drawing, and of several other arts, even though the persons to whom these talents are imparted have not the slightest intention of becoming painters or professional musicians? Why should these agreeable talents not be joined by another that is no less agreeable and, furthermore, eminently useful? Is this because its acquisition would be a longer and more difficult process? A perusal of the present work will suffice to convince the reader of the contrary; but, even if this fear were well founded, what an advantage it would be, in every nation, if those men who are destined by nature to occupy the first positions in society—and to whom it consequently falls to set in hand the construction of buildings of great importance—might be enabled to select the best architects and the best designs from those submitted to them? Would their fame not be greatly enhanced? Would not even those who are never called upon to exercise such exalted functions find the reward of their studies in the pleasure of discoursing from genuine knowledge on a subject that is as much favored in polite society as it is imperfectly understood? Would there not be a more tangible reward, should they ever need to order building works for themselves, whether for pleasure or for business?

But, some will say, would not architects and architecture suffer if the art were thus, to some degree, popularized? We do not think so; but, even supposing this to be true, either society is made for architecture and for architects, or architecture and architects are made for society: is there any man worthy of the name of architect who can hesitate for one moment in this matter? After all, what would he have to lose? A little empty praise, all too often conferred by ignorance and folly. In its place would be sincere expressions of esteem and gratitude, fully adequate to reward his heart for any injury to his amour propre. Such will be the lot of any architect who exercises this noble art with talent and with honor, when the art comes to be generally known.

Notice

Recueil et parallèle des édifices de tout genre, anciens et modernes, remarquables par leur beauté, par leur grandeur ou par leur singularité, et dessinés sur une même échelle
(Collection and Parallel of Buildings of Every Genre, Ancient and Modern, Remarkable for Their Beauty, Greatness of Size, or Singularity, and Drawn to a Common Scale)

—by J.-N.-L. Durand
Architect and Professor of Architecture at the École Polytechnique

It is of the utmost importance to architects, to civil and military engineers, to those students of the École Polytechnique who are destined to become architects and engineers, to painters of history and landscape, to sculptors, to draftsmen, to stage decorators—in a word, to all those who have to construct or to represent buildings and monuments—to study and to become acquainted with all the most interesting productions of architecture in every country and in every age.

But the buildings that deserve notice are mingled with a crowd of others that are in no way remarkable; and what is more, they are scattered through nearly three hundred volumes, for the most part folios, which would cost an enormous sum to collect; so that artists can never gain a complete knowledge of them except in libraries.

This expedient would require unlimited time, and even then it would be practicable only for those artists who live in large cities. What is more, even if all were in a position to make use of it, the consequent advantages might well fall far short of rewarding them adequately for their trouble. And this is the reason: often a given volume is composed of objects of different kinds, and those that are of the same kind are scattered through a large number of volumes. It will be apparent that in such a case comparisons, which alone can enable the mind to judge and to draw conclusions, become drawn out, laborious, imperfect, and unfruitful: and the difficulty is compounded by disparities of scale.

This being so, we concluded that if we were to detach from the three hundred volumes just mentioned only those objects that must be known and to collect them in a single volume at a price equal at most to that of an ordinary architectural work, we should be able to offer to artists in general, and to the students of the École Polytechnique in particular, a complete and inexpensive image of architecture: an image that they might peruse in a short time, examine without labor, and study with profit, especially if buildings and monuments were to be classified by genres, juxtaposed in accordance with their degree of analogy, and reduced to a single scale: and this is what we have undertaken to do. To reach this end with greater certainty, we have excluded from the collection not only all those objects that offered no interest in themselves, but also those that, being more or less similar to other objects of greater interest, would only serve to swell the book without increasing the quantity of ideas.

It may be that some buildings will be found in this collection that will appear uninteresting; but, as they are almost the only extant representatives of their genre, we have considered it necessary to include them, in order to draw attention to the genre of architecture concerned.

Some restorations will be found here that are unauthentic, like those of the Thermae by Palladio, and those of a number of buildings in ancient Rome by Piranesi, Pirro Ligorio, and so on. We did not wish to deprive students or architects of the fine opportunities that these restorations present, of which they can make frequent and happy use.

We have, however, taken the liberty of simplifying them and of adding others that are almost entirely our own work. If it is understood that—far from attempting to correct those great masters—we have sought only to make more evident the spirit that prevails in their magnificent productions, we shall readily be pardoned for our presumption in setting ourselves alongside them.

This work is composed of fifteen fascicles, each of six plates:

The first comprises the Egyptian, Greek, and Roman temples, and those of Solomon, of Baalbek, and of Palmyra.

The second, public squares, forums, marketplaces, market halls, bazaars, city halls, basilicas, palaestrae, schools, porticoes, and bourses.

The fourth, Egyptian, Greek, Indian, Turkish, Persian, and Roman tombs; triumphal arches, bridges, aqueducts, and so on.

The fifth, harbors, lighthouses, towers, cisterns, wells, water towers, barracks, arsenals, prisons, hospitals, lazar houses, caravansaries, and cemeteries.

The sixth, thermae, nymphaea, and baths.

The seventh, theaters, both ancient and modern; amphitheaters; naumachiae; and circuses.

The eighth, ninth, and tenth, houses; castles; mansions; and palaces, both ancient and modern.

Finally, the eleventh, twelfth, thirteenth, fourteenth, and fifteenth offer, drawn to an identical, larger, modular scale, all the details of buildings that deserve to be made known.

The work is to be purchased from the author, at the École Polytechnique, in Paris.

The price of each fascicle is twelve francs. That of the whole work is one hundred and eighty francs.[57]

Editorial Notes

1. The preface was omitted from the 1813 edition of the *Précis,* which would form the basis of subsequent editions. Its content was largely moved to the introduction, together with a "Continuation of the Introduction" in which, notably, Durand included his ideas on drawing. For a detailed comparison of the original and 1813 editions, see Werner Szambien, *Jean-Nicolas-Louis Durand, 1760–1834: De l'imitation à la norme* (Paris: Picard, 1984), 200–201. ED.

2. In Durand's time, the importance of the engineers employed by the French state, and notably those who belonged to two corps of Ponts et Chaussées and Génie, was a very real one. It had been officially recognized under the ancien régime; and a draft edict of 1780 provided for all public building projects to be restricted to members of the Ponts et Chaussées. Laurent Pelpel, ed., "La formation architecturale au dix-huitième siècle en France," research report, Paris, 1980, 41–42. ED.

3. This assertion notwithstanding, the time devoted by École Polytechnique students to architecture was far from negligible. Durand's argument was intended, above all, to justify his own method. See Fernand de Dartein, *Observations sur le cours d'architecture de l'École Polytechnique et sur le programme de ses leçons* (Paris: Imprimerie de Simon Raçon, 1874), 41–42. ED.

4. Here Durand differs from the generation of his own teachers, Boullée and Ledoux, who insisted on the importance of drawing and painting in the training of an architect. ED.

5. This emphasis on the coordination of different representations is in the spirit of Gaspard Monge's descriptive geometry, in which these shared lines, or *traits de rappel,* play a fundamental role. See Joël Sakarovitch, *Épures d'architecture: De la coupe des pierres à la géométrie descriptive, XVIᵉ–XIXᵉ siècles* (Basel: Birkhäuser, 1998). ED.

6. Jean-Nicolas-Louis Durand, Jacques-Guillaume Legrand, *Recueil et parallèle des édifices de tout genre, anciens et modernes, remarquables par leur beauté, par leur grandeur ou par leur singularité, et dessinés sur une même échelle* (Paris: Gillé fils, 1799–1801). ED.

7. Jean-Baptiste Maudru was a man of letters and the author of a *Nouveau système de lecture applicable à toutes les langues* (Paris: Mérigot, Rondonneau, & Girardin, Year VIII [1799–1800]). It was in this capacity that Durand secured his assistance in revising the manuscript of the *Précis* and seeing it through the press. See Szambien (note 1), 91–92. ED.

8. Here Durand is echoing the celebrated dictum of his own teacher, Étienne-Louis

Boullée: "*Il faut concevoir pour exécuter.*" (You must conceive in order to execute.) Boullée, *Architecture: Essai sur l'art,* ed. Jean-Marie Pérouse de Montclos (Paris: Hermann, 1968), 46. ED.

9. The following passage stems from the *Essai sur l'architecture* of the Abbé Laugier. Marc-Antoine Laugier, *Essai sur l'architecture* (Paris: Duchesne, 1753; 2d ed., 1755), 8–10. ED.

10. Durand here draws fairly freely on the translation of Vitruvius by Claude Perrault, regarded as an authority among French architects. Marcus Vitruvius Pollio, *Les dix livres d'architecture,* trans. Claude Perrault (Paris: J.-B. Coignard, 1673), 100–104. ED.

11. The word *fitness,* as used in architectural discussion in Durand's day, seems to me to be an exact historical equivalent for the French *convenance.* In such a context *fitness,* like *convenance,* means not only "fitness for purpose" (i.e., functionality) but also "decorum": what is appropriate, fitting, and proper. TRANS.

12. Durand's criticisms of Soufflot's church of Sainte-Geneviève, renamed Panthéon under the French Revolution, agree with those of a whole generation of architects who rejected the kind of constructional tours de force that it typified. Here, Durand is particularly close to Charles-François Viel de Saint-Maux and to his treatise *De l'impuissance des mathématiques pour assurer la solidité des bâtimens, et recherches sur la construction des ponts* (Paris: the author and Veuve Tilliard, 1805). On the reception accorded to Soufflot's building in the nineteenth century, see Barry Bergdoll, ed., *Le Panthéon, symbole des révolutions: De l'église de la nation au temple des grands hommes* (Paris: Picard, 1989). ED.

13. In the 1813 edition of the *Précis,* most of the detailed information on materials is relegated to the end of volume 1. This information is not essential to a training in composition. The survey of constructional techniques provided by Durand is in any case far less comprehensive than that given by Rondelet in his *L'art de bâtir* from 1802 onward. ED.

14. This whole section on materials is difficult to negotiate, and here we agreed to abandon the search for English equivalents. TRANS.

15. The small space devoted to lime is particularly revealing of Durand's comparative lack of interest in constructional matters. In Britain as well as in France, research into limes, mortars, and cements was at its height at the turn of the nineteenth century. Those involved included scientists such as the Frenchman Barthélemy Faujas de Saint-Fond and inventors such as the Englishmen James Parker and Joseph Aspdin. See André Guillerme, *Bâtir la ville: Révolutions industrielles dans les matériaux de construction, France–Grande-Bretagne (1760–1840)* (Paris: Champ Vallon, 1995); C. Simonnet, "Matériau et architecture: Le Béton armé: Origine, invention, esthétique," doctoral diss., École des Hautes Études en Sciences Sociales, Paris, 1994. ED.

16. The iron-reinforced colonnades described by Durand are common in seventeenth- and eighteenth-century French architecture, especially in Paris, where the use of iron allowed wider and wider spans. The most celebrated of these colonnades are those of the Louvre, the Place Louis XV (now de la Concorde), and Sainte-Geneviève (now Panthéon). Pierre Patte discusses them at length in his *Mémoires sur les objets les plus importants de l'architecture* (Paris: Rozet, 1769). ED.

17. The return to favor of the *plafond à la française,* that is, the ceiling with exposed beams, was of a piece with the neoclassical architects' interest in traditional, and even vernacular, building techniques. On this see Jean-Marie Pérouse de Montclos, "Innovation technique et archéologie des techniques dans l'architecture néoclassique," *Les cahiers de la recherche architecturale,* no. 18 (1985), 44–49. However, Durand's defense of exposed beams did not meet with universal assent. It was criticized in an article in the *Journal des bâtiments, des monumens et des arts,* 28 Floréal An XI (17 May 1802). ED.

18. Pendentives, rear vaults, and skew and surbased vaults were part of the basic vocabulary of stereotomy. The latter underwent a rapid decline at the turn of the nineteenth century, at the very time when Monge's descriptive geometry was taking up and systemizing the drafting methods on which it was founded. On the importance of stereotomy in French architecture, see Jean-Marie Pérouse de Montclos, *L'architecture à la française XVᵉ, XVIIᵉ, XVIIIᵉ siècles* (Paris: Picard, 1982). ED.

19. Having taken charge of building works at the Panthéon, Rondelet was well versed in the theory and practice of vaulting because he had to tackle the structural problems raised by Soufflot's building. However, he did little to advance the theory of the subject. Here, the most innovative contribution was made by Charles-Augustin Coulomb, who was the first to employ the calculus of variations in his "Essai sur une application des règles de maximis et minimis à quelques problèmes de statique, relatifs à l'architecture," 1773. Coulomb's essay was rediscovered by structural theorists in the early 1820s. See J.-M. Delbecq, "Analyses de la stabilité des voûtes en maçonnerie de Charles Augustin Coulomb à nos jours," *Annales des Ponts et Chaussées,* no. 19 (1981), 36–43; Edoardo Benvenuto, *La scienza delle costruzioni e il suo sviluppo storico* (Florence: Sansoni, 1981). ED.

20. Durand probably has the Panthéon and its structural shortcomings in mind when he denies the ability of iron to reinforce vaults. ED.

21. The Philibert truss, the system described by Philibert de l'Orme in his *Nouvelles inventions pour bien bastir et à petits fraiz* of 1561, had in fact been used by Legrand and Jacques Molinos to cover the central yard of Le Camus de Mézières's Halle aux Blés in 1783. See Mark Deming, *La Halle au Blé de Paris 1762–1813* (Brussels: Archives d'Architecture Moderne, 1984). See also, more generally, Jean-Marie Pérouse de Montclos, "La Charpente à la Philibert de l'Orme: Réflexions sur la fortune des techniques en architecture," in idem, *Les chantiers de la Renaissance: Actes des colloques tenus à Tours en 1983–1984* (Paris: Picard, 1991), 27–50. ED.

22. Here Durand refers to Pierre Patte, *Mémoires sur les objets les plus importants de l'architecture* (Paris: Rozet, 1769), and above all to Patte's continuation of Jacques-François Blondel's *Cours d'architecture.* ED.

23. This profession of faith calls to mind the rationalism of Viollet-le-Duc, but it needs to be seen in relative terms. The ordonnances presented by Durand seldom rely on the straightforward expression of constructional logic. With him, any such expression always has an additional, basically geometrical character. ED.

24. As I have stressed in my introduction, this tripartite notion of beauty owes much to the theory set out by Claude Perrault in the notes to his translation of Vitruvius (see note 10), and in his *Ordonnance des cinq espèces de colonnes selon la*

méthode des Anciens (Paris: J.-B. Coignard, 1683); translated by Indra Kagis McEwen as *Ordonnance for the Five Kinds of Columns after the Method of the Ancients*, ed. Alberto Pérez-Gómez (Santa Monica: Getty Center for the History of Art and the Humanities, 1993). ED.

25. Where Perrault relied on *Les édifices antiques de Rome*, by Antoine Desgodets, to exemplify the variety of proportions used by the ancients in their orders, Durand bases himself on *Ruines des plus beaux monuments de la Grèce*, by the architectural theorist Julien-David Le Roy. Le Roy's influence is evident in many passages of the *Précis*. ED.

26. As with Perrault, the proportions of the orders follow a regular progression from the sturdiest to the lightest. However, the Tuscan is placed after the Doric, and the Composite disappears. ED.

27. This reference to Egyptian architecture, as revealed by Bonaparte's expedition, disappears from the 1813 edition of the *Précis*, as if the experiment had proved inconclusive. ED.

28. An interaxis is the distance from the axis of one column (or wall, or opening) to the next. The English word is cited by the *Oxford English Dictionary* from Joseph Gwilt's *Encyclopaedia of Architecture* (1842–76). Here the interaxis serves as the basic unit of an interaxial grid. TRANS.

29. Durand had attended Julien-David Le Roy's classes as a student of the Académie d'Architecture. The quotation that follows is taken from Le Roy's *Histoire de la disposition et des formes différentes que les Chrétiens ont donné à leurs temples depuis le règne de Constantin le Grand jusqu'à nous* (Paris: Desaint & Saillant, 1764), 63. ED.

30. In fact, the leeway allowed between plan and elevation in the *Précis* is markedly greater than Durand says here. See my introduction. ED.

31. This is one of the comments that indicate that Durand visited Italy in the course of his training, although the precise date is not known. ED.

32. This third section, on the *ensemble* or edifice as a whole, was considerably reworked for the 1813 edition. Additional plates were inserted, including the famous "Ensembles d'édifices résultants de diverses combinaisons horizontales et verticales" (Whole Buildings, Derived from a Variety of Horizontal and Vertical Combinations), and "Marche à suivre dans la composition d'un projet quelconque" (Procedure to Be Followed in the Composition of Any Project). ED.

33. For Durand, as for Jacques-François Blondel before him, talent takes precedence over genius: in other words, methodical reasoning is to be preferred to intuition. On the notion of talent in Blondel, see Antoine Picon, *Architectes et ingénieurs au siècle des Lumieres* (Marseilles: Parenthèses, 1988); translated by Martin Thom as *French Architects and Engineers in the Age of the Enlightenment* (Cambridge: Cambridge Univ. Press, 1992), 92–94. ED.

34. The two main schools to which Polytechnique graduates proceeded, the École des Ponts et Chaussées and the École de l'Artillerie et du Génie, had architecture courses of their own. On the training dispensed at the École Polytechnique and its associated establishments in the early nineteenth century, see my introduction; also Bruno Belhoste, Amy Dahan Dalmedico, and Antoine Picon, eds., *La formation polytechnicienne, 1794–1994* (Paris: Dunod, 1994). ED.

35. More explicitly than at the end of volume 1 of the *Précis,* Durand here sets out the importance of the definition of axes for his method of composition. Axiality was also to be a characteristic of the large-scale compositions designed within the ambit of the École des Beaux-Arts. ED.

36. Durand's views on city design are far less progressive than the protofunctionalist theses sustained by Pierre Patte in his *Mémoires sur les objets les plus importants de l'architecture* (see note 22). In saying that the rules of urban composition do not differ fundamentally from those of the composition of buildings, the author of the *Précis* reveals the limitations of his argument all too clearly. He is talking about embellishment, in the ancien régime's sense, rather than urban transformation on a large scale. ED.

37. The Pont de Neuilly and the Pont Louis XVI, renamed Pont de la Concorde under the Revolution, are both by Jean-Rodolphe Perronet, the founder and first director of the École des Ponts et Chaussées. Before Durand, Boullée had already criticized the Pont Louis XVI and its decoration, which was intended to harmonize with the adjacent square and its buildings, designed by Jacques-Ange Gabriel. ED.

38. This remark might well be taken as an indication that Durand was an atheist. It would, in any case, have been unsurprising to have it from the pen of a notorious eighteenth-century materialist such as Helvétius or Holbach. ED.

39. In the mid–eighteenth century, the dome of Saint Peter's had had to be reinforced with circular iron bands. The controversy prompted by this piece of restoration foreshadowed the polemics that arose a few decades later over the construction of Soufflot's Church of Sainte-Geneviève (Panthéon). On this, see Alberto Pérez-Gómez, *Architecture and the Crisis of Modern Science* (Cambridge, 1983; reprint, Cambridge: MIT Press, 1984), 248–53. On the technical side, see also Edoardo Benvenuto, *An Introduction to the History of Structural Mechanics* (New York: Springer, 1991), 2:351–71. ED.

40. Durand's admiration for the structural qualities of Gothic architecture is entirely in keeping with the tradition of the eighteenth-century rediscovery of Gothic. On the multiple dimensions of that rediscovery, see *Le "Gothique" retrouvé avant Viollet-le-Duc,* exh. cat. (Paris: Caisse nationale des monuments historiques et des sites, 1979); Anne Coste, *L'architecture gothique: Lectures et interprétations d'un modèle* (Saint-Étienne: Publications de l'Université de Saint-Étienne, 1997). ED.

41. Durand's palace is inspired by a composition for Saint-Cloud designed by Boullée in 1785. A comparison between the two projects will be found in Werner Szambien, "Durand and the Continuity of Tradition," in Robin Middleton, ed., *The Beaux-Arts and Nineteenth-Century French Architecture* (London: Thames & Hudson, 1982), 19–33, esp. 24. ED.

42. The courthouse and magistrate's court projects presented in the *Précis* are designs by Durand and Thibault that date from the competitions organized by the revolutionary government in the Year II (1793–94). See Szambien (note 1), 50. ED.

43. Durand's institute design is a simplified version of the monument to assemble the academies, with which Charles Percier had won the Grand Prix de l'Académie in 1786. Durand reused it in 1813 to exemplify his "Procedure to Be Followed in the Composition of Any Project." See my introduction, page 42 and figure 21. ED.

44. The museum in the *Précis* derives from projects submitted by Delannoy, Gisors, and Durand himself for the Grand Prix in 1779. See Szambien (note 1), 50. ED.

45. On the Paris Observatory, one of the few seventeenth- or eighteenth-century monuments in Paris for which Durand has a good word to say, the reader may consult Michael Petzet, "Claude Perrault als Architekt des Pariser Observatoriums," *Zeitschrift für Kunstgeschichte* 30, no. 1 (1967): 1–54; Antoine Picon, *Claude Perrault, 1613–1688; ou, La curiosité d'un classique* (Paris: Picard, 1988). ED.

46. See Deming (note 21). ED.

47. The idea of covering a theater with an iron roof to avoid fires was current in Durand's day. Victor Louis had been one of the first to resort to iron for this purpose, at the Théâtre Français in the late 1780s. See Bertrand Lemoine, *L'architecture du fer: France, XIXᵉ siècle* (Seyssel: Champ Vallon, 1986), 7, 69. ED.

48. On the debates concerning hospital building at the turn of the nineteenth century, see Michel Foucault, ed., *Les machines à guérir: Aux origines de l'hôpital moderne* (Brussels: P. Mardaga, 1979). Durand's hospital composition is inspired by Bernard Poyet's project of 1787 for the rebuilding of the Hôtel-Dieu at La Roquette. ED.

49. For his prison, Durand again uses a project devised for one of the Year II competitions. See Szambien (note 1), 50–51. ED.

50. The architect here is Détournelle. Durand's version of the project is much simplified by comparison with the original. ED.

51. Plate 23 shows the Maison Lathuille, one of the few buildings that Durand built in Paris. ED.

52. The version of Pliny's letters to his friends Apollinaris and Gallus given by Durand is so free that it is more or less impossible to identify the translation on which he bases himself. ED.

53. The translation follows Durand's version except for the words printed in brackets [thus], which are essential to the sense but were omitted by Durand. TRANS.

54. If this is hard to visualize, it is because the translation of Pliny ought to read something like this: "There is also a bedchamber, with doors into the gallery and windows overlooking the parterre." TRANS.

55. The surprising reference to "men's quarters" seems to have been a traditional misreading of Pliny. The word in the Latin text, *andron*, means a passageway. TRANS.

56. The reorganization of the École Polytechnique mentioned here took place at the beginning of the Restoration period; it was mainly a process of demilitarization. ED.

57. This notice appeared, with slight variations, in each of the volumes. The version translated is from the first volume of the *Précis*. ED.

Plates to *Précis*, Part I
Elements of Buildings

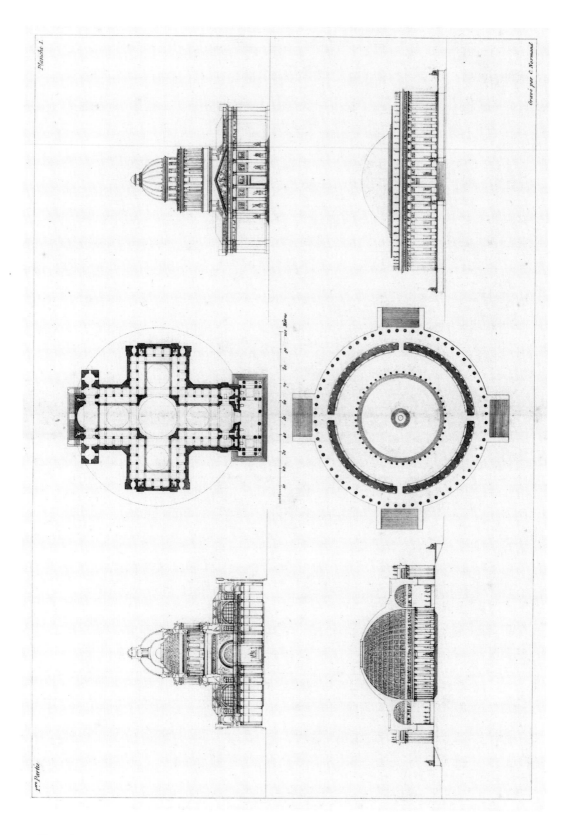

Plate 1

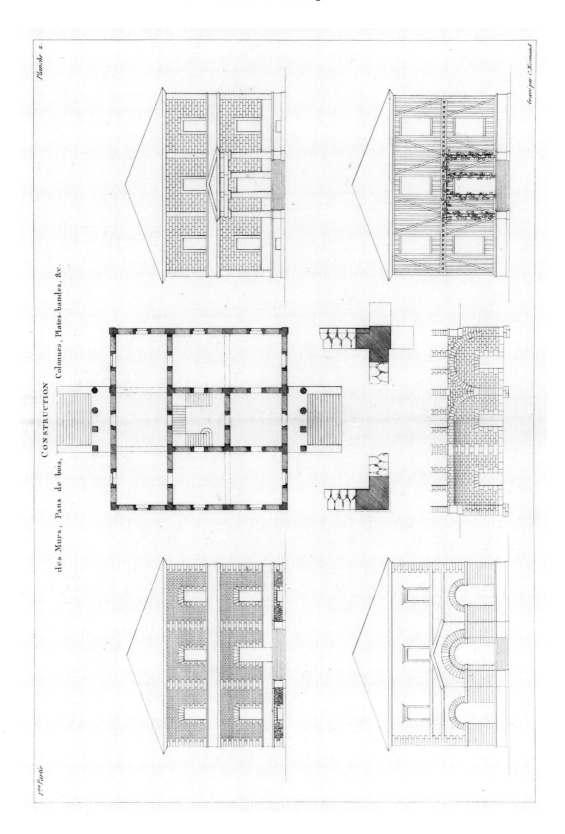

Plate 2

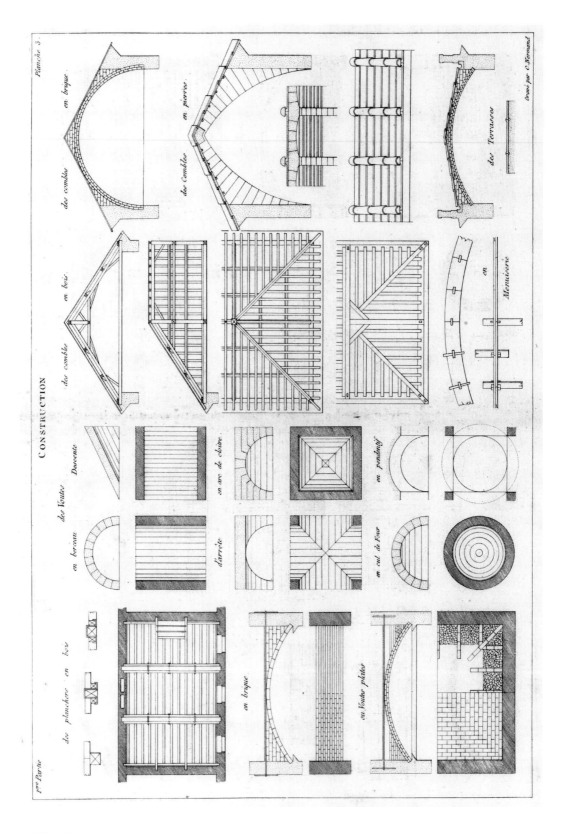

Plate 3

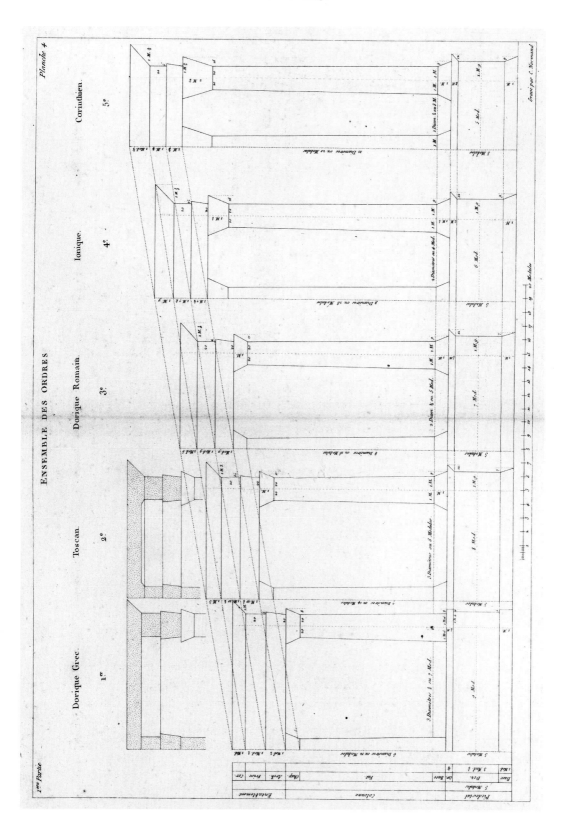

Plate 4

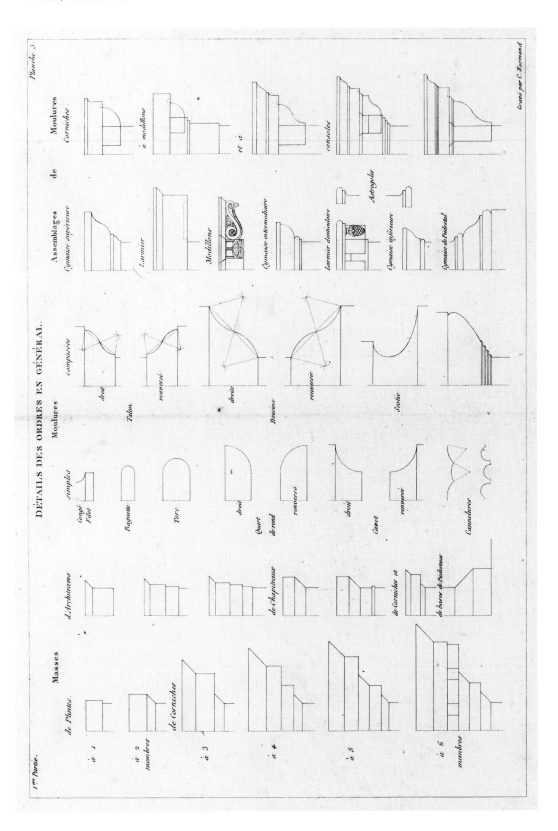

Plate 5

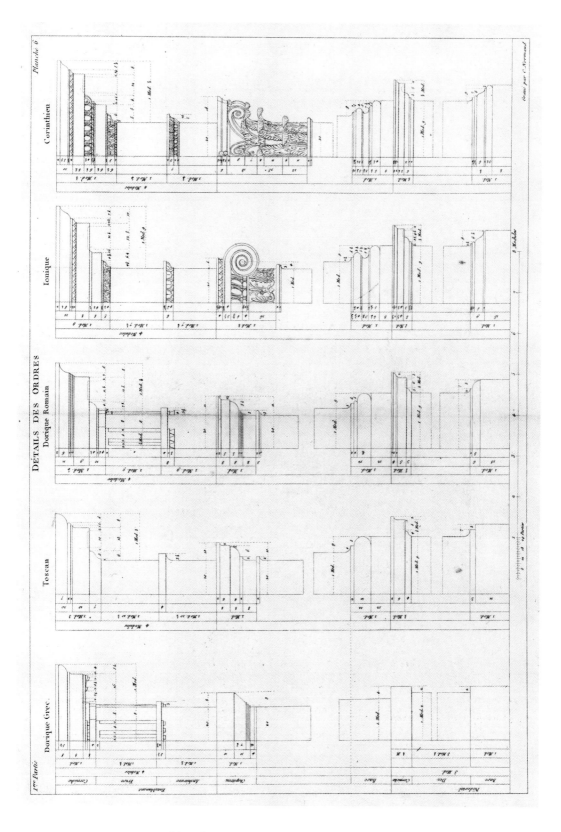

Plate 6

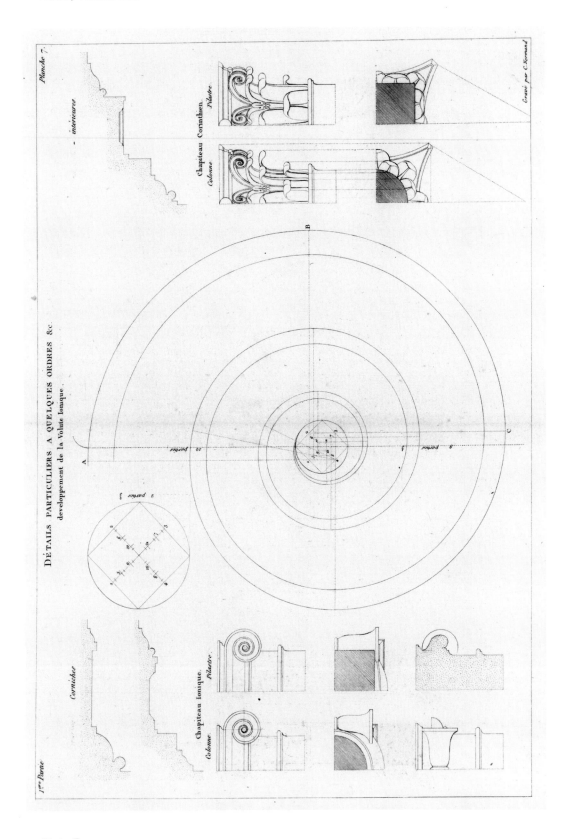

Plate 7

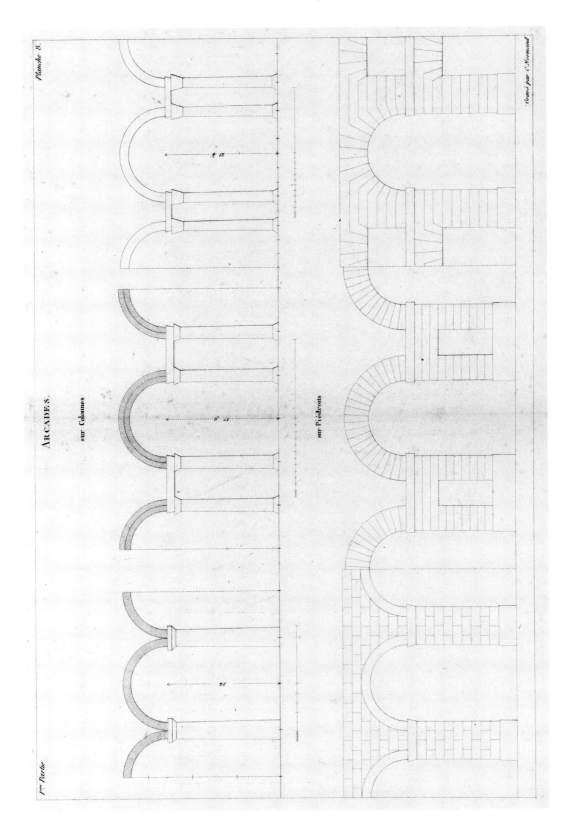

Plate 8

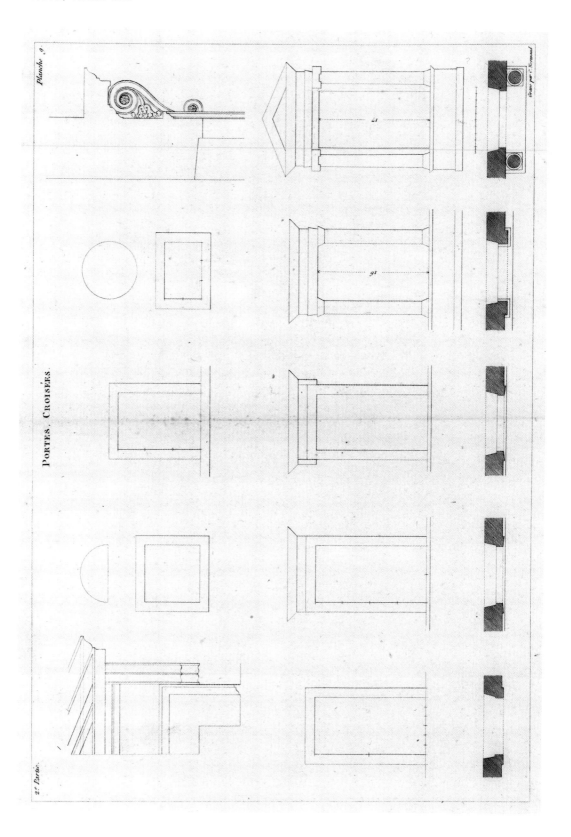

Plate 9

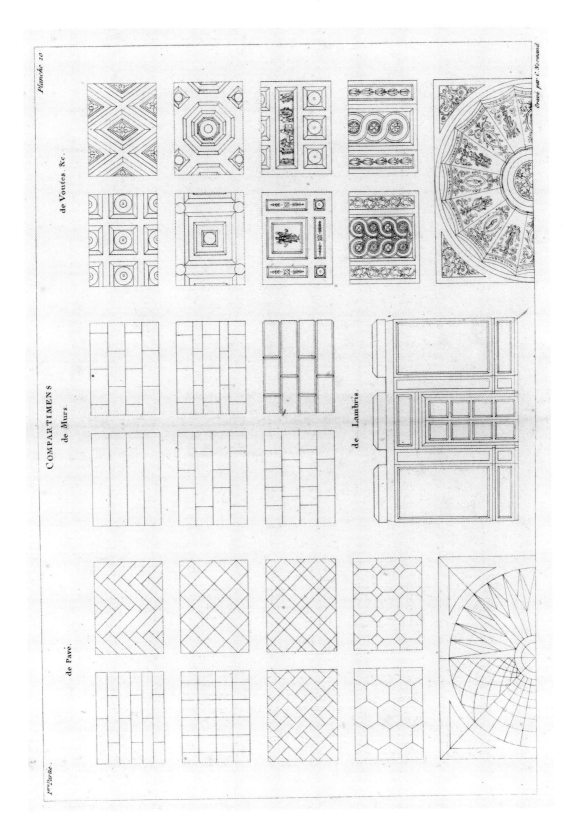

Plate 10

Plates to *Précis*, Part II
Composition in General

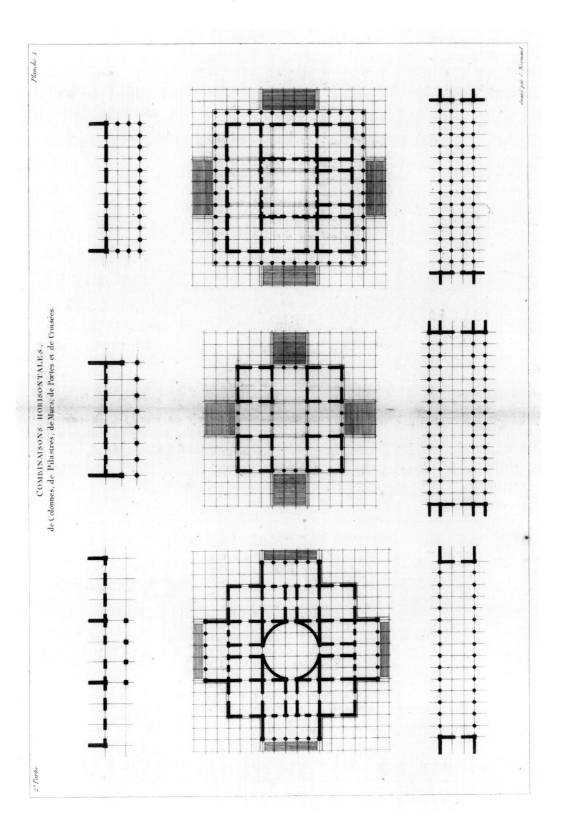

Plate 1

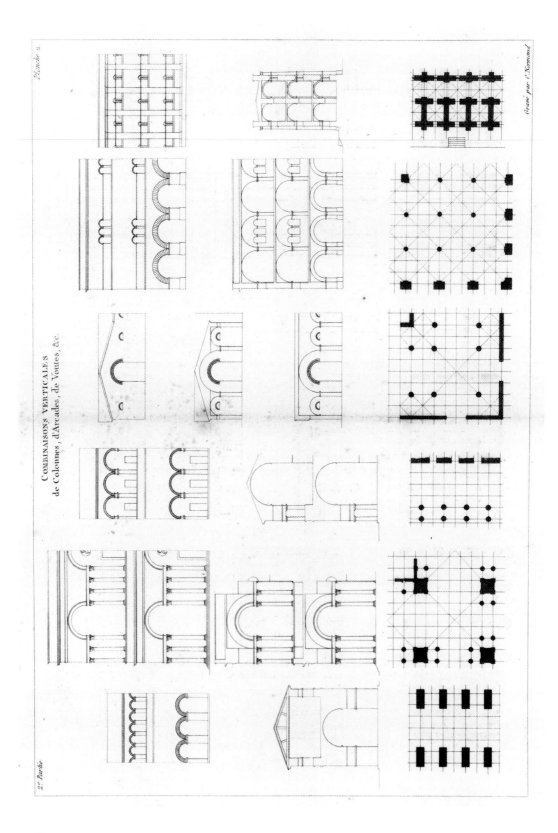

COMBINAISONS VERTICALES
de Colonnes, d'Arcades, de Voutes, &c.

Plate 2

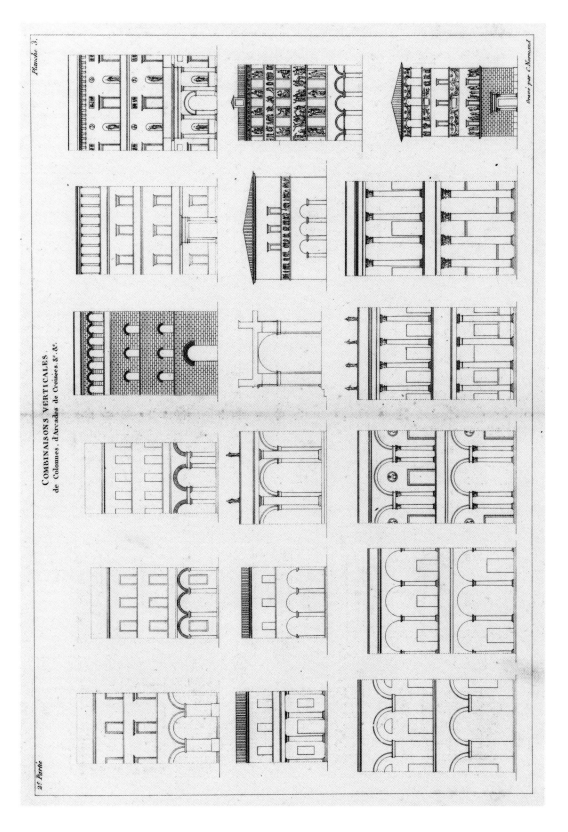

Plate 3

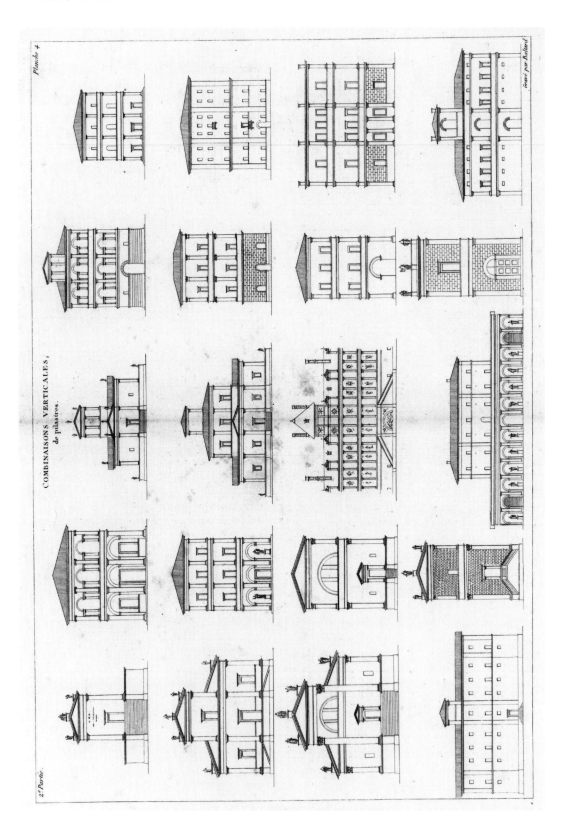

Plate 4

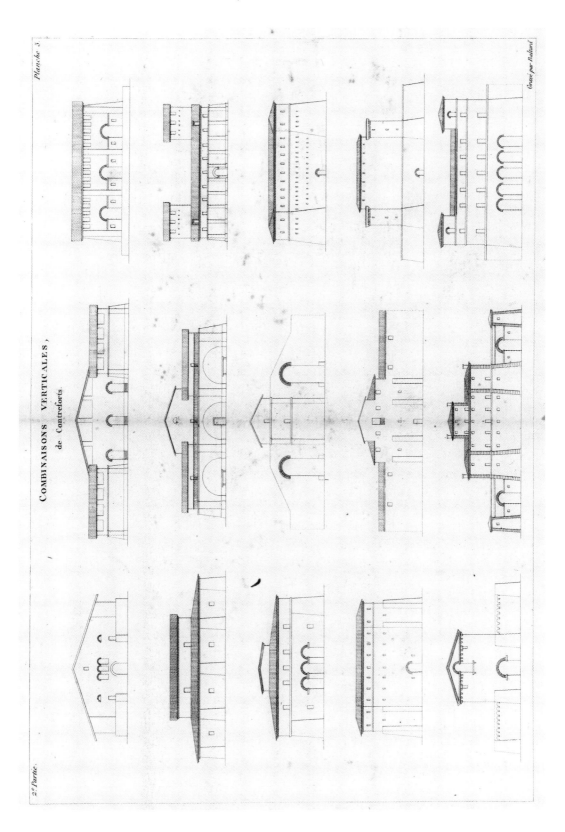

Plate 5

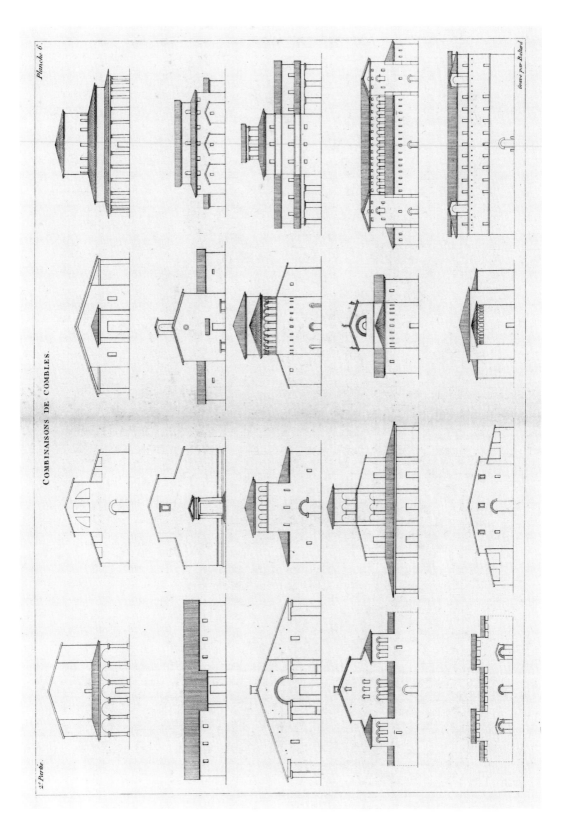

Plate 6

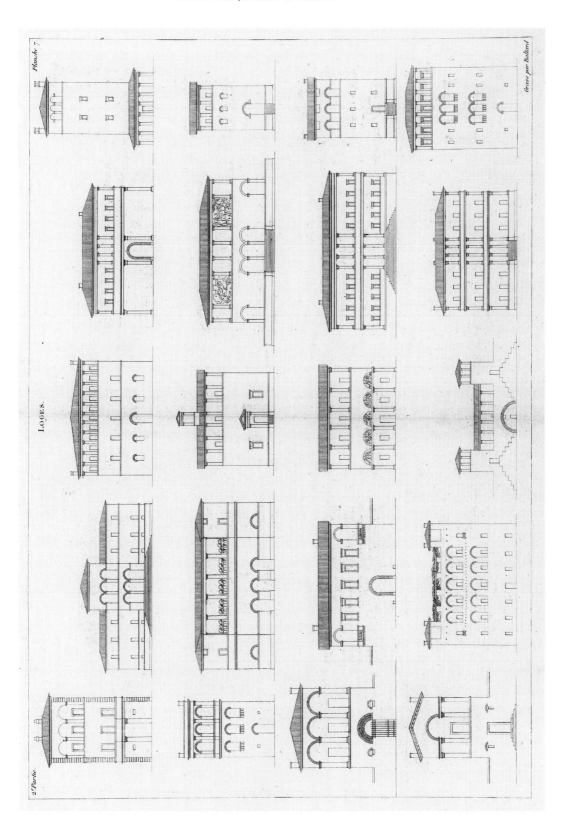

Plate 7

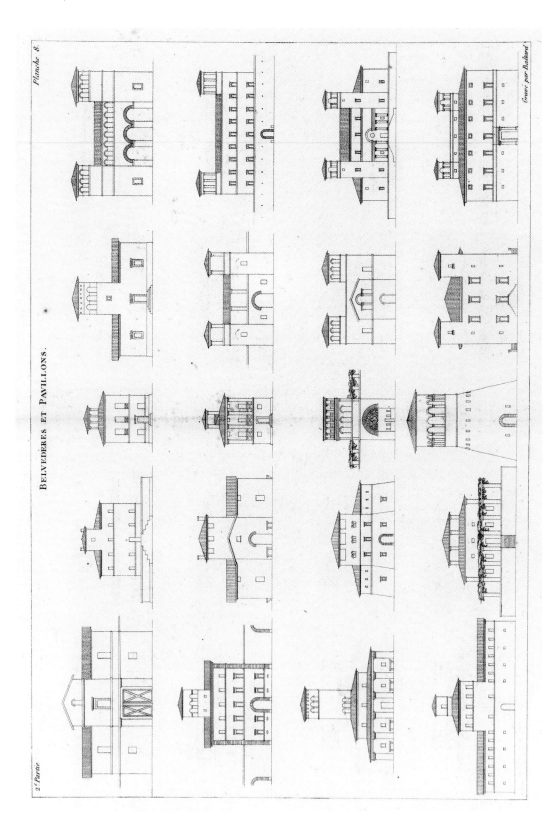

Plate 8

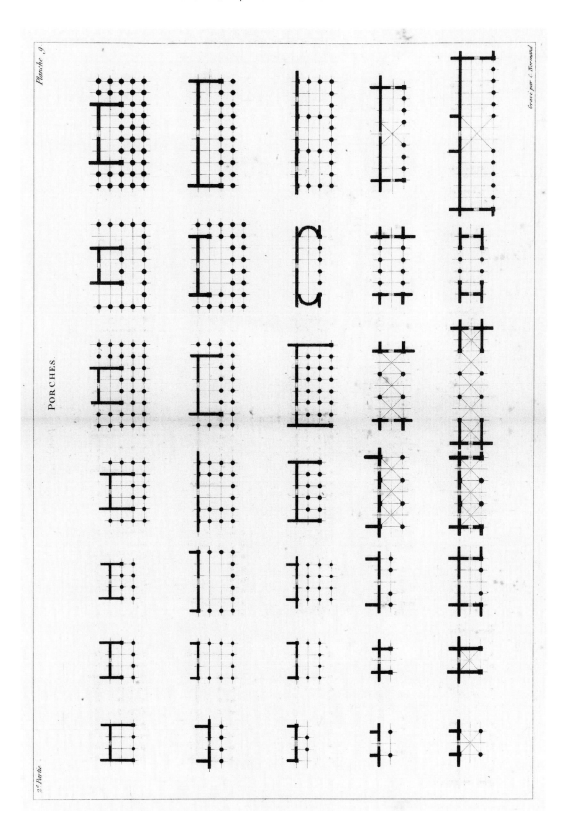

Plate 9

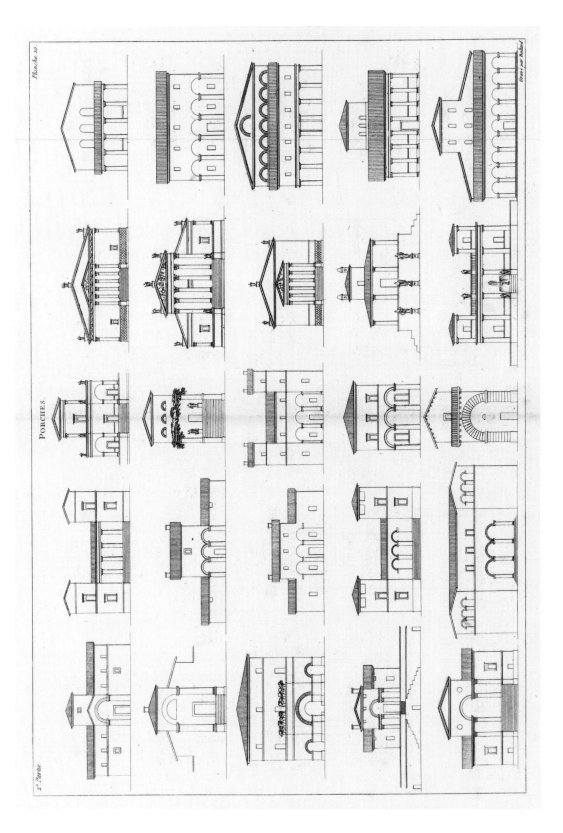

Plate 10

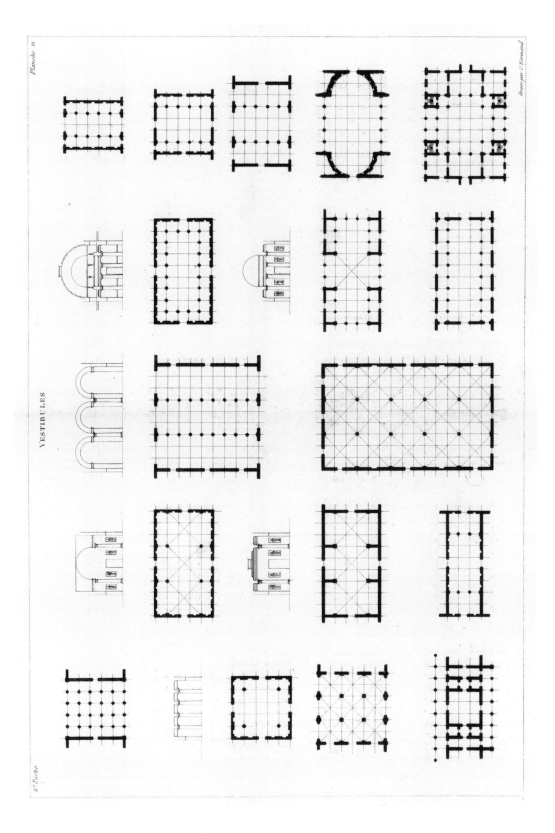

Plate 11

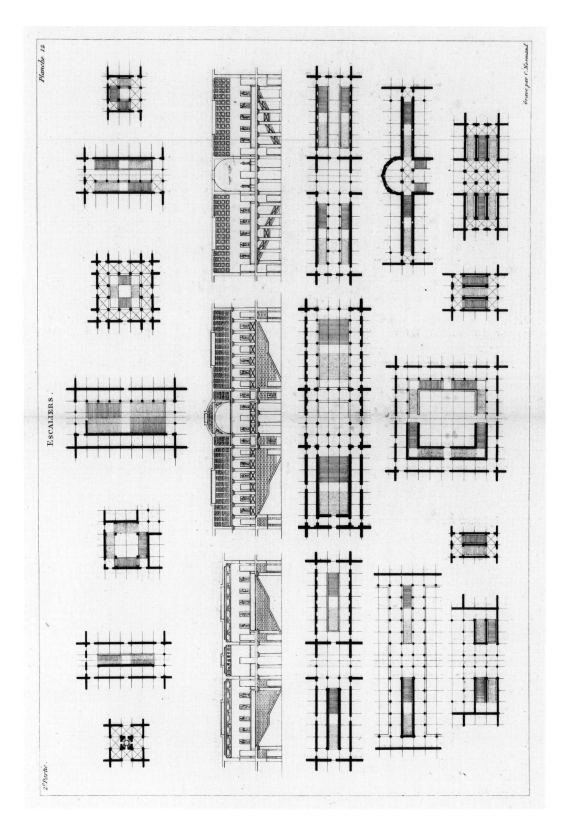

Plate 12

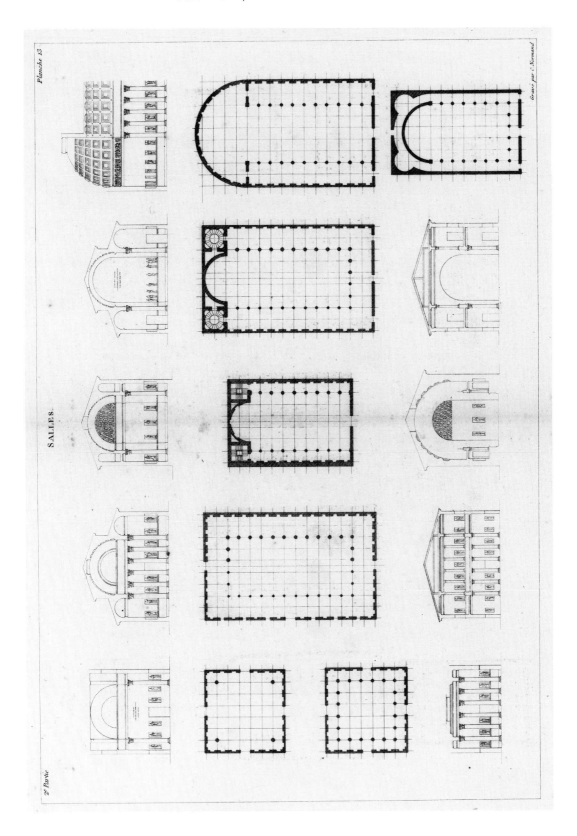

Plate 13

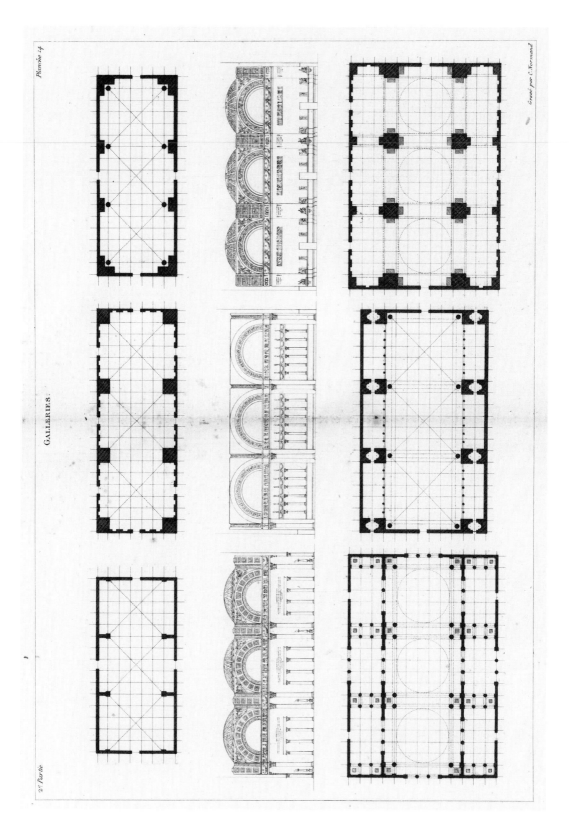

Plate 14

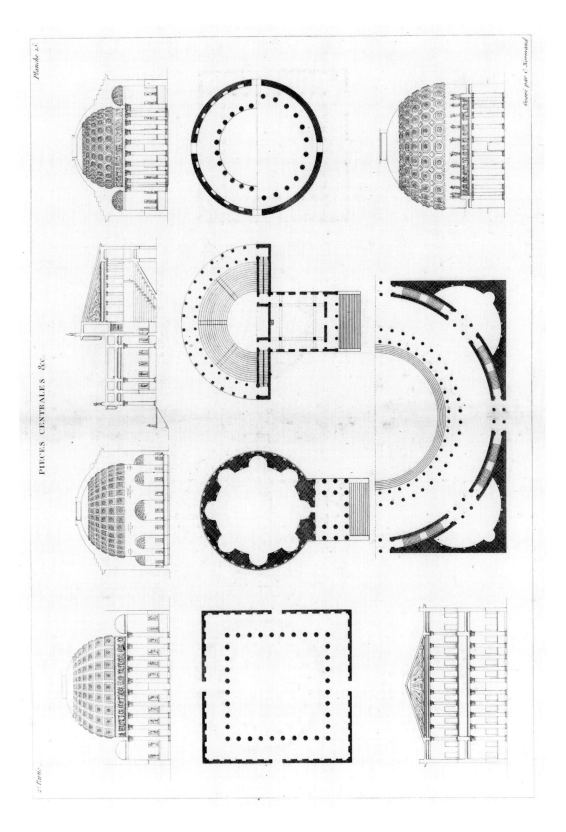

Plate 15

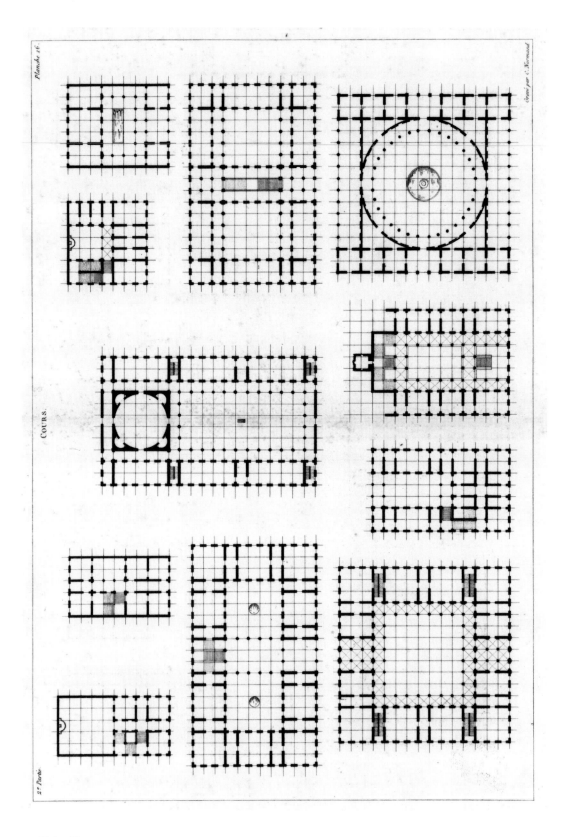

Plate 16

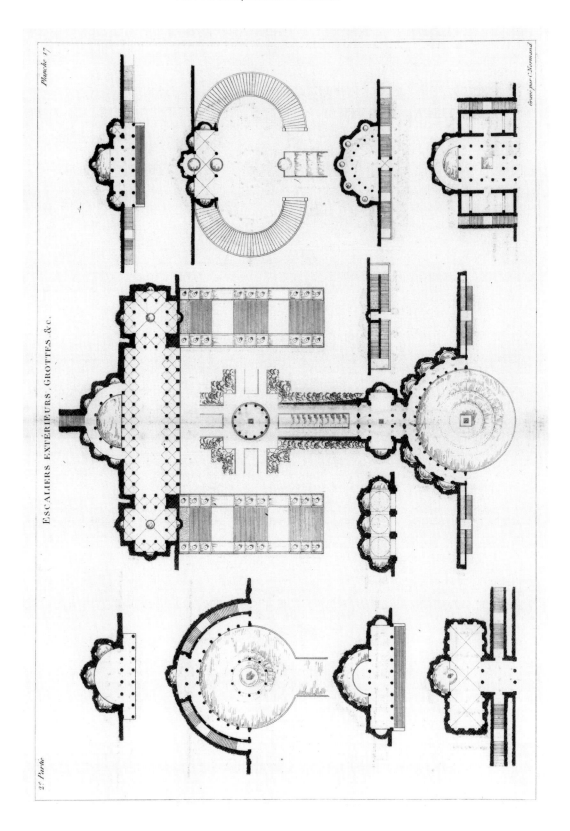

Plate 17

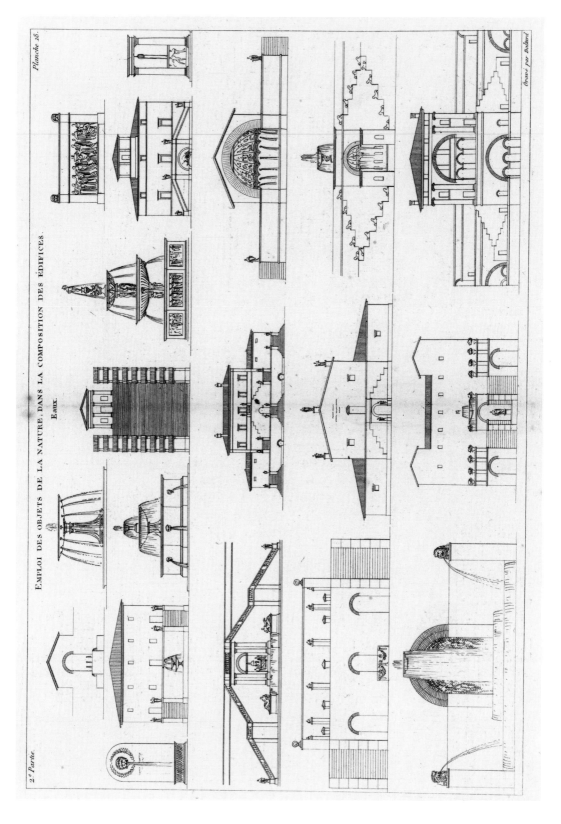

Plate 18

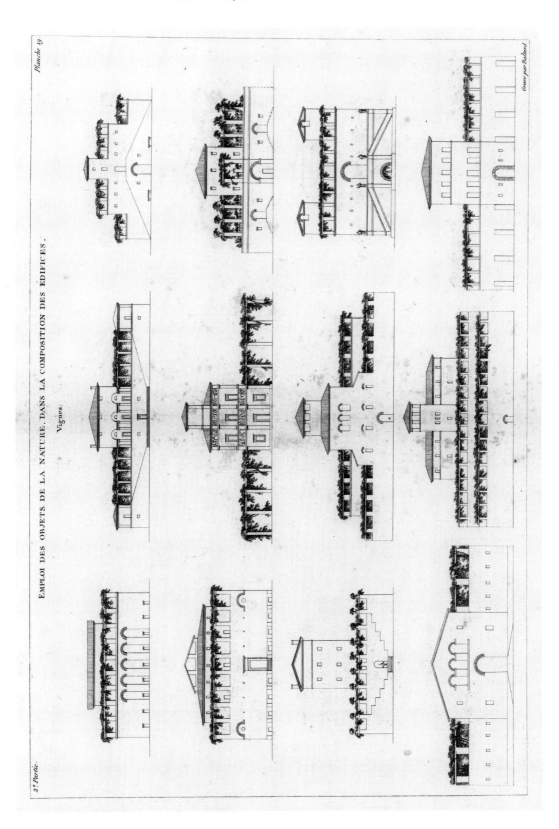

Plate 19

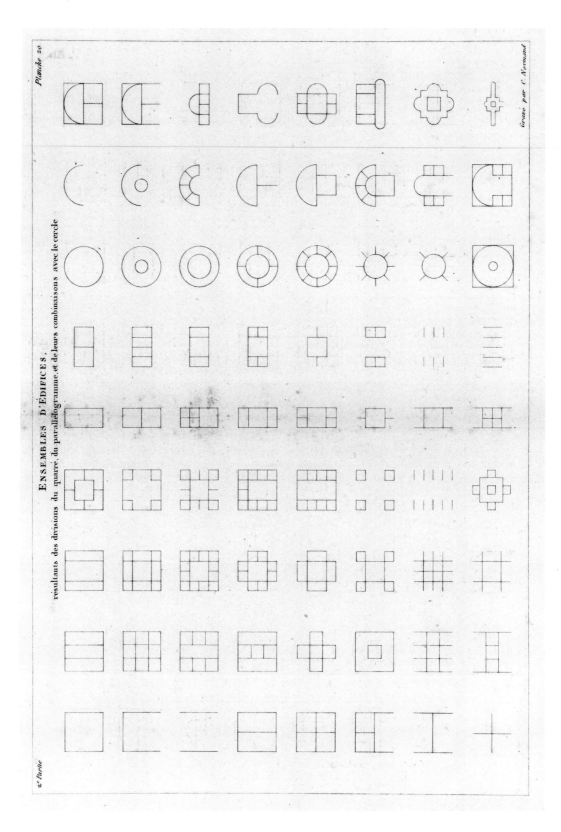

Plate 20

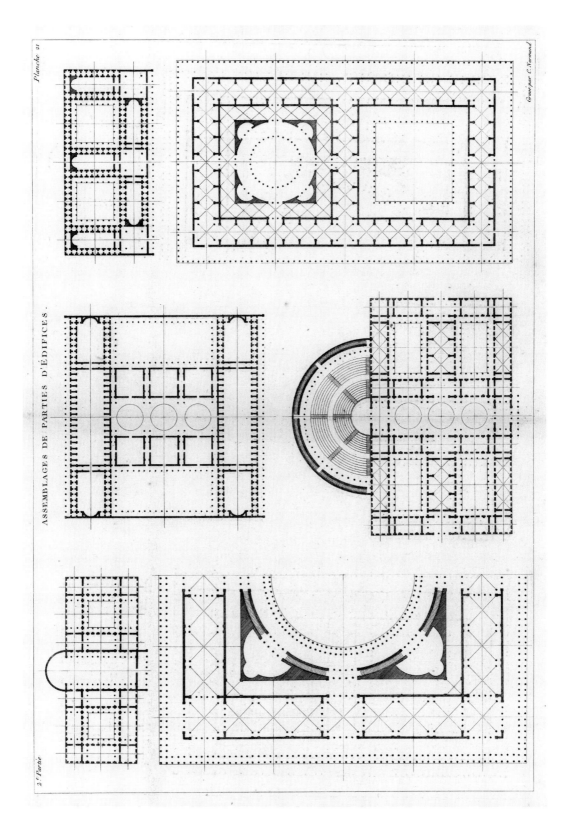

Plate 21

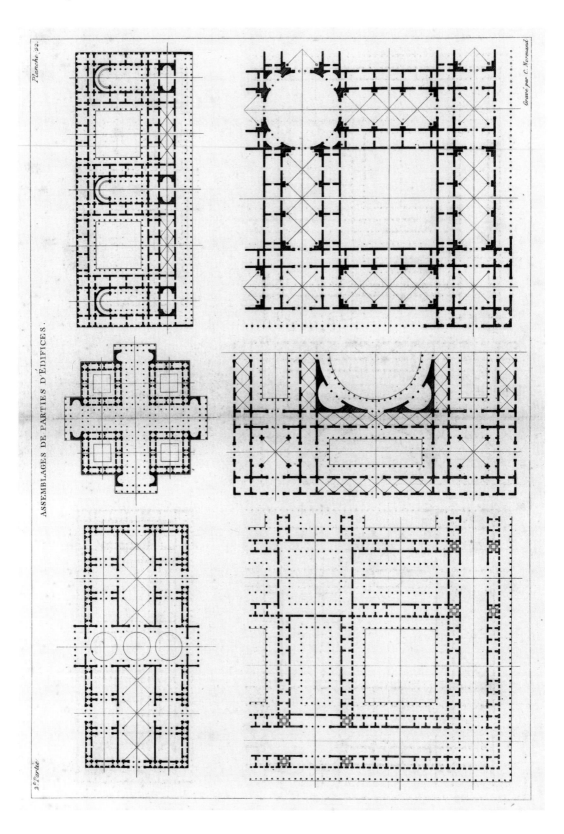

ASSEMBLAGES DE PARTIES D'ÉDIFICES.

Planche 22.

Gravé par C. Normand.

2.e Partie.

Plate 22

Plates to *Précis*, Part III
Examination of the Principal
Kinds of Building

Plate 1

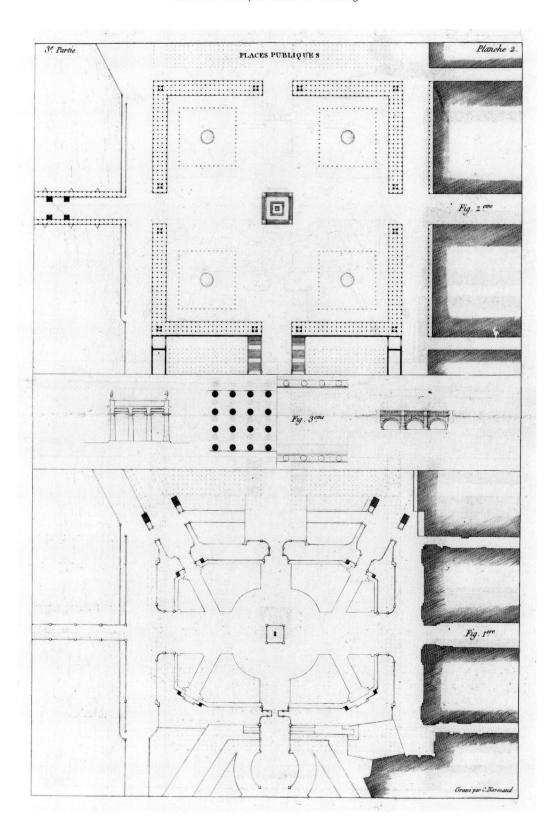

Plate 2

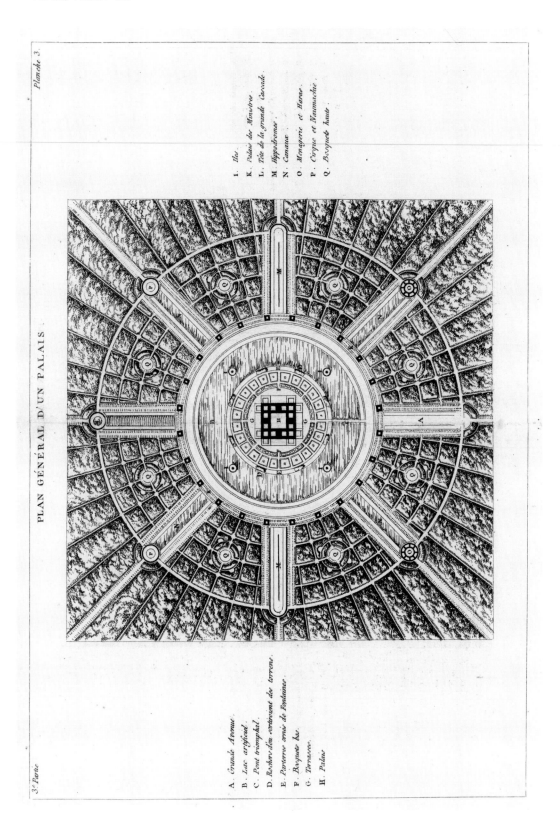

PLAN GÉNÉRAL D'UN PALAIS.

Planche 3.

3.ᵉ Partie

A. Grande Avenue.
B. Lac artificiel.
C. Pont triomphal.
D. Rochers d'où sortirent des torrens.
E. Parterres ornés de Fontaines.
F. Bosquets bas.
G. Terrasses.
H. Palais.

I. Iles.
K. Palais des Ministres.
L. Tête de la grande Cascade.
M. Hippodromes.
N. Canaux.
O. Menagerie et Harus.
P. Cirque et Naumachie.
Q. Bosquets hauts.

Plate 3

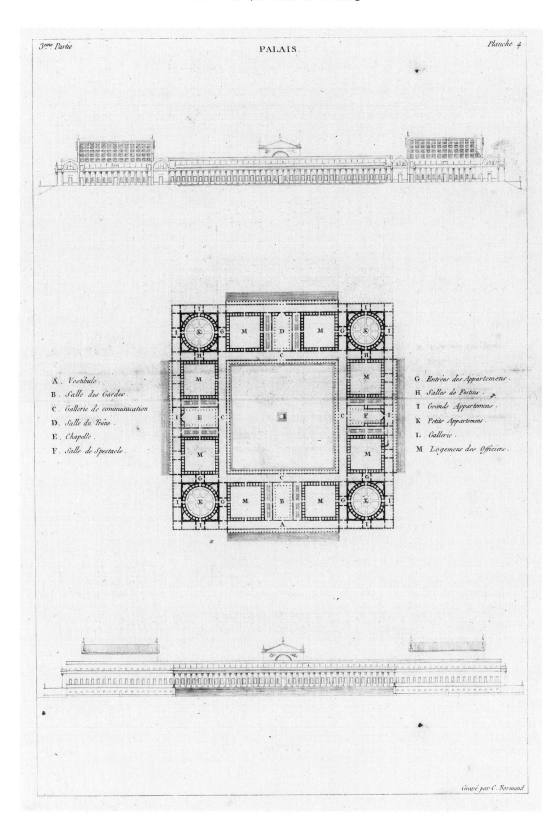

Plate 4

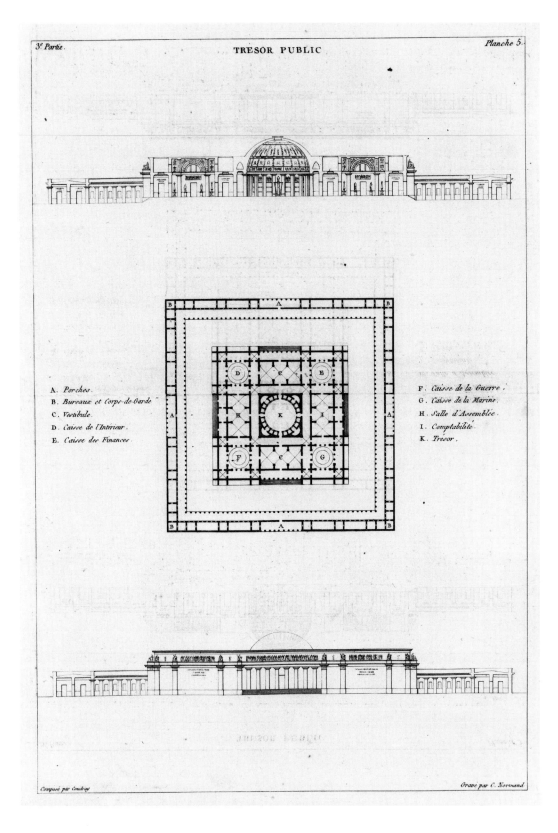

Plate 5

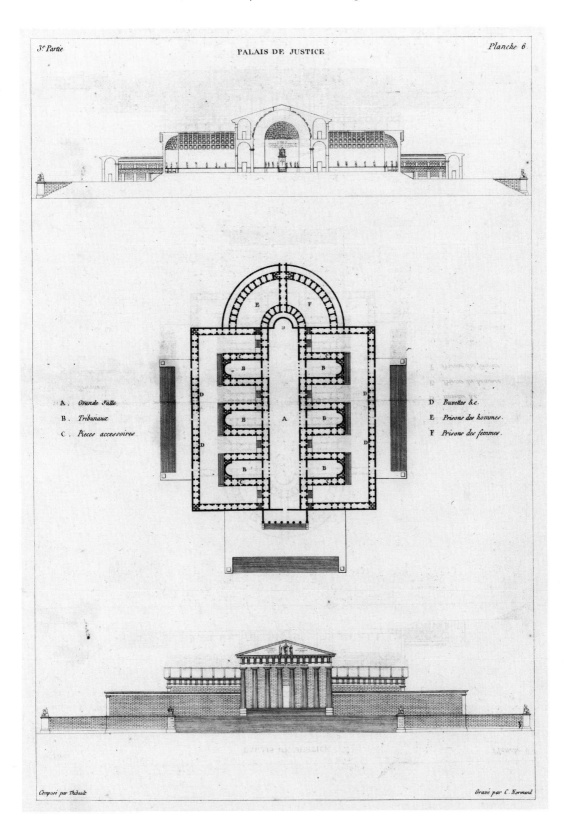

PALAIS DE JUSTICE

A . Grande Salle

B . Tribunaux

C . Pieces accessoires

D . Buvettes &c.

E . Prisons des hommes.

F . Prisons des femmes.

Composé par Thibault

Gravé par C. Normand

Plate 6

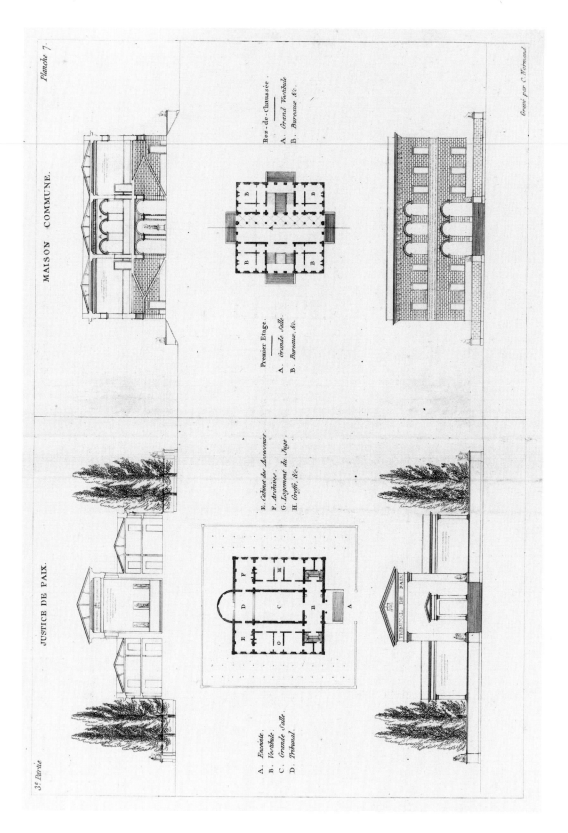

Planche 7.

MAISON COMMUNE.

Rez-de-chaussée.

A. Grand Vestibule.
B. Bureaux &c.

Premier Étage.

A. Grande Salle.
B. Bureaux. &c.

Gravé par C. Normand.

3.ᵉ Partie

JUSTICE DE PAIX.

E. Cabinet des Assesseurs.
F. Archives.
G. Logement du Juge.
H. Greffe. &c.

A. Enceinte.
B. Vestibule.
C. Grande Salle.
D. Tribunal.

Plate 7

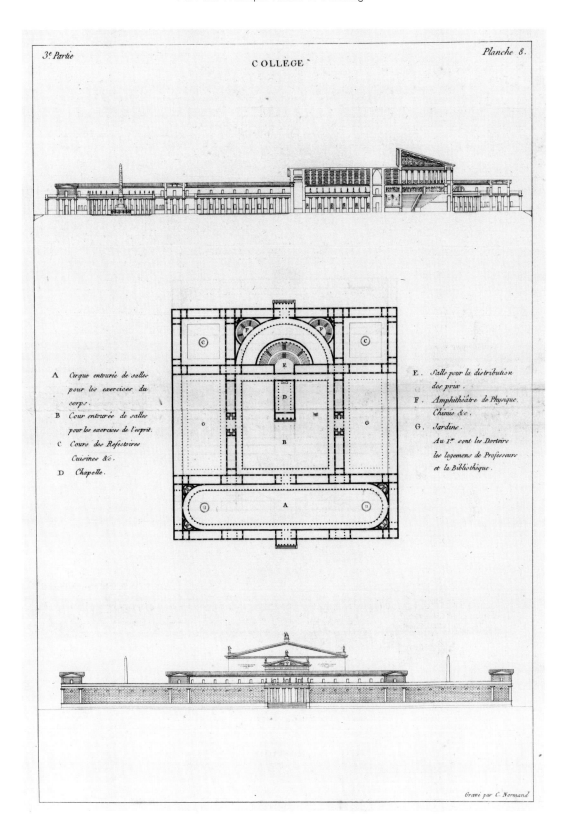

Plate 8

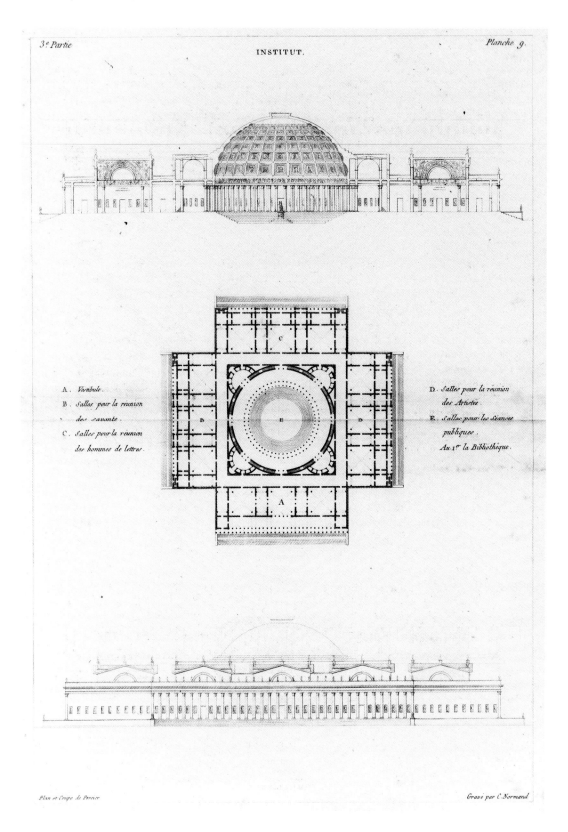

INSTITUT.

A . Vestibule .

B . Salles pour la réunion
    des savants .

C . Salles pour la réunion
    des hommes de lettres .

D . Salles pour la réunion
    des Artistes .

E . Salles pour les Séances
    publiques .
    Au 1.ᵉʳ la Bibliothèque .

Plan et Coupe de Percier .

Gravé par C. Normand .

Plate 9

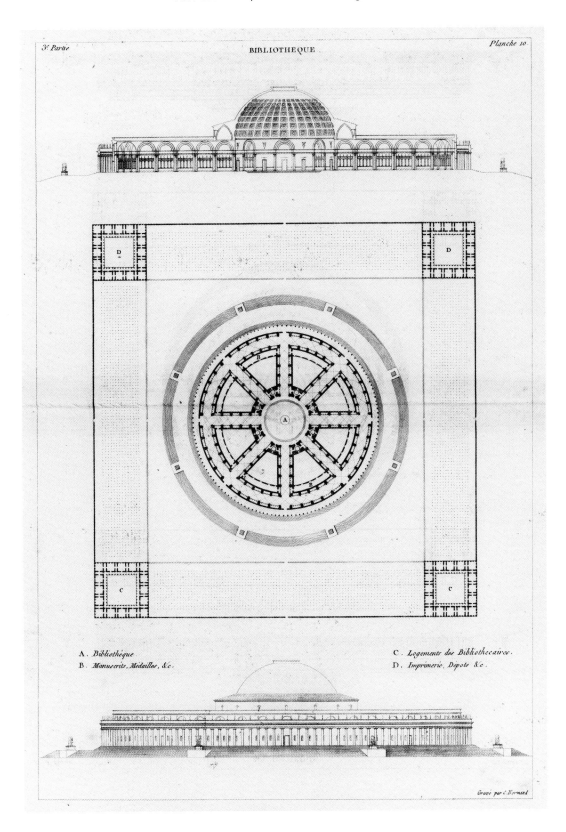

Plate 10

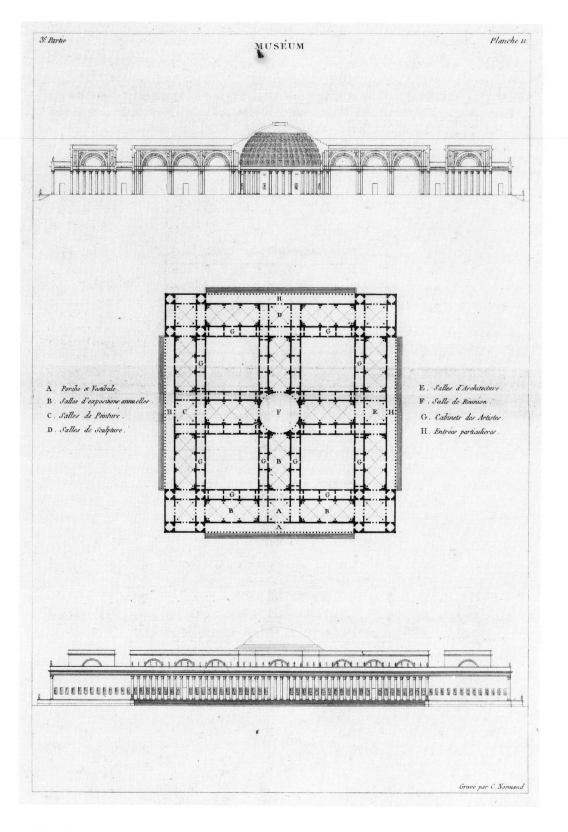

A. Porche et Vestibule.
B. Salles d'expositions annuelles.
C. Salles de Peinture.
D. Salles de Sculpture.

E. Salles d'Architecture.
F. Salle de Réunion.
G. Cabinets des Artistes.
H. Entrées particulieres.

Gravé par C. Normand.

Plate 11

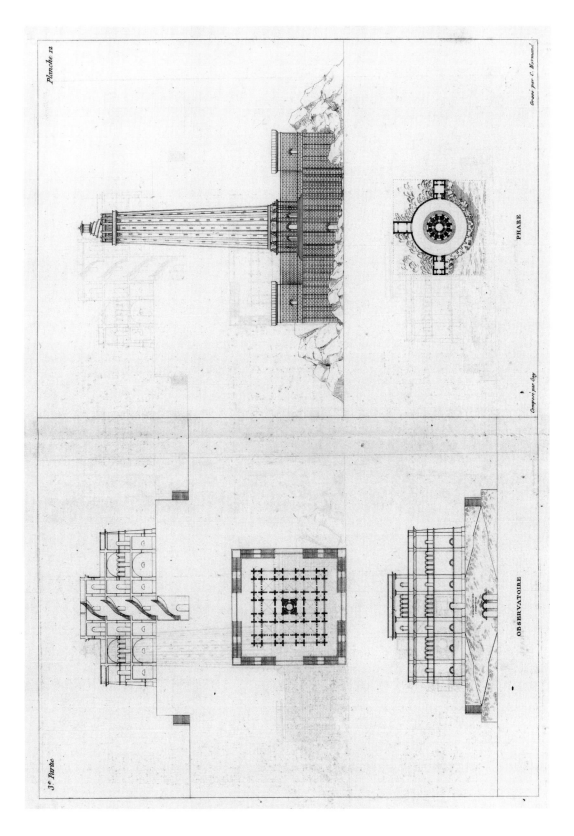

Plate 12

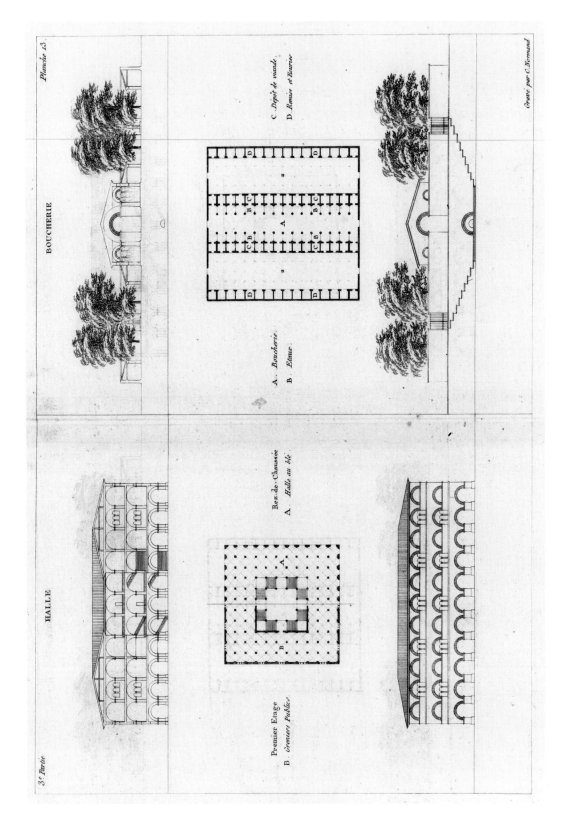

Plate 13

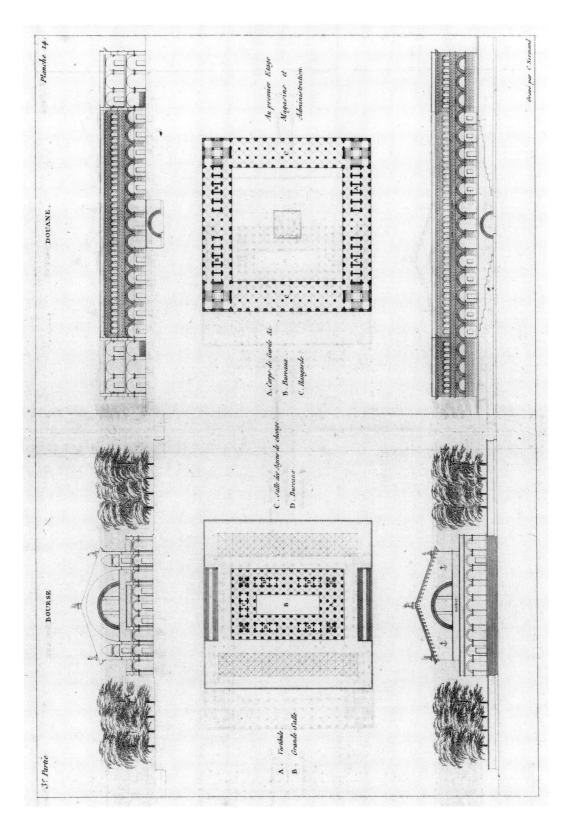

Plate 14

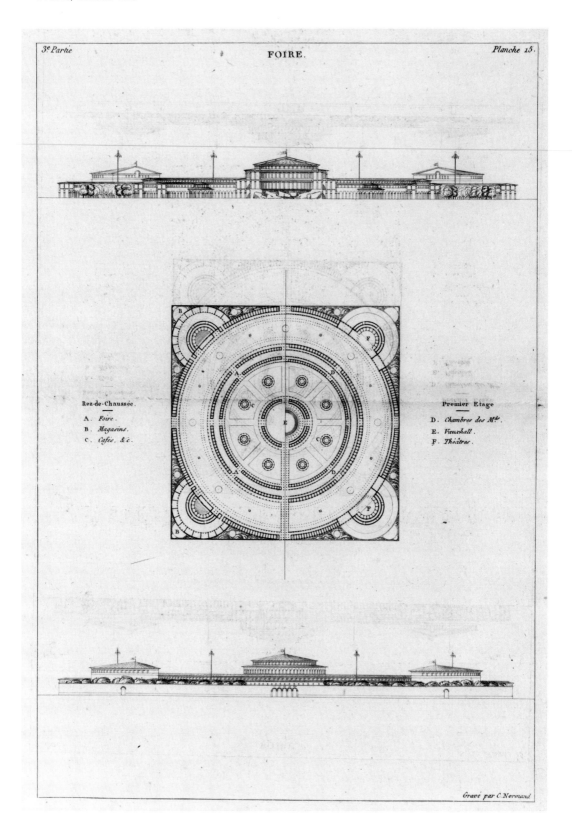

Plate 15

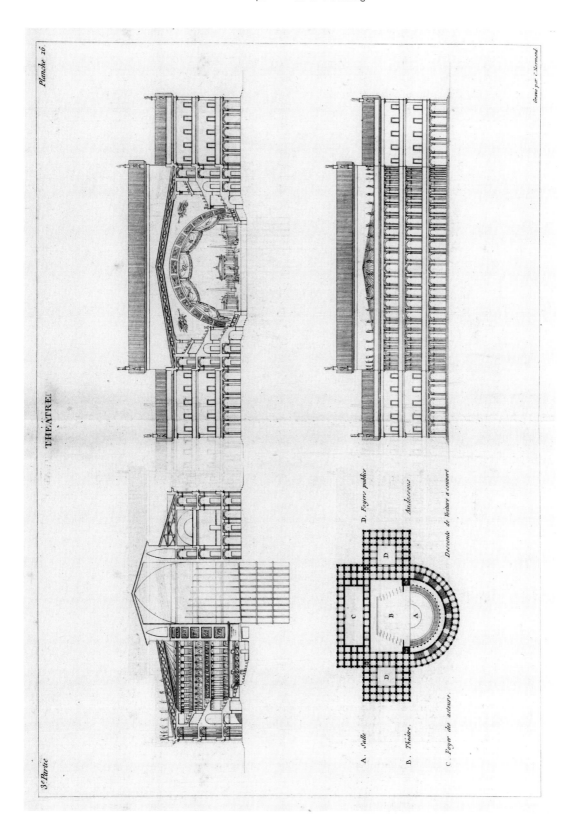

THÉATRE

Planche 16.

3.ª Partie

Gravé par C. Normand

A. Salle

B. Théâtre.

C. Foyer des acteurs.

D. Foyer public

Ambocoeur

Descente de Voiture a couvert.

Plate 16

A   Esplanade.
B   Administration.
C   Pièce d'eau pour la joute.
D   Bains des hommes.

E   Bains des femmes.
F   Bains découverts.
G   Restaurateur.
H   Cafés, Jeux &c.

Gravé par C. Normand.

Plate 17

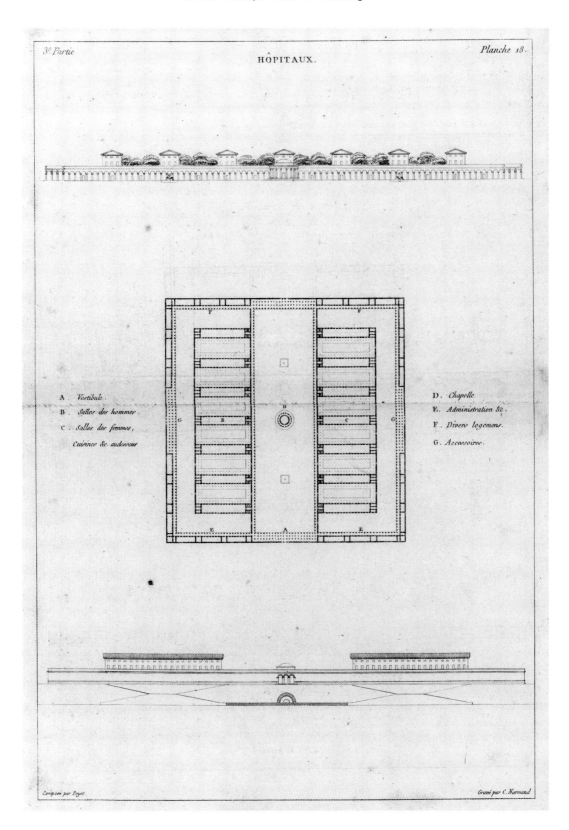

Plate 18

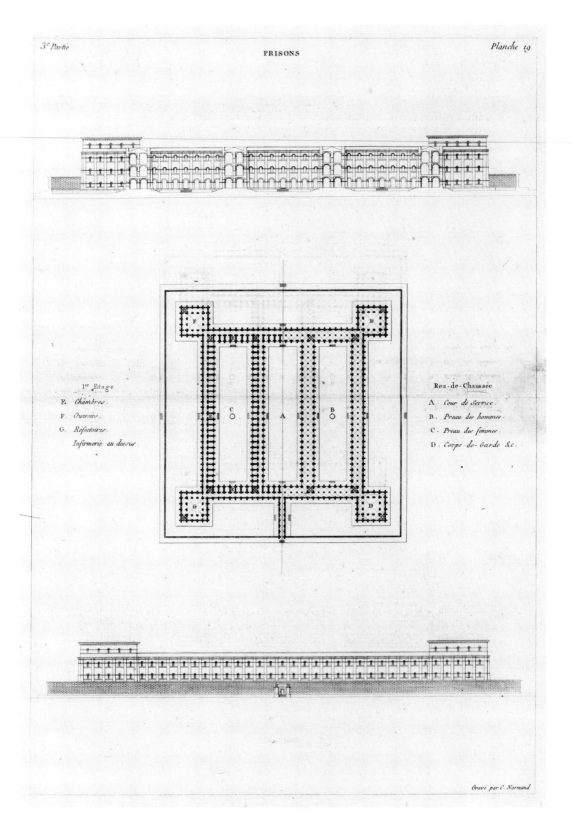

PRISONS

1ᵉʳ Etage

E. Chambres.
F. Ouvroire.
G. Réfectoires.
   Infirmerie au dessus.

Rez-de-Chaussée

A. Cour de Service.
B. Preau des hommes.
C. Preau des femmes.
D. Corps-de-Garde &c.

Gravé par C. Normand

Plate 19

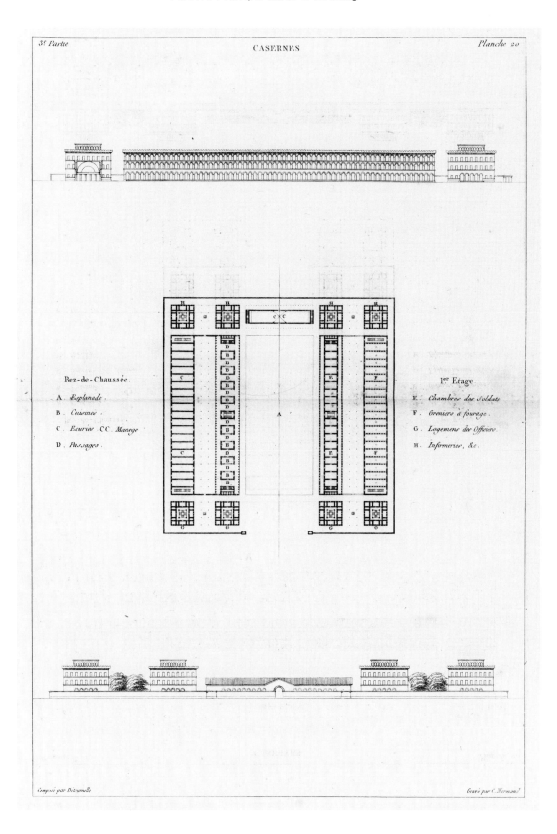

Rez-de-Chaussée.

A. Esplanade.

B. Cuisines.

C. Ecuries CC. Manege.

D. Passages.

1ᵉʳ Etage.

E. Chambres des Soldats.

F. Greniers à fourage.

G. Logemens des Officiers.

H. Infirmeries, &c.

Composée par Détournelle   Gravé par C. Normand

Plate 20

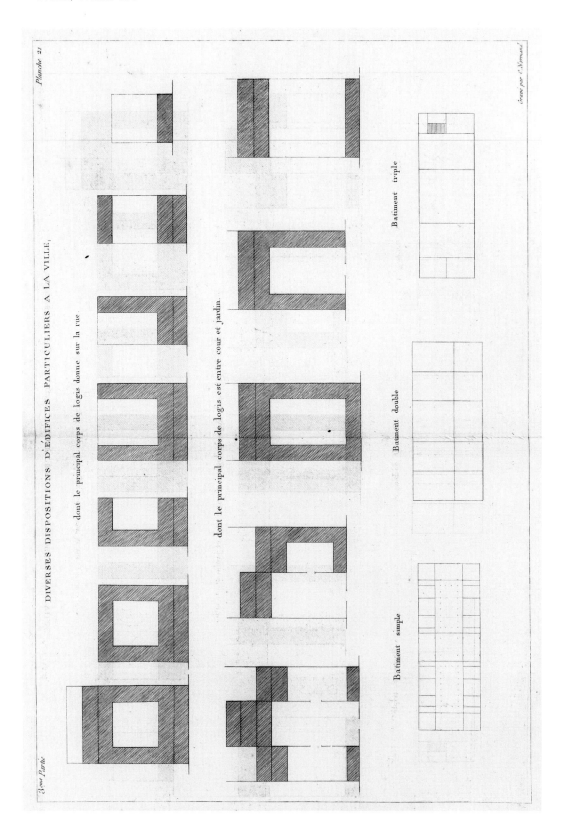

DIVERSES DISPOSITIONS D'ÉDIFICES PARTICULIERS A LA VILLE.

dont le principal corps de logis donne sur la rue.

dont le principal corps de logis est entre cour et jardin.

Bâtiment triple

Bâtiment double

Bâtiment simple

Planche 21

3ᵐᵉ Partie

Gravé par C.Normand.

Plate 21

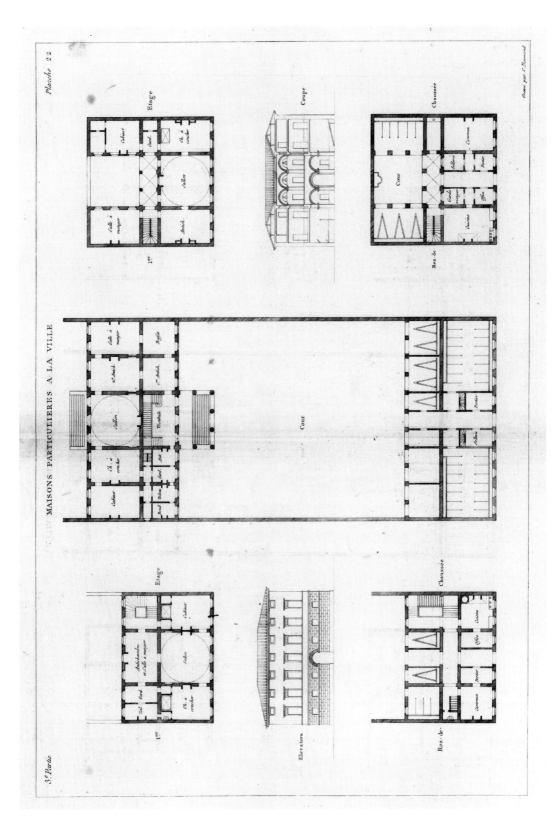

Plate 22

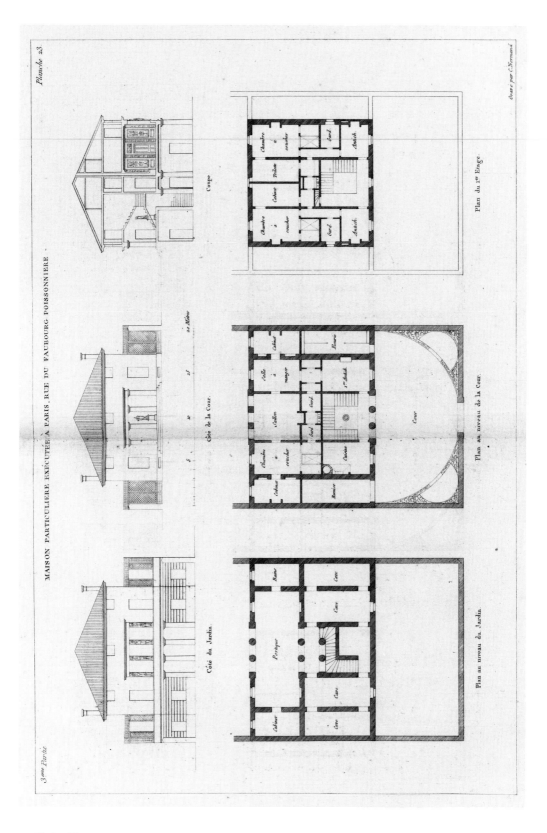

Plate 23

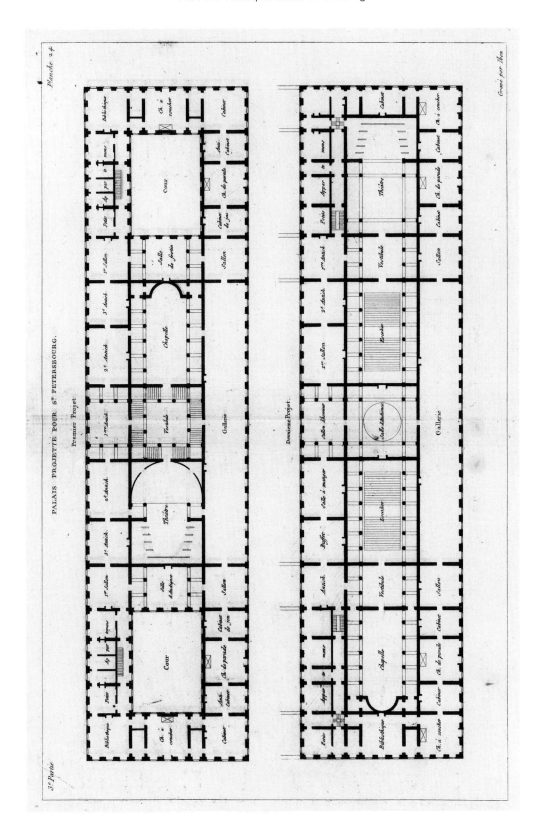

Plate 24

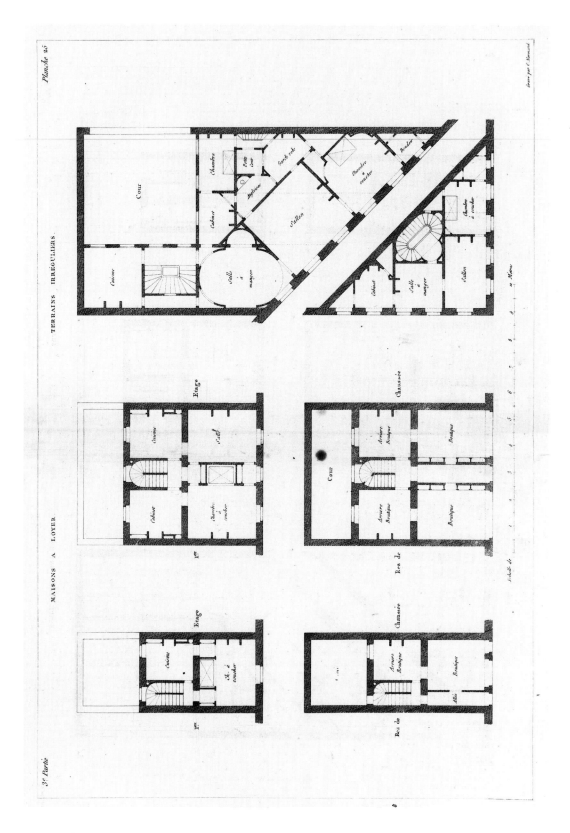

Plate 25

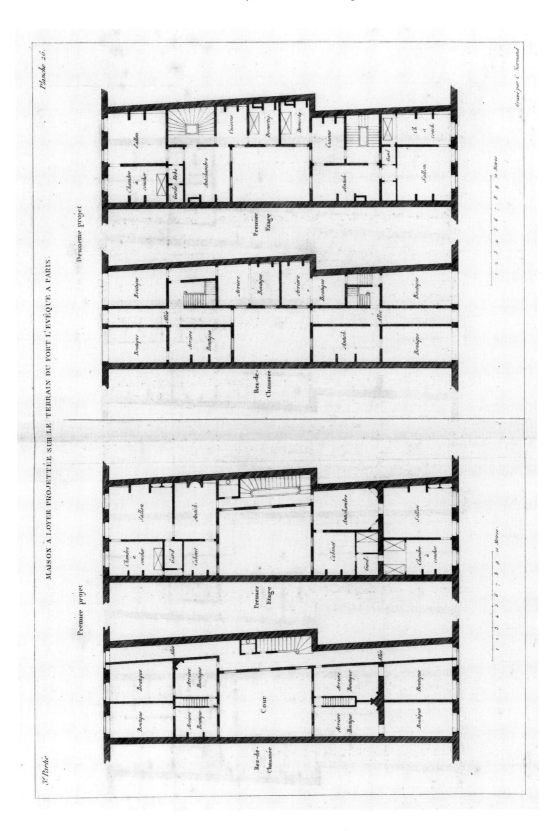

Plate 26

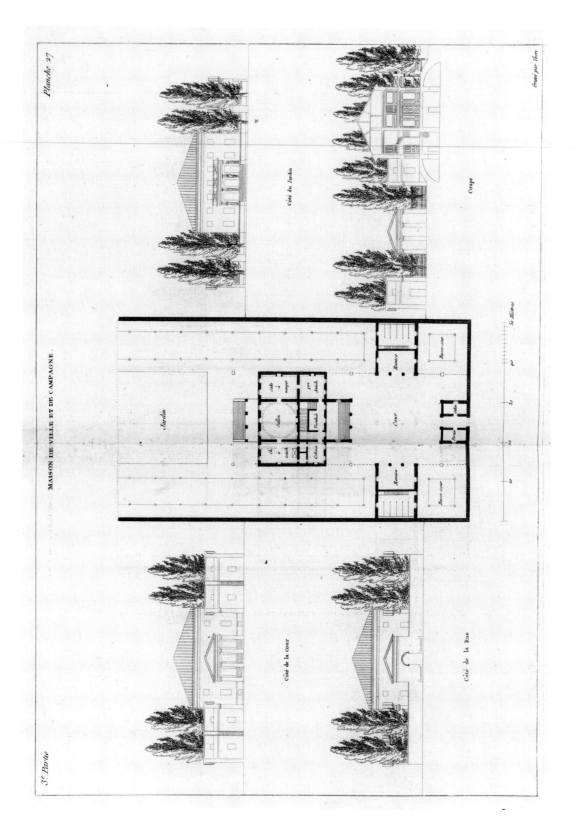

Plate 27

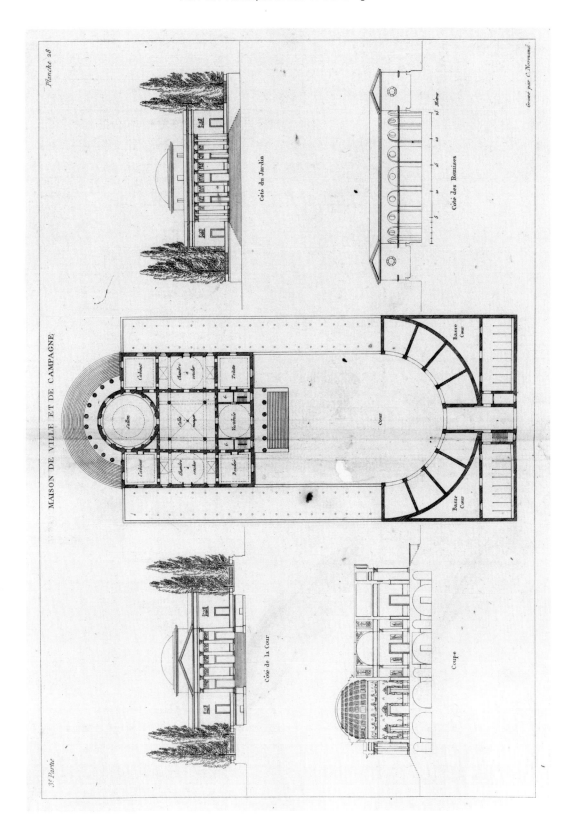

Planche 28

Gravé par C. Normand

Côté du Jardin

Côté des Remises

MAISON DE VILLE ET DE CAMPAGNE

Cabinet

Chambre à coucher

Salon

Ville à manger

Toilette

Vestibule

Cabinet

Chambre à coucher

Boudoir

Basse Cour

Cour

Basse Cour

3e Partie

Côté de la Cour

Coupe

Plate 28

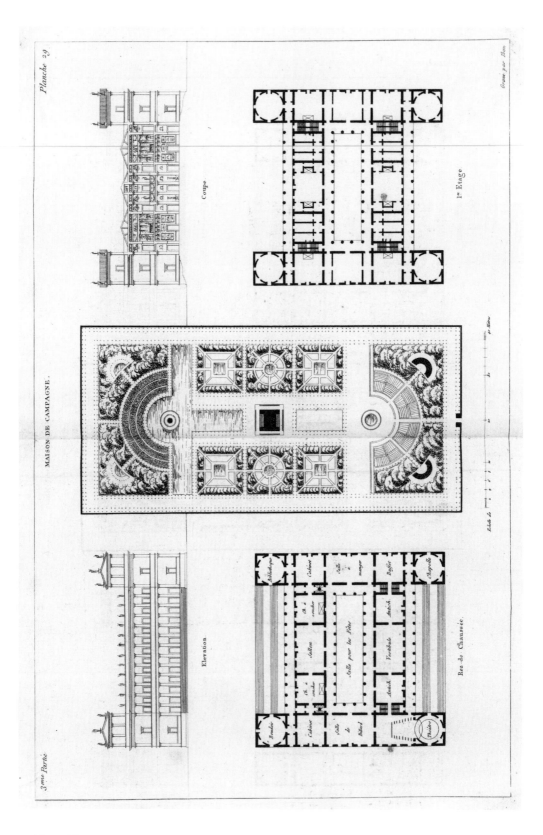

Plate 29

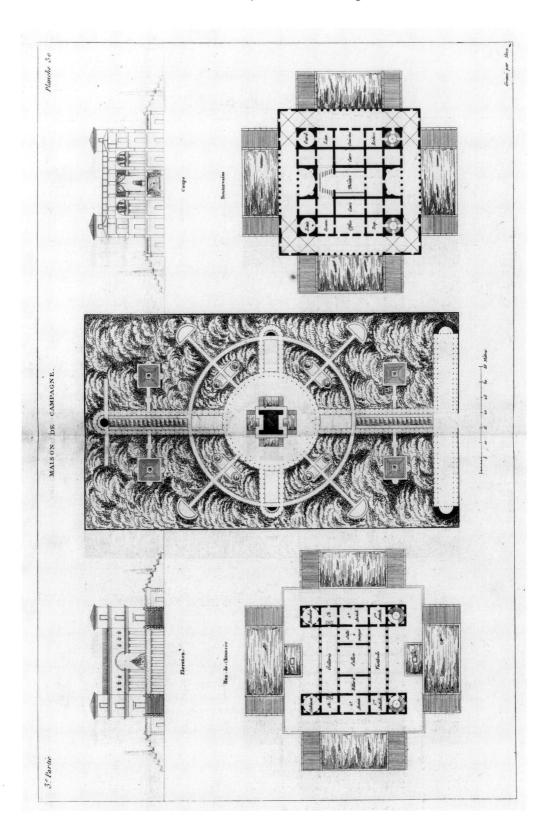

Plate 30

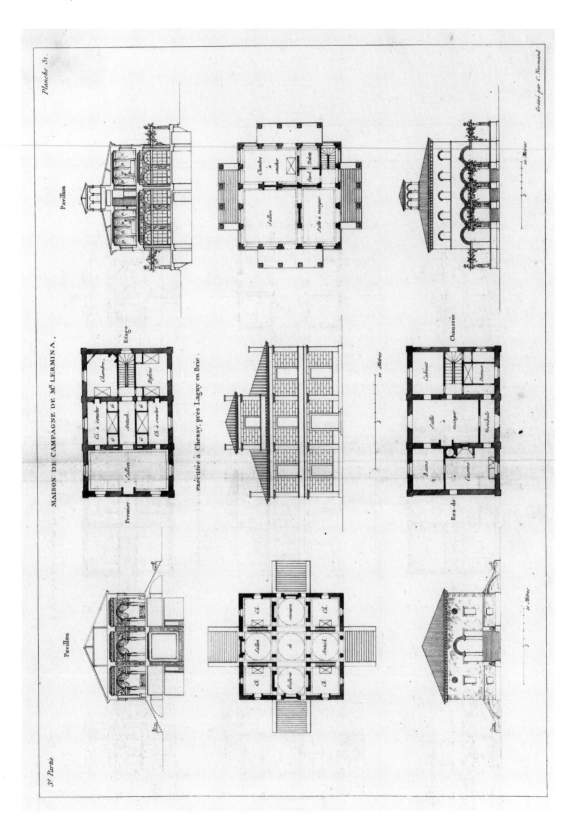

MAISON DE CAMPAGNE DE Me LERMINA,

exécutée à Chessy, près Lagny en Brie.

Planche 31.

Gravé par C. Normand.

Plate 31

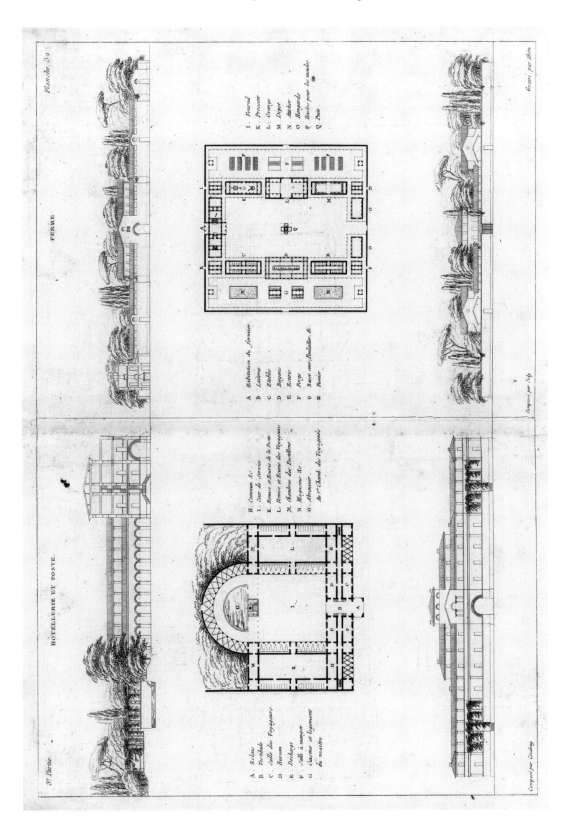

Plate 32

Plates to *Graphic Portion*

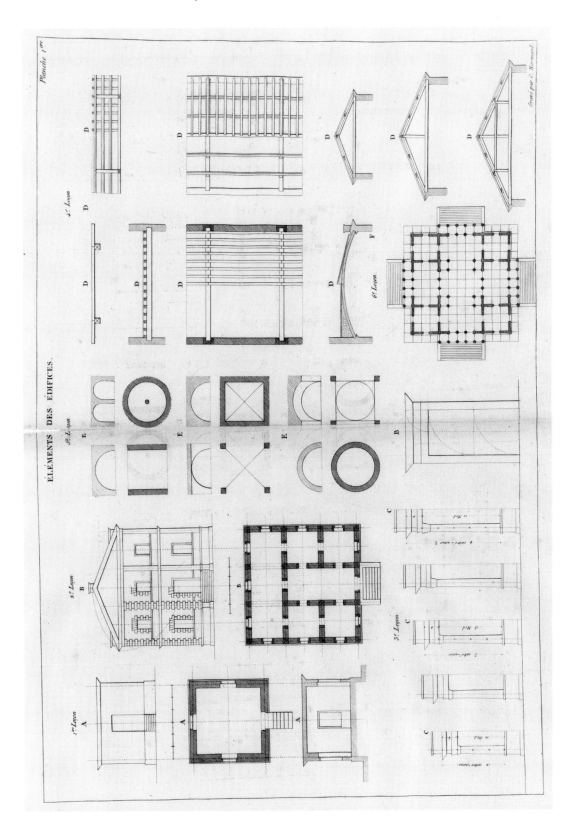

Plate 1

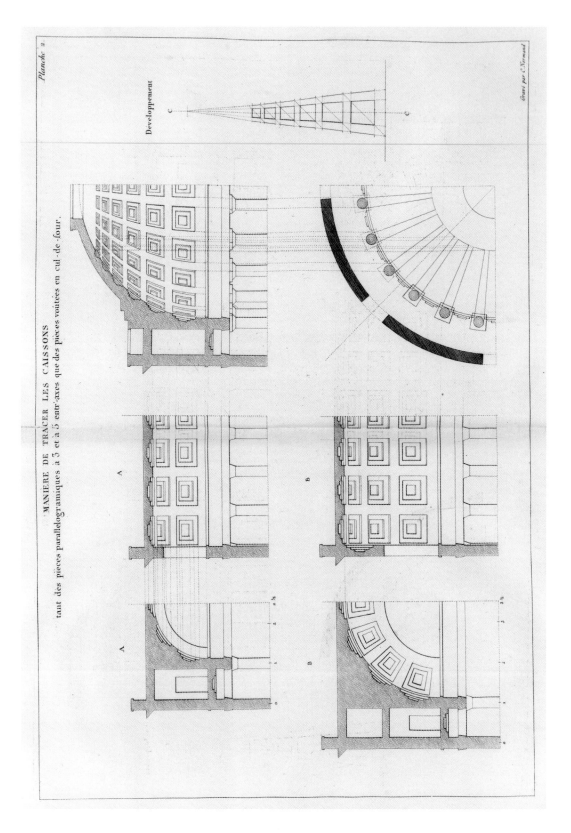

Plate 2

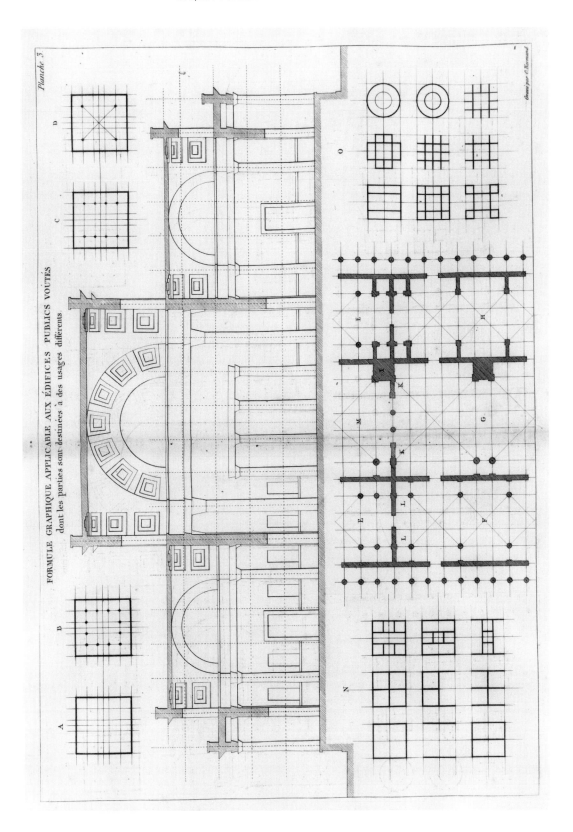

Plate 3

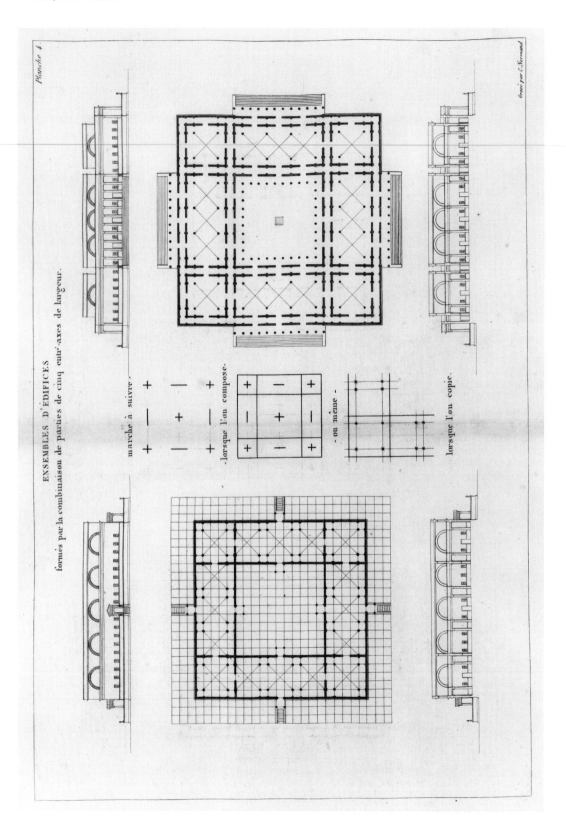

Plate 4

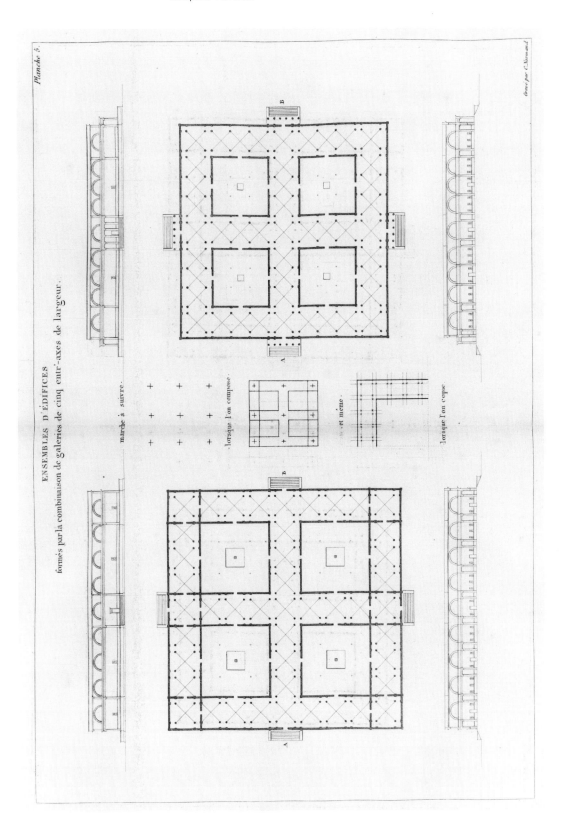

Plate 5

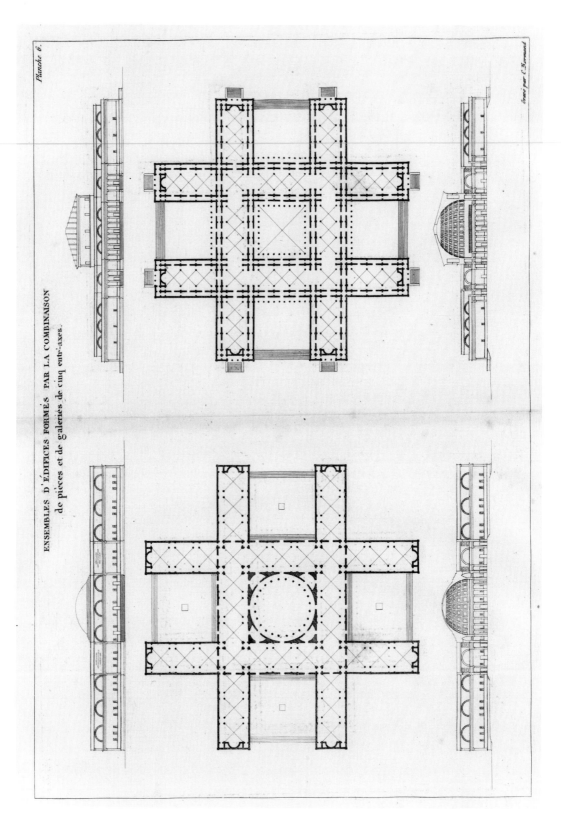

ENSEMBLES D'ÉDIFICES FORMÉS PAR LA COMBINAISON
de pièces et de galeries de cinq entr'-axes.

Planche 6.

Gravé par C.Normand

Plate 6

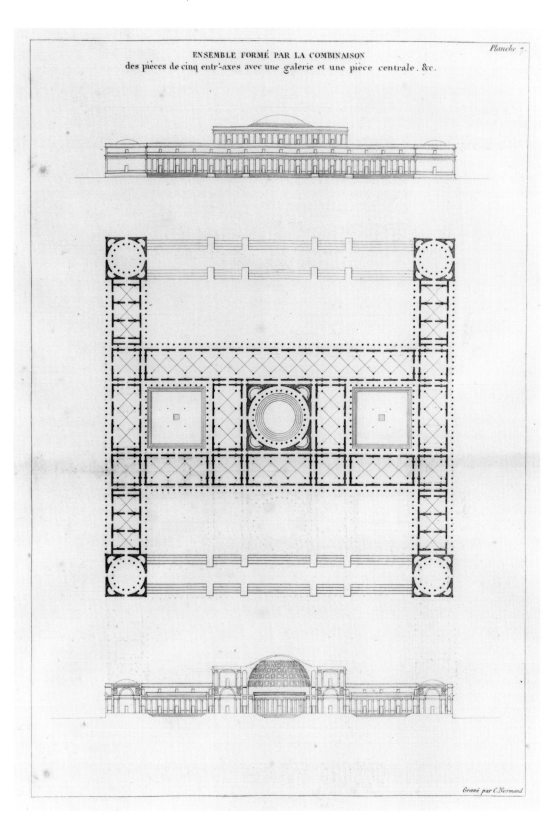

Plate 7

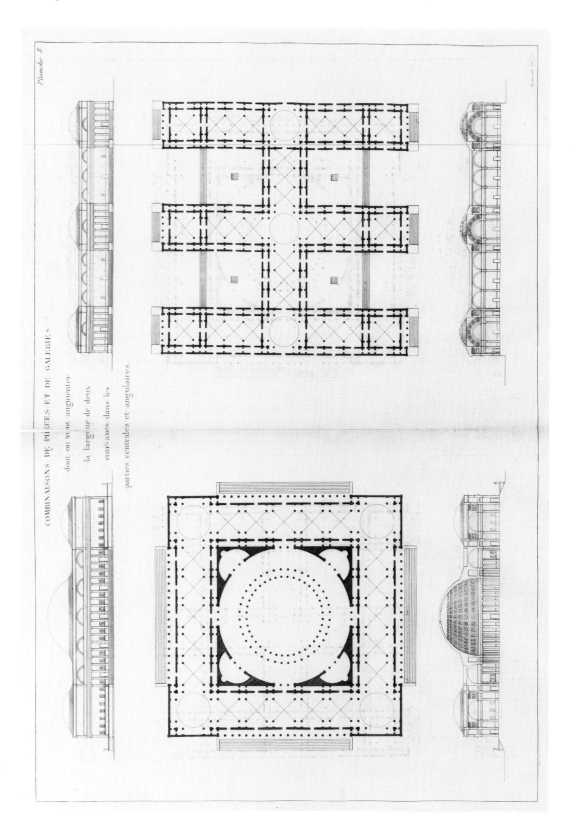

Plate 8

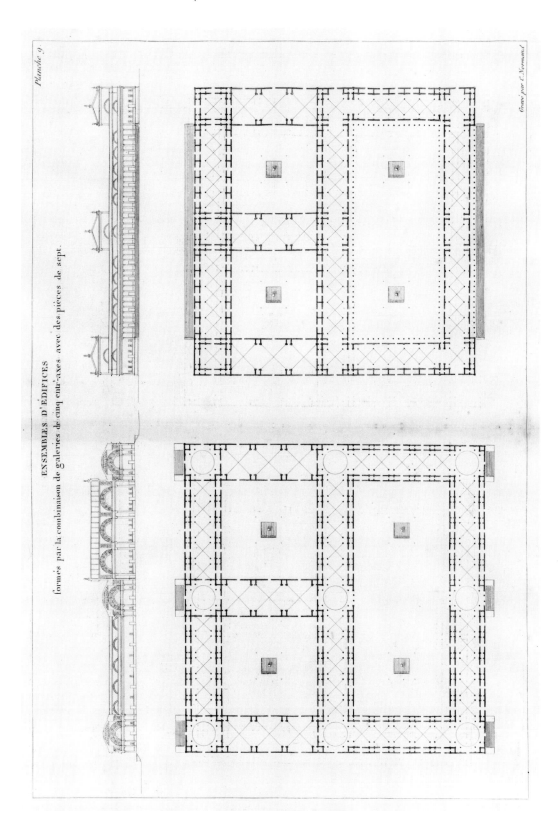

Plate 9

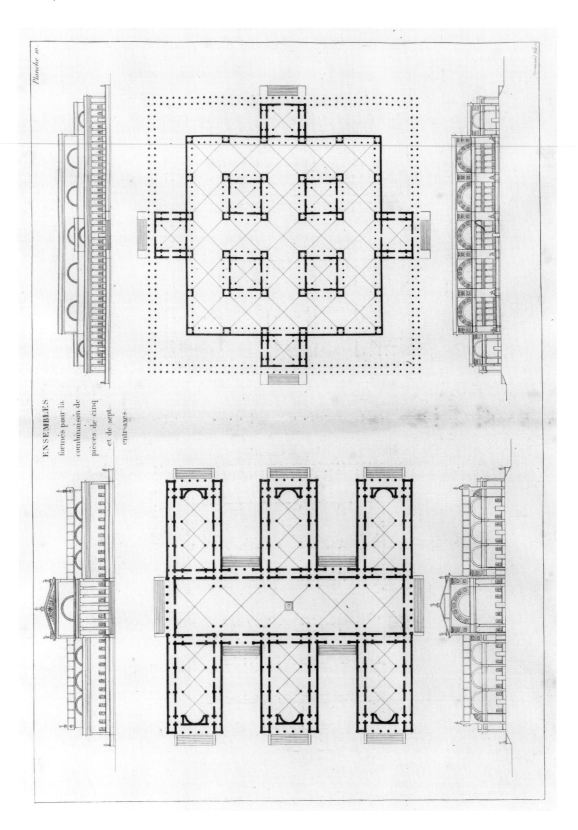

Plate 10

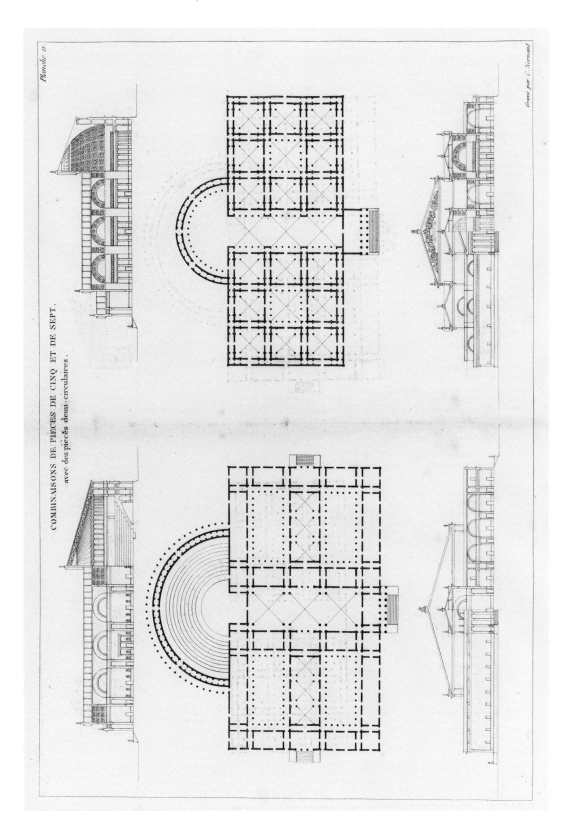

Plate 11

Plate 12

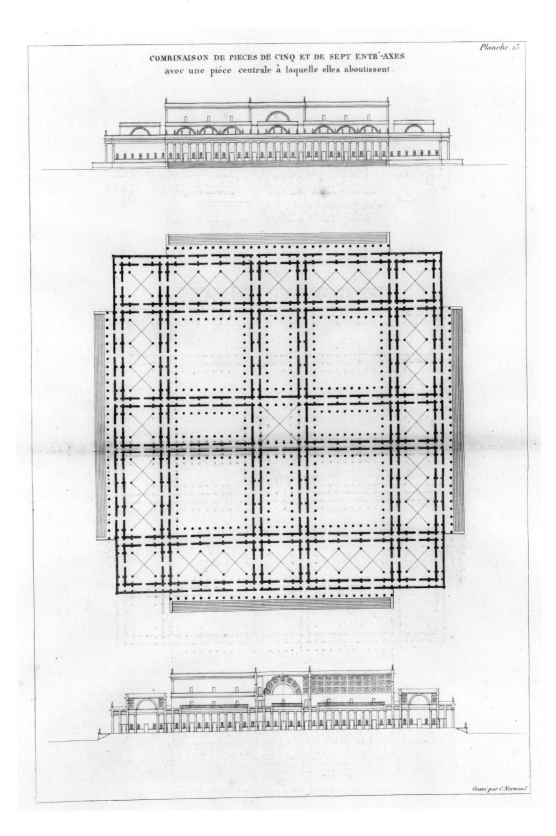

Plate 13

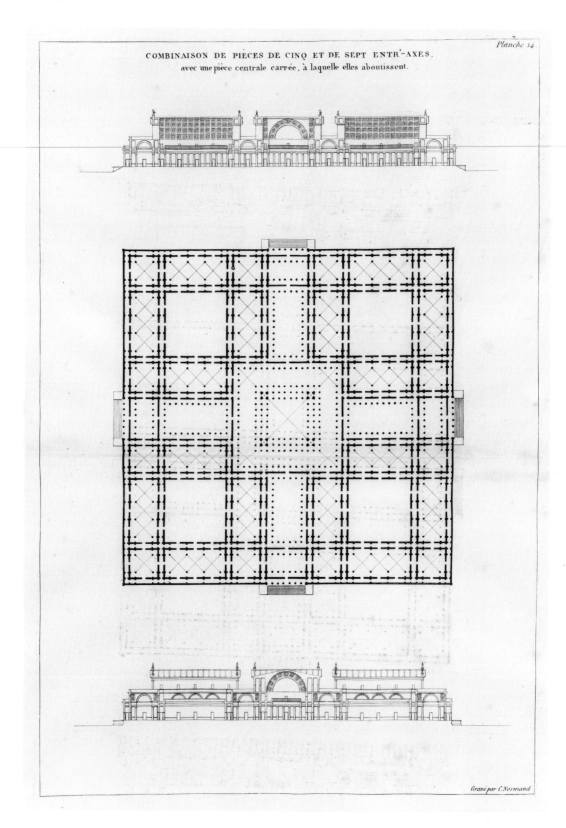

COMBINAISON DE PIÈCES DE CINQ ET DE SEPT ENTR'-AXES,
avec une pièce centrale carrée, à laquelle elles aboutissent.

Gravé par C.Normand.

Plate 14

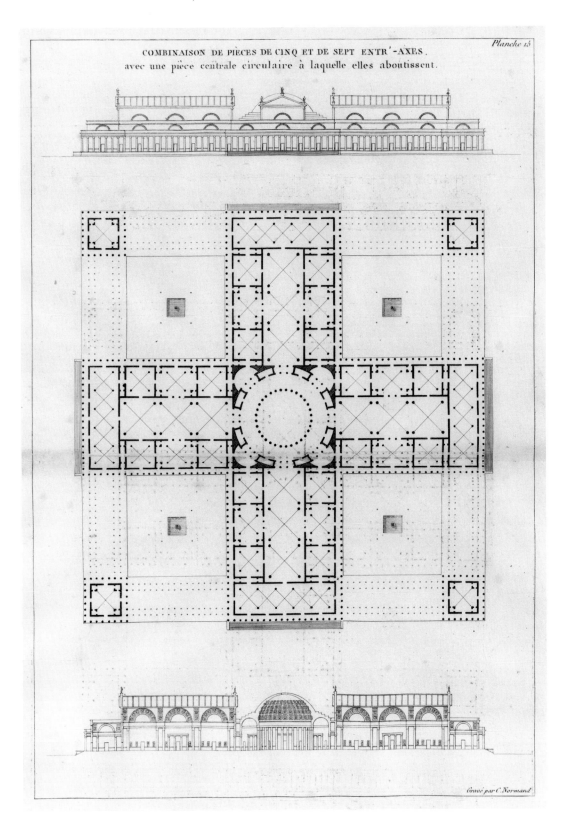

Plate 15

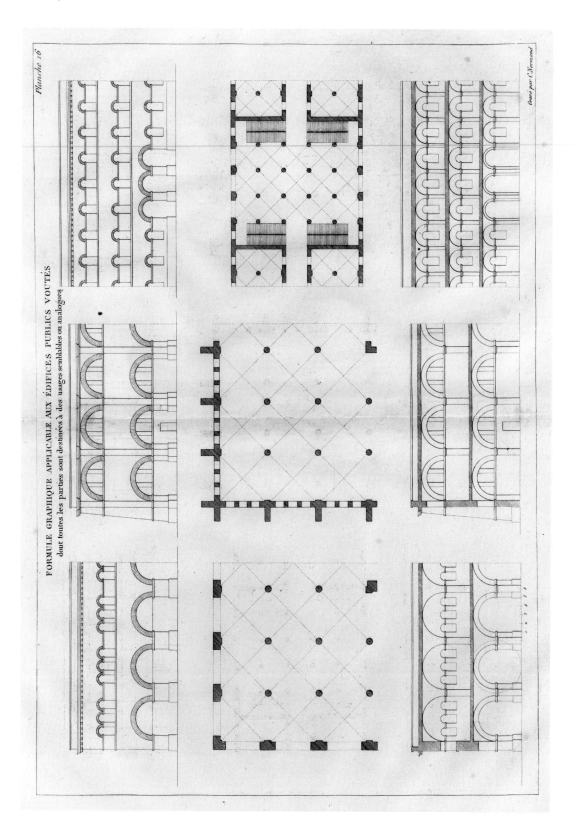

Plate 16

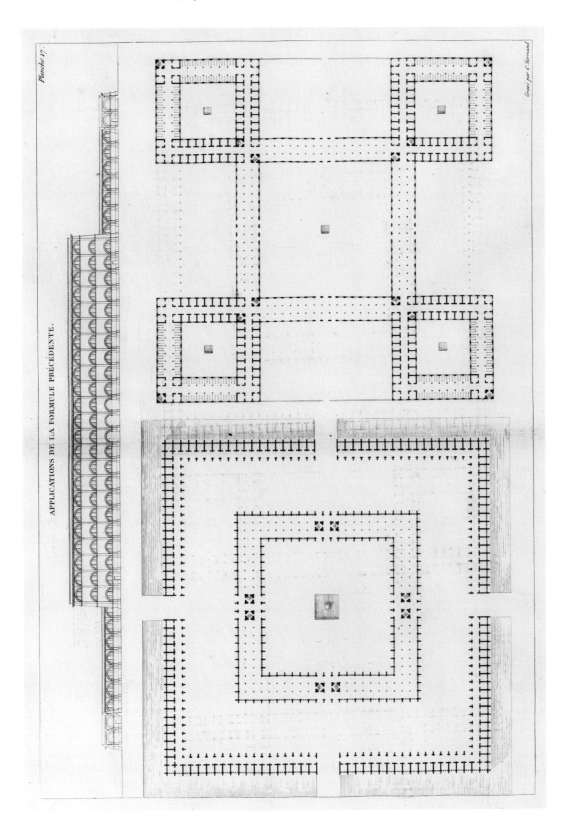

Plate 17

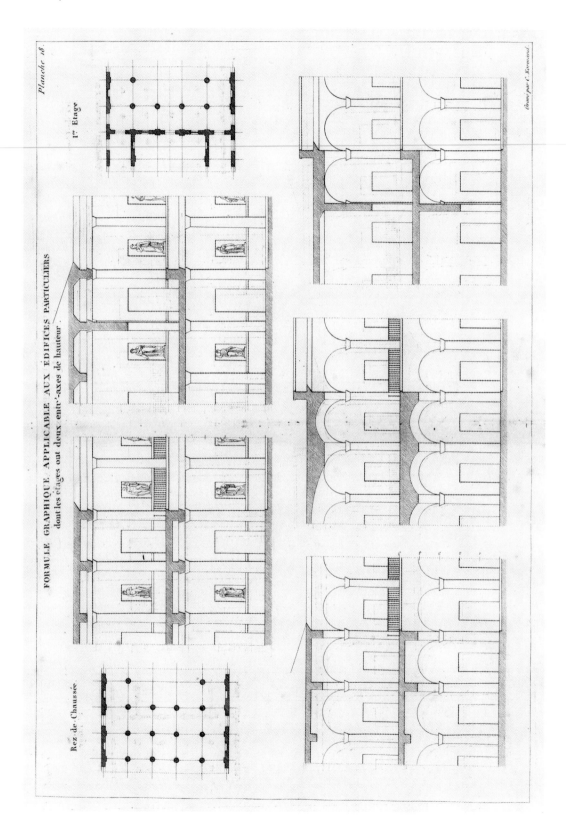

Plate 18

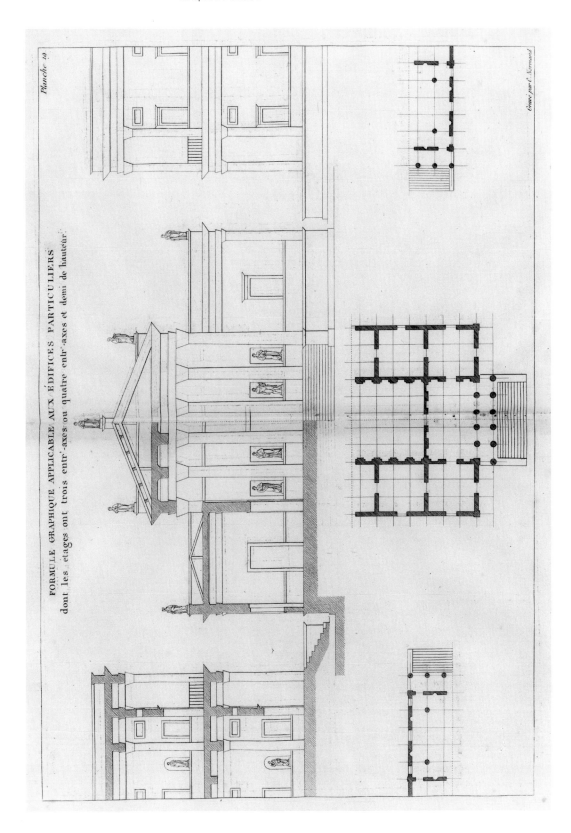

Planche 19

FORMULE GRAPHIQUE APPLICABLE AUX ÉDIFICES PARTICULIERS
dont les étages ont trois entr'axes ou quatre entr'axes et demi de hauteur.

Gravé par L. Normand.

Plate 19

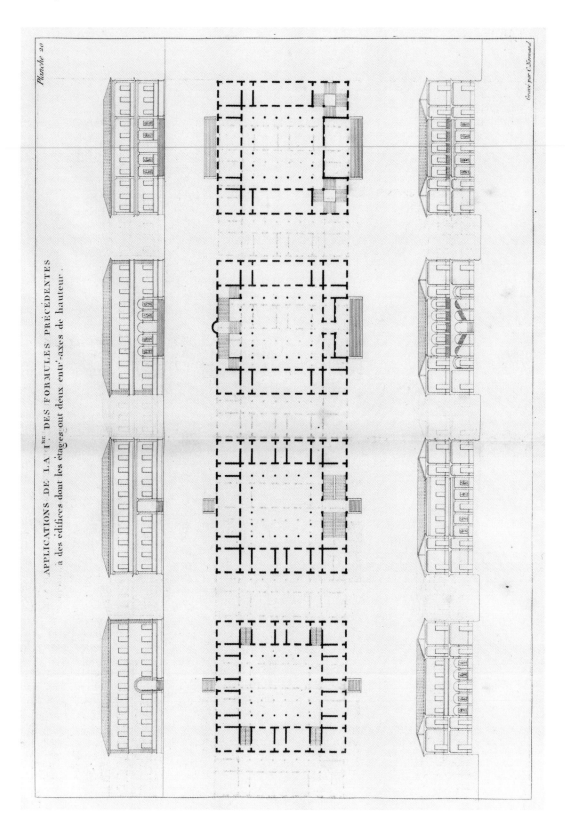

Plate 20

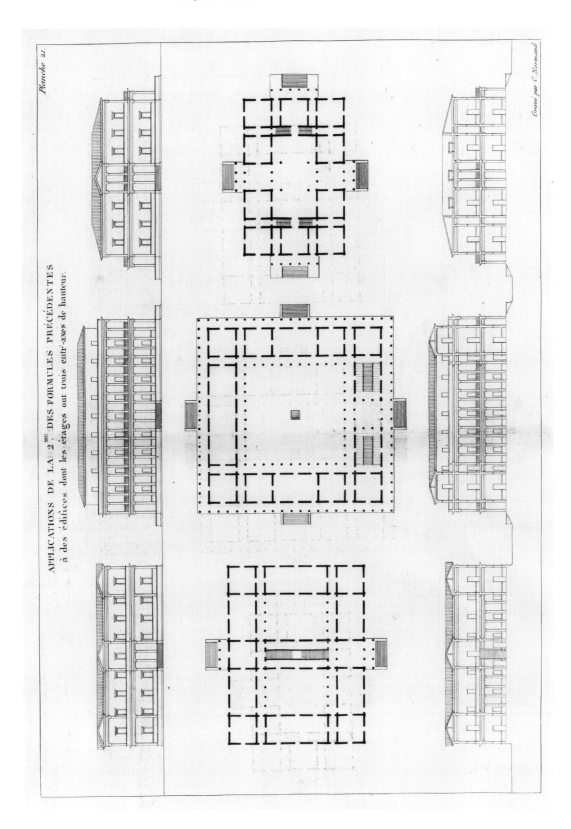

Plate 21

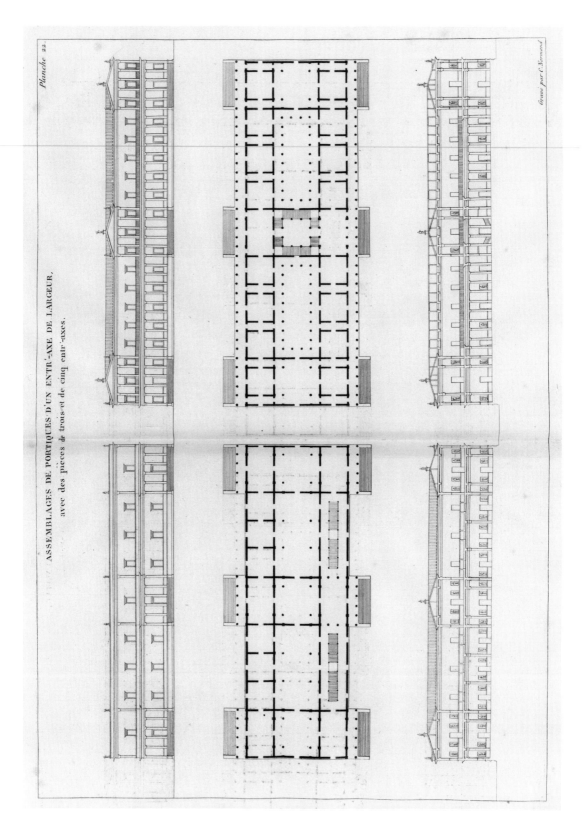

Plate 22

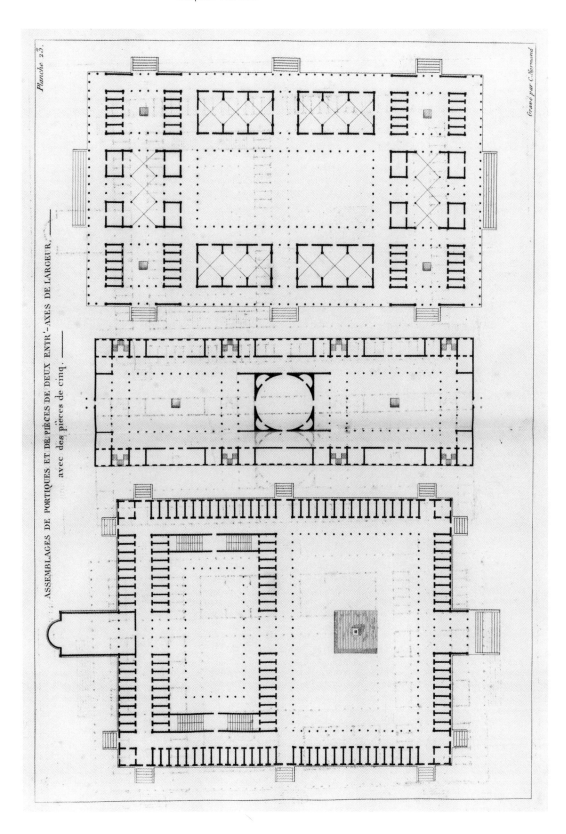

ASSEMBLAGES DE PORTIQUES ET DE PIÈCES DE DEUX ENTR'-AXES DE LARGEUR, avec des pièces de cinq.

Planche 23.

Gravée par C. Normand.

Plate 23

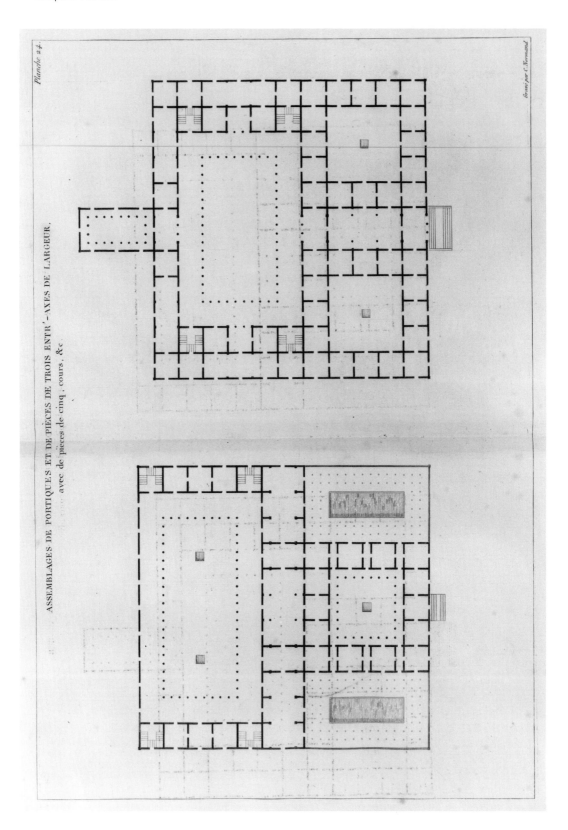

Plate 24

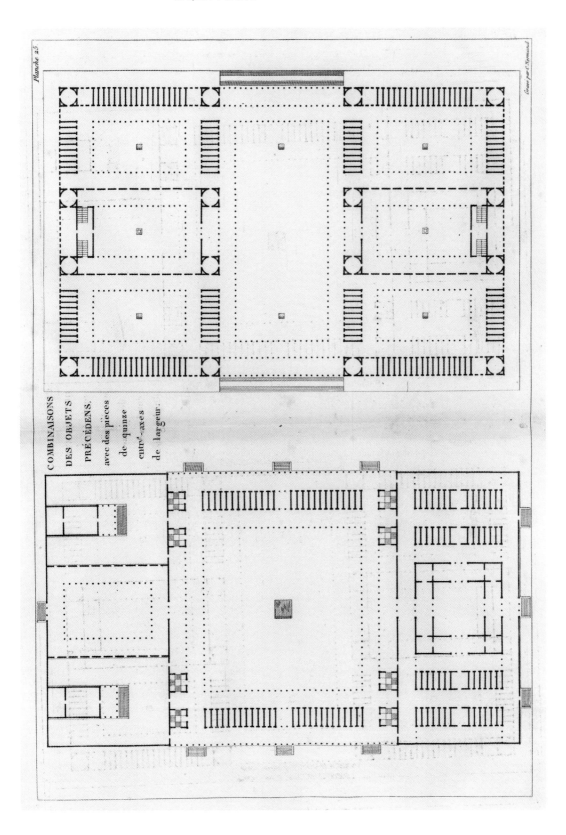

Plate 25

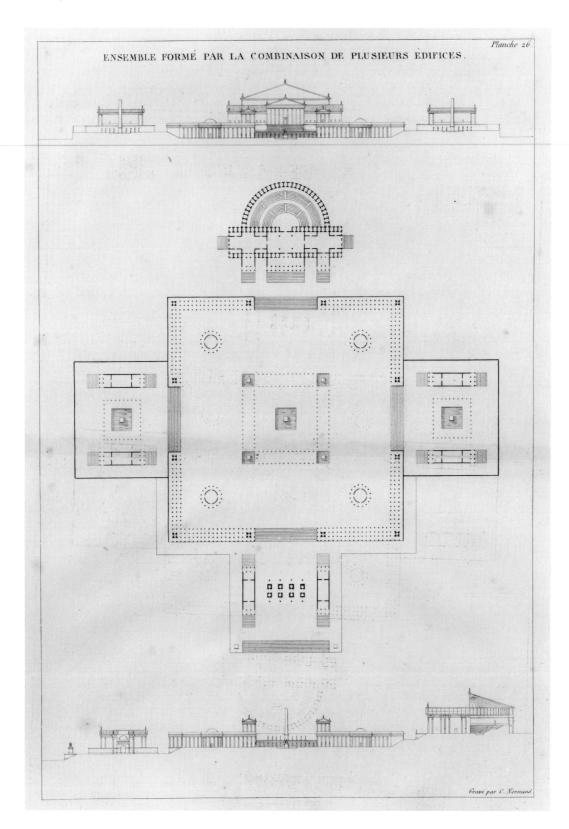

Plate 26

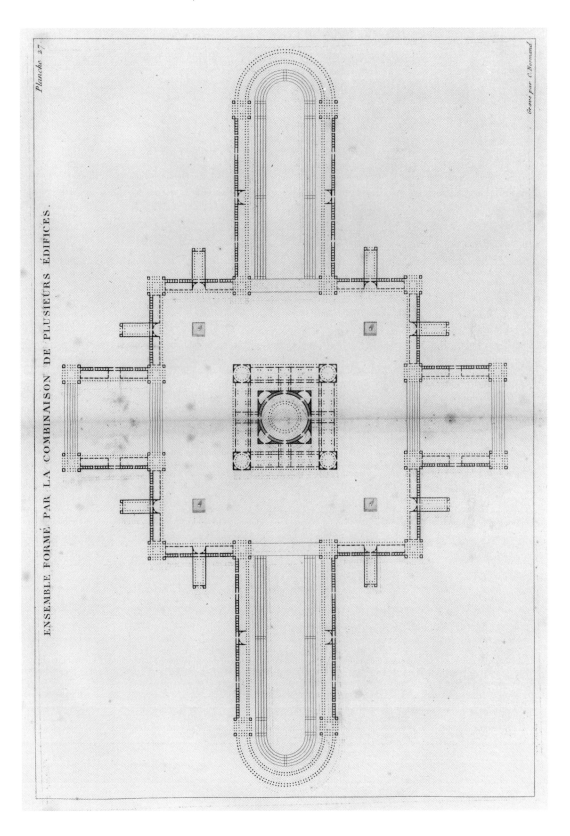

ENSEMBLE FORMÉ PAR LA COMBINAISON DE PLUSIEURS ÉDIFICES.

Planche 27.

Gravé par C.Normand.

Plate 27

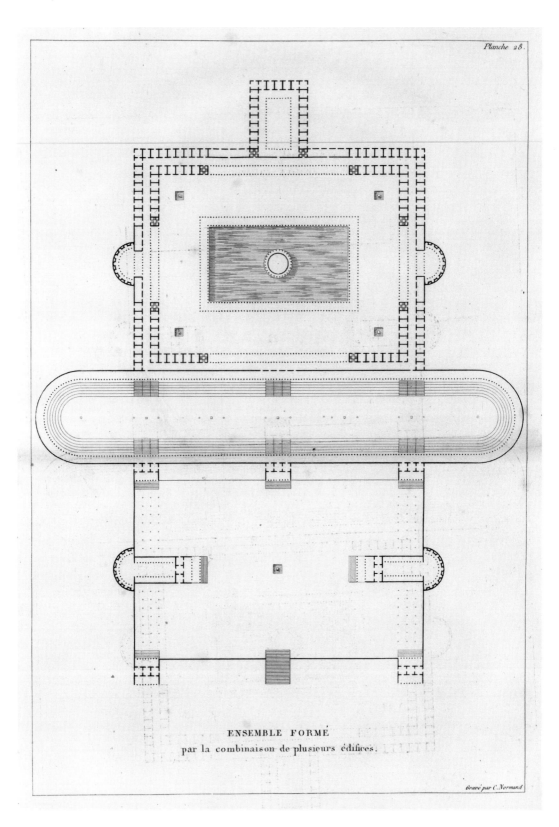

ENSEMBLE FORMÉ
par la combinaison de plusieurs édifices.

Gravé par C. Normand.

Plate 28

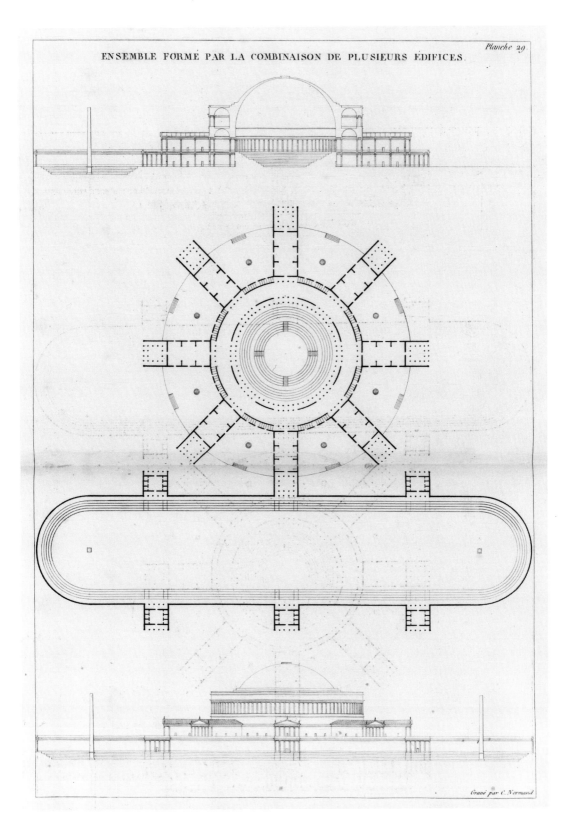

Plate 29

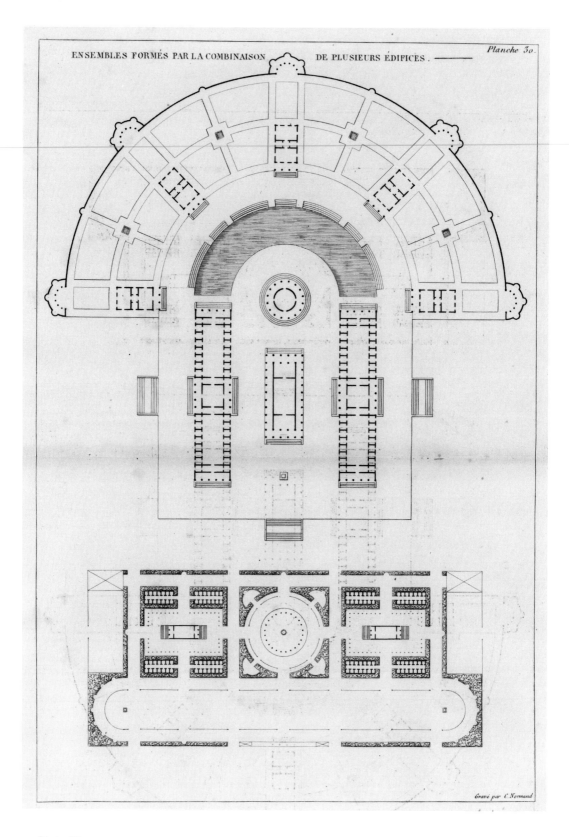

ENSEMBLES FORMÉS PAR LA COMBINAISON — DE PLUSIEURS ÉDIFICES. —————

Planche 3o.

Gravé par C. Normand.

Plate 30

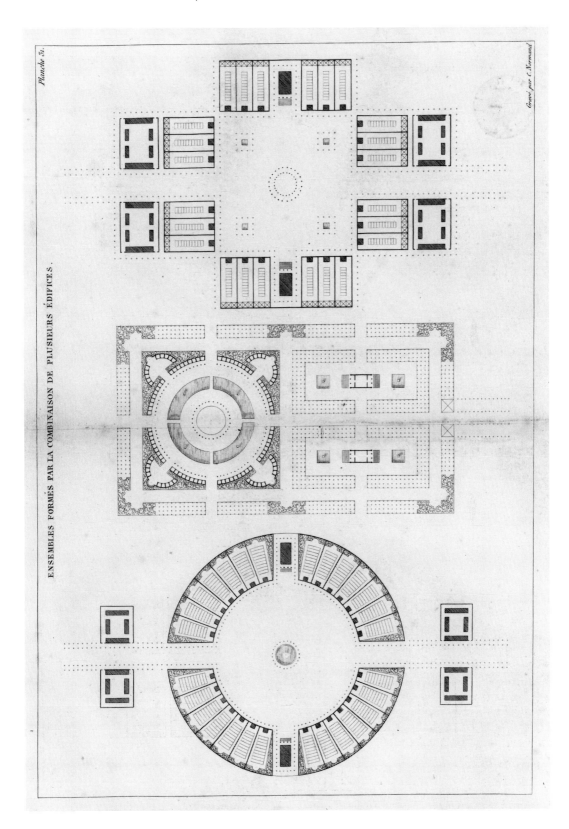

Plate 31

ENSEMBLE FORME PAR LA COMBINAISON DE PLUSIEURS ÉDIFICES.

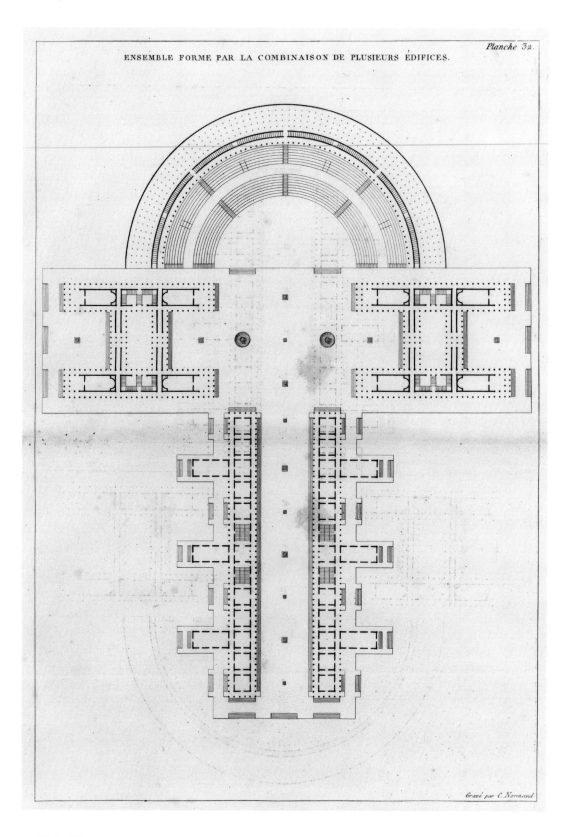

Gravé par C. Normand.

Plate 32

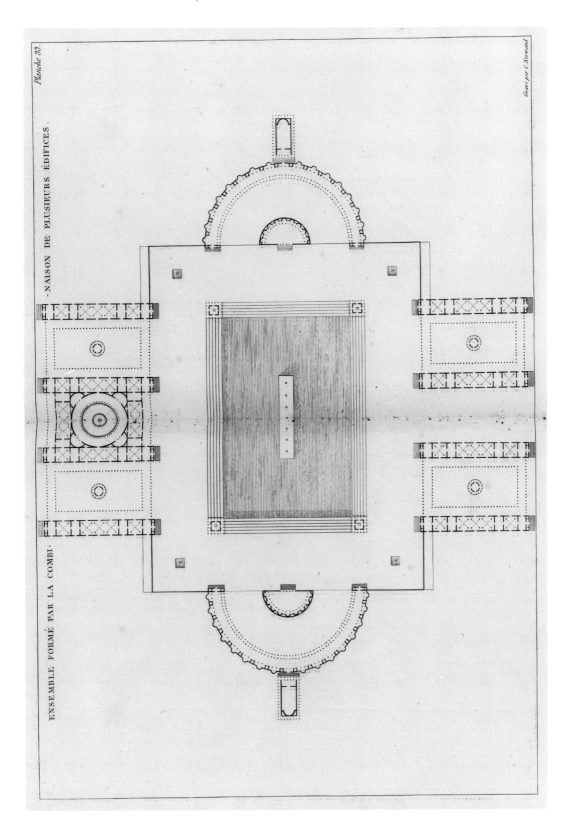

Planche 33.

NAISON DE PLUSIEURS ÉDIFICES.

ENSEMBLE FORMÉ PAR LA COMBI-

Gravé par C. Normand.

Plate 33

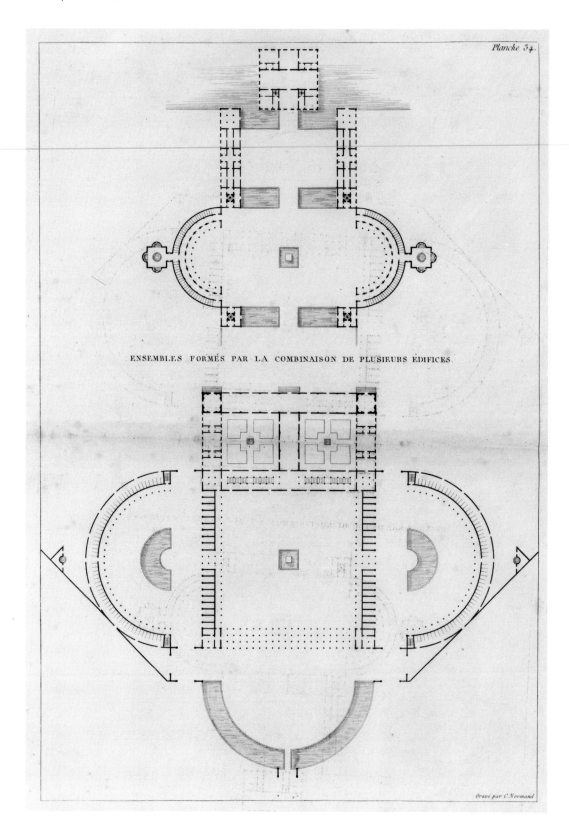

Planche 34.

ENSEMBLES FORMÉS PAR LA COMBINAISON DE PLUSIEURS ÉDIFICES

Gravé par C. Normand.

Plate 34

Works by Durand

Books and Contributions to Books

With Jean-François Janinet, engraver. *Vues des plus beaux édifices publics et particuliers de la ville de Paris.* Paris: Esnauts & Rapilly, 1787.

With Jean-François Janinet, engraver. *Vues pittoresques des principaux édifices de Paris.* Paris: Campion frère & fils, [1792].

With Jacques-Guillaume Legrand. *Recueil et parallèle des édifices de tout genre, anciens et modernes, remarquables par leur beauté, par leur grandeur ou par leur singularité, et dessinés sur une même échelle.* Paris: Gillé fils, Year IX [1800/1801].

Précis des leçons d'architecture données à l'École Polytechnique, 2 vols. Paris: the author, Year X [1802]–Year XIII [1805]. Additional editions of volume 1 in 1809, 1813, 1819, 1823, 1840. Additional editions of volume 2 in 1817, 1823, 1825, 1840.

Choix des projets d'édifices publics et particuliers composés par MM. les élèves de l'École Polytechnique. Paris: Gaucher, 1816.

Partie graphique des cours d'architecture faits à l'École Royale Polytechnique depuis sa réorganisation, précédée d'un sommaire des leçons relatives à ce nouveau travail. Paris: the author and the École Royale Polytechnique, 1821.

Architectural Projects

This section is based on the list of Durand's works in Werner Szambien, *Jean-Nicolas-Louis Durand, 1760–1834: De l'imitation à la norme* (Paris: Picard, 1984), 198. Where possible, we have included references to original drawings, copies, and engravings that are thought to represent or relate to the known projects.

Unrealized

Museum, 1779

> Plan by Durand: India ink with pink wash, 221 × 157 cm, Paris, École Nationale Supérieure des Beaux-Arts, inv. PRA 096a. Section by Durand: India ink with gray, blue, and bister wash, 62 × 170 cm, Paris, École Nationale Supérieure des Beaux-Arts, inv. PRA 096b. Elevation by Durand: India ink with gray and bister wash, 62.5 × 171 cm, Paris, École Nationale Supérieure des Beaux-Arts, inv. PRA 096c.

College, 1780

    Plan of first floor by Durand: India ink with pink wash and blue, green, and ocher watercolor highlights, 161.3 × 172.5 cm, Paris, École Nationale Supérieure des Beaux-Arts, inv. PRA 099a. Plan of second floor by Durand: India ink with gray wash, 122 × 127 cm, Paris, École Nationale Supérieure des Beaux-Arts, inv. PRA 099b. Section by Durand: India ink with gray and pink wash, 60 × 180 cm, Paris, École Nationale Supérieure des Beaux-Arts, inv. PRA 099c. Elevation by Durand: India ink with gray wash, 58 × 262.5 cm, Paris, École Nationale Supérieure des Beaux-Arts, inv. PRA 099d.

Bourse, ca. 1782

    Engraving by Charles-Pierre-Joseph Normand of section, plan, and elevation in Durand, *Précis,* vol. 2 (1805), pl. 14.

House on the site of the For-l'Évêque, after 1783 (with Étienne-Louis Boullée?)

    Engraving by Charles-Pierre-Joseph Normand of plans of first and second floors for each of two designs in Durand, *Précis,* vol. 2 (1805), pl. 26.

Library, ca. 1787

    Engraving by Charles-Pierre-Joseph Normand of section, plan, and elevation in Durand, *Précis,* vol. 2 (1805), pl. 10.

Rudimenta operis magni et disciplinae, ca. 1790

    Nine rows of ten drawings by Durand: Black chalk, 40.0 × 59.5 cm, Rouen, Musée des Beaux-Arts, Collection Baderou, inv. 975-4-1256. Six rows of thirteen drawings by Durand: Black chalk, 39.0 × 59.0 cm, Rouen, Musée des Beaux-Arts, Collection Baderou, inv. 975-4-1257.

Town and country houses, 1790s (with Étienne-Louis Boullée?)

    Engraving by Auguste Hibon of three elevations, a plan, and a section for a town or country house in Durand, *Précis,* vol. 2 (1805), pl. 27; engraving by Charles-Pierre-Joseph Normand of two elevations, two sections, and a plan of a town or country house in ibid., pl. 28; engraving by Auguste Hibon of an elevation, three plans, and a section of a country house in ibid., pl. 29; engraving by Auguste Hibon of an elevation, three plans, and a section of a country house in ibid., pl. 30.

Customhouse, ca. 1794

    Engraving by Charles-Pierre-Joseph Normand of section, plan, and elevation in Durand, *Précis,* vol. 2 (1805), pl. 14.

Designs for the Year II, 1794 (with Jean-Thomas Thibault)

    Column for the Panthéon

        Copy by Clemens Wenzeslaus Coudray of elevation: Pencil on tracing paper, 49.5 × 32 cm, Biberach an der Riss, Braith-Mali-Museum, Coudray-Mappe, no. 4, inv. 1983/163. Copy by Leo von Klenze of elevation: Pen and black ink with gray watercolor and gold highlights, 54.5 × 41.9 cm, Munich, Staatliche Graphische Sammlung, inv. 27154.

Common house 1

Engraving of plan in G.-E. Allais, A. Détournelle, and A.-T.-L. Vaudoyer, *Projets d'architecture*... (Paris: Détournelle, 1806), pl. 33; engraving of section and elevation in ibid., pl. 34.

Common house 2

Copy by Clemens Wenzeslaus Coudray of elevation, plan, and section (together with hall, justice of the peace, and section assembly): Pen and black and red ink with black, gray, and pink wash, 59.0 × 43.0 cm, Weimar, Kunstsammlungen, inv. Ka. B 183. Engraving by Charles-Pierre-Joseph Normand of section, plan, and elevation in *Précis,* vol. 2 (1805), pl. 7.

Courthouse

Copy by Clemens Wenzeslaus Coudray of section and elevation (together with prison): India ink on colored paper, 22 × 32 cm, Biberach an der Riss, Braith-Mali-Museum, inv. 26. Copy by Clemens Wenzeslaus Coudray of plan (together with prison): India ink on tracing paper, 22 × 32 cm, Biberach an der Riss, Braith-Mali-Museum, inv. 27. Engraving by Charles-Pierre-Joseph Normand of section, plan, and elevation in *Précis,* vol. 2 (1805), pl. 6.

Fountains and public baths

Engraving of elevations and plans for each of three designs in G.-E. Allais, A. Détournelle, and A.-T.-L. Vaudoyer, *Projets d'architecture*... (Paris: Détournelle, 1806), pl. 40. Engraving by Charles-Pierre-Joseph Normand of elevation for the second design in C.-P. Landon and J.-G. Legrand, *Annales du Musée et de l'École Moderne des Beaux-Arts,* coll. 1, vol. 6 (Paris: C.-P. Landon, 1804), pl. 40; engraving by Devilliers jeune of elevation for the third design in ibid., vol. 8 (Paris: C.-P. Landon, 1805), pl. 68. Engraving by Charles-Pierre-Joseph Normand of elevation and plan for the third design in A. Détournelle, *Nouveau vignole au traits; ou, Élemens des ordres* (Paris: the author, Year VII [1803–4]), pl. 10.

Hall

Copy by Clemens Wenzeslaus Coudray of plan, section, and elevation (see details for second common house above). Engraving by Charles-Pierre-Joseph Normand of section, plan, and elevation in *Précis,* vol. 2 (1805), pl. 13.

Justice of the peace

Copy by Clemens Wenzeslaus Coudray of plan, section, and elevation (see details for second common house above). Engraving by Charles-Pierre-Joseph Normand of section, plan, and elevation in *Précis,* vol. 2 (1805), pl. 7.

Primary assembly

Copy by Clemens Wenzeslaus Coudray of the elevation: Pen and black ink with gray and light gray wash, 19.0 × 44.6 cm, Weimar, Kunstsammlungen, inv. Ka. A 1447.

Primary school

> Engraving by [Étienne-Jules?] Thierry of the plan in A. Détournelle, *Recueil d'architecture nouvelle* (Paris: the author, 1805), pl. 52; engraving by Auguste Hibon of elevation and section in ibid., pl. 53.

Prison

> Copies by Clemens Wenzeslaus Coudray of section and elevation and of plan (see details for courthouse above). Engraving by Charles-Pierre-Joseph Normand of section, plan, and elevation in *Précis,* vol. 2 (1805), pl. 19.

Public baths

> Plan, section, and elevation by Durand: Pen and ink with green watercolor wash and highlights, 59.4 × 44.6 cm, Paris, École Nationale Supérieure des Beaux-Arts, inv. EBA 1850. Engraving by Charles-Pierre-Joseph Normand of two elevations and a plan in Durand, *Précis,* vol. 2 (1805), pl. 17.

Section assembly

> Copy by Clemens Wenzeslaus Coudray of plan, section, and elevation (see details for second common house above).

Temple for *décadi* (final day of the week in the revolutionary calendar) 1

> Engraving of plan in G.-E. Allais, A. Détournelle, and A.-T.-L. Vaudoyer, *Projets d'architecture . . .* (Paris: Détournelle, 1806), pl. 31; engraving of section and elevation in ibid., pl. 32. Engraving by Charles-Pierre-Joseph Normand of the elevation in C.-P. Landon and J.-G. Legrand, *Annales du Musée et de l'École Moderne des Beaux-Arts,* coll. 1, vol. 5 (Paris: C.-P. Landon, 1803), pl. 20.

Temple for *décadi* 2

> Section and elevation by Durand: Pen and ink with wash, 57.5 × 95 cm. Paris, Musée Carnavalet, Cab. Est., carton des dessins d'architecture anonymes, très grande réserve, D. 8208. Engraving by [Étienne-Jules?] Thierry of the plan in A. Détournelle, *Recueil d'architecture nouvelle* (Paris: the author, 1805), pl. 91; engraving by Auguste Hibon of section in ibid., pl. 92; engraving by Auguste Hibon of elevation in ibid., pl. 93.

Temple of equality/Temple of public felicity

> Copy by Leo von Klenze of elevation: Pen and black ink with gray wash, 63.6 × 92.3 cm, Munich, Staatliche Graphische Sammlung, inv. no. 27000. Copy by unknown artist of elevation: Pen and black ink and pencil, 25.8 × 43.2 cm. Vizelle, Musée de la Révolution française, inv. 84262. Copy by Coudray of elevation: Pencil on tracing paper, 11 × 16 cm, Biberach an der Riss, Braith-Mali-Museum, inv. no. 222. Copy by Clemens Wenzeslaus Coudray of elevation: Weimar, Herzogin Anna Amalia Bibliothek, inv. 1477. Engraving of section and plan in G.-E. Allais, A. Détournelle, and A.-T.-L. Vaudoyer, *Projets d'architecture . . .* (Paris: Détournelle, 1806), pl. 27; engraving of elevation in ibid., pl. 28; engraving of longitudinal section in ibid., pl. 29.

Triumphal arch

> Copy by Clemens Wenzeslaus Coudray of plan: Pen and brush with black ink, gray wash over graphite, on two sheets joined together, 18.2 (max.) to 17.3 (min.) 63.8 cm, Stiftung Weimarer Klassik, inv. 1464. Copy by Clemens Wenzeslaus Coudray of elevation: Graphite, pen and brush with black and brown ink, 29 × 56.7 cm, Stiftung Weimarer Klassik, inv. 1466. Copy by Clemens Wenzeslaus Coudray of section: Pen and gray and black ink with gray wash over black chalk, graphite, watercolor, 28.7 × 54.8 cm, Stiftung Weimarer Klassik, inv. 1474.

Town houses, ca. 1796 (with Étienne-Louis Boullée?)

> Engraving by Charles-Pierre-Joseph Normand of plans of first and second floors, elevation, and plan for two designs in Durand, *Précis,* vol. 2 (1805), pl. 22.

Apartment building, ca. 1800

> Engraving by Charles-Pierre-Joseph Normand of plans for three designs in Durand, *Précis,* vol. 2 (1805), pl. 25.

College, ca. 1800

> Engraving by Charles-Pierre-Joseph Normand of section, plan, and elevation in Durand, *Précis,* vol. 2 (1805), pl. 8.

Museum, ca. 1800 (after his own museum of 1779)

> Engraving by Charles-Pierre-Joseph Normand of section, plan, and elevation in Durand, *Précis,* vol. 2 (1805), pl. 11.

Public baths, ca. 1800

> Engraving by Charles-Pierre-Joseph Normand of two elevations and a plan in Durand, *Précis,* vol. 2 (1805), pl. 17.

Slaughterhouse, ca. 1800

> Engraving by Charles-Pierre-Joseph Normand of section, plan, and elevation in Durand, *Précis,* vol. 2 (1805), pl. 13.

Theater, ca. 1800

> Engraving by Charles-Pierre-Joseph Normand of transverse section, longitudinal section, plan, and elevation in Durand, *Précis,* vol. 2 (1805), pl. 16.

Tombs and triumphal arches, ca. 1800

> Engraving by Charles-Pierre-Joseph Normand of elevations and section in Durand, *Précis,* vol. 2 (1805), pl. 1.

Observatory, ca. 1802

> Engraving by Charles-Pierre-Joseph Normand of section, plan, and elevation in Durand, *Précis,* vol. 2 (1805), pl. 12.

Fair, ca. 1803 (after Clemens Wenzeslaus Coudray)

> Engraving by Charles-Pierre-Joseph Normand of section, plan, and elevation in Durand, *Precis,* vol. 2 (1805), pl. 15.

Triumphal arch for the Place de l'Étoile, 1807

> Elevation by Durand (?): Pen and black ink with gray and black wash, 48.2 × 62.8 cm, location unknown.

Realized

Lathuille House, Paris, 1788

Engraving by Charles-Pierre-Joseph Normand of plans, elevations, and section in Durand, *Précis,* vol. 2 (1805), pl. 23. Engraving by Pierre-Nicolas Ransonnette of two plans, two elevations, and a section in J.-C. Krafft and N. Ransonnette, *Plans, coupes et élévations des plus belles maisons* . . . (Paris: the authors and F. Benoist, 1801?), pl. 13. Engraving by [Jean?] Adam of elevation and profile in J.-C. Krafft, *Recueil des plus jolies maisons de Paris et de ses environs,* pt. 2 (Paris: J.-L. Scherff, 1809), pl. 33; engraving by [Jean?] Adam of detail, profile, and elevation in ibid., pl. 34.

Lermina House, Chessy, Seine-et-Marne, after 1801

Engraving by Charles-Pierre-Joseph Normand of plan, section, and elevation in Durand, *Précis,* vol. 2 (1805), pl. 31.

House, Thiais, Val-de-Marne, before 1811

Durand House, Thiais, Val-de-Marne, 1820

Engraving by Louis-Marie Normand of site plan in idem, *Paris moderne . . . ,* vol. 3 (Paris: the author, 1849), pl. 46; engraving by Louis-Marie Normand of plans for the basement and first and second floors, in ibid., pl. 47; engraving by Louis-Marie Normand of elevation and section, in ibid., pl. 48.

Durand Country House, Thiais, Val-de-Marne, 1825

Engraving by Louis-Marie Normand of site plan in idem, *Paris moderne . . . ,* vol. 3 (Paris: the author, 1849), pl. 143.

Panorama, 1828

Elevation and section by Durand (?) with Charles O. Barbaroux: Pen and ink, 46.5 × 29 cm, Archives de l'Institut National de la Propriété Industrielle. Patent application for portable panorama, 29 April 1828 by Barbaroux, Paris, rue Notre-Dame de Nazareth, no. 13.

Selected Bibliography

Primary Sources

Alembert, Jean Le Rond d'. "Élémens des sciences." In *Encyclopédie; ou, Dictionnaire raisonné des sciences, des arts et des métiers,* vol. 5, 491–97. Paris: Briasson, 1755.

Bélidor, Bernard Forest de. *La science des ingénieurs dans la conduite des travaux de fortification et d'architecture civile.* Paris: Claude Jombert, 1729. 2d ed., edited by Claude-Louis-Marie-Henri Navier, Paris: F. Didot, 1813. Reprint of 1st ed., Paris: Hachette, 1979.

Blondel, Jacques-François. *Cours d'architecture; ou, Traité de la décoration, distribution et construction des bâtiments.* Paris: Desaint, 1771–77.

Bossuet, Jacques-Bénigne. *Introduction à la philosophie; ou, De la connoissance de Dieu, et de soi-mesme.* Paris: R.-M. d'Espilly, 1722.

Boullée, Étienne-Louis. *Architecture: Essai sur l'art.* Edited by Jean-Marie Pérouse de Montclos. Paris: Hermann, 1968. Translated by Sheila de Vallée in Helen Rosenau, ed., *Boullée and Visionary Architecture,* 81–116. London: Academy Editions; New York: Harmony Books, 1976.

Bruyère, Louis. *Études relatives à l'art des constructions.* Paris: Bance, 1823–28.

Cabanis, Pierre-Jean-Georges. *Rapports du physique et du moral de l'homme.* Paris: Crapelet, 1802. Reprint, Paris: Slatkine, 1980. Translated by Margaret Duggan Saidi as *On the Relations between the Physical and Moral Aspects of Man.* Edited by George Mora. 2 vols. Baltimore: Johns Hopkins Univ. Press, 1981.

Chaptal, Jean-Antoine-Claude. *Élémens de chymie.* 2d ed. Paris: Deterville, 1794. Translated by W. Nicholson and James Woodhouse as *Elements of Chemistry.* 4th American ed. 2 vols. Philadelphia: Benjamin & Thomas Kite, Bartram & Reynolds, 1807. Reprint, Worcester, Mass.: American Antiquarian Society, 1968.

Condillac, Étienne Bonnot de. *Essai sur l'origine des connoissances humaines.* Amsterdam: Pierre Mortier, 1746. Reprint, Paris: Galilée, 1973. Translated by Thomas Nugent as *An Essay on the Origin of Human Knowledge.* London: J. Nourse, 1756. Reprint, New York: AMS Press, 1974.

———. *Œuvres philosophiques de Condillac.* Paris: Presses Universitaires de France, 1947–51.

Coulomb, Charles-Augustin. "Essai sur une application des règles de maximis et minimis à quelques problèmes de statique, relatifs à l'architecture." In

Mémoires de mathématiques et de physique, présentés à l'Académie Royale des Sciences, par divers savans: Année 1773, 343–82. Paris: Imprimerie Royale, 1776. Translated by Jacques Heyman in *Coulomb's Memoir on Statics: An Essay in the History of Civil Engineering*, 41–69. River Edge: Imperial College Press, 1997.

Daly, César. *Ingénieurs et architectes (un toast et son commentaire)*. Paris: Ducher, 1877.

Desgodets, Antoine. *Les édifices antiques de Rome dessinés et mesurés très exactment*. Paris: J.-B. Coignard, 1682. Reprint, Portland: Collegium Graphicum, 1972. Translated by George Marshall as *The Architectural Antiquities of Rome, Accurately Measured and Delineated*. 2 vols. London: The Architectural Library, 1835.

Destutt de Tracy, Antoine-Louis-Claude. *Élémens d'idéologie*. Paris: Courcier, 1803. Translated by Thomas Jefferson as *A Treatise on Political Economy*. Georgetown: J. Milligan, 1817.

Détournelle, Athanase. "Architecture, second volume du *Précis*." *Journal des arts, des sciences et de littérature* (30 March 1805): 25–30.

Diderot, Denis. *Pensées sur l'interprétation de la nature*. [Paris]: n.p., 1754. Partial translation by Jean Stewart and Jonathan Kemp in *Diderot, Interpreter of Nature: Selected Writings*. Edited by Jonathan Kemp. New York: International Publishers, 1943.

Dubut, Louis-Ambroise. *Architecture civile: Maisons de ville et de campagne de toutes formes et de tous genres*. Paris: J.-M. Eberhart, 1803. Reprint, Unterschneidheim: Walter Uhl, 1974.

Fischer von Erlach, Johann Bernhard. *Entwurff einer historischen Architectur, in Abbildung unterschiedener berühmten Gebäude, des Alterthums, und fremder Völcker, umb aus den Geschicht- Büchern, Gedächtnüss-Müntzen, Ruinen und eingeholten wahrhafften Abrissen, vor Augen zu stellen*. Vienna: n.p., 1721. Translated by Thomas Lediard as *A Plan of Civil and Historical Architecture, in the Representation of the Most Noted Buildings of Foreign Nations, Both Ancient and Modern*. Farnborough: Gregg Press Ltd., 1964.

Fourcy, Ambroise. *Histoire de l'École Polytechnique*. Paris: the author, 1828. Reprint, Paris: Belin, 1987.

Garat, Joseph-Dominique. "Analyse de l'entendement: Programme." In *Séances des Écoles Normales, recueillies par des sténographes, et revues par les professeurs*, 1:138–69. Paris: L. Reynier, [ca. 1795].

Hachette, Jean-Nicolas-Pierre. *Notice sur la création de l'École Polytechnique*. Paris: Decourchant, 1828.

Krafft, Jean-Charles. *Recueil des plus jolies maisons de Paris et de ses environs*. Paris: J.-L. Scherff, 1809. Reprint, Nördlingen: Alfons Uhl, 1992.

Laplace, Pierre-Simon. *Essai philosophique sur les probabilités*. Paris: Courcier, 1814.

Laugier, Marc-Antoine. *Essai sur l'architecture*. Paris: Duchesne, 1753. Reprint, Brussels: P. Mardaga, 1979. Translated by Wolfgang and Anni

Herrmann as *An Essay on Architecture*. Documents and Sources in Architecture 1. Los Angeles: Hennessey & Ingalls, 1977.

Le Camus de Mézières, Nicolas. *Le génie de l'architecture; ou, L'analogie de cet art avec nos sensations*. Paris: the author & B. Morin, 1780. Translated by David Britt as *The Genius of Architecture; or, The Analogy of That Art with Our Sensations*. Santa Monica: Getty Center for the History of Art and the Humanities, 1992.

———. *Le guide de ceux qui veulent bâtir: Ouvrage dans lequel on donne les renseignements nécessaires pour se conduire lors de la construction, et prévenir les fraudes qui peuvent s'y glisser*. Paris: the author & B. Morin, 1786. Reprint, Geneva: Minkoff, 1972.

Ledoux, Claude-Nicolas. *L'architecture considérée sous le rapport de l'art, des mœurs et de la législation*. Paris: the author, 1804. Reprint, Paris: Hermann, 1997.

Le Roy, Julien-David. *Histoire de la disposition et des formes différentes que les Chrétiens ont donnés à leurs temples, depuis le règne de Constantin le Grand jusqu'à nous*. Paris: Desaint & Saillant, 1764.

———. *Les ruines des plus beaux monuments de la Grèce*. 2 vols. 2d ed. Paris: H.-L. Guérin & L.-F. Delatour, 1770.

L'Orme, Philibert de. *Nouvelles inventions pour bien bastir et à petits fraiz*. Paris: Morel, 1561. Reprint, Paris: Léonce Laget, 1988.

Mandar, Charles-François. *Études d'architecture civile*. Paris: Carilian-Gœury, 1826.

Monge, Gaspard. "Géométrie descriptive: Programme." In *Séances des Écoles Normales, recueillies par des sténographes, et revues par les professeurs*, 1:49–64. Paris: L. Reynier, [ca. 1795]. Translated by J. F. Heather as *Descriptive Geometry: With a Theory of Shadows and of Perspective*. Revised ed. London: Crosby Lockwood & Son, 1899.

Ouvrard, René. *Architecture harmonique; ou, Application de la doctrine des proportions de la musique à l'architecture*. Paris: R.-J.-B. de la Caille, 1679.

Patte, Pierre. *Mémoires sur les objets les plus importants de l'architecture*. Paris: Rozet, 1769. Reprint, Geneva: Minkoff, 1973.

Perrault, Claude. *Essais de physique; ou, Recueil de plusieurs traitez touchant les choses naturelles*. Paris, J.-B. Coignard, 1680–88.

———. *Mémoires pour servir à l'histoire naturelle des animaux*. 2 vols. Paris: Imprimerie Royale, 1671–76. Translated by Alexander Pitfield as *Memoires for a Natural History of Animals*. N.p., 1687.

———. *Ordonnance des cinq espèces de colonnes selon la méthode des Anciens*. Paris, J.-B. Coignard, 1683. Translated by Indra Kagis McEwen as *Ordonnance for the Five Kinds of Columns after the Method of the Ancients*. Santa Monica: Getty Center for the History of Art and the Humanities, 1993.

Quatremère de Quincy, Antoine-Chrysostôme. *Essai sur la nature, le but et les moyens de l'imitation dans les beaux-arts*. Paris: Treuttel et Wurtz, 1823.

Reprinted as *De l'imitation, 1823*. Brussels: Archives d'Architecture Moderne, 1980. Translated by J. C. Kent as *An Essay on the Nature, the End, and the Means of Imitation in the Fine Arts*. London: Smith, Elder, 1837. Reprint, New York: Garland, 1979.

Reynaud, Léonce. *Traité d'architecture contenant des notions générales sur les principes de la construction et sur l'histoire de l'art*. 2 vols. Paris: Carilian-Gœury & Victor Dalmont, 1850–58.

Rondelet, Antoine-Jean-Baptiste. *Traité théorique et pratique de l'art de bâtir*. Paris: the author, 1802–17.

Saint-Simon, Claude Henri de Rouvroy, comte de. *Lettres d'un habitant de Genève à ses contemporains*. N.p., [1803]. Reprint, Paris, F. Alcan, 1925. Translated by Valence Ionescu as "Letters from an Inhabitant of Geneva to His Contemporaries," in *The Political Thought of Saint-Simon*. Edited by Ghita Ionescu, 65–81. London: Oxford Univ. Press, 1976.

Viel de Saint-Maux, Charles-François. *De l'impuissance des mathématiques pour assurer la solidité des bâtimens et recherches sur la construction des ponts*. Paris: the author & Veuve Tilliard, 1805.

———. *Lettres sur l'architecture des Anciens, et celle des Modernes*. Paris: n.p., 1787. Reprint, Geneva: Minkoff, 1974.

Villalpando, Juan Bautista. *In Ezechielem explanationes et apparatus urbis ac templi hierosolymitani*. Rome: A. Zannetti, 1596–1604.

Viollet-le-Duc, Eugène-Emmanuel. *Dictionnaire raisonné de l'architecture française du XIe au XVIe siècle*. Paris: B. Bance & A. Morel, 1854–68.

———. *Entretiens sur l'architecture*. 2 vols. Paris: A. Morel, 1863–72. Translated by Benjamin Bucknall as *Lectures on Architecture*. 2 vols. New York: Dover Publications, 1987.

———. *Lettres addressées d'Allemagne à Monsieur Adolphe Lance, architecte*. Paris: B. Bance, 1856.

Vitruvius. *Les dix livres d'architecture*. Translated by Claude Perrault. Paris: J.-B. Coignard, 1673. Translated by Ingrid D. Rowland as *Ten Books of Architecture*. New ed. New York: Cambridge Univ. Press, 1999.

Secondary Sources

Les architectes de la liberté, 1789–1799. Exhibition catalog. Paris: École Nationale Supérieure des Beaux-Arts, 1989.

Avril, Jean-Louis, and Monique Mosser. *De Ledoux à Le Corbusier: Origine et développement de l'architecture autonome*. Paris: L'équerre, 1981.

Baker, Keith Michael. *Condorcet: From Natural Philosophy to Social Mathematics*. Chicago: Univ. of Chicago Press, 1975.

Balan, Bernard. *L'ordre et le temps: L'anatomie comparée et l'histoire des vivants au XIXe siècle*. Paris: Vrin, 1979.

Belhoste, Bruno. *Cauchy, 1789–1857: Un mathématicien légitimiste au XIXe siècle*. Paris: Belin, [1985]. Translated by Frank Ragland as *Augustin-Louis Cauchy: A Biography*. New York: Springer, 1991.

———. "Du dessin d'ingénieur à la géométrie descriptive: L'enseignement de

Chastillon à l'École Royale du Génie de Mézières." *In Extenso* 13 (1990): 103–28.

———. "Les origines de l'École Polytechnique: Des anciennes écoles d'ingénieurs à l'École Centrale des Travaux Publics." *Histoire de l'éducation* 42 (1989): 13–53.

———, Amy Dahan Dalmedico, and Antoine Picon, eds. *La formation polytechnicienne, 1794–1994.* Paris: Dunod, 1994.

———, Antoine Picon, and Joël Sakarovitch. "Les exercices dans les écoles d'ingénieurs sous l'Ancien Régime et la Révolution." *Histoire de l'éducation* 46 (May 1990): 53–109.

Benjamin, Walter. *Das Passagen-Werk.* Edited by Rolf Tiedemann. 2 vols. Frankfurt: Suhrkamp, 1982. Translated by Howard Eiland and Kevin McLaughlin as *The Arcades Project.* Cambridge, Mass.: Belknap Press, 1999.

Benvenuto, Edoardo. *La scienza delle costruzioni e il suo sviluppo storico.* Florence: Sansoni, 1981.

———. *An Introduction to the History of Structural Mechanics.* 2 vols. New York: Springer, 1991.

Bergdoll, Barry. *Léon Vaudoyer: Historicism in the Age of Industry.* New York: Architectural History Foundation; Cambridge: MIT Press, 1994.

Blondel, Christine, and Dörries Matthias, eds. *Restaging Coulomb: Usages, controverses et réplications autour de la balance de torsion.* Biblioteca di Nuncius, Studi e testi 15. Florence: L. S. Olschki, 1994.

Boudon, Philippe, Jacques Guillerme, and René Tabouret. "Figuration graphique en architecture: Le théâtre de la figuration." Paris: Délégation Générale à la Recherche Scientifique et Technique, 1976.

Braham, Allan. *The Architecture of the French Enlightenment.* Berkeley: Univ. of California Press, 1980.

Bresler, Henri. "Dessiner l'architecture: Point de vue des Beaux-Arts et changement de point de vue." In *Images et imaginaires d'architecture: Dessin, peinture, photographie, arts graphiques, théâtre, cinéma en Europe aux XIXe et XXe siècles,* 33–37. Exhibition catalog. Paris: Centre Georges Pompidou, 1984

Bressani, M. "Science, histoire et archéologie: Sources et généalogie de la pensée organiciste de Viollet-le-Duc." Ph.D. diss., Université de Paris IV-Sorbonne, Paris, 1997.

Cabestan, J.-F. "L'architecture à Paris au XVIIIe siècle, distribution et innovation." Ph.D. diss., Université de Paris I-Sorbonne, Paris, 1998.

Callebat, Louis, et al. *Histoire de l'architecte.* Paris: Flammarion, 1998.

Comité de la Recherche et du Développement en Architecture. "La formation architecturale au dix-huitième siècle en France." [Paris]: [Fondation Royaumont], 1980.

Coste, Anne. *L'architecture gothique: Lectures et interprétations d'un modèle.* Saint-Étienne: Publications de l'Université de Saint-Étienne, 1997.

[Dartein, Fernand de]. *M. Léonce Reynaud: Sa vie et ses œuvres par l'un de ses élèves.* Paris: Dunod, 1885.

———. *Observations sur le cours d'architecture de l'École Polytechnique et sur le programme de ses leçons*. Paris: Simon Raçon, 1874.

Daudin, Henri. *Cuvier et Lamarck: Les classes zoologiques et l'idée de série animale, 1790–1830*. Paris: F. Alcan, 1926.

———. *De Linné à Lamarck: Méthodes de classification et idée de série en botanique et en zoologie, 1740–1790*. Paris: F. Alcan, 1926–27.

Delbecq, Jean-Michel. "Analyse de la stabilité des voûtes en maçonnerie de Charles Augustin Coulomb à nos jours." *Annales des ponts et chaussées* 19 (1981): 36–43.

Demangeon, Alain, and Bruno Fortier. *Les vaisseaux et les villes*. Brussels: P. Mardaga, 1978.

Deming, Mark K. *La Halle au Blé de Paris, 1762–1813: "Cheval de Troie" de l'abondance dans la capitale des Lumières*. Brussels: Archives d'Architecture Moderne, 1984.

Dhombres, Nicole, and Jean Dhombres. *Naissance d'un pouvoir: Sciences et savants en France, 1793–1824*. Paris: Payot, 1989.

Drexler, Arthur, ed. *The Architecture of the École des Beaux-Arts*. New York: Museum of Modern Art, 1977.

Dufour, Claude. *Louis Bruyère et la direction des travaux de Paris*. Thesis for degree of archivist, École Nationale des Chartes, Paris, 1998.

Éleb-Vidal, Monique, and Anne Debarre-Blanchard. *Architectures de la vie privée: Maisons et mentalités, XVIIe–XIXe siècles*. Brussels: Archives d'Architecture Moderne, 1989.

Fortier, Bruno. "Logiques de l'équipement: Notes pour une histoire du projet." *Architecture-Mouvement-Continuité* 45 (1978): 80–85.

Foucault, Michel. *L'archéologie du savoir*. Paris: Gallimard, 1969. Translated by A. M. Sheridan Smith as *The Archaeology of Knowledge*. New York: Pantheon Books, 1972.

———. *Les mots et les choses: Une archéologie des sciences humaines*. Paris: Gallimard, 1966. Translated as *The Order of Things: An Archaeology of the Human Sciences*. New York: Vintage Books, 1970.

———, ed. *Les machines à guérir: Aux origines de l'hôpital moderne*. Brussels: P. Mardaga, 1979.

Gallet, Michel. *Les architectes parisiens du XVIIIe siècle: Dictionnaire biographique et critique*. Paris: Mengès, 1995.

———. "Blondel (Jacques-François), 1705–1774." In *Encyclopaedia Universalis*, vol. 5, 735–37. Paris: Encyclopaedia Universalis, 1988.

———. *Claude-Nicolas Ledoux, 1736–1806*. Paris: Picard, 1980.

———, ed. *Architecture de Ledoux: Inédits pour un tome III*. Paris: Éditions du Demi-Cercle, 1991. Translated by Michael Robinson as *Claude-Nicolas Ledoux, Unpublished Projects*. Berlin: Ernst & Sohn, 1992.

Germann, Georg. *Einführung in die Geschichte der Architekturtheorie*. 2d ed. Darmstadt: Wissenschaftliche Buchgesellschaft, 1987. Translated by Michèle Zaugg and Jacques Gubler as *Vitruve et le Vitruvianisme:*

Introduction à l'histoire de la théorie architecturale. Lausanne: Presses Polytechniques et Universitaires Romandes, 1991.

Gillmor, C. Stewart. *Coulomb and the Evolution of Physics and Engineering in Eighteenth-Century France.* Princeton: Princeton Univ. Press, 1971.

Le "Gothique" retrouvé avant Viollet-le-Duc. Exhibition catalog. Paris: Caisse Nationale des Monuments Historiques et des Sites, 1979.

Gouhier, Henri Gaston. *La jeunesse d'Auguste Comte et la formation du positivisme.* 3 vols. Paris: Vrin, 1933–41.

Guigueno, Vincent, and Antoine Picon. "Entre rationalisme et éclectisme: L'enseignement d'architecture de Léonce Reynaud." *Bulletin de la Société des amis de la bibliothèque de l'École Polytechnique* 16 (December 1996): 12–19.

Guillerme, Andre. *Bâtir la ville: Révolutions industrielles dans les matériaux de construction, France-Grande-Bretagne, 1760–1840.* Paris: Champ Vallon, 1995.

Guillerme, Jacques. "Notes pour l'histoire de la régularité." *Revue d'esthétique* 3 (1971): 383–94.

Gusdorf, Georges. *Les principes de la pensée au siècle des Lumières.* Vol. 4 of *Les sciences humaines et la pensée occidentale.* Paris: Payot, 1971.

Herrmann, Wolfgang. *Laugier and Eighteenth Century French Theory.* London: A. Zwemmer, 1962.

——. *The Theory of Claude Perrault.* London: A. Zwemmer, 1973.

Hitchcock, Henry Russell. *Architecture: Nineteenth and Twentieth Centuries.* 4th ed. New Haven: Yale Univ. Press, 1987.

Jacques, Annie, and Miyake Riichi. *Les dessins d'architecture de l'École des Beaux-Arts.* Paris: Arthaud, 1988.

Jones, Caroline A., and Peter Galison, eds. *Picturing Science, Producing Art.* New York: Routledge, 1998.

Kaufmann, Emil. "Three Revolutionary Architects: Boullée, Ledoux, and Lequeu." *Transactions of the American Philosophical Society,* n.s., 42, pt. 3 (1952).

——. *Von Ledoux bis Le Corbusier: Ursprung und Entwicklung der Autonomen Architektur.* Vienna: Passer, 1933.

Krier, Robert. "Façades pour un palais." *Archives d'architecture moderne* 11 (1977): 25–32.

Kruft, Hanno-Walter. *Geschichte der Architekturtheorie: Von der Antike bis zur Gegenwart.* Munich: C. H. Beck, 1985. Translated by Ronald Taylor, Elsie Callander, and Antony Wood as *A History of Architectural Theory: From Vitruvius to the Present.* London: A. Zwemmer; New York: Princeton Architectural Press, 1994.

Langins, Janis. *La République avait besoin de savants: Les débuts de l'École Polytechnique, L'École Centrale des Travaux Publics et les cours révolutionnaires de l'an III.* Paris: Belin, 1987.

Lavin, Sylvia. *Quatremère de Quincy and the Invention of a Modern Language of Architecture.* Cambridge: MIT Press, 1992.

Lemoine, Bertrand. *L'architecture du fer: France, XIXᵉ siècle.* Seyssel: Champ Vallon, 1986.

Lipstadt, Hélène, et al. *Architecte et ingénieur dans la presse: Polémique, débat, conflit.* Paris: Institut d'Études et de Recherches Architecturales et Urbaines, 1980.

Mantion, Jean-Rémy. "La solution symbolique: Les *Lettres sur l'architecture* de Viel de Saint-Maux (1787)." *VRBI* 9 (1984): 46–58.

Mathurin Crucy, 1749–1826: Architecte nantais néo-classique. Exhibition catalog. Nantes: Musée Dobrée, 1986.

Middleton, Robin. "The Abbé de Cordemoy and the Graeco-Gothic Ideal: A Prelude to Romantic Classicism." *Journal of the Warburg and Courtauld Institutes* 25 (1962): 278–320; 26 (1963): 90–123.

———, ed. *The Beaux-Arts and Nineteenth-Century French Architecture.* Cambridge: MIT Press, 1982.

Morachiello, Paolo, and Georges Teyssot. *Nascita delle città di stato: Ingegneri e architetti sotto il Consolato e l'Impero.* Rome: Officina, 1983.

Moravia, Sergio. *Il pensiero degli Idéologues: Scienza e filosofia in Francia, 1780–1815.* Florence: La Nuova Italia, 1974.

———. *Il tramonto dell'Illuminismo: Filosofia e politica nella società francese, 1770–1810.* Rome: Laterza, 1968.

Mosser, Monique. "Situation d'Emil K." In idem and Jean-Louis Avril, *De Ledoux à Le Corbusier: Origine et développement de l'architecture autonome.* Paris: L'équerre, 1981.

———. "Le rocher et la colonne: Un thème d'iconographie architecturale au XVIIIᵉ siècle." *Revue de l'art* 58–59 (1982–83): 55–74.

Le Panthéon, Symbole des révolutions: De l'Église de la Nation au temple des grands hommes. [Paris]: Picard, 1989 .

Pérez-Gómez, Alberto. *Architecture and the Crisis of Modern Science.* 2d ed. Cambridge: MIT Press, 1984.

———. Introduction to *Ordonnance for the Five Kinds of Columns after the Method of the Ancients,* by Claude Perrault. Santa Monica: Getty Center for the History of Art and the Humanities, 1993.

Pérouse de Montclos, Jean-Marie. *L'architecture à la française XVIᵉ, XVIIᵉ, XVIIIᵉ siècles.* Paris: Picard, 1982.

———. "La charpente à la Philibert de l'Orme: Réflexions sur la fortune des techniques en architecture." In *Les chantiers de la Renaissance: Actes des colloques tenus à Tours en 1983–1984,* 27–50 . Edited by Jean Guillaume. Paris: Picard, 1991.

———. *Étienne-Louis Boullée, 1728–1799: De l'architecture classique à l'architecture révolutionnaire.* Paris: Arts et Métiers Graphiques, 1969.

———. "Innovation technique et archéologie des techniques dans l'architecture néo-classique." *Les cahiers de la recherche architecturale* 18 (1985): 44–49.

———, ed. *'Les Prix de Rome': Concours de l'Académie Royale d'Architecture au XVIIIᵉ siècle.* Paris: Berger-Levrault, École Nationale Supérieure des Beaux-Arts, 1984.

Petit, A. "Heurs et malheurs du positivisme: Philosophie des sciences et politique scientifique chez Auguste Comte et ses premiers disciples, 1820–1900." Ph.D. diss., Université de Paris I-Sorbonne, Paris, 1993.

Petzet, Michael. "Claude Perrault als Architekt des Pariser Observatoriums." *Zeitschrift für Kunstgeschichte* 30, no. 1 (1967): 1–54.

———. *Soufflots Sainte-Geneviève und der französische Kirchenbau des 18. Jahrhunderts.* Berlin: Walter de Gruyter, 1961.

Picavet, François Joseph. *Les Idéologues.* Paris: F. Alcan, 1891.

Pickering, Mary. *Auguste Comte: An Intellectual Biography.* Cambridge: Cambridge Univ. Press, 1993.

Picon, Antoine. *Architectes et ingénieurs au siècle des Lumières.* Marseille: Parenthèses, 1988. Translated by Martin Thom as *French Architects and Engineers in the Age of the Enlightenment.* Cambridge: Cambridge Univ. Press, 1992.

———. "Charles-François Mandar, 1757–1844; ou, L'architecture dans tous ses détails." *Revue de l'art* 109 (1995): 26–39.

———. *Claude Perrault, 1613–1688; ou, La curiosité d'un classique.* Paris: Picard, 1988.

———. "Gestes ouvriers, opérations et processus techniques: La vision du travail des encyclopédistes." *Recherches sur Diderot et sur l'Encyclopédie* 13 (October, 1992): 131–47.

———. *L'invention de l'ingénieur moderne: L'École des Ponts et Chaussées, 1747–1851.* Paris: Presses de l'École Nationale des Ponts et Chaussées, 1992.

———. "Un moderne paradoxal." Introduction to *Mémoires de ma vie,* by Charles Perrault, 1–107. Paris: Macula, 1993.

———. "Towards a History of Technological Thought." In *Technological Change: Methods and Themes in the History of Technology,* edited by Robert Fox, 37–49. London: Harwood Academic Publishers, 1996.

———. "'Vers une architecture classique': Jacques-François Blondel et le *Cours d'architecture.*" *Les cahiers de la recherche architecturale* 18 (1985): 28–37.

Potié, Philippe. *Philibert de l'Orme: Figures de la pensée constructive.* Marseille: Parenthèses, 1996.

Roger, Jacques. *Buffon: Un philosophe au jardin du roi.* Paris: Fayard, 1989. Translated by Sarah Lucille Bonnefoi as *Buffon: A Life in Natural History.* Edited by L. Pearce Williams. Ithaca: Cornell Univ. Press, 1997.

Rykwert, Joseph. *On Adam's House in Paradise: The Idea of the Primitive Hut in Architectural History.* New York: Museum of Modern Art, 1972.

Saboya, Marc. *Presse et architecture au XIXe siècle: César Daly et la Revue générale de l'architecture et des travaux publics.* Paris: Picard, 1991.

Sakarovitch, Joël. *Contribution à l'histoire de la géométrie descriptive: Origine et destin d'une discipline polymorphe.* Documents assembled for accreditation to direct research at the École des Hautes Études en Sciences Sociales. Paris, 1997.

———. *Épures d'architecture: De la coupe des pierres à la géométrie descriptive, XVIe–XIXe siècles.* Basel: Birkhäuser, 1998.

Shinn, Terry. *L'École Polytechnique, 1794–1914.* Paris: Presses de la Fondation Nationale des Sciences Politiques, 1980.

Simonnet, C. *Matériaux et architecture: Le béton armé; Origine, invention, esthétique.* Ph.D. diss., École des Hautes Études en Sciences Sociales, Paris, 1994.

Soufflot et l'architecture des Lumières. Supplement to *Cahiers de la recherche architecturale* 6–7. Paris: 1980.

Szambien, Werner. "Architekturdarstellung an der Pariser École Polytechnique zu Beginn des 19. Jahrhunderts." *Daidalos* 11 (1984): 55–64.

———. "Aux origines de l'enseignement de Durand: Les cent soixante-huit croquis des *Rudimenta operis magni et disciplinae.*" *Études de la revue du Louvre 1 (1980): 122–30.*

———. Jean-Nicolas-Louis Durand, 1760–1834: De l'imitation à la norme. Paris: Picard, 1984.

———. "Napoléon, ville-modèle?" *303: Recherches et créations* 12 (1987): 123–32.

———. "Notes sur le recueil d'architecture privée de Boullée, 1792–1796." *Gazette des Beaux-Arts,* 6th ser., 97, no. 1346 (March 1981): 111–24.

———. *Les projets de l'an II: Concours d'architecture de la période révolutionnaire.* Paris: École Nationale Supérieure des Beaux-Arts, 1986.

———. *Symétrie, goût, caractère: Théorie et terminologie de l'architecture à l'âge classique, 1500–1800.* Paris: Picard, 1986.

——— and Simona Talenti. "Durand, Quaet-Faslem et Dartein; ou, L'influence européenne de Durand." *Bulletin de la Société des amis de la bibliothèque de l'École polytechnique* 16 (1996): 1–11.

Taton, René. *L'œuvre scientifique de Monge.* Paris: Presses Universitaires de France, 1951.

——— et al. *Enseignement et diffusion des sciences en France au XVIIIe siècle.* Paris: Hermann, 1964.

Vacchini, Livio. "Letzte Etappe der 'Primarschule ai Saleggi' in Locarno TI." *Werk, Bauen und Wohnen* 4 (1981): 17–21.

Van Eck, Caroline. *Organicism in Nineteenth-Century Architecture: An Inquiry into Its Theoretical and Philosophical Background.* Amsterdam: Architectura & Natura Press, 1994.

Van Zanten, David. *Designing Paris: The Architecture of Duban, Labrouste, Duc, and Vaudoyer.* Cambridge: MIT Press, 1987.

Vidler, Anthony. *Claude-Nicolas Ledoux: Architecture and Social Reform at the End of the Ancien Régime.* Cambridge: MIT Press, 1990.

———. *The Writing of the Walls: Architectural Theory in the Late Enlightenment.* Princeton, N.J.: Princeton Architectural Press, 1987.

Villari, Sergio. *J.-N.-L. Durand, 1760–1834: Arte e scienza dell'architettura.* Rome: Officina, 1987. Translated by Eli Gottlieb as *J. N. L. Durand, 1760–1834: Art and Science of Architecture.* New York: Rizzoli, 1990.

Index

Précis of the Lectures on Architecture
with
Graphic Portion of the Lectures on Architecture
Jean-Nicolas-Louis Durand
Introduction by Antoine Picon
Translation by David Britt

Antoine Picon is a professor at the École Nationale des Ponts et Chaussées, Paris, where he teaches the history of architecture and engineering. He received his doctoral degree from the École des Hautes Études en Sciences Sociales, Paris, 1991. Recent publications include *French Architects and Engineers in the Age of the Enlightenment* (Cambridge Univ. Press, 1992), *L'invention de l'ingénieur modern* (Presses de l'École Nationale des Ponts et Chaussées, 1992), and articles in many journals, including *Casabella, Revue de l'art, Sciences et techniques en perspectives, Annales des Ponts et Chaussées, The Architectural Review, Visa pour la Cité,* and *Revue de synthèse.*

David Britt was an editor of art books at Thames & Hudson in London for more than twenty years; since 1987 he has been translating full-time. His translations in the Getty Research Institute's Texts & Documents series include titles by Aby Warburg, Friedrich Gilly, and Nicolas Le Camus de Mézières.

Texts & Documents
A Series of the Getty Research Institute Publications and Exhibitions Program
Julia Bloomfield, Kurt W. Forster, Harry F. Mallgrave, Thomas F. Reese, Michael S. Roth, and Salvatore Settis, *Editors*

In Print
Otto Wagner, *Modern Architecture* (1902)
Introduction by Harry Francis Mallgrave
ISBN 0-226-86938-5 (hardcover), ISBN 0-226-86939-3 (paper)

Heinrich Hübsch, Rudolf Wiegmann, Carl Albert Rosenthal, Johann Heinrich Wolff, and Carl Gottlieb Wilhelm Bötticher, *In What Style Should We Build? The German Debate on Architectural Style* (1828–47)
Introduction by Wolfgang Herrmann
ISBN 0-89236-199-9 (hardcover), ISBN 0-89236-198-0 (paper)

Nicolas Le Camus de Mézières, *The Genius of Architecture; or, The Analogy of That Art with Our Sensations* (1780)
Introduction by Robin Middleton
ISBN 0-89236-234-0 (hardcover), ISBN 0-89236-235-9 (paper)

Claude Perrault, *Ordonnance for the Five Kinds of Columns after the Method of the Ancients* (1683)
Introduction by Alberto Pérez-Gómez
ISBN 0-89236-232-4 (hardcover), ISBN 0-89236-233-2 (paper)

Robert Vischer, Conrad Fiedler, Heinrich Wölfflin, Adolf Göller, Adolf Hildebrand, and August Schmarsow, *Empathy, Form, and Space: Problems in German Aesthetics, 1873–1893*
Introduction by Harry Francis Mallgrave and Eleftherios Ikonomou
ISBN 0-89236-260-X (hardcover), ISBN 0-89236-259-6 (paper)

Friedrich Gilly: Essays on Architecture, 1796–1799
Introduction by Fritz Neumeyer
ISBN 0-89236-280-4 (hardcover), ISBN 0-89236-281-2 (paper)

Hermann Muthesius, *Style-Architecture and Building-Art: Transformations of Architecture in the Nineteenth Century and Its Present Condition* (1902)
Introduction by Stanford Anderson
ISBN 0-89236-282-0 (hardcover), ISBN 0-89236-283-9 (paper)

Sigfried Giedion, *Building in France, Building in Iron, Building in Ferroconcrete* (1928)
Introduction by Sokratis Georgiadis
ISBN 0-89236-319-3 (hardcover), ISBN 0-89236-320-7 (paper)

Hendrik Petrus Berlage, *Thoughts on Style, 1886–1909*
Introduction by Iain Boyd Whyte
ISBN 0-89236-334-7 (paper)

Adolf Behne, *The Modern Functional Building* (1926)
Introduction by Rosemarie Haag Bletter
ISBN 0-89236-364-9 (paper)

Aby Warburg, *The Renewal of Pagan Antiquity* (1932)
Introduction by Kurt W. Forster
ISBN 0-89236-537-4 (hardcover)

Alois Riegl, *The Group Portraiture of Holland* (1902)
Introduction by Wolfgang Kemp
ISBN 0-89236-548-X (paper)

Walter Curt Behrendt, *The Victory of the New Building Style* (1927)
Introduction by Detlef Mertins
ISBN 0-89236-563-3 (paper)

In Preparation
Karel Teige, *Modern Architecture in Czechoslovakia and Other Writings* (1923–30)
Introduction by Jean-Louis Cohen

Gottfried Semper, *Style in the Technical and Tectonic Arts; or, Practical Aesthetics* (1860–63)
Introduction by Harry Francis Mallgrave

Designed by Bruce Mau Design Inc.,
Bruce Mau with Chris Rowat and Catherine Rix
Coordinated by Stacy Miyagawa
Type composed by Archetype in Sabon and News Gothic
Printed and bound by Thomson-Shore on Cougar Opaque and Fortune Matte
Cover printed by Phoenix Color

Texts & Documents
Series designed by Bruce Mau Design Inc., Toronto, Canada